D0926929

Imagining the World from Behind the Iron Curtain

Imagining the World from Behind the Iron Curtain

Youth and the Global Sixties in Poland

MALGORZATA FIDELIS

OXFORD
UNIVERSITY PRESS

OXFORD
UNIVERSITY PRESS

Oxford University Press is a department of the University of Oxford. It furthers
the University's objective of excellence in research, scholarship, and education
by publishing worldwide. Oxford is a registered trade mark of Oxford University
Press in the UK and certain other countries.

Published in the United States of America by Oxford University Press
198 Madison Avenue, New York, NY 10016, United States of America.

© Oxford University Press 2022

CIP data is on file at the Library of Congress
ISBN 978–0–19–764340–2

DOI: 10.1093/oso/9780197643402.001.0001

1 3 5 7 9 8 6 4 2

Printed by Integrated Books International, United States of America

For Krzysztof and Jan

Contents

Acknowledgments   ix

Introduction: Poland and the Global Sixties   1

1. The Polish Thaw: Youth Carnival, Domestic Revolution, and
   Cross-border Encounters   14

2. Youth as Modernity: Envisioning Young People after the Thaw   39

3. Window to the World: Youth Magazines and the Politics of
   Apolitics   61

4. Bohemians and Discontents: The Making of a Student
   Community   81

5. Tensions of Transnationalism: Youth Rebellion, State Backlash,
   and 1968   102

6. The Counterculture: Hippies, Artists, and Other Subversives   127

7. The World in the Village: Rural Rebels in Search of Modernity   156

8. Domesticating the Sixties: Youth Culture, Globalization, and
   Consumer Socialism in the 1970s   184

Conclusion: Imagining the World after the Sixties   202

Abbreviations   209
Notes   211
Bibliography   267
Index   283

Acknowledgments

The idea for this book has been with me for a long time. I became interested in the sixties when I moved to the San Francisco Bay Area in the early 1990s. Walking by the remnants of American counterculture, I had a vague memory of hippies from my own childhood while growing up in Poland. I was always fascinated by a picture in a family photo album that my parents had taken while on vacation in Yugoslavia, which featured one of these long-haired and colorfully dressed people on the streets of Dubrovnik. What did parallel youth movements look like in places far away from the American West Coast? How did young people imagine alternative social and political organization on the opposite sides of the Cold War? And why was no one talking about Polish or Yugoslav hippies?

I put those questions aside. Many years after, I learned that people were actually talking and writing not just about the American sixties but the global sixties. In 2007, I participated in an amazing international conference at Queens University in Kingston, Canada, which exposed me to new and vibrant research on the sixties in many parts of the world. But even there, one was under the impression that the sixties upheavals had barely touched the Soviet-dominated communist camp. Out of more than 500 papers presented, only two focused on Eastern Europe, including my own. Just a year later, in August 2008, I found myself in Prague, attending a workshop on protest movements in Europe at the invitation of Martin Klimke (now at New York University Abu Dhabi), whom I had met in Kingston. Being in Prague on the fortieth anniversary of the Warsaw Pact invasion of Czechoslovakia and interacting with scholars of protest movements and a few activists from the 1960s was an unforgettable experience. It was this scholarly gathering that finally set me on the path to finding the sixties in Poland. This book is the fruit of that search.

Research for this book was supported by a grant from the National Council for Eurasian and East European Research in 2012–2013; and the Stefan and Lucy Hejna Endowment in Polish Studies and the LAS Dean Award for Faculty Research in the Humanities, both at the University of Illinois at Chicago. I was able to draft a substantial part of the book thanks to a residential fellowship at the UIC Institute for Humanities in 2014–2015. I am immensely grateful to the then director of the Institute, Susan Levine, and all the fellows for their constructive and encouraging feedback on early chapter drafts.

The Department of History at UIC provided a supportive and intellectually stimulating environment for working on this book. My colleagues were always ready to discuss ideas, ask questions, and challenge me. I am especially grateful to Keely Stauter-Halsted, Marina Mogilner, Jonathan Daly, Michal Wilczewski, Jennifer Brier, Joaquin Chavez, Laura Hostetler, Lynn Hudson, Mark Liechty, Kevin Schultz, and Jeffrey Sklansky. I benefited from feedback from faculty and students I received at the Brown Bag seminars in my department, and various conferences and workshops organized by the Hejna Chairs in Polish Studies at UIC, Keely Stauter-Halsted and Michał Paweł Markowski. Some of the most critical ideas and perspectives in this book took shape through discussions with students in my graduate colloquium on the Global Sixties in the fall of 2015, and the spring of 2021. I owe gratitude to my research assistants: Mikołaj Czerwiński, for his patient and skillful work of transcribing the recorded interviews, and Frankee Lyons, for her insights and her excellent work on this book's index.

I am grateful to my colleagues from outside UIC who invited me to share my work with a variety of audiences: John Connelly at UC Berkeley; Andrea Rees Davies at Stanford University; Agnieszka Mrozik at the Institute for Literary Research, Polish Academy of Sciences in Warsaw; Mark Keck-Szajbel and Dagmara Jajeśniak at the European University Viadrina in Frankfurt-Oder; the Graduate Organization for the Study of Europe and Central Asia at the University of Pittsburgh; Ewa Domańska at the Adam Mickiewicz University in Poznań; Kathryn Ciancia and David Danaher at the University of Wisconsin-Madison; Kyrill Kunakhovich at the University of Virginia; Ulf Brunnbauer at the Leibnitz Institute for East and Southeast European Studies in Regensburg; Katherine Lebow at Oxford University; Michelle Nickerson at Loyola University Chicago; Tomasz Zarycki at the Robert Zajonc Institute for Social Studies in Warsaw; Jakub Szumski and Jochen Böhler at the Imre Kertesz Kelleg in Jena; Przemysław Wielgosz at Le Monde Diplomatique in Warsaw; and Monika Zbytniewska at the Polonium Foundation in Zurich.

I deeply appreciate the work and assistance of the archivists at the Archive of New Documents and the Institute for National Remembrance, both in Warsaw; the Open Society Archives in Budapest; and the state archives in

Białystok, Kraków, and Wrocław. Szczepan Świątek at the State Archive in Kraków went out of his way to find relevant documents and put me in touch with former participants in student artistic and cultural initiatives in Kraków. Without the generosity and professional assistance of Dariusz Wierzchoś at the Archive of New Documents in Warsaw, I would not have been able to access thousands of handwritten memoirs by rural young people. I also thank the librarians at the National Library in Warsaw, the Warsaw University Library, and the Library of the Institute of Philosophy and Sociology at the Polish Academy of Science in Warsaw for their assistance in accessing the relevant materials. Marta Przybyło at the Archeology of Photography Foundation in Warsaw helped with locating the copyright owners of many images in this book.

During my frequent field trips to Poland, I benefited from conversations with and help from many people. First and foremost, I would like to thank all the individuals who agreed to be interviewed. My perspective and the questions I explore have been greatly influenced by my conversations with those who personally experienced the sixties as young people, not all of them directly quoted here. I also benefited from informal conversations with scholars, artists, and friends, including Grzegorz Sołtysiak, Tom Junes, Piotr Kosicki, Patryk Wasiak, Małgorzata Mazurek, Dobrochna Kałwa, Rafał Mierzejewski, Edyta Kozak, and Roland Rowiński. Maciej Wysocki helped organize a number of interviews, and he shared insights and memories that helped guide some of these conversations. Natalia Jarska provided thoughtful feedback, and she helped me obtain key documents. I am grateful to scholars at the Center for Cultural and Literary Studies on Communism at the Institute for Literary Research of the Polish Academy of Sciences in Warsaw for sharing their work and inviting me to their seminars and workshops. Their sophisticated cultural analysis of communism made an imprint on my thinking. I also would like to thank Joanna Sadowska and Andrzej Sadowski at Białystok University and Monika Piotrowska-Marchewa at the University of Wrocław. The research and writing of this book overlapped with another project—a book on the history of women in Poland, 1945–1989. In the process, I found the intellectual exchange with my coauthors, Katarzyna Stańczak-Wiślicz, Piotr Perkowski, and Barbara Klich-Kluczewska, incredibly helpful to this book. My gratitude goes to Katarzyna especially for her assistance in obtaining materials from Polish libraries at the last stages of this book that I was not able to access personally because of the COVID-19 pandemic.

Several people read portions of this book when it was in progress. I thank Brian Porter-Szűcs, Theodora Dragostinova, Jill Massino, Colleen McQuillen, Michał Kwiecień, and Lukas Dovern for their insightful feedback. Words cannot describe my gratitude to my beloved remote writing group, who have provided sustained intellectual engagement and moral support for more than a decade: Kathryn Ciancia, Irina Gigova, Emily Greble, Maureen Healy, Katherine Lebow, and Andrea Orzoff. These amazing scholars and friends painstakingly read my early chapter drafts or just collections of ideas, provided detailed critique, and kept me focused.

A slightly modified version of chapter 5 appeared as "Tensions of Transnationalism: Youth Rebellion, State Backlash and 1968 in Poland," *American Historical Review* 125, no. 4 (October 2020): 1232–1259. Some of the material from other chapters appeared in the following publications: "Red State, Golden Youth: The Student Culture and Political Protest in Poland in the 1960s," in *Between the Avant-Garde and the Everyday: Subversive Politics in Europe, 1958–2008*, edited by Timothy Scott Brown and Lorena Anton (Oxford: Berghahn Books, 2011), 145–153; "The Other Marxists: Making Sense of International Student Revolts in Poland in the Global Sixties," *Zeitschrift für Ostmitteleuropa-Forschung* 62 (2013): 425–449; and "Jugend Moderne und die Welt. Die polnische Jugend an der Schwelle der Long Sixties. Historische Berachtungen," in *Nouvelle Vague Polonaise? Auf der Suche nach einem flüchtigen Phänomen der Filmgeschichte*, edited by Margarete Wach (Marburg: Schüren, 2015), 80–100.

At Oxford University Press, I thank the anonymous readers for their constructive suggestions and for pushing me to sharpen my arguments. My immense gratitude goes to my editor, Susan Ferber, whose dedication, professionalism, and support made the revision and publication process a true delight I never expected.

My husband, Krzysztof, and my son, Jan, have been the most wonderful companions on this intellectual journey that I could have imagined. They went to research trips and conferences with me, constantly serving as a sounding board for ideas and a source of practical help in getting me between the archives and the wilderness, where some of my interlocutors resided. Jan's bilingualism and a penchant for writing helped improve my awkward translations from Polish and the articulation of some key ideas on paper. I dedicate this book to Krzysztof and Jan.

Imagining the World from Behind the Iron Curtain

Introduction

Poland and the Global Sixties

It was a summer morning when an overnight train approached its final station at Kłodzko, Poland, a quiet medieval town near the Czechoslovak border.
Suddenly, a distant rumbling startled its passengers awake. When eighteen-
year-old Jerzy looked out the train's window, all he could see was a swarm of
military helicopters overhead. A fellow passenger turned on the radio, from
which a stern voice announced the Warsaw Pact invasion of Czechoslovakia.
It was August 21, 1968, a long-anticipated day for Jerzy. With long hair and
colorful clothes, he was one of hundreds of Polish hippies, who on that day
headed to the picturesque Karkonosze Mountains to gather as a community
and escape social isolation and the harassment they faced from the political
police. By early afternoon, Jerzy and other hippies reached the meeting point
at the base of Muflon Mountain, but they found themselves surrounded by a
Polish military unit. The commander of the unit ordered them to disperse.
Reluctantly, they left the meeting point, picking flowers along the way to the
nearby park. "We gave the flowers to passersby," Jerzy recalled. A young man
played Jimi Hendrix's "Hey Joe" on a guitar, and the hippies broke out into
dance.[1]

Jerzy's disrupted attempt to join a hippie gathering in 1968 is just one of
countless examples of how young people in Poland engaged with the political and cultural upheavals of the global sixties. Polish hippies saw themselves as a community of shared values and creative lifestyles rather than
as rebels against the capitalist system and middle-class norms as American
and Western European hippies usually did. Yet they often made hand-drawn
posters of sixties icons such as Allen Ginsberg, Jimi Hendrix, Angela Davis,
and Mao Tse Tung to establish their connection to the global community of
dissent. Indeed, if there was one thread that ran through the diverse ideas
and practices of young people in 1960s Poland, it was the desire to be part of
the larger world and transcend the Cold War divide.

Imagining the World from Behind the Iron Curtain. Malgorzata Fidelis, Oxford University Press. © Oxford University Press
2022. DOI: 10.1093/oso/9780197643402.003.0001

This book offers a new perspective on Poland and Eastern Europe during the "long sixties" that spans the mid-1950s through the early 1970s. It does so by putting young people and their engagement with international youth culture at the center of the story.[2] Long seen as the subjects to an isolationist and "totalitarian" regime, young people in Poland, in fact, were active participants in global conversations, including nonconformist lifestyles, experimentation with consumer products and technology, counterculture, and leftist politics. This book situates them in the "global sixties," a term that refers not simply to the decade of the 1960s but to a conceptual model to study what historian Timothy Brown identified as "the global/local intersections" or "moments in which transnational exchanges result in actors in one local terrain . . . coming into contact with, adopting, rejecting, or otherwise responding to, exogenous influences."[3] Such global/local intersections were central to shaping the subjectivity of young people in Eastern Europe while also showcasing the agency of actors in the periphery of the American-Soviet superpower conflict.

These young people often framed their local circumstances within the larger context of world events, which shaped their collective desires and practices. In postwar Eastern Europe, opportunities for personal travel and interaction with international actors were limited, so global symbols from blue jeans and miniskirts to Allen Ginsberg and Che Guevara formed part of a powerful transnational imagination.[4] Imagining the world played a critical role not only in shaping desires and practices but also in defining the broader relations between state and society and the trajectory of the political opposition.

The turning point that stimulated Polish youth's transnational imagination in the postwar era came in the summer of 1955 with the Fifth World Youth and Students Festival. Nearly 27,000 young people from 116 countries descended upon Warsaw, creating an unprecedented youth carnival and celebration of cultural diversity. In the wake of the festival, young Poles flooded the state's passport bureau with applications and launched a public campaign for the right to travel abroad as part of socialist education. Seeking to renew the communist system after the death of Iosif Stalin in 1953, Polish political elites responded to such desires by modifying their attitude toward the youth: they deemphasized explicit political and ideological agendas in favor of cultural engagements, educational leisure, and allowing access to selective Western trends.[5]

Consequently, those growing up in sixties Poland enjoyed a great deal of exposure to mass media that were not limited to domestic popular productions but also included Radio Luxembourg, American and British television shows, and French and Italian films. At the same time, the Polish popular press reported on youth culture in the West, from the beat poets to rock 'n' roll. In addition, student clubs under the patronage of the official Polish Student Association provided a space where young elites could listen to jazz, learn how to dance the twist, or exchange vinyl records brought by those who traveled to the West.

Although most of the young people in Poland could only engage in "virtual" tourism, actual foreign travel became more accessible to Polish citizens after 1956, when Poland began to open its borders gradually to individual travel abroad by liberalizing its passport policy and signing agreements with neighbors for tourism exchange. Young people had more opportunities than other demographics to travel abroad since they could join organized tours for youth and students to other European countries. Such trips often gave them eye-opening exposure to life beyond the Eastern bloc and to global youth culture.

While scholars have paid growing attention to the Global South and the interaction between the Third World and the First World, Eastern Europe and the Second World have persistently been marginalized in studies of the global sixties and globality in general.[6] This book aims to recover Eastern European experiences of culture and politics in the sixties and to show how they can enrich our understanding of global connections. Recent work on the "socialist sixties" has illuminated the impact of transnational ideas and commodities on Soviet and Eastern European societies, from popular culture and consumption to protest movements and anticolonial revolutions.[7] It is now clear that the Iron Curtain was not a sufficient barrier against outside influence, and that young people, from hippies to mainstream youth in miniskirts and blue jeans, saw themselves as part of a global community of like-minded people, in addition to concerning themselves with myriad local issues.[8] This book aims to delve more deeply into the transnational sixties moment in Poland, examining how contemporary actors understood the increasingly interconnected world in their specific localities and how they used these understandings to propel their agendas.

For much of the Second World, the cultural and political turbulence started during the Thaw, in the mid-1950s. In Poland, 1954 saw the first signs of pluralist cultural expression after Stalinism and the empowerment of young people through grassroots initiatives, from artistic activity and critical journalism to new forms of leisure and crosscultural encounters. The

Polish Thaw officially ended in late 1957, when the new leader Władysław Gomułka consolidated his power under the slogan of the "Polish Road to Socialism." Yet the legacy of the Thaw cultivated more relaxed cultural styles and contested ideas of modernity. While 1968 marked a turning point in postwar Polish history—with nationwide student and youth demonstrations and an antisemitic campaign launched by the state against these protestors—it was not the end of the global sixties in Poland. The hippie counterculture, for example, continued to flourish. The demise of sixties upheavals and the high point of "normalization" took place in the early 1970s, under the new Party leader, Edward Gierek. At the time, many aspects of youth rebellion came to be depoliticized and incorporated into the official model of "consumer socialism." Moreover, the Gierek regime promoted a new engagement with the world that extended beyond cultural interaction and pushed Poland into active participation in the global market.

Youth in an Era of Change

In 1965, a collection of sociological studies was published in Poland that heralded young people as the embodiment of the unprecedented dynamism of the postwar world. The authors of these studies titled *Youth in an Era of Change* argued that this demographic could not be studied or understood apart from global developments beyond Polish borders.[9] Sociologists and other intermediaries between young people and the state, such as journalists, writers, and educators, helped shape ideas about youth while drawing connections between young people and what they believed was a new type of postwar modernity centered on the values of peace and material well-being.

This was not the first time youth came to the forefront of public debates in Poland or other European countries. In the interwar period, both fascist and communist leaders had mobilized scores of young men and women for their movements and singled them out as potent symbols of the revolutions and future societies they wanted to create. In interwar Poland, youth occupied a prominent place in public debates as the first generation to come of age in independent Poland after 1918. At that time, however, young people were often categorized according to their social and ethnic identifications with the culturally Polish young intelligentsia holding an elevated position as future leaders of the nation.[10] World War II helped mythologize young people as resisters and fighters against the Nazi occupiers. The Warsaw

Uprising against the Germans in August 1944, in particular, became a powerful symbol of the "flower of Polish intelligentsia" sacrificing their lives for the nation.[11]

While building on these domestic traditions, a new conceptualization of youth emerged after the war. Young people were instead understood as a separate social category, regardless of their class or ethnic origin, and a potential force of renewal in the world. This new approach to youth was common in Eastern and Western Europe as well as other parts of the world.[12] The spread of mass media, popular culture, and consumption provided new spaces for the manifestation of what became known as youth culture.

In sixties Poland, "youth" was defined broadly to include teenagers, university students, and working people in their twenties. Sociologists defined youth as those between the ages of 15 and 29. Communist youth organizations, such as the Socialist Youth Association (Związek Młodzieży Socjalistycznej; ZMS) and the Rural Youth Association (Związek Młodzieży Wiejskiej; ZMW), employed a similar definition, recruiting members who were between fifteen and thirty years old.[13] This book does not deal with any specific "generation" but with multiple age cohorts who fit the Polish definition of "youth" during the two decades between the mid-1950s and the mid-1970s. Depending on the context, some groups of young people became more important than others in public discourse, for example university students during the March 1968 protests or young male professionals in the official project of building a "Second Poland" in the early 1970s.

These chapters do not aim to provide a comprehensive overview of Polish youth. Young industrial workers, for example, do not figure prominently. Most of the characters are university students and rural youth, who numerically represented a significant segment of this age group at the time. Moreover, these two groups embodied, in many ways, emancipatory trends of the socialist sixties. While young workers, many of them migrants from the countryside, had been the primary beneficiaries of social advancement in the early 1950s as a result of the Stalinist industrial drive, the post-Stalinist era offered a different kind of emancipation, one centered on cultural opportunity, consumer choice, and access to the outside world. The number of university students, many of them coming from working-class and rural backgrounds, skyrocketed through the 1960s. Young women entered higher education in unprecedented numbers, posing new challenges to young male elites. In Poland, as elsewhere, students became a group likely to engage in protest and rebellion. They stood at the forefront of the Thaw, hoping to build a genuine workers' democracy after the death of Stalin, and later led the protests of 1968. Rural young people, at the same time, found emancipation through increased opportunities for education, mobility, and the cultural modernization campaign in the countryside.

Young women often experienced emancipation and modernity in different ways from men. Gender played an important role in countercultural imagery and texts produced by students and young intelligentsia. Moreover, gender identity often determined the kind of possibilities available to individuals. For rural young women, in particular, the sixties opened up an unprecedented opportunity to break away from roles their families, villages, and the church had traditionally demanded. Claiming the roles of "modernizers" in the countryside, young women attempted to take control over their lives and bodies.

In Search of Socialist Modernity

A distinct understanding of modernity informed young people's engagements with the outside world. The quest for modernity was, of course, not new to Poland. Heated debates about industrialization, urbanization, and secularization have raged in Poland since the early nineteenth century.[14] Some of the first calls for modernity (*nowoczesność*) during the Thaw came from artists, designers, and literary scholars, for whom "modernity" was synonymous with "freedom" and, more precisely, with the rebellion against the dogma of socialist realism that was imposed on Polish arts and literature during the Stalinist period.[15] Public conversation in the late 1950s responded to these calls by adopting the term "modernity" to denote a post-Stalinist renewal of the socialist system. But the concept of modernity was fluid enough to produce multiple interpretations. For young people, it became a helpful tool for asserting themselves. As in the past, modernity remained not only a subjective and contested concept but also an aspirational one. Modernity was always a work in progress, an ongoing search rather than an accomplished fact.

This book uses the phrase "socialist modernity" to distinguish the Polish project from the hegemonic Western one.[16] This term was rarely used in Poland at the time, as most believed that modernity was not inherently "socialist" or "capitalist" but universal and global. Józef Tejchma, member of the Politburo of the Polish United Workers' Party (PZPR, the ruling party in Poland until 1989) and minister of culture in the early 1970s, insisted that he and other political leaders were seeking at the time not a distinct brand of "socialist culture" but rather "culture in socialism."[17] Such phrasing is significant, as it recognized the possibility of multiple and divergent forms of cultural content and expression depending on the political context.

It was in the framework of socialist modernity—understood as intersecting but not necessarily overlapping with the Western one—that Polish actors confronted contemporary global connections. The term "globalization" has been commonly associated with the economic and financial interdependence that accelerated in the early 1970s, but global cultural exchange forged through travelers, consumer goods, ideas, and images is a much older phenomenon.[18] In the second half of the twentieth century, the rapid spread of mass media created an unprecedented cultural interconnectedness, prompting Canadian philosopher Marshall McLuhan to coin the term "global village" in 1964.[19] The Iron Curtain notwithstanding, this book argues that Poland was part of that "global village."

Eastern Europe presents fertile ground for the exploration of international youth culture. Tensions between internationalism and nationalism have been embedded in the communist project from the very beginning. On the one hand, communism was a global movement that endorsed class revolution that would transcend national boundaries. On the other, anywhere communism was implemented it aimed at sealing borders and eliminating alternative points of view. Ironically, building the new, ostentatiously internationalist system required vigilance and distrust of outsiders.[20] Young people were very much aware of these tensions while constructing their own ideas about "isolation" and "catching up" with what they perceived as the modern world to which they wished to belong.

How did young people in Poland imagine the world? The Polish term świat ("the world") casually meant anything outside one's specific locality. For Polish youth it meant breaking away, whether temporarily or permanently, from the confines of their specific place, be it a village, a town, a narrowly conceived nation, or a communist camp. These were all seen as impediments to the meaningful self-expression of young people. Imagining "the world" in the socialist Polish context often meant implicitly imagining "the West," a term that was frequently used to refer to the modern, the progressive, the fashionable, and the urban.

But the Global South was not absent from the mental geography of young Poles. The Third World and especially anticolonial struggles, such as the Cuban Revolution and the Vietnam War, remained under the purview of state propaganda that proved particularly difficult to challenge from below.[21] Under the policy of peaceful coexistence and, later, détente, the Soviet Union and the Eastern European countries cultivated a range of relationships with newly decolonized nations in Africa and Asia. In the process, the Third World became a prominent area of competition between communist and capitalist states, from economic and cultural influence to political and military assistance.[22] In addition to official speeches in support of decolonization and state visits to newly independent countries, the Global South began to work its way into Polish popular culture. Spread through the pages of youth magazines, it appeared in the form of news items, recipes for African dishes, adventure short stories, reportage, and color photographs of exotic places and people. Young people's fascination with the non-European world is evidenced in the popularity of such reading material. Yet the dominant discourses positioned Poles as agents of modernization from whom postcolonial peoples were supposed to learn. In a way, the Poland depicted in youth magazines was intended to assume the imaginary place of the West, offering newly decolonized states a European "civilization" free from the burden of capitalism or the legacy of overseas colonial conquest.

Young people, especially those identifying with leftist politics, did attempt to forge alternative connections to the Global South. The hippie movement looked to international countercultures, pacifism, and Eastern philosophies in constructing their everyday nonconformist practices. The official culture, however, remained dominated by the state's vision of internationalism and anticolonialism. In the wake of student demonstrations in March 1968, the state was able to effectively deploy and weaponize the transnational imagination to stigmatize youth rebellion as a foreign infiltration. Party leaders denigrated Polish students as unpatriotic cosmopolitans and connected them to the international and allegedly misguided "New Left" in order to delegitimize the young rebels and fuel moral anxiety among the traditional public.

Such multiple uses of transnational imagination demonstrated that the engagement with the world was diverse and uneven in Poland. Imagining the world did not always mean producing or acquiring a more open outlook or embracing cultural diversity. Despite its professed internationalism, the Polish state often proved effective in suppressing expressions of international solidarity from below, especially if young people ventured into expression that went beyond personal style or cultural taste and into political thinking. Similarly, the state's eagerness for Poland to become more open to global trends often aimed to overcome regionalism and produce a uniform national self-identification rather than cultural openness or cosmopolitan outlooks. Rather than idealize Polish youth's engagements with the world, this book explores the tensions that arose from the ways the world made its way in sixties Poland.

Recovering the Polish Sixties

In order to capture these tensions, the following chapters draw on a variety of sources. These include records of the Party-state institutions and youth organizations, contemporary sociological research and sex education manuals, youth magazines and the popular press, and memoirs and oral histories. To gain a more transnational perspective, I explored the holdings of the Vera and Donald Blinken Open Society Archives in Budapest with special attention to materials compiled by the Radio Free Europe/Radio Liberty Research Institute.[23]

Personal stories, such as the one told by Jerzy at the beginning of this introduction, are central to my analysis of youth subjectivities and the global/local intersections that shaped them. Many of the personal testimonies that I used came from a collection of handwritten memoirs and diaries by rural youth submitted to state-organized competitions in the late 1960s and early 1970s, now housed at the Archive of New Documents in Warsaw. Village authors wrote their autobiographies for a specific audience: the state-sponsored commission that usually consisted of sociologists, writers, and journalists. As such, the autobiographies often followed a script of accepted vocabulary that rarely challenged the political power of the Party-state. Yet reducing these memoirs to their performative aspects would be not only incorrect but also unfair to the authors. They devoted considerable space to their personal lives, hidden emotions, and everyday routines in ways that put their own subjectivity at the center.

In addition, I conducted more than twenty interviews with former students and other participants in sixties youth culture during my travels to Poland in 2011–2016. I am fully aware that my interlocutors' perspectives were mitigated by later experiences, individual and collective remembering, and the interaction with me as an interviewer from the American academic world. In my interviews, I usually started by asking open-ended questions, and then I let the interlocutors speak about the things they considered important. I was interested in what they remembered and how they remembered it more than in extracting information on specific facts or evaluating their memory of communism. My goal was to recover subjective emotions and meanings that they assigned to their experiences. These personal conversations were supplemented by published collections of interviews conducted by other researchers in Poland.[24]

Personal testimonies about communism present distinct methodological challenges, from the need to consider the role of censorship and auto-censorship in autobiographies written for public consumption to issues of nostalgia that may affect testimonies gathered after the collapse of the system. In working with autobiographies, I was not looking for "authentic" or "representative" testimonies but for a range of possible perspectives and understandings of oneself and the world around one. In doing so, I followed the approach that scholars have called "empathetic reconstruction" or "refeeling" of one's personal world. Applying this approach does not mean that we simplify personal experiences or "dispense with the rational elements of historical analysis" but that we enrich the study of the past with multiple perspectives.[25]

Exploring young people's subjective worlds allows us to uncover the complexity of individuals and society that may be less evident in institutional documents or conventional narratives of political history. For example, the flourishing of youth culture in Poland attests to the successes of secularization in Poland, which was overshadowed by the dramatic rise of the Catholic Church's political and economic power after the collapse of communism. As a result of World War II, Polish society became nearly ethnically and religiously homogenous, with 98 percent of the population declaring themselves Roman Catholics by the end of the 1940s. But Catholicism has traditionally been a social identity for most Poles rather than a spiritual or moral one. Through the sixties, the Church proved as powerless as the state in controlling young people's embrace of modern lifestyles and outlooks. The dominant self-identification of young Poles as Catholics did not prevent scores of young women from wearing miniskirts, engaging in premarital sex, and dancing the twist, despite the Church's condemnation of these trends. As sociological research consistently showed, close to 70 percent of young people who considered themselves practicing Catholics supported divorce and the right to abortion.[26]

It is also clear from personal testimonies that the sixties presented a unique moment when the novelty of mass media and consumer objects stimulated rather than suppressed youth activity and creativity. Young people's interactions with Western popular music or consumer commodities often created a distinct feeling of "freedom" and a desire for action. In that sense, this book argues against the paradigm of depoliticization through popular culture and consumption put forward by such authors as Alexei Yurchak and Paulina Bren. Focusing on late socialism in the Soviet Union and Czechoslovakia, respectively, Yurchak and Bren have highlighted the consumer turn as instrumental in the socialist regimes' successes to secure the conformity of society.[27] While acknowledging the fluid boundaries between "official" and "unofficial" cultures and between state and nonstate actors that Yurchak and Bren underline in their works, I look at consumption, both material and cultural, as a creative endeavor and a statement about one's subjectivity. In doing so, I draw on anthropological work by Krisztina Fehérváry, who has stressed the complex meaning of consumer goods and their role in fostering nonmaterial needs and desires in socialist and postsocialist Hungary.[28] Exploring the many ways consumption served to express agency, I show the potential for contingency and alternative developments.

This book aims to capture the dynamism of the sixties in Poland through eight thematic chapters. Chapter 1 focuses on the cosmopolitan dimension of the Polish Thaw and the transborder contacts that, ironically, shaped the launching of "the Polish Road to Socialism." These included the Fifth World Youth and Student Festival in Warsaw in 1955 and Polish youth's involvement in the Hungarian Revolution in November 1956. The festival accelerated cultural liberalization and youth's desire for mobility across borders, whereas the Soviet invasion of Hungary, as witnessed by Polish students and young journalists reporting from Budapest, set limits on these newly acquired freedoms. Chapter 2 looks at public projections of youth identity in Polish popular writings, sociological research, and sex education manuals in an effort to show how the state, despite cracking down on the Thaw and youth "radicalism," created an environment in which new ways of imagining the young selfhood became possible. Sociologists, writers, and educators helped promote the idea of youth as the embodiment of a new type of socialist modernity that embraced moderate consumption, educated leisure, and moral values. New youth magazines that covered a range of cultural developments in the West while also building connections between the Second World and the Third World are the topic of Chapter 3. Analyzing several youth magazines, such as *Around the World*, *Radar*, and *ITD*, this chapter traces the specific ways in which domestic forms of modernity interacted with international youth culture. Ultimately, rather than "normalizing" society through a socialist culture of consumption, I argue, youth magazines helped readers imagine themselves as part of a global community beyond the Iron Curtain.

No wonder that young people asserted themselves through nonconformist cultural expression and a new relationship with consumer products and technology. Chapter 4 looks at the state-sponsored student clubs that offered students a unique "freedom" that was more extensive and more transnational than the opportunities granted to other groups. These new spaces, however, also produced new hierarchies and exclusions, as women and students from rural backgrounds often struggled to be seen as equals in urban student milieux. This chapter also introduces students' political circles, which continued the Thaw-era search for leftist ideas as alternatives to those professed by the state socialist regime. Chapter 5 examines leftist students' attempts to challenge the state's hegemony with their own interpretations of socialism and internationalism. This challenge culminated in student and youth demonstrations in March 1968, to which the state reacted with violence and a powerful antisemitic campaign that stigmatized young rebels as Zionists and foreign agents alien to the Polish national community.

While political groups tended to turn inward after 1968, the search for transnational engagement survived in hippie communities. Chapter 6 follows the hippie counterculture from the creation of unique personal styles and the formation of communes to experimentation with sex and drugs. It draws on hippie interactions with Polish society, from the security apparatus and the Church to their parents and older generations. This chapter also uncovers the influence of this counterculture on the wider society, including youth styles in the early 1970s and state-sponsored international festivals of avant-garde theater held in the city of Wroclaw. Chapter 7 turns to rural youth and the ways the world entered the traditional Polish village. This occurred, to a large extent, through state-supported cultural modernization, which included the spread of education, television, and club-cafés. Young rural women were critical to introducing modern lifestyles to the countryside, from coffee drinking and dating to new household technologies and courses on female health and reproduction. While inspiring global connections, however, the world in the village also served to minimize regional identities and solidify the link between the rural population and the modern Polish nation. Chapter 8 returns to public projections of youth culture and how they changed at the time of the global turmoil of the 1960s. It shows how the Polish state, under the leadership of the new Party secretary, Edward Gierek, who assumed power in December 1970, proved successful in absorbing many elements of youth culture into the official culture, including hippie fashion, rock music, and more relaxed private lifestyles. The Gierek regime also promoted a new kind of global engagement in which Poland served as the epitome of a modern socialist country: a champion of détente, open to the world and the global market. The book ends in 1974, arguably the heyday of Polish consumer socialism, before the protests and dissent of the second half of the 1970s and the 1980s.

Contrary to the popular narratives of Poland's "isolation" from the West propagated after the fall of communism in 1989, this book shows how much Poland was part of the global story even when the Iron Curtain was standing. From the perspective of youth culture, this book argues, the postcommunist transition often dubbed as "the return to Europe" was less of a breakthrough than of a continuation and modification of earlier trends catalyzed by the global sixties.

1

The Polish Thaw

Youth Carnival, Domestic Revolution, and Cross-border Encounters

In January 1954, less than a year after the death of Stalin, a new illustrated magazine, *Around the World* (Dookoła Świata) captivated the Polish public. "Warsaw has new fun," writer and jazz lover Leopold Tyrmand recorded in his diary. "Today, the third issue of this magazine came out and was, literally, snatched from newsstands in less than an hour." The magazine differed from the typical state publications of the day, since none of its articles called on readers to build socialism or worship the leader. "Ninety-five percent of this magazine is free from political propaganda," Tyrmand explained. "It is an imitation of all kinds of entertainment and sensationalist press of the world. . . . Sports, short stories, a lot of stories from real life, from games, from entertainment; pictures from parties, cafés, and restaurants; practical advice . . . funnies . . ."[1] No wonder young people dubbed the new magazine "The Voice of the Bikini Boy," referring to the contemporary youth subculture in Poland, the equivalent of the zoot-suiters in the United States, zazou in France, and Teddy boys in England.[2]

Around the World was an early sign of the relaxation of the Stalinist grip on East European societies that soon became known as the Thaw. The "Thaw"— a term taken from the title of a socialist realist novel by the Soviet writer Ilya Ehrenburg published in the fall of 1954—captured the attention of the public across multiple nations. Tadeusz Mazowiecki, a young journalist at the time, read the Polish translation of Ehrenburg's novel and felt that it meant for him "coming out of the era of fear and nonsense."[3] Soon, the Polish term Odwilż, a literal translation of the Russian Ottepel (Thaw), was adopted in mainstream culture to articulate a widespread sense of a new beginning. Youth magazines, student periodicals, music, films, and grassroots theater quickly became the heart and soul of this emergent movement.

Imagining the World from Behind the Iron Curtain. Malgorzata Fidelis, Oxford University Press. © Oxford University Press 2022. DOI: 10.1093/oso/9780197643402.003.0002

The spark that ignited the Thaw could be found in the cautious reforms, known as Malenkov's New Course, undertaken by the Kremlin shortly after Stalin's death on March 5, 1953.[4] These included economic reforms aimed at boosting the consumer sector of the economy, the decentralization of governance, and the dismantling of the terror machine. Soviet and East European societies carefully watched the signals from the top and began to see a growing atmosphere of opening in everyday life.[5] At the threshold of 1954, reforms of the Moscow-directed New Course took hold in Poland. The relentless industrial drive of the Stalinist era subsided, as did the massively unpopular collectivization of agriculture. In personal narratives, the year 1954 has often been described as a hopeful moment, a time when "there was something in the air."[6]

Whereas the Soviet Thaw has often been described in cultural terms as the "revival of intelligentsia," the Polish Thaw ushered in a political revolution that brought to power the Polish "national" communist Władysław Gomułka in October 1956.[7] The gradual buildup to this event included Nikita Khrushchev's "Secret Speech" in February 1956 and the workers' uprising in Poznań in western Poland the following June. An ardent advocate of the "Polish road to socialism," Gomułka was a victim of Stalinism, having been purged from the Party in 1951 and held under house arrest until December 1954. His political takeover in October 1956 marked the official end of Stalinism in Poland and has been considered a moment when both the population and domestic political leaders stood up to the Soviets. For large segments of Polish society, Gomułka represented the end of Soviet-imposed order and the "Polish revolution."[8] But as Gomułka and others quickly discovered, for some young people, this revolution barely addressed the radical social and political change they desired.

Liberation 1954

For young people, the Thaw was not just about changes in political leadership.[9] It was also about new sensations: the sound of jazz on the radio, the taste of coffee at a newly opened student club, and the thrill of discovering the world through popular magazines, music, and movies. These trends had started prior to October. In spring of 1953, a group of young journalists at the biweekly periodical the *Generation* (Pokolenie) had proposed a new illustrated magazine devoted to international travel and popular entertainment.

On the announcement of the idea, readers suggested the title for the new magazine: *Around the World*.[10] Connecting to the outside world was key to the new project. As soon as these journalists received permission from the state to publish, they embarked on collecting "the most interesting photographs from the foreign press" to feature in the magazine's pages. One journalist anticipated with excitement the first issue of *Around the World*: "can't wait for January, can't wait for January / Fashion, adventure, the journey into the unknown, some song, humor and sport."[11] The magazine promised not only to expose Poles to foreign cultures but also to make them part of the global community of mass media audiences.

From the beginning, *Around the World* suggested the possibility of an open, international community for Poles far removed from the rigid and insular structures imposed by the previous Stalinist order. It also established the Polish audience as distinctly Western vis-à-vis the non-European world. The cover of the first issue depicted a snake charmer in India with the caption "This Hindu fakir does not even suspect that he has just been 'immortalized' in the photograph, and . . . by a Polish journalist no less."[12] The encounter with what Poles perceived as an exotic Hindu symbolized the understanding of new freedoms bringing cultural diversity and personal mobility, but it also included Poles among the Western audience of the Orient.

A commentary by journalist Kazimierz Koźniewski affirmed the widespread desire of young people to travel. "Looking at the cover, you see a snake charmer," Koźniewski wrote. "You would like to be there and see him with your own eyes, wouldn't you? Who wouldn't?"[13] Koźniewski praised Poland's friendly relations "with Asian countries" and the supposed opportunities for travel based on achievement, "be it scientific, industrial, technical, artistic," rather than wealth, as had been the case in precommunist Poland. But he was quick to note that personal travel was not essential to experiencing "a splendid adventure." "You have read the *Adventures of Tom Sawyer*, haven't you?" he asked. "[These adventures] all happened within a small town, but they were no less enthralling."[14]

For the majority of young Poles who, like Tom Sawyer, had little choice but to stay in their own localities, *Around the World* offered opportunities for imaginary travel. Its issues featured ample photo-reportage by Polish and foreign authors traveling to foreign lands.[15] Foreign material was combined with images of everyday life in Polish cities, symbolically making Poland part of the "world" that young people were encouraged to explore.[16]

Travel literature was not simply escapism, but a way for young people to conceptualize a broader world. In its early editions, *Around the World* devoted considerable attention to the non-European world. Photographs from Africa, Asia, and Latin America, often featured on the front cover, depicted native populations, mostly women and children in regional dress, engaging in traditional work or cultural rituals such as dancing.[17] Occasionally, short notes compared the suppression of native revolts such as the Mau Mau Uprising in Kenya against the British to the Polish experience of the German occupation during World War II. "Look at the pictures featured here," one commentary stated. "They remind us vividly of the tragic snapshots from the gloomy occupational past; long columns of people with their hands behind their heads and with machine gun muzzles pointed at them."[18] Articulating connections between contemporary colonial oppression and Polish wartime suffering, *Around the World* encouraged its readers to identify with the experiences and struggles of the Global South.

Alongside *Around the World*, young people engaged in other transgressive activities. Students and young artists began producing a range of experiments in theater that became known as Student Theater. Spearheaded by a group at Warsaw University under the name of the Student Theater of Satirists (Studencki Teatr Satyryków), the first premiere of this type of theater in May 1954 was titled *Youth Is Coming* (To idzie młodość). The group relied on help from professional script writers and directors, which initially suggested a cautious approach toward their unconventional production. In November, the Student Theater of Satirists staged its first independent show, *The Simple People* (Prostaczkowie), written, directed, and performed entirely by students.[19] Similar theater groups emerged in Gdańsk, Kraków, Poznań, Wrocław, and other cities. Resisting the existing models of institutional or amateur theater, young people sought their own voice through new forms of theatrical expression.[20]

Youth and student periodicals published reviews of performances and information on the Student Theater. Even if one had no opportunity to attend the plays, print culture conveyed what the performances looked like and how they impacted audiences. Young actress Halina Mikołajska, for example, attended a performance by the Gdańsk-based theater Bim-Bom and vividly detailed her reaction in the widely read official student weekly *Po prostu* (Straight talk) in May 1956:

A group of young people wearing colorful tights runs onto the stage. They are beautiful. Young women have long, beautiful legs, high hips, and slim shoulders. They all have child-like faces. With the waltz playing in the background, they dance in a simple and relaxed manner holding a balloon. A balloon, in its essence, is nice and light. It is as light as air, and almost as light as a dream. It shines in light. Children like the balloon, because it is as if it were from a fairy tale. These young people on the stage are at times awkward in their child-like charming gesture. And this is beautiful too. Suddenly, a man walks onto the stage. He is serious. He does not make faces. Slowly, he approaches the little balloon. He tries to frighten it with a cigarette. He wants to destroy the little balloon. For a moment, the beautiful people are hovering over the beautiful toy. Eventually, the balloon bursts under the shoe of the man. The man quietly leaves the stage. A small scrap of the balloon remains on the floor. A young girl stands in front of the group. She extends a terribly empty hand after the departing man. The forestage becomes dark. With a bright horizon in the background, two figures swing steady like the pendulum of a clock. The time passes by. The curtain falls. The first act is over.[21]

Another viewer, Stanisław Jonas, could not shake what he saw for several weeks after attending the same performance in a crowded hall "with no chance to find a sitting spot." For Jonas, the movements and metaphors described by Mikołajska were more than an aesthetic experience but a call to engage. "The constant change of scenes, dimming the lights, closing the curtain do not weary the audience," Jonas explained, "because these intermissions are needed to absorb the content of the previous scene, to calm down after the shocking but very authentic ending, and *to formulate one's own conclusions (yes!)*."[22]

Several actors from the Student Theater made their way into movies and soon became idols of the young generation. The most famous of them was Zbyszek Cybulski, a cofounder of the Bim-Bom in Gdańsk, who embodied youth rebellion on stage and off. Years before his memorable role in *Ashes and Diamonds*, the young actor began to build his credentials as a male existentialist rebel in live performance. Wearing dark glasses and a leather jacket, he became a symbol of the era in Poland not unlike James Dean in contemporary American films.[23]

Given the enthusiasm that the Student Theater generated among performers and audiences alike, communist leaders had little choice but to incorporate the new artistic initiative into state structures. The official Polish Student Association (Związek Studentów Polskich; ZSP) soon took charge of the Student Theater. The move exposed the ambiguous boundaries between the state and its young subjects. Situated at the intersection between culture and politics, and between grassroots initiatives and official activism, the Student Theater was an important outlet for younger generations for years to come.

Writing the Revolution

On September 4, 1955, *Po prostu* changed the color of the subheading background in its front cover title from red to green. What looked like a simple alteration amounted to nothing short of a revolution. *Po prostu* to date had served as a mouthpiece of state propaganda. The color green not only marked a break with that formula but also signaled the beginning of critical journalism, which soon became the hallmark of the Polish Thaw. Young journalists at *Po prostu* published critical commentary on current events, unembellished reporting from factories and villages, and debates on Marxism. Within weeks, the circulation of the new *Po prostu* reached 150,000 copies, one of the highest among all Polish periodicals at the time.[24]

The renewed *Po prostu* inspired a wave of similar publications by students in all large cities in Poland. These included *Fresh Start* (Od nowa) in Warsaw; *Zebra* in Kraków; *Rough Road Ahead* (Wyboje) in Poznań; *Views* (Poglądy) in Wrocław; *Against the Wind* (Pod wiatr) in Lublin; and *Contrasts* (Kontrasty) on the Baltic coast. Students took charge of every step in the process of writing, publication, and distribution. As Bogusław Litwiniec, a student-journalist at *Views* recalled, in addition to reporting, writing, and editing, he also delivered copies from the printer to various newsstands in the city of Wrocław by bicycle.[25]

How was the independent student press possible under state censorship? The Thaw generated a new political climate in which censors found themselves disoriented by the changes and uncertain of what exactly was allowed. Young journalists recalled that at first, censors accepted critical articles for publication in *Po prostu* because they assumed that these texts had already been approved by Party officials. Censors operated according to the conventional process, in which the editor-in-chief "cleared" the pieces with his or her patron in the Party structures before submitting the material to the censors. The censorship office then usually gave the material another reading to ensure that politically unacceptable statements did not slip in. They especially watched for critical remarks about the Soviet Union, which were not allowed in print.[26] Ultimately, the responsibility for a controversial text rested with the editor-in-chief. This process was unexpectedly interrupted by the personnel changes in the Party-state institutions and the liberalizing signals from Moscow. It took some time for the censors to catch up.[27] When they did, "they took off not only individual articles, but entire pages," recalled one journalist at *Po prostu*. "With time, however . . . we worked out a strategy for action," he continued. "For small matters, it was enough to convince the censor that he did not really understand what we wrote. In other cases, however, one had to intervene with the higher-ups."[28] During the Thaw, such interventions often worked as the highest echelons of the Party acknowledged the need for more openness.

Being part of critical journalism was a way of life, as was the case for those involved in Student Theater. The Lublin students who published *Against the Wind* declared their commitment to progress: "*Against the Wind* always wants to be dissatisfied with the current state of affairs—it wants to gather people, who believe that standing in one place really means backtracking."[29] The editors of *Zebra*, a magazine published by young artists in Kraków, believed in empowerment through art: "we are a group of young people. We paint, sculpt, write. . . . We would like our journal to become a weapon in the struggle for truth, justice, and human dignity."[30] But even those journals that were not produced by the artistic milieu celebrated the transformative power of art and literature. All student periodicals featured poetry, drawings, and photographs by young artists. In that sense, the student press of the Thaw saw cultural revolt as a necessary precursor of the political revolution, the notion that would permeate global protest culture over the next decade and beyond.

A key question debated in the student press was how to rekindle the true revolutionary spirit of the youth. Student journalists argued that the rigid Stalinist approach to youth organizations turned the revolution into a matter of routine and bureaucracy. In June 1956, *Po prostu* published a piece on the need to abolish the Polish Youth Association (Związek Młodzieży Polskiej; ZMP), modeled on the Soviet Komsomol, and to create a new organization based on ideas from below. The Leninist title, "What Is To Be Done?," pointed to the urgency and gravity of the issue as much as to the socialist nature of the initiative.[31] At the center of the demand to redefine the organizational formula was the need to reclaim the physical space of youth activism and move the revolution to the club.

Po prostu inspired the creation of the Clubs of Young Intelligentsia (Kluby Młodej Inteligencji) to facilitate an open discussion among young professionals and students about political and social matters. Such discussion clubs were not limited to large cities, but often became gathering spots in small towns throughout Poland.[32] The clubs also facilitated diverse intellectual and social pursuits. Tadeusz Mazowiecki and his friends, for example, formed a Catholic discussion club inspired by French philosopher Emmanuel Mounier.[33] Students opened their own clubs, which typically included discussion rooms, bridge and chess rooms, dancing halls, and a room to play jazz. Jazz became the symbol of new freedoms after being banned to the public during the Stalinist era.

Critical journalism was not just a diatribe against those in power. Rather, political debate went hand in hand with new notions of the relationship between the self and the possibilities of the modern world. Student periodicals incorporated contemporary popular culture inspired by the West, with the back cover of issues usually being devoted to advertising, humor, and sexual innuendo. In one advertisement for the state-run men's fashion house AS in Kraków, the drawing showed Adam and Eve naked with their genitalia covered by fig leaves. The caption read: "PARADISE:—Here is a suit from "AS." You will finally look like a human being."[34] The ad was accompanied by another drawing depicting a woman in scant clothing bending and showing her knee. She stood next to a lantern, with the Barbakan, a medieval landmark in Kraków, in the background. The caption read: "Kraków is a city full of beautiful historic buildings."[35]

The mixing of "low" and "high" art was used to celebrate eroticism and gender difference. Student periodicals, created and edited predominantly by men, featured reports on female beauty pageants staged in different Polish cities, complete with photographs of the winner and the runners-up and details on their measurements.[36] In *Views*, winners of the Miss Polonia beauty contest in 1957 were presented next to the article about the history of the female nude in art under the title "The History of the Nude: Short Course." The title parodied a well-known book, the *History of the Communist Party of the Soviet Union (Bolsheviks): Short Course*, commissioned by Stalin in 1938. Photographs of the beauty pageant contestants were arranged in such a way as to merge with reprints of Renaissance paintings of nude women.[37]

Fig. 1.1 "A History of the Nude in Art: Short Course," *Views*, 20 August 1957. Warsaw University Library, Warsaw.

Such images and commentary could not be exclusively attributed to the reassertion of heterosexual masculinity in reaction to Stalinist policies of gender equality. Rather, these images helped define men as producers and consumers of the anti-Stalinist revolution, which would indeed liberate them personally and bring more pleasure in life. At the same time, eroticized female bodies served as both the objects and subjects of the anti-Stalinist revolt. As art historians have noted, styling themselves after Western film stars became an important element of Polish female artists' self-representation during and after the Thaw. By wearing leopard dresses and modeling their hairstyles after Brigitte Bardot, female artists provided a contrast to the austerity the Stalinist industrialization had generated. In this way, they enacted their own strategy of resistance.[38] Participants in the beauty pageants featured in the student press adopted a similar style of Western "bombshells."[39] Expressing female agency in this way, however, proved to be precarious. Images of bombshells and nude women were soon adopted by state publications, making the objectification of women an inherent part of the Polish public culture under communism. During the Thaw, such images served the state's agenda to neutralize calls for liberalization by showing that personal styles and sexual matters had already been "liberalized."[40]

Alongside the new self-expression embedded in global popular culture, rebellious journalists also confronted national myths about the recent past. *Po prostu* helped initiate the process of rehabilitating the Home Army (Armia Krajowa), the noncommunist Polish resistance movement under Nazi occupation. Under Stalinism, members of the Home Army had experienced persecution, including prison terms and executions as "reactionaries" and "fascists." Those who escaped prison or death faced marginalization and condemnation in the official media. In March 1956, *Po prostu* was the first periodical to publicly call for restoring the Home Army, one of the largest underground movements in occupied Europe, to its proper place in the "chain of national and revolutionary tradition."[41]

Rehabilitating the Home Army was not hero worship devoid of criticism, however. Writing the revolution entailed creating historical narrative that reckoned with the good and bad sides of Polish history. This was important for the Thaw leaders both as a protest against the Stalinist attempt to erase the truth and as an act of claiming a leftist ethical stance. While recognizing Polish struggles and sacrifices during the war, young journalists also invited reflection on less admirable aspects of Poles' wartime behavior. Some of the most compelling pieces featured in *Po prostu* dealt with Polish antisemitism and complicity in the Holocaust.[42]

As many of the writers and readers of *Po prostu* knew, in the aftermath of World War II, antisemitism persisted across Poland in many forms, from prejudice and discrimination to pogroms.[43] Since the late nineteenth century, Polish national thought had framed the Jew as "the other," an idea that endured but was rarely expressed in public.[44] Moreover, suspicion and distrust toward Jewish comrades was not uncommon among Polish communists, with Polish Jews being labeled in internal Party documentation as "of Jewish descent" (*osoby pochodzenia żydowskiego*) or "of Jewish nationality" (*osoby narodowości żydowskiej*), while Polish Catholics were simply called "Poles."[45] This had profound consequences for the way the Polish communist state addressed—or rather, silenced—narratives of the Holocaust. Only approximately 10 percent of the 3.5 million Polish Jews survived the Holocaust. Facing hostility in postwar Poland, the vast majority of survivors emigrated. Tens of thousands were aided in the process by a secret agreement between Poland and Israel in 1949.[46] Jewish issues, however, were largely absent from public discussion during the Stalinist period, not least because of antisemitism in the communist circles. Emboldened by the revelations of Khrushchev's "Secret Speech," young Polish leftists believed that the renewal of socialism required confronting the dark side of the past and reconciling with the Jewish community.

In May 1956, *Po prostu* published parts of the diary of Hanka Szwarcman, a young Polish Jewish woman, who had spent the war years in hiding in France but returned to her homeland in the summer of 1954. Her relatives in France had advised her to change her last name to a Polish-sounding one to avoid being a target of antisemitism, but she refused. "I have nothing to be ashamed of," she responded. "Shame on those who profess such reprehensible feelings, 'feelings' that . . . motivated some to denounce Jewish children [during the Nazi occupation of Poland], and not always in exchange for a kilogram of sugar, but sometimes 'unselfishly,' out of conviction."[47] When Szwarcman arrived in Poland, she soon learned that her relatives had a point. The father of her Polish fiancé stopped speaking to his son on learning that he "wanted to marry a Jewish woman."[48]

Szwarcman's diary was not a lamentation on popular antisemitism, however abhorrent. She accused those in power of allowing such attitudes to go unchecked and for not reckoning with their own problematic relationship with the Jews. When she went to the official commemorations of the thirteenth anniversary of the Warsaw Ghetto Uprising in April 1956, she could not understand why "the commemoration was a purely Jewish event." Moreover, she explicitly referred to antisemitism as instrumental in the Stalinist terror machine and to Stalin's close associate, Lavrentiy Beria, largely responsible for antisemitic purges. "Why is there no conversation about Beriaism [Beriowszczyzna], which disseminated antisemitism along with committing other crimes?" she asked.[49]

As young journalists at *Po prostu* argued, building a genuine socialist state required not just a political revolution but also a rethinking and reframing of Polish communism. Embracing the Home Army was as important as embracing Polish Jews as an integral part of Polish society and history. Indeed, the survival of socialism depended on rebuilding its moral center. Szwarcman declared: "if the guarantee for change is the uncovering and condemning of evil, then only an open conversation about the symptoms of antisemitism will uproot it from the consciousness of the people."[50] Young philosopher Leszek Kołakowski echoed this message in the subsequent issue of *Po prostu* by claiming that even the most "benign" forms of anti-Jewish prejudice "can lead to the most heinous crimes" since "tolerating antisemitism even in its most mild forms is tolerating future pogroms." According to Kołakowski, antisemitism was "anticulture, antihumanity, antiphilosophy and antiscience."[51] In openly confronting antisemitism, the student movement pushed the boundaries of acceptable topics of conversation, creating new norms for what was public and what was silenced. In doing so, young leftists such as Szwarcman and Kołakowski revealed the darker side of Polish memory and history.

The mixing of styles and messages suggests a new type of youth self-expression that crossed geopolitical boundaries. To take just one example, the mixing of styles and themes—"youth revolution and popular culture, sexual provocation and political critiques of postcolonial warfare"—were crucial markers of the underground student press that emerged in West Germany in the early 1960s, including the periodicals *Spiegel*, *Stern*, *Pardon*, *konkret*, and *Twen*.[52] The political and cultural demands of West German students were more radical than Polish students' idealistic calls for "democratization" and "humanism" in the mid-1950s, but the idea of critical journalism as a tool to change society and challenge Cold War politics was strikingly similar.

Crossing Borders: From the World Youth Festival to the Hungarian Revolution

The World Youth and Student Festival that took place in Warsaw in the summer of 1955 was a key catalyst for the explosion of critical journalism. If *Around the World* offered virtual travel to foreign lands through photographs and reports, contact with the outside world through such a mass event created new opportunities for personal interaction with young people from many nations. The world youth festivals, although dismissed by the American and British governments as nothing more than communist propaganda events, were an important tool of Cold War cultural diplomacy, or "the exercise of soft power," across the East-West divide.[53] The festivals originated when the United Nations established the World Federation of Democratic Youth in November 1945. Two years later, it joined with the International Union of Students to create a platform for young people from all parts of the world, including capitalist and socialist countries, that underscored world peace and an antinuclear agenda. In the early postwar period, festivals were held in the capitals of socialist countries: in 1947 in Prague; in 1949 in Budapest; in 1951 in East Berlin; and in 1953 in Bucharest. The Warsaw festival took place between July 31 and August 15, 1955, bringing together an estimated 26,600 participants from 116 countries. In addition, 150,000 youths from different parts of Poland joined the celebrations.[54]

Fig. 1.2 Opening of the World Youth and Student Festival at the Tenth-Anniversary Stadium, Warsaw, 1 August 1955. Photo by Mariusz Szyperko. Courtesy of Polish Press Agency.

The World Youth Festival embraced a stunning array of arts and culture, including Summer Olympics–style sports, music, theater, film, fine art, and photography, all in combination with "political education" and "mass demonstrations." Gathering under the slogan "Peace and friendship," the festivals' official aim was to enable young people from all over the world to meet one another, learn about different cultures, and "in doing so, reduce the likelihood of future global conflict."[55] Participants in the Warsaw festival came from all continents and political systems, including the United States, Western Europe, the Soviet Union, China, Syria, Egypt, Israel, Brazil, Mexico, Sudan, and Nigeria. Many belonged to communist organizations, but representatives of the YMCA, YWCA, social democrats, Zionists, and the Polish diaspora could also be found among the attendees. Festivities took place not only in meeting halls and public squares but also in newly created cafés and student clubs. The Bim-Bom arrived from Gdańsk to give performances, and

Fig. 1.3 The Ball of One Hundred Nations at the World Youth and Student Festival, Warsaw, 1 August 1955. Photo by Bolesław Miedza. Courtesy of Polish Press Agency.

a young Arab man by the name of Yasser Arafat came to watch a play by the Student Theater of Satirists and befriended the student-actors.[56]

The Polish media celebrated the meeting of cultures, especially the encounter with the non-Western world. The cover of *Around the World* for the first week of August 1955 showed a group of racially diverse participants having fun at the festival. At the forefront, a white female and a black male embraced, suggesting that there were no barriers to interracial interaction. The caption read: "exotic instruments, dark faces, foreign melodious speech . . . Brazil? A village on the Amazon? No. This is Marszałkowska street in August."[57] The issue projected official support for internationalism and antiracism while publicizing an internationalized, progressive, and anti-Western Poland. The idea of being "like a village on the Amazon" explicitly rejected racial ideologies prevalent among the Whites in the European colonies and the United States. The Third World, as hosted in Warsaw, became an object of admiration and curiosity and a metaphor for social emancipation at home.

This gathering of young people from all over the world made a lasting impression on young Poles. The collective memory of the Warsaw festival

Fig. 1.4 Cover of *Around the World*, 7 August 1955. Racially diverse participants at the World Youth and Student Festival in Warsaw. Photo by J. Napiórkowski. National Library, Warsaw.

is strikingly similar to the memory of the Sixth World Youth and Student Festival, held in Moscow two years later.[58] Male participants typically recall the Warsaw festival as the scene of a realization of their sexual fantasies. According to one of them, Stanisław Manturzewski, the festival was "one big alcoholic-erotic party, a sort of sexual-artistic uncorking."[59] A large banner with the words "baise-moi" (kiss me) was displayed in the center of Warsaw. The erotically charged climate was not absent from the official coverage of the festival. Newsreels showed couples hugging and kissing. In one report, the audience saw the participants playing "a new Polish game: I choose who." It was not clear how the game worked, but one could see young women and men first walking in circles, and then forming couples. They hugged, kissed, and danced together. The voice-over explained to the audience that the Polish young women were acting as "teachers" and men from different countries were pretending to be their "students."[60]

Such fantasies of transnational and interracial intimacy became an important part of celebrating socialist internationalism.[61] Exotic foreign women drew particular attention. Journalist Wojciech Giełżyński's report, published in *Around the World* during the festival, featured photographs of several young women from different countries in their national costumes. The author started with a poetic confession: "I wanted to write about the beauty of girls from Asia, Africa, and America. . . . But I set my pen aside. I cannot. One cannot articulate with words the beauty of roses, chrysanthemums, and orchids."[62] Giełżyński nevertheless described the said beauties using superficial stereotypical features of the cultures and nationalities they came from.

In the report, dark skin was fetishized and endowed with the highest aesthetic qualities. "Amid the delegates from Guadeloupe, Paule Palantin is probably the darkest and the most beautiful," Giełżyński wrote about the woman featured on the cover of this issue of *Around the World*. He then turned to young women from India, who "do not walk, but rather they glide, or—if you will—they have a majestic stride." Hindu women also "did not laugh out loud, but rather only smiled with the most beautiful eyes in the world that even a doe would be jealous of."[63] As such commentary suggested, communist antiimperialism could easily turn into colonial fantasizing. The two could reinforce each other by projecting an attractive image of the Third World according to the new standards of popular media culture and entertainment.[64] In this sense, the World Youth Festival offered a new way to celebrate internationalism, not through worn-out appeals to working-class solidarity but through gendered and racialized fantasies of male desire.

The festival fueled young people's longing for more interaction with the world. More than a year later, in December 1956, student Andrzej Konopacki fondly recalled the festivities as a turning point that changed the self-definition of young people like him. "The Warsaw Festival knocked out a huge hole in the hermetically sealed iron curtain," he wrote in the student magazine *Contrasts*, directly challenging the Cold War binary. "What remained is nostalgia for foreign lands, newly made friends—sustained by letters peppered with colorful stamps from all over the world. We alone know

Fig. 1.5 Cover of *Around the World*, 14 August 1955. Paule Palentine from Guadeloupe at the World Youth and Student Festival in Warsaw. Photo by J. Napiórkowski. National Library, Warsaw.

how many evenings we spent studying the world map and foreign dictionaries. Life acquired new colors."[65] Andrzej articulated a strong link between bridging Cold War divides and a fulfilling personal life.

In the wake of the festival, thousands of young people flooded the state's Passport Bureau with applications and letters demanding that international travel become an integral part of socialist education. *Around the World* soon launched a public campaign for the right to travel under the slogan "Travel is Education" (*Podróże kształcą*). In May 1956, the editorial board published an open letter to the minister of the interior on behalf of the magazine's readers. "One should not have a difficult time convincing anyone," the first line of the letter read, "that the love of travel, the desire to see the world—is an indispensable part of youth." The letter recognized the expanded opportunity for organized travel but demanded easing restrictions on individual travel. "Many young people, who met each other during the Festival or on another occasion," the editors continued, "equally dream of visiting each other. They exchanged letters; they came up with the necessary financial quotas; they agreed on all kinds of details. . . . *And here the state bureaucracy trumps their friendships.*"[66] The petition continued in capital letters: "CITIZEN MINISTER, PLEASE TELL US WHY ONE DEPRIVES THE YOUNG PEOPLE OF THE VALUABLE, MEMORABLE EXPERIENCES ASSOCIATED WITH GETTING TO KNOW THE WORLD?" The letter ended by asking the minister to make "the relevant decisions that would allow . . . the desires and dreams of many young people to come true."[67]

The following month, the state did indeed ease travel restrictions, but the public campaign for the right to travel soon faded in the face of the political revolution that broke out in Hungary.[68] If the World Youth Festival exposed young people's desires to cross geopolitical barriers, the Hungarian Revolution showed a more dangerous and politicized side to transnational encounters. Just a few days after the Eighth Plenary Meeting of the Central Committee in October 1956, at which Gomułka was elected by the Politburo to head the Polish ruling party, Hungarians rose up against the Stalinist regime in their country. The Hungarian "national" communist Imre Nagy had been expelled from the government and the Party in 1955 but was gaining support from reformist circles within the Party and the general population, including the Thaw-inspired youth movements. As popular discontent grew, in July 1956, the Hungarian leadership replaced General Secretary Matyas Rákosi with Ernő Gerő. Unfortunately, the change did little to alleviate popular anger, since Gerő was another notorious Stalinist determined to suppress any reforms.

Inspired by the events in Poland and the coming to power of Gomułka there, Hungarian students held a demonstration in Budapest, on October 23, calling for the withdrawal of Soviet troops from Hungary and the implementation of democratic reforms, including free elections. The protestors began the demonstration near the monument of Sándor Petőfi, a Hungarian Romantic poet who perished in one of the last battles of the Hungarian War of Independence in 1849. They then marched to the monument of another hero of the Hungarian War of Independence, Polish general Józef Bem, who had fought alongside Lajos Kossuth (the leader of the Hungarian War of Independence) and Petőfi. A small group of Polish students in Hungary joined the demonstration, and one of them reported in the Lublin student magazine *Against the Wind*: "not without emotion we read [the slogans on the banners]: 'Long live Poland! Long live Polish Youth! Long-Live the Polish-Hungarian friendship!'"[69] For a short period of time, the Polish and Hungarian revolutions generated transnational youth solidarity of a type that would come to be associated with 1968. The Polish student continued: "we march in procession under the Polish flag. Ecstatic faces of young Hungarian men and women surround us. We are infected with the zeal and enthusiasm of the crowd."[70]

Under pressure, Gerő appointed Imre Nagy as head of the Hungarian government the next day. But Gerő also called on the Soviet military stationed in Hungary to help suppress the revolt. By that point the police and portions of the Hungarian Army had joined the protestors. Some of the first casualties occurred on October 25, when security forces fired on the crowd, leaving dozens dead. Yet the uprising continued, with workers joining the students and forming their own revolutionary councils.

On October 26, the first Polish plane carrying medical supplies in anticipation of possible bloodshed landed in Budapest. Two journalists, Marian Bielicki from Polish Radio and *Po prostu* and Roman Kornecki from the main Party daily *The People's Tribune* (Trybuna Ludu), were also on board.[71] Assisted by a Soviet escort, the journalists were transported to the Polish embassy. Along the route, they passed alternating Soviet and Hungarian checkpoints scattered through the city. They also noted Hungarian national flags with the Soviet coat of arms cut out and an empty post on which the monument of Stalin had stood until just a few days earlier. "On the base of the statue," they reported, "only Stalin's boots remained where a Hungarian flag was planted."[72] A few days later, Bielicki and Kornecki were joined by several other Polish journalists, including "the passionately pro-Hungarian" journalist Hanka Adamiecka, who worked for the communist youth daily the *Banner of Youth* (Sztandar Młodych).[73] Adamiecka walked around Budapest with a Hungarian tricolor cockade pinned to her chest. Her colleague Wiktor Woroszylski described her as "an inexhaustible enthusiast . . . always being on the right side of the cause. . . . Without people like Hanka, revolutions would not have been possible. In Budapest, there must be more than one bright-haired Hungarian girl like Hanka."[74]

In Polish reports, Adamiecka became a revolutionary heroine ready to put her life on the line to transmit the truth about the Hungarian Revolution to the outside world. Stories about her helped romanticize the Hungarian struggle and a Polish-Hungarian solidarity. In one scene reported in *Around the World*, in order to send a dispatch to Warsaw, Adamiecka made her way by crawling along the ground several hundred meters, under heavy gunfire, to the headquarters of the independent Hungarian newspaper *Szabad Nep*. "The insurgents greeted her with a standing ovation," the report stated. "They helped her start the teleprinter, on which she typed her correspondence to the *Banner of Youth*." The insurgents even brought her food, "including a lemon, which they had somehow miraculously acquired."[75]

Alongside Szwarcman, Adamiecka became a powerful female figure of the Thaw revolution. Whereas Szwarcman's writings in *Po prostu* gave voice to the Holocaust survivors, Adamiecka spoke on behalf of the Hungarian revolutionaries and showcased, in her understanding, a transnational struggle of young people for democratic socialism. While at *Szabad Nep*'s headquarters, she interviewed the leader of the squad of Hungarian revolutionaries, Jozsef Dudas, whose communist credentials dated back to the interwar period. She also visited György Lukács, the prominent writer and minister of culture in Nagy's cabinet, who told her that the Hungarian Uprising "was an indirect path, but without a doubt, a path to socialism." Lukács supported Hungarian independence from the dominant international alliances. "We have to maintain the balance of neutrality, with no tilting to the east or west," he told Adamiecka.[76]

Imre Nagy's decision on November 1 to withdraw Hungary from the Warsaw Pact prompted the Soviets to launch a full-fledged military invasion three days later. The invasion was a graphic display of brute force as the Soviet army shot directly into buildings and killed and wounded people inside. In less than a week, the Hungarian Revolution was crushed.[77] On Saturday, November 10, the Soviets ordered Adamiecka and other Polish journalists to leave Hungary. By that afternoon, they were on their way to Belgrade.[78] Polish journalists were devastated by what they saw in Budapest. On her way home from Belgrade, Adamiecka compared the Soviet attack on Hungarian fighters and civilians to "fascism" in a private letter written to a friend. After her return to Warsaw, she continued to maintain contacts with the leaders of the Hungarian Revolution, who went into exile. In early 1957, she began publishing her diary of the Hungarian Revolution, titled "I Saw Hungary," in the *Banner of Youth*. After the seventh installment, however, the series was halted. On June 1, 1957, Hanka Adamiecka committed suicide at the age of 26.[79] Although it is difficult to establish a direct connection between the Soviet crushing of the Hungarian Revolution and Adamiecka taking her own life, there is no doubt that the Hungarian experience affected her in a dramatic way.

News of the Soviet invasion of Hungary in November 1956 sparked street demonstrations in Poland. In Kraków, the crowd carried Polish and Hungarian flags tied with black crêpe.[80] On learning about the Hungarian defeat, Kraków students organized the Student Committee to Assist the Fighting Hungarians. Years later, a former member of the Committee, Stefan Bratkowski, recalled "collecting things" and "collecting blood" for the Hungarians.[81] When the Committee's delegation was about to leave for Budapest on November 26, crowds of people came to the train station to present "patriotic speeches and flowers." The local military garrison provided sleeping mattresses, sheepskin coats, and food for the student mission. By the end of the day, four train cars, each carrying twenty tons of flour, ten tons of apples, and four tons of salt, bacon, sugar, lard, and other supplies left the station.[82]

The mission to Hungary facilitated personal encounters between Polish students and other Eastern bloc citizens: first Czechs and Slovaks and then Hungarians. Yet if the Polish-Hungarian encounter demonstrated potential for transnational solidarity and cooperation against the Soviet empire, meetings with Czechs and Slovaks did not. As Polish students learned, not everyone in the bloc rebeled against Stalinism the way they did. When the transport from Kraków reached Czechoslovakia, students saw "monuments and portraits of Stalin . . . red stars and banners declaring the eternal love for the USSR . . . no sympathy for the Hungarians existed here." Polish students also learned that the Czechoslovak communist regime effectively exploited national tensions between Czechs and Hungarians and between Czechs and Poles. In the regime's official messages, the revolts in Poland and Hungary were depicted not just as reactionary and antisocialist but also as explicitly anti-Czechoslovak. Referring to the events of March 1939, when Poland and Hungary had joined Nazi Germany in partitioning the interwar Czechoslovak Republic, the Czechoslovak regime claimed that Poles and Hungarians were about to start a new world war and to enact another "partition of Czechoslovakia."[83]

No wonder Czechoslovak officials and workers obstructed the Polish students' journey to Hungary in every possible way. At one station, students were refused water. At another, they barely escaped arrest. Participant Andrzej Bratkowski recalled: "during a fiery exchange of words with a stationmaster, a portrait of Stalin fell from the wall; they [Czechoslovak officials] almost arrested us for offending the leader."[84] The mood changed as the young Poles reached the Hungarian border at Komárom on the Danube. Here Polish students were greeted by "enthusiastic crowds of Hungarians" waving Polish flags. "Women carried out large trays with cookies from the bakery," Bratkowski continued, "and men put glasses filled with wine in our hands."[85] Such a vivid contrast between Czechoslovak and Hungarian citizens underscored for students the tragic solitude of Hungarian rebels and their own heroism in supporting them. Even if the contrast was oversimplified, participants were painfully aware that their enthusiasm and hope were not shared by others and that the Iron Curtain was not the only border to be overcome. While many Poles and Hungarians saw the Thaw as a release of youthful and socialist energies, others in the Eastern bloc interpreted it as a retreat from socialism and a return to nationalist antagonisms of the prewar era.

Cross-border encounters defined the possibilities and limits of the Polish Thaw. Celebrating cultural and racial diversity, the World Youth and Student Festival accelerated cultural and political liberalization. In contrast, the Soviet invasion of Hungary in November 1956, as witnessed by Polish students and young journalists, set limits on the newly acquired freedoms. Ultimately, the two experiences demonstrated two distinct paths for transnational encounters. One was the power of youth from different parts of the world to overcome political barriers; the other was the determination of the Cold War superpowers—the invading Soviets in this case—to cut short any such possibility.

The Frost

The precarious nature of the Thaw was captured by two Soviet dissidents, Ludmila Alexeyeva and Paul Goldberg, who recalled their participation in the cultural revival of the era this way: "a thaw, Lenin Library smokers concurred, was not quite spring. The spring is cyclical and irreversible, and it turns to summer as surely as night turns to day. But a thaw is tenuous. A frost could strike any day."[86] The quote aptly describes the Polish Thaw. By early 1957, the youth rebellion in Poland had lost momentum. The suppression of the Hungarian Revolution had sent a clear signal to Eastern European leaders as to what might happen if movements from below went too far from the Soviet perspective. The Eighth Plenary Meeting of the Polish ruling Party that brought Gomułka to power was the high point of the Polish Thaw. Soon, Gomułka used his popular support to consolidate power. The new regime quickly curtailed the freedom of the media, including the student press. Already on November 1, Gomułka established the Press Bureau as part of Party structures and the Press Commission, an advisory body within the Central Committee, to deal with the sphere of publishing that, in his mind, had got out of control.

Young rebels watched with dismay as Gomułka further legitimized his power in the elections to the Sejm (the lower house of Parliament) on January 20, 1957. The elections included a democratic component but were still controlled by the ruling Party. Instead of the customary one-candidate-per-one-place rule, the number of candidates in each district could be two-thirds higher than the number of seats. If no names were crossed out on the ballot, the candidate in the first position won. To help boost popular legitimacy for the elections, the Party formed the Front of National Unity, in which different political groups were invited to participate (including nominal Catholic and agrarian parties). A few days before the elections, Gomułka appealed to the public to vote without crossing out names. So great was the public's trust in Gomułka that more than 94 percent of eligible voters went to the polls and close to 90 percent of them voted following Gomułka's instruction.[87]

This was not what young rebels imagined democratic socialism would look like. Yet they abstained from further protests, largely as a result of not wanting to share the fate of the Hungarians. In May 1957, *Po prostu* wrote about student clubs and the Clubs of the Young Intelligentsia as "victims of stabilization." In Częstochowa, for example, young people had pressured local officials that October to organize "free elections" to the city government, but then the young woman who had spearheaded those efforts gave up. "One cannot break the wall with one's head," she noted. Other young people, "the most aggressive and revolutionary . . . Jacobins" from the time of the Thaw, claimed not to "give a damn" about political discussion at the club. The only thing left for them was "playing bridge."[88]

Soon, debates over the meaning of the Thaw disappeared from public view. The Gomułka leadership cracked down on critical journalism, shutting down *Po prostu* in November 1957. The main charge against it was that it continued to pursue radical politics despite regime change, which according to the Press Bureau had resolved Poland's political problems and thus eliminated the need for critique.[89]

The suppression of critical journalism had far-reaching consequences. It meant not only the silencing of the debates about the Thaw but also an end to the public reckoning with the past, including the troubling legacy of interwar and wartime antisemitism. In this way, the Gomułka regime made sure that the "Polish Road to Socialism" would leave national myths intact and the departure from "errors and distortions" would not include the reckoning with antisemitism within the Party that *Po prostu* had called for. Silencing discussions about memory would help ease the way for a powerful antisemitic campaign when the Party faced another youth rebellion in 1968.

Po prostu did not go down without a fight. When the Press Bureau halted its publication in September 1957, the editors appealed directly to Gomułka, but to no avail. Students then organized a public demonstration in Warsaw in support of the weekly, but the militia put it down. In October 1957, Gomułka told journalists to obey the hard line: "either you are with the party or against the party. Either you are with socialism, or against socialism."[90] Nearly all independent student periodicals soon shared the fate of *Po prostu*. The last issue of *Views* came out in December 1957. Kraków-based *Zebra* survived only a few months longer; its final edition was April-May 1958. When student-journalists objected to the shutting down of their papers, Party leaders lamely blamed a shortage of printing paper.[91]

This crackdown on critical journalism, while silencing the younger Poles' voices, exposed the power of the printed word as an instrument of change. Stalinist uniformity would never return. Rather, Gomułka envisioned a degree of guided pluralism, in which a new space for "depoliticized" publications opened up. Although *Po prostu* was eliminated, *Around the World* was allowed to remain in circulation because a magazine about travel and entertainment was not considered a threat to socialism. Like the clubs, the press was encouraged to divert its creative energy away from "Jacobinism" and toward "playing bridge."

* * *

The Polish Thaw encompassed the shedding of Stalinism and the "nationalization" of Polish communism. But the meaning of the new "Polish road" to communism was a work in progress, contested and negotiated by multiple players. Many young people believed that the authentic version of socialism demanded not only political and cultural freedoms but also an active engagement with the world. The Polish Thaw therefore was full of internal tensions: the national project was also a cosmopolitan one, and cross-border interaction shaped the new post-Stalinist environment.

Print culture became an important forum where young people contested the ideologies and policies emanating from above. While entertainment-oriented periodicals suggested new relationships between young people in Poland and the modern world, critical journalism aimed at revolution-izing politics and culture through the printed word—inspired and ener-gized by new opportunities for crosscultural interaction such as the World Youth and Student Festival. Practitioners of critical journalism brough to-gether domestic and foreign content in their publications: consumer culture and Western-style bombshells alongside critical texts about Polish wartime memory and the "antihumanity" of antisemitism. More than a year after the Warsaw festival, the news of the Hungarian Revolution provided a chance for some young Poles to participate in an actual transnational effort to enact a version of democratic socialism. Young Hungarian and Polish leftists bonded over what they considered to be genuine socialist values and used national symbols that harkened back to the Romantic era of antiimperialist struggles in 1848–1849.

To this day, the image of Soviet tanks rolling into Budapest in November 1956 serves as a powerful symbol of the tragic end of the Hungarian Revolution and the hopes of the Thaw in all of Eastern Europe. For these reasons, scholars often see the Thaw as a movement abruptly put down from above, a "silenced spring," to use the words of political scientist Kathleen F. Smith.[92] The decline of the Polish Thaw has been expressed through a sim-ilar though less imaginative metaphor of "the retreat from October." The metaphors of "silencing" and "retreat," however, tell us only a part of the story. After the crushing of the Hungarian Revolution, the Polish Thaw in-deed faded away, but it left a fertile environment for a pluralist culture and new opportunities for self-expression. The intellectual challenge of the Thaw persisted and became visible in the youth culture that emerged at the intersec-tion of domestic forms of socialist humanism and crossborder encounters.

2

Youth as Modernity

Envisioning Young People after the Thaw

On March 24, 1959, the port city of Gdańsk became the site of an unusual performance. During an annual competition of jazz and dance bands, organized by the *Banner of Youth*, six young men, who called themselves Rhythm and Blues, came to the stage. Music critic Roman Waschko was present at the event and reported that the audience sensed that "something unexpected was going to happen." As soon as the musicians struck the opening chords, "cheers of enthusiasm filled the gigantic tent under which the bands played. The public unmistakably recognized the lively rock 'n' roll."[1] Thus far such music could be heard mainly on Western radio stations or on vinyl records that some travelers brought in from the West.[2] But here was a Polish band creating these sounds and putting the audience "in such a frenzy that one could only hear one unceasing cheer."[3] Shortly after this performance, Rhythm and Blues played two concerts in the nearby resort town of Sopot, where audiences stood up and sang "One Hundred Years" (Sto lat)—the Polish version of "Happy Birthday"—to honor the band.[4] Flowers were presented to the musicians, and a few young men got on stage attempting to toss them into the air in celebration (they were stopped by the security personnel). As Rhythm and Blues began to tour the country, audience members often became so excited that they broke chairs and vandalized concert halls.[5] Such reactions were familiar to Poles from press reports on rock 'n' roll concerts in the West, where uncontrolled youth behavior was blamed on the commercial and demoralizing aspects of capitalism. But why were youths in socialist Poland acting the same way?

The political upheaval of the Thaw was over, but the troubling youth behavior that characterized it was not. Not only did young people go crazy when they heard rock 'n' roll but also more and more teenage girls were seen wearing pants in public. Others put on red pantyhose, a wardrobe item that scandalized parents and teachers. Soon, young women and men were dancing the twist, while those more intellectually inclined spent their time

Imagining the World from Behind the Iron Curtain. Małgorzata Fidelis, Oxford University Press. © Oxford University Press 2022. DOI: 10.1093/oso/9780197643402.003.0003

in smoke-filled cafés discussing existentialists like Jean-Paul Sartre. During the summer, numerous young people carrying backpacks and guitars were spotted hitchhiking or going camping, often in mixed gender groups.

Not unlike the Thaw rebels, young people in the late 1950s and early 1960s engaged with the outside world and blurred the boundaries between politics and everyday life. But they did so largely by creating their own styles with the use of selected consumer products like young people in other parts of the world. By the end of the 1950s, politicians and other commentators finally thought they knew what they were witnessing: young people practiced "modernity" (*nowoczesność*) of a new type, one that transcended national boundaries and geopolitical divisions. As part of universal progress, these observers thought, it could not be stopped. Rather, the challenge was to appropriate and manage modernity in a noncapitalist society. By the early 1960s, not one day went by without the popular media celebrating the encroachment of modernity on almost every human activity, from technological innovation and aesthetic taste to clothing styles and ways of drinking coffee. As Teresa Bochwic, who turned eighteen in 1965, remarked, "modernity was a magic word of our generation."[6] In Poland, a socialist version of modernity, as envisioned by political and cultural elites, entailed balancing Western influences with domestic culture, while also ensuring that young people remained committed to the collective well-being of society. The idea of modernity was flexible enough, however, to encompass a range of meanings, which were shaped as much by official discourses as by pluralist popular culture and young people themselves.

The term "globalization" was not yet part of the Polish public vocabulary, but commentators spoke about "integration" of the "technological-cultural base" as a defining feature of "a new type of civilization of the second half of the twentieth century."[7] Communist politician Włodzimierz Sokorski, who in 1956 became the head of the Commission for Radio and Television and was a frequent commentator on the topic of youth, maintained that this new type of civilization "doesn't just have to do with the size of our pants and the silhouette of the modern woman, but also with the contemporary notions of modernity as much as in architecture, music, and painting, as in lifestyle, the style of speech, and especially the style of dance." He also believed that the shape of modernity depended on the political and ideological context. The "mutual osmosis and influence," according to this line of reasoning, "would not change the fact of friction and debate about social questions nor would it change philosophical arguments."[8] The idea of socialist "integration" was therefore grounded in the logic of the Cold War. The insistence on "friction and debate" could enrich the global community, but such a stance also contained seeds of antiglobalism. Commentators such as Sokorski insisted that the socialist world would always remain separate from the capitalist one.

Polish communist leaders responded to post-Thaw youth desires for the engagement with the modern world by deemphasizing political and ideological agendas in favor of cultural engagement, secular ethics, and educational leisure. Youth activists, writers, educators, sociologists, and journalists became key players in this endeavor, creating an environment in which new ways of imagining the young selfhood became possible.

Defining a Young Socialist Citizen

The Thaw sparked rethinking of young socialist citizenship on many levels. After all, some of the most prominent Thaw rebels came from the all-youth organization the Stalinist ZMP. In June 1956, they began forming "revolutionary committees" to challenge the Stalinist dogma and rigid structure of their own organization.[9] In January 1957, amid tumultuous debates between young activists and the Party, the ZMP was dissolved and replaced with a new organization, the ZMS. It was a far cry from the rebels' demands for the creation of a genuinely socialist and democratic youth movement but nevertheless promised a less intrusive ideological agenda than the ZMP. Alongside the ZMS, the state agreed to establish three other organizations to serve specific groups of young people: the ZMW, the ZSP, and the Polish Scouts Association (Związek Harcerstwa Polskiego; ZHP).[10] Although still under the state's control, young people were granted official recognition of their diverse needs and interests.

But if young people ceased to be the avant-garde of the communist revolution, who would they be now? Some suggestions came from contemporary popular culture, especially film. Whether they belonged to youth organizations or not, young people's entanglements with the modern world in Polish cinema were increasingly expressed through depictions of consumption and leisure. The turn of the 1960s in Poland ushered in a new genre of feature film "about the young and for the young."[11] These films did not focus on labor heroes, who had populated socialist realist films during Stalinism, nor did they explore the dilemmas of the wartime generation as did the contemporary Polish Film School.[12] On the contrary, films by directors such as Roman

Polański, Andrzej Wajda, Janusz Morgenstern, and Tadeusz Konwicki often depicted young male rebels situated in a context of leisure. Polansky's *Knife in the Water* (1961), for example, told a story of two men and a woman spending a weekend on a sailboat, while Wajda's *Innocent Sorcerers* (1960) revolved around a young medical doctor who devoted much of his time to listening to jazz, socializing in student clubs, and searching for romance.[13]

A new model of Polish masculinity emerged from those films that significantly departed from tragic male heroes of wartime Poland. Male subjectivity was defined not through serving the nation but through relationships with consumer objects, which had been associated with the feminine. A good example is *Knife in the Water*, where male fashions and consumer styles defines the two protagonists, an older journalist and a young hitchhiker. Literary scholar Elżbieta Ostrowska notes that in the opening scene, the journalist is shown "in a bright . . . casual suit, and the Boy in blue jeans, sweater, and sneakers." Later in the movie, both men make sure "that their dress style matches their circumstances. Right after reaching the harbor, the journalist changes into white jeans and a cotton pullover. And the Boy, who had already said he was a hiker and had nothing in common with water, finds . . . swimming shorts in his backpack, which he shows up in on the deck."[14]

The so-called young film was often vilified by Party officials and film critics for its ambiguous moral messages. But youth publications had a more flexible understanding of young people's desires and needs. They often promoted engagement with both foreign consumer commodities and education about the world as equally beneficial to young people. In January 1959, the youth magazine *Radar* directly called on its readers to acknowledge the presence of the world in their own immediate surroundings. "Look around your room" the article—titled "A Geography of Thinking"—began. "There is much from abroad here." The anonymous author continued: "You have a TESLA radio [Czechoslovak-made tube radio] on your shelf, and next to it, there is a box with tests and records of the Linguaphone for Languages [a British company specializing in foreign language education]. One could also see a Swiss watch and the Brockhaus Encyclopedia [a German-language encyclopedia]. There is nothing one can do about it: the world is international. And the conditions of our lives rest on international achievements—regardless of marked and unmarked borders on the map."[15] International interconnectedness, as many commentators argued, was a fact of modern life, and young people had no choice but to embrace it in an informed way. Not only did popular publications point to the media as an invaluable resource to learn about the world but also leaders of the official youth association, the ZMS, did the same. In the words of one activist in 1961, the purpose of the media was no longer crude propaganda but "creating an inspiration, not the one limited to 'dos' and 'don'ts', but the one that assumes independent thought . . . a critical assessment of things" on the part of the audience.[16] Accordingly, exposure to Western content was not undesirable. Many believed that after the initial fascination with the West, young Poles would be more aware of "colonial exploitation and fascist political tendencies" and would opt for socialism.[17]

Responding to Thaw-era youth's demands for more open borders, the new youth organizations encouraged international travel. In 1957, the state opened the Bureau of Foreign Tourism for Youth with the aim of facilitating domestic and foreign travel for secondary school and university students. By 1959, more than 2,000 young people took advantage of the Bureau's program. Most tours went to other socialist countries, but soon the Bureau offered select Western European destinations. In 1960, for example, a group of forty people traveled to Rome to watch the Summer Olympics.[18]

Such an exchange and frame of mind fit the new doctrine of peaceful co-existence that was being promoted by the communist camp. Under the new general secretary of the Soviet Party, Nikita Khrushchev, the Eastern bloc accepted the "two-system" world and sought to demonstrate the superiority of socialism through peaceful means rather than a military confrontation. A telling call for bridging Cold War divisions came at the ZMS city chapter meeting in Kraków in June 1959, when some activists condemned a black-and-white understanding of the Cold War as "a huge blunder" of the past. It was wrong to teach young people that "evil is situated according to geo-graphical zoning," one activist contended. He warned that such "uncritical zoning . . . of good and bad" could be counterproductive, as it hindered the progress of socialism by preventing constructive criticism and "correction."[19]

Understanding young people in this new international context required not just familiarity with Marxist-Leninist tenets but also, above all, studying the psychology, practices, and beliefs of these young subjects. This was be-cause youth behavior, many believed, primarily stemmed from contempo-rary global shifts. As the head of the Commission for Radio and Television, Włodzimierz Sokorski, contended in 1963, "one cannot understand youth or help young people without understanding the modern world."[20] It was with this assumption that researchers, educators, and journalists began to ex-amine youth behavior, opening new ways to shape a modern socialist citizen.

Youth as an Object of Study

In postwar Europe and the United States, the concept of "youth culture" emerged in public discussions to describe what the older generation saw as the new and often socially and morally concerning behavior of young people. As Stuart Hall and other British sociologists argued in the 1970s, youth "appeared as an emergent category in post-war Britain, one of the most striking and visible manifestations of social change in the period."[21] By the early 1950s French commentators had adopted the concept of *nouvelle vague* (the New Wave) to denote "anything having to do with the idea of youth or involving young people."[22] In Poland, prominent sociologist Józef Chałasiński called attention to youth as a powerful repository of cultural meaning in 1948. "Youth [Młodość]," he wrote, "is not a natural physiological and hormonal condition, but an element of culture, a social 'institution.' " He continued: "Just like wisdom, gender [płeć] or beauty, these are social imaginaries, social values, which are shaped in diverse ways depending on the structure and culture of different societies."[23]

The quote is significant for its early articulation of gender as a cultural category. Although Chałasiński provided no further explanation as to how exactly gender and youth might function as "elements of culture," he nevertheless opened a way to examine seemingly unquestionable biological concepts as unfixed and fluid. Both gender and youth, he argued, belonged to the same realm of social and cultural imagination that could be studied and understood in their specific temporal contexts. Through the 1960s, Polish scholars followed suit by producing substantial research on youth as both a distinct social group and a cultural symbol.[24]

Scholars have interpreted the rise of youth culture in the West as an outgrowth of the postwar economic boom.[25] A comparable economic prosperity would have been difficult to find in Poland at the time. Poles still struggled with wartime devastation and the austerity of the Stalinist industrialization. "There is no country as devastated as ours [due to World War II] in the entire orbit of capitalism," wrote one journalist in *Around the World* in August 1956. Rather, one should search for a relevant comparison "beyond Europe . . . somewhere in Asia, Africa, or Latin America."[26] For sociologist Aleksander Kamiński, Poland was a country "halfway through" its quest for material improvements and modern lifestyles.[27] Yet political leaders, like their Western counterparts, encountered similar effects of rising consumer aspirations and expanded imaginations stimulated by the mass media.[28]

Kamiński's metaphor of the "halfway through" can help explain the birth of postwar consumer society in Poland. While many commentators acknowledged the slow pace of material advancement, the observation "halfway through" meant that some milestones had been achieved. Important changes took place as a result of the Party-led de-Stalinization after 1953 and increased attention to the consumer sector of the economy. Between 1955 and 1960, the production of consumer goods in Poland increased by 63 percent.[29] In 1956, the state halted the collectivization of agriculture and allowed private ownership of land. At the same time, the number of private enterprises in urban areas increased from 42,000 in 1955 to 76,000 in 1960, while the number of employees in private businesses doubled.[30] Poland was gradually becoming industrial and urban. Although the most powerful wave of migration from villages to cities took place during the intense industrialization of the Six-Year Plan (1950–1955), the process continued throughout the following decade. Each year an average of 100,000 people migrated from rural areas to urban centers; more than 40 percent of them were young people under the age of twenty-six.[31]

More important than the actual numbers was the subjective sense of material improvement and opportunity for advancement. When in 1961 a group of Warsaw sociologists conducted a nationwide survey on the perception of social change, they found that respondents in all social groups expressed optimism about the future and the expectation of upward mobility. The majority saw their own social position as higher than that of their parents and expected their children to attain an even higher social and material standard.[32] Many valued the expanded access to education and anticipated that their children would enter a university. Most respondents also believed that Polish society had become more egalitarian after the war but "the process of egalitarianism" had not been completed.[33] Regardless of the sincerity of such responses, the survey revealed shared aspirations on both sides of the Iron Curtain: the value of material standards, a commitment to egalitarianism, and an expectation of state-guaranteed economic security and opportunities for education.[34] In this context, youth culture became a pan-European phenomenon resulting from the shared commitment to peace and prosperity regardless of actual levels of economic development or consumer satisfaction.

The revival of Polish sociology helped to facilitate the new understanding of youth and modernity. Sociology had been banned under Stalinism, but when it returned to research institutions in 1956, the discipline became especially open to American sociological empiricism and survey methods that targeted diverse populations.[35] For Polish sociologists, youth became an urgent focus of research that would help assess and assist with the social, cultural, and material progress of society.

Some of the first sociological studies after 1956 centered on young people. In 1958, a group at the Warsaw University under the direction of Stefan Nowak launched a monumental research project, The Students of Warsaw (Studenci Warszawy), with the goal of detecting "socio-political attitudes of the future intelligentsia."[36] Alongside political views and religious outlooks, leisure and everyday life became part of the study, reflecting the expert interest in a range of self-expression by the young generation.[37] When in that same year the Center for Research on Public Opinion (OBOP) or the "Polish Gallup" opened up, one of its surveys was directed at young people.[38] Titled "The Worldview of Youth," the study asked close to 3,000 young people between the ages of fifteen and twenty-four from diverse social backgrounds about their political beliefs and moral values.[39]

"The Worldview of Youth" set the tone for subsequent research on youth that was disassociated from the political turmoil of the Thaw. The results of the survey revealed weak commitments to politics and ideology. As many as 68 percent of the respondents denied strong political convictions. Only 3.5 percent of male and 1.1 of female respondents identified themselves as communists. A slightly larger group, 7.7 percent of men and 3.2 percent of women, considered themselves socialists. Those who supported capitalism were a similar minority: 5.3 percent of men and 3.2 percent of women. Many respondents looked for more encompassing designations, with 16 percent of men and 16.5 percent of women preferring to think of themselves as "democratic."[40]

Ambivalence toward clear political designations was built into the survey. The makers of the multiple-choice questionnaire created an answer that provided a safe way for the respondents to declare political neutrality. In the survey, alongside conventional categories such as "communist," "socialist," and "capitalist," respondents could choose to identify themselves as "an apolitical supporter of the socialist system." In a way, young people were invited to simultaneously declare political loyalty to the Party-state while also claiming political distance. The designation "apolitical," formulated by the sociologists, signaled a new relationship between the individual and the state. Since reports on the survey appeared in official publications that had to be approved by the censorship, the Party-state must have at least tacitly accepted the idea that focusing on personal goals was sufficient for inclusion in the socialist polity.

The choice of "apolitical supporter of the system" proved attractive. As many as 26.3 percent of men and 28.7 percent of women marked that option. At the same time, the largest segment, 30 percent of men and nearly 47 percent of women, claimed no attachment to any political views.[41] As other parts of the survey revealed, young Poles wanted to "accumulate wealth, achieve professional credentials, and be in love." The desire "to lead a fulfilling life" appeared as the foremost priority in almost all the responses.[42]

Such responses diverged little from contemporary findings in other European countries. In 1957 in France, a major study conducted by L'Express in collaboration with the Institut Francais d'Opinion Publique demonstrated "political disenchantment" among youth, as well as desires for material comfort and success, although young people "did not believe either could guarantee personal fulfillment."[43] The communist camp registered a similar retreat from overt politics. Just a few years before the Prague Spring, a poll conducted among university students in the Czechoslovak capital showed 61 percent of respondents believing "that students in Czechoslovakia had no chance at all to influence political developments." Like their counterparts in Poland, they "prefer to pursue their leisure in private pastimes, they regard work in an organization as futile, and they are afraid to offer political comment."[44] Young people's orientation toward consumption and leisure were not absent from Soviet research either.[45] At the threshold of the 1960s, on both sides of the Iron Curtain, researchers and others discovered various forms of "apolitics" as the defining feature of the young generation.

Sociologists not only produced a wealth of empirical data but also contributed to designating the contemporary generation of youth as unprecedented in the history of the world. When in 1965 a group of sociologists published *Youth in an Era of Change*, they reinforced the belief that new lifestyles among young people were rooted in the unprecedented dynamism of the modern world. The book featured research on different aspects of young people's lives, from ethical systems and religion to dating and leisure. It focused on different age groups, ranging from high school students to university students, and on a variety of social environments, from cities to small towns and villages. The study demonstrated that it was impossible to study Polish youth without looking at them in the context of international youth culture, notably the fascination with rock 'n' roll, film stars, and youth fashion.

One of the most illustrative studies in the collection analyzed the entries by young women in the 1957 national contest titled "Beautiful Girls to the Screen." Only a year after the official end of Stalinism in Poland, the study by sociologist Ryszard Kołodziejczyk revealed just how much Western film culture had penetrated Polish society. Aspiring to greater participation in the global media, Polish film critics and directors advertised the contest through the popular weekly *Film*. Recognizing that the "nation" was coming to be increasingly represented on the global stage by national stars and celebrities, the campaign sought to identify and recruit Polish "beautiful girls" to play parts in Polish films in the hopes of finding a new type of national star, such as the French actress Brigitte Bardot or Italian Gina Lollobrigida. Young women were encouraged to send their photographs to *Film*, and readers would then vote for the most beautiful ones, who would be recommended to filmmakers.

As Kołodziejczyk showed, the campaign generated something of a craze among young women across Poland. Female respondents typically sent photographs and letters in which they described their physical features and artistic talents. Many presented themselves as avid readers of *Film* and other popular magazines. Most important, however, female contestants likened themselves to foreign stars. A twenty-two-year-old Lucjanna from Poznań claimed that she turned heads of foreign visitors as she walked down the streets of her city during the International Poznań Fairs. She believed that Poland needed "a female artist that is the pride of America and other countries, as exemplified by Marilyn Monroe and Jayne Mansfield, who remind me of myself the most."[46] In a similar way, seventeen-year-old Helena wrote that her girlfriends called her Brigitka (little Brigitte): "they say that I possess certain features and qualities of BB."[47] And eighteen-year-old Maja from a small village claimed that her girlfriends "tell me that I look like [Giulietta] Masina."[48] The study affirmed a significant influence of the "cinema world" on "shaping opinions and attitudes."[49]

What did the Polish fascination with the "cinema world" mean? Did young women in socialist Poland succumb to the capitalist-driven commodification of the female body? The objectification of women, including reducing their worth to body appearance and sexual functions, has been a central theme in feminist scholarship.[50] Some scholars, however, suggest a more nuanced interpretation of female sex symbols in film. They argue that the antidomestic and sexualized femininity featured in the Hollywood films of the 1950s was an important prefiguration of future feminist and queer politics.[51] Similarly, Brigitte Bardot, who embodied a "sexually predatory young woman," suggested a new empowerment of female sexuality that challenged its traditional associations with reproduction.[52] The desire on the part of many young women around the world to become like Bardot did not necessarily suggest the uncritical internalization of gender stereotypes. Rather, it could indicate a new-found source of sexual agency that young female audiences found attractive.

Polish young women styling themselves after Bardot could evoke ridicule and contempt but rarely struck commentators as a danger to public morality, as was often the case in the West.[53] While journalists and scholars recognized consumer aspirations as common to youth everywhere, they agreed that such aspirations acquired a different and more noble meaning under socialism. Sociologist Mikołaj Kozakiewicz believed that when young people in Poland wanted fashionable clothes or a motorcycle or even a car, they expressed "quite a rational and healthy desire to raise the standard of living, to possess a minimum of resources and tools, which . . . are considered normal and necessary as the life equipment of a modern human being."[54] Such statements suggested the normalization of modernity while at the same time repudiating perceived "excesses" of Western youth as deviations from the modern path.

Most Polish commentators believed in the fundamental goodness of youth on both sides of the Iron Curtain. Juvenile delinquency was of limited concern in Polish public discourse prior to 1968. To be sure, throughout the 1960s, the word "hooligan" was commonly used to describe a variety of undesirable youth behavior from breaking the law to men wearing long hair, but commentators warned against overhyping the problem of "bad youth." They believed that the Western press publicized "bad" behavior of young people for sensationalist reasons. Rather than analyzing "congregations of several hundred American beatniks," sociologist Kozakiewicz argued in the popular weekly *Polityka*, American researchers would be better advised to conduct "equally detailed studies and surveys of normal American youth."[55]

Polish commentators saw the turning away from politics and ideology and toward consumption and lifestyle as irreversible. They also believed that the socioeconomic conditions of socialism moderated how Polish youth embraced modern trends. Yet the process could not be left entirely to some presumed natural course. While accepting the desire for consumer goods and entertainment as part of healthy modernity, commentators warned against replacing "the view of the world" with material concerns. "A young person," the editor-in-chief of the *Banner of Youth*, Jerzy Feliksiak, wrote in 1966, "must see the connection between personal interest and the general social benefit, and when necessary—put the interest of society above one's own."[56] In short, the project of socialist modernity was also the project of socialist morality.

Modernity as Morality

While political leaders recognized international youth culture as an integral part of modernity, they agreed that it required national adjustment. Such an approach was not unique to Poland. Fears of "Americanization" permeated Western European public responses to youth's enthusiastic embrace of rock 'n' roll, Coca-Cola, and Hollywood movies.[57] Shortly after the successes of the band Rhythm and Blues, youth leaders and others worked hard to Polonize the transatlantic language of rock 'n' roll. Journalist Franciszek Walicki invented a new Polish term for rock 'n' roll music: "big beat" (*mocne uderzenie*). The term referred to the "beat boom" that was associated with British groups such as the Beatles and the Rolling Stones.[58] In Polish usage, however, big beat (sometimes spelled "bigbit") typically meant a rock 'n' roll–style pop song with Polish lyrics performed by Polish artists. Rhythm and Blues soon changed its name to a Polish-sounding one: Czerwono-Czarni (the Red and Blacks). Other bands followed suit, adopting similar names: Niebiesko-Czarni (the Blue and Blacks), Czerwone Gitary (the Red Guitars), and Trubadurzy (the Troubadours), to name a few. While touring the country, the new bands helped make big beat a democratic endeavor that attracted young Poles. Within less than a year, the managers of the Red and Blacks launched a competition titled "We are looking for young talents," in which everyone with musical inclination was invited to participate. Thousands of young women and men vied for a chance to sing or play with the bands.[59]

Polish rock 'n' roll became a collective effort to promote Polish culture and meaningful leisure for young people. Walicki insisted that big-beat performances "due to their mass following and lively reactions from the audience resembled, in some sense, spectator sports."[60] Others suggested that big beat could be used to educate young people in music and the English language. Journalist Roman Waschko reminded the public about the "interwar traditions of the English language school [in Poland] run by Methodists, where the language was taught with the help of texts from contemporary

Fig. 2.1 A concert by the Blue and Blacks, Warsaw, September 1962. Photo by Jarosław Tarań. Taran_0171. Courtesy of KARTA Center Foundation.

popular songs. The results were fantastic."[61] Walicki, who was instrumental in promoting Rhythm and Blues as part of the Jazz Club in Gdańsk, pledged to uphold the artistic qualities of the new genre by strengthening its connection to jazz, which would allow the bands "to have a more ambitious program devoid of trashy and simplistic features."[62] Thus rock 'n' roll concerts did not have to "Americanize" young people or create public disorder. On the contrary, they could serve constructive purposes: getting healthy exercise, learning English, and enhancing musical skills.

Embracing modernity required harmonizing it with the national tradition as much as with state socialist ethics. Soon, political leaders, academics, journalists, educators, and other public figures were all competing for a chance to speak about and with the youth. Perhaps it was not a coincidence that the leading voice in defining socialist modernity for the young was the man who managed the mass media revolution in Poland: Włodzimierz

Fig. 2.2 A concert by the Blue and Blacks. Warsaw, September 1962. Photo by Jarosław Tarań. Taran_0172. Courtesy of KARTA Center Foundation.

Sokorski. In 1956 Sokorski, the minister of culture under Stalinism, became the head of the National Committee for Radio and Television, a post he held until 1972. He was the key political figure to support the revival of Polish sociology and made extensive use of sociological material in his articles and radio broadcasts addressed to young audiences. In the early 1960s, he began writing regular columns in youth magazines urging his readers to embrace the proper version of modernity. He also traveled around the country to meet with young people in cities, towns, and villages to help shape what he considered a healthy relationship between personal lives and the modern world.

Sokorski's commentary often focused on global transformations as the key to understanding the young generation. Despite the existence of a "two-system world," he argued, "there is a common technological base which gives an immense platform for coexistence, competition, and struggle. Only then when all of these things are working together can a clear image of modernity arise."[63] He repeatedly acknowledged the pivotal impact of decolonization and the economic advancement of the non-European world on young people and their disorientation in the modern world. "How did one make sense of liberation movements in Africa," he asked, "where new nations were moving straight from tribal relations to modern socio-national movements in defiance of existing economic and political theories?" This was all in addition to space exploration and "the power of the television." From the perspective of young people, he argued, "the world is being made," and "the modern man [has] stopped being surprised."[64] Unable to comprehend the multitude and magnitude of change, young people had all the right to feel "cheated," "frustrated," and "ideologically insensitive."[65]

For socialist modernity to prevail, however, the project had to rest on more than an allegiance to a particular political and ideological camp. For Sokorski and others, being modern required a distinct moral code that defined the identity of young socialist citizens. Indeed, socialism and morality became equivalent as Sokorski repeatedly declared that "the problem of youth" was "an issue of morality."[66] The morality in this case was grounded in gender difference and in an ordered sexual life. For Sokorski, modernity as morality was a hypermasculine project. He often chastised teenage girls as "ideologically indifferent," "excessively independent," and "obligatory smokers." Such young women allegedly "set the tone" for the young generation.[67] He echoed the anxieties over young women's uncontrolled sexuality that had permeated the communist project from the very beginning.[68] He specifically warned against the "moral-sexual havoc" that left "a lasting impact" on young people and was "the source of tragedy; in the case of young women—often [a source of] an irreversible tragedy."[69] The commitment to higher moral values allegedly marked the superiority of socialist youth over their Western counterparts, who were believed to be more prone to sexual promiscuity. In this way, the adherence to the specific moral code became an indelible mark of a young and gendered socialist citizen.

The Discovery of Sex

While commentators agreed that young people, especially young women, needed to control their sexual impulses, they did not advocate a return to traditional morality based on the sexual double standard and women's subordinate position. Ironically, the focus on modernity as morality opened a

new way for female commentators to advocate sexual autonomy and reproductive rights as inherent markers of modern femininity. By the late 1950s,
sex education had become an area where writers and educators sought to establish a new moral code supported by science-based knowledge.

The new prominence of sexual morality—articulated so clearly by
Sokorski—provided an opening for interwar feminist and birth control activist Irena Krzywicka to enter the conversation. Krzywicka, too, traveled
around the country to speak with young people, but unlike Sokorski she did
not chastise teenage girls for practicing a misguided version of modernity.
Instead, she embraced female autonomy as the essence of modernity. In 1962,
she published a book under the deceptive title *Love . . . Marriage . . . Children*,
which in many ways read like a modern-day feminist manifesto on reproductive rights as human rights. She urged her readers not to take for granted
the fact that they lived in an unprecedented time when "Love . . . becomes
the stronghold of equal partners, in which each member represents a high
degree of humanity."[70] This was significant, Krzywicka believed, for women,
who could finally, due to technological advances and progressive social
views, exercise control over their bodies. Reproductive rights, which she
understood as a conscious choice to give birth, created the conditions that
allowed women "to be recognized as true human beings rather than beings
forced into an unending cycle of torture due to their physiology." If women
were able to exercise control over their reproductive functions, "humanity
will go through one of the most important revolutions in its existence."[71]

Such statements indicated that breaking taboos was a lasting legacy of
the Thaw. Stalinism had projected a conservative sexual agenda that was
expressed in a nearly total ban on abortion, the promotion of large families,
and the exclusion of the topic of sex from public discourse. At the same time,
Stalinist industrialization worked against that vision as millions of young
people moved from villages to cities, finding more personal and sexual autonomy in the process. In that sense, the Polish case fits the argument that
in socialist societies sexual revolution resulted from changes in individual
behavior rather than from legislative reforms and the spread of contraception as in Western Europe and the United States.[72] Polish sociologist Hanna
Malewska, who conducted research on female sexuality from 1959 to 1963,
found that 65 percent of Polish women had sexual intercourse before marriage.[73] She believed that "we are dealing with a change in moral standards"
whereby the Catholic emphasis on procreation was being challenged by secular ethics.[74]

The liberalization of the abortion law in April 1956 was a major departure from the Stalinist antiabortion policy. The Polish penal code of 1932 had provided for legal abortions on two grounds: when the mother's health was in danger and when the pregnancy was a result of rape or incest. Under this law, certifications from three doctors, including at least one gynecologist, were required to obtain an abortion on medical grounds. Public prosecutors authorized abortions in cases of incest or rape.[75] While the legal grounds for terminating pregnancy did not change after the war, the Ministry of Health, following the Stalinist antiabortion legislation in the Soviet Union, restricted abortion rights in 1948 by requiring special abortion commissions to approve each petition. In April 1956, that law was liberalized to allow women the right to abortion due to "difficult life conditions."[76]

This liberalization of the abortion law at first was not meant to make the procedure available on demand. For the first several years, legal access to abortion was restricted to married women with health problems and those who had already given birth to at least three children. These abortion rights were expanded in 1960 to allow women rather than doctors to make the decision about whether to undergo the procedure. This practically made abortion in the first trimester legal and solely a woman's choice. Yet the state persistently sought to limit the number of procedures. The state carefully monitored demographic factors and became preoccupied with a pronatalist stance when birth rates dropped in the late 1960s.[77] In addition, many doctors and others still feared that abortions had bad physical and moral effects on women.

Access to legal abortion made the need for sex education a pressing concern in the eye of the state. One way to limit the demand for abortion was to make contraception more widely available. In 1957, the state resurrected the Society for Conscious Motherhood (Towarzystwo Świadomego Macierzyństwa; TŚM), an organization devoted to family planning, first established in 1932.[78] The TŚM, composed primarily of medical professionals, began publicizing knowledge about reproduction and distributing contraceptive devices while at the same time discouraging abortion. The leaders of the TŚM stressed that their purpose "is not to provide information, but rather an education that puts value on the experiences people go through."[79]

By the late 1950s, scholars and educators were expressing alarm at the limited knowledge of anatomy and sexuality among Poles of all ages. According to Malewska, only 25 percent of her female respondents possessed what she described as "the correct information" about sexual intercourse, childbirth, and their own anatomy and physiology.[80] Despite the TŚM efforts to popularize birth control, Poles rarely used modern contraceptives. Until the late 1960s, the pill was not produced in Poland and could be obtained only through the TŚM and selected pharmacies in large cities that sold imported medications.[81] Most of the birth control distributed by the TŚM consisted of unreliable spermicides and IUDs.[82]

In the absence of readily available modern contraception, unwanted pregnancies were frequent, and abortion remained a common way to deal with them. In the late 1950s, the official number of abortions in Poland stood at 700,000 per year. On average, every tenth woman in Poland underwent at least one abortion.[83] More and more voices, including youth periodicals, called for sex education, especially for young women, who were more directly affected by the consequences of sexual ignorance.[84]

When Krzywicka began traveling around the country in the mid-1950s to speak about sex education, she applauded what she saw as progressive attitudes on the part of young people in the audience. She was asked questions on a wide variety of topics, including puberty, contraception, marriage, and "the lesbian disease."[85] Krzywicka supported the youth's openness to sexual matters as a normal part of life. "Sexual matters are no longer hidden in a smoke screen of taboo and mystery as in the past," she noted. "They can be placed in categories of issues to be discussed and pondered over, like choice of occupation or how to deal with day-to-day life."[86] Such interests required not only scientifically informed answers but also an ethical framework.

Krzywicka and other female educators believed that modernity required a new system of sexual ethics that would fight widespread ignorance and dispel religious teachings on sex as procreation. Indeed, many believed that sexual ethics were more fundamental to sex education than knowledge about physiological functions or birth control methods. Journalist Anna Lanota, who wrote a sex education handbook for parents in 1960, warned her readers against exclusively focusing on the physical aspects of sexuality such as "the anatomy and function of reproductive organs."[87] Likewise, popular writer Elżbieta Jackiewiczowa claimed that "physical maturity" for young women was not as important as "the maturity of the heart."[88]

The emphasis on ethics should not come as a surprise. In a nominally communist country, in which Catholic teachings on morality dominated, experts considered the creation of a new secular framework for sexual behavior an urgent matter. Such ethical dimensions guided the first regular column on sex education that appeared in the progressive youth magazine *Radar* in 1957, under the title "Conversations with Diotima" (Dialogi Diotimy). The column featured a dialogue between Diotima and "Man" (Człowiek), in which Man typically asked questions about puberty and sexual behavior, while Diotima responded as the authority on love. The "Conversations" were inspired by Plato's *Symposium*, which includes the exchange between Socrates and Diotima of Mantinea, Greek priestess and philosopher.

The text was not an original creation of *Radar*'s editors but a translation of the popular 1930 book *The School of Love* (Schule der Liebe) by the German author Gilbert Otto Nauman-Hoffer, written under the pen name Diotima. The book was translated for *Radar* by Andrzej Dołęgowski, who explained that he chose the text because Diotima rejected contemporary sexologists, for whom "love is a function of physiology." Instead "the school of love" was "a school of feelings and common sense in love."[89] To highlight the contemporary relevance of Diotima's wisdom, *Radar* sometimes featured letters from readers as well as pieces written by medical doctors.

The sexual ethics proposed by Diotima featured first and foremost a healthy relationship encompassing both physical and emotional aspects. To this end, Diotima supported premarital sex within a loving heterosexual relationship. "Both sexual restraint (incorrectly thought of as the condition of a happy marriage)," Diotima argued, "and lighthearted, characteristic of young people, promiscuity—do not offer the kind of knowledge about the matters of spirit and body which is provided by a long-term (even if this lasts only for a few months) relationship with one person."[90] In short, premarital sex within a loving relationship helped form happy marriages.

The normalization of premarital sex, however, required creating and reinforcing categories of "abnormal" sexual behavior. The socialist sexual ethics, although in many ways progressive and egalitarian, included a strict set of sexual activities deemed "deviant." Nearly everything that did not conform to heterosexual intercourse was considered pathological and harmful to society, including "excessive" masturbation, homosexuality, and sex without emotional attachments. Such "deviant practices" disturbed the correct sexual relations and contributed to personal unhappiness.[91] Articles about deviance in *Radar* were usually authored by medical doctors, who in a way provided modern updates and warnings to Diotima's philosophical exaltation of love.

Gender difference loomed large in sexual advice, as many authors believed that the different physiological and social experiences of girls and boys required different guidelines. Sometimes, separate handbooks on sexual ethics were published for young women and men.[92] Diotima believed that girls were more vulnerable to sexual pathologies than boys, because of their distinct emotional states, combined with the new personal freedoms they were acquiring in modern times. In one conversation, Man worried about new practices among young women, such as "going camping in groups" or "hanging out in cafés . . . until late in the evening," customs that had been unthinkable to the older generations.[93] Despite her feminist messages, Irena Krzywicka considered young women to be "neophytes of progress" and therefore more prone than boys to "make mistakes." After all, as she explained, "they belonged only to the third generation of independent women at best."[94] As young women had been trained to be mothers for "thousands of years," Krzywicka believed that young women' minds and bodies responded to "a shock of modernity" in unpredictable ways. Such young women needed extra effort and vigilance in adjusting their "psychophysical distinction" to new social conditions.[95]

Although Diotima and others reinforced gender difference by stressing physiological and emotional differences between women and men, the strong moral vision of sexuality allowed many authors to dispense with the double moral standard. Instead, they insisted that both girls and boys needed to save sexual experiences for meaningful relationships. Sexual restraint became as much part of the advice for boys as for girls. "My book is not intended for mama's boys," Jan Łopuski wrote in *What Every Boy Wants to Know*, "who suffer from the lack of courage and the lack of determination."[96] He encouraged boys to practice sexual restraint as part of cultivating genuine masculine traits, including self-discipline and responsibility for a future family. Accordingly, respect for women was a sign of healthy masculinity, "because only a lowlife, who rates women on appearance like wares in a sex market, shows women disdain."[97] Young women, at the same time, needed to stop acting like "dolls" or "kittens," Jackiewiczowa argued in her sex education manual for young women. "A young woman [who is] dumb and empty headed," she insisted, "only holds the attention of a man for the short term. But a woman—who is thoughtful, and a companion, can cultivate a relationship for the rest of her life."[98]

Reproductive choice was the centerpiece of the new sexual ethics. Krzywicka was not alone in arguing for women's control over their bodies as an essential human right. Jackiewiczowa also believed that women had the right and a duty to decide whether they wanted to be mothers or not. "Not always when we are in love, do we want to become mothers," she wrote. "And we have the right to decide in these matters. That is why birth control . . . is necessary and normal, [it is] the right of a thinking human being."[99]

This idea of reproductive rights was remarkable for this time and place. Scholars have traditionally argued that abortion in the Soviet Union and Eastern Europe was conceptualized primarily in economic and medical terms rather than as a woman's right to choose. But a recent study on Czechoslovakia has found that demographers and female Party activists "were more rights driven than contemporary scholars usually acknowledge."[100] This early evocation of human rights in Poland and Czechoslovakia suggests an important corrective to understandings of the language of human rights in the region as originating at the intersection of male-dominated dissident movements and the Helsinki Accords of the 1970s. The writings on sex education in the late 1950s and early 1960s suggest that the concept of human rights entered the public sphere earlier, if only in a limited way, and that it was distinctly related to the female body and what we today would call reproductive justice. Moreover, the language of reproductive rights came neither directly from the state nor the dissidents but from those who were the intermediaries between the state and society.

Popularizing sex education in print culture generated anxieties in many quarters, among not only the Catholic clergy but also the Party leadership. When the Party Press Bureau evaluated *Radar*, "Conversations with Diotima" came under particular scrutiny. The internal reviewer for the Bureau, journalist Janusz Kolczyński, praised the magazine for taking up the topic of sex education, at the same time scolding the editors for "the excessively extensive focus on sexual deviance." He believed that discussing a variety of sexual practices such as masturbation and homosexuality introduced "elements of cheap sensation to the magazine."[101]

The prominence of a female voice as the authority on sex might have been an additional source of irritation for male elites. By late 1958, Diotima had disappeared from the pages of *Radar*. She was soon replaced by the male sociologist and educator Mikołaj Kozakiewicz, whose new column, titled "Sentimental Education" (Edukacja sentymentalna) reasserted the primacy of emotions in sexual relations.[102] The basic message about premarital sex changed little but was delivered by a male expert rather than an imagined priestess. Signaling a gradual shift in sex education toward reliance on male experts, the new column covered a variety of themes from the cultural history of love to personal hygiene and sexual "pathologies." By the late 1960s, sexual advice in youth magazines had become the prerogative of sexology. Moral teachings were expressed through a scientific vocabulary often focused on gender difference. Sexual advice departed from the ideas of Krzywicka and

other female educators, who had prioritized female independence and reproductive justice. Male experts instead reasserted traditional gender roles and
advocated for female submissiveness as a condition of a happy relationship.

* * *

At the threshold of the 1960s, political leaders, sociologists, journalists, and
writers conceptualized youth as central part of modernity on many levels,
from rethinking the organized youth movement to popular writings on
sexual ethics. Rather than rejecting Western influences, young people were
encouraged to embrace them selectively. A Polonized version of rock 'n' roll
was one way to do that, as was informed interaction with foreign consumer
commodities and the mass media. Yet even as modernity was heralded as
a universal project that promoted "civilizational integration," systemic
differences needed to be maintained. Young socialist citizens, Party officials
and others agreed, could not uncritically absorb Western popular culture and
consumption. Rather, they required moral guidance from experts. Growing
up modern in a socialist society required not only moderation in consumer
behavior but also a new set of morals centered on heterosexual love, access to
birth control and abortion, and egalitarian gender relations.

Polish scholars have often juxtaposed the politically engaged youth
of the Thaw era with the allegedly "depoliticized" young generation that
followed.[103] The emphasis on youth's political passivity goes hand in hand
with the broader metaphor of the "small stabilization," after the upheavals
of Stalinism, that has been used to encapsulate the Gomułka era between
1956 and 1970 in dominant Polish narratives.[104] By contrast, this chapter has
shown the dynamism of this time and the global connectivity that inspired
the new youth's practices. For young people, the era was arguably not one
of stability but of a turbulent engagement with postwar modernity. While
promoting youth as modernity, the Polish state opened new ways for young
people to define themselves. The new "apolitical" style that many young
people declared in sociological surveys became a new kind of politics that
allowed for testing the boundaries of acceptable modern behavior.

3

Window to the World

Youth Magazines and the Politics of Apolitics

By the late 1950s, *Around the World*, the illustrated magazine that had made
such big impression when it was launched in January 1954, was no longer a
unique "window to the world." A number of new periodicals had emerged
to engage with young readers not as political or ideological subjects but as
individuals with diverse emotional and social needs. The extent to which,
prior to 1989, photos of Western film, rock stars, and celebrity gossip (things
often publicly repudiated by Party leaders) populated the pages of the Polish
popular press still seems striking today, several decades after the fall of communism. Youth magazines covered a range of Western culture. Some were
reprints of articles from French, British, and American press. In other cases,
Polish correspondents wrote detailed reports on recent developments in
literature, film, dance, and fashion that they encountered in places such as
Paris, London, Los Angeles, and New York. These were complemented by
updates on decolonization and colorful photo-reportage on Polish visitors to
countries in the Global South. Editors and journalists devoted limited space
to the coverage of political news and ideological pronouncements and, instead, like so many of their young readers, openly claimed "apolitics" as the
guiding principle for their worldviews.

One may be tempted to see these Polish youth magazines as an expression
of the internationalism—conventionally defined as friendship and cooperation among socialist states—and cultural diplomacy that all the communist governments pursued at the time. In the Soviet Union, internationalism
was officially expanded in the post-Stalinist era to include cultural exchange
with capitalist countries. Yet the Polish youth magazines went well beyond
accepting the "carefully measured and censored" Soviet cultural exchange
with the West.[1] Rather, these publications invited readers to participate in
the global community of youth, who bonded over the same symbols of emergent youth culture, from pop music and fashion to debates about changing
lifestyles and morality. Even if the language of internationalism helped the

Imagining the World from Behind the Iron Curtain. Malgorzata Fidelis, Oxford University Press. © Oxford University Press
2022. DOI: 10.1093/oso/9780197643402.003.0004

editors explain the magazines' content to their superiors, these publications are better understood as "transnational transmitters of youth culture," to use Gerd-Rainer Horn's term for the contemporary youth magazines in the West.[2] This is not to suggest an "imitation" of the Western press on the part of Polish editors, but their attempt to promote global youth culture filtered through the lens of the socialist political context.

Youth magazines became a prominent space where multiple actors, including Party-state officials, journalists, editors, censors, and readers contested and negotiated youth identity and its relationship with the world. While state officials often believed that distance from politics could be an effective antidote to potential youth radicalism, others used the notion of apolitics to broaden the sphere of cultural pluralism. Ultimately, rather than creating "depoliticized" consumers, the Polish youth magazines helped produce multiple understandings of the self and the possibilities of the modern world.

In Defense of Mass Culture

The idea of the seemingly apolitical mass culture guided Poland's embrace of global youth culture. In 1963, prominent Polish sociologist Antonina Kłoskowska published a breakthrough book, *Mass Culture: Critique and Defense*, in which she argued for the universal quality of mass culture as a natural development in all modern societies regardless of political or economic systems. Her work reinvigorated a public debate in Poland about the place of mass culture in socialist societies.[3] How should mass culture be defined and practiced in a society that was not supposed to be governed by the rules of commerce and the market?

After 1956, the definition of culture in Poland shifted from a strictly ideological project to one centered on aesthetics, taste, morality, and education. At a meeting of the Party Press Bureau in 1959, prominent Marxist intellectual Stefan Żółkiewski noted that "what we call the culture of masses is misleading, because in those societies that are highly industrialized, the culture of masses is simply modern culture."[4] According to this reasoning, mass culture was defined as a part of universal modernity rather than in terms of any specific political system. The state was acknowledged as a facilitator of cultural production, but the shape and content of that production was to be determined by intellectuals, artists, writers, and other professionals rather than politicians.

The Ministry of Culture and Art was formally in charge of cultural policy in Poland, but in August 1957, a decree of the Council of Ministers decentralized the decision process by delegating local cultural activity to National Councils in different parts of Poland. Local National Councils were put in charge of organizing and overseeing local concerts and entertainment events as well as regional theaters, operas, and music halls. Only a handful of institutions "of national significance" remained under the direct purview of the Ministry, such as the Warsaw National Theater and the Jewish Theater.[5]

In addition, several advisory bodies composed of experts were established: the Commission of Culture as part of the Party Central Committee, the Commission of Culture as part of the Sejm (lower house of Parliament), and, in 1958, the Council of Culture and Art, which worked directly with the Minister of Culture and Art. Composed of delegates from official artists' unions and major cultural institutions, the Council in 1964 was composed of eighty-eight professionals in literature, theater, art, architecture, industrial design, and other artistic realms.[6] From the beginning, members criticized the limited autonomy of this body. Regardless of the specific powers granted to the Council, what mattered was the official recognition that cultural matters rested with the experts rather than with political leaders.

Many, in fact, believed that expert knowledge combined with freedom from arbitrary market forces provided a unique opportunity to create a version of mass culture that was educational, moral, and progressive. Even before Kłoskowska published her book, liberal Catholic intellectuals associated with the periodical Bond (Więź), edited by Tadeusz Mazowiecki, agreed that embracing modern trends in consumption and popular culture was not a choice, since "it is not possible to choose something that is inevitable in the historical process as one does not choose the place and time of one's birth."[7] Catholic intellectuals proposed instead to shape "the proper attitude of the human being [toward mass culture], and the hierarchy of values."[8]

The most vocal supporter of mass culture in the political circles remained the Marxist Stefan Żółkiewski. He argued that mass culture acquired a different meaning in socialist societies as it helped create a "socialized" human being.[9] At the meeting of the Council of Culture and Art in May 1964, he underscored the unique ability of mass culture in the age of mass media to cross borders and class lines, since "a son of a worker listens to the same kind of jazz as a son of a millionaire in a capitalist system" and "here in Warsaw we can watch the same kind of American western as people in Bangkok."[10] Other professionals concurred, claiming that mass culture was key to "**breaking**

parochialism" and to providing opportunities for Polish citizens to participate in the global cultural life.[11]

However, no one arrived at a clear definition of what mass culture was or
ought to be in a socialist society. What content specifically counted as educational and liberating from "parochialism"? No clear guidelines emerged from
these debates or the Party headquarters. In April 1965, *Nowe Drogi* (New
Paths), the Party Central Committee monthly, did little more than reiterate
arguments familiar to readers of the periodical press. Literary critic Jerzy
Adamski wrote in *Nowe Drogi:* "our goal is not only to transmit cultural commodities on a massive scale but also to inspire cultural needs, and a cultural
movement." Party leaders expressed confidence in the socialist system as a
powerful shaper of mass culture. "The correctly understood 'mass-quality'
is not solely dependent on the mass media technology," Adamski continued,
"but on the social conditions, in which [the media] operate. Socialism has
the power to shape these conditions." But even the ruling Party left the definition of mass culture unfixed. "The problem of mass culture in the socialist
model of culture remains open," Adamski concluded.[12]

The Politics of Apolitics

Soliciting expert knowledge never meant the state giving up control over cultural production. The creation of the Press Bureau in November 1956 was
a clear signal that the state was determined to reestablish control over the
press after the unbridled "radicalism" of the Thaw. By 1958, the process of
eliminating independent student periodicals was complete. New decrees and
a barrage of public pronouncements against "Marxist revisionism" and the
"snobbish" following of Western trends continued through the early 1960s.
However, studying Party instructions and decrees with regard to cultural
policy is misleading when these are not considered alongside the actual cultural products available to the Polish public.[13]

Although scholars have typically dismissed popular magazines as less significant than the daily press or sociocultural periodicals aimed at the general
educated public, these publications offer a unique window onto the everyday
lives of ordinary people.[14] In the popular press, readers and editors discussed
topics ranging from their cultural tastes and interests to private and intimate
matters. After all, it was the youth magazine *Radar* that took up the subject of
sex education for the first time in postwar Poland in 1957.

Polish youth magazines catered to different audiences, but all of them featured a great deal of international content to help readers imagine themselves in a global sphere.[15] *Radar*, which in the early 1960s carried the subtitle "Youth of the World" (Młodzież Świata) began publishing in 1954. Designed as an intellectually ambitious monthly promoting "knowledge of the world," *Radar* paid particular attention to "matters of youth in different countries."[16] Along with its aim to inspire "an active attitude toward the problems of the age of the atom and sputniks," it included regular updates on jazz, rock 'n' roll, and movie stars.[17] A popular biweekly for teenage girls, *Filipinka*, created in 1957, was shaped primarily by the correspondence between the editors and young female readers.[18] Discussion of new youth styles and outlooks was important there, too, with regular debates on what it meant to be a "modern girl."[19] In October 1960, the ZSP began publishing a new biweekly for students, *ITD* (Polish for the Latin *ETC*) with the goal of educating the future intelligentsia.[20] Like *ITD*, all the youth magazines enjoyed the patronage of official youth organizations. *Around the World* was published by ZMS, and *Radar* was under the patronage of the Polish branch of the WFDY. These patronages formally linked these magazines to state organizations, a standard practice in socialist countries.

Youth magazines featured a wide variety of topics and a mixture of styles. Sports, short stories, entertainment news, and gossip were frequently accompanied by essays on literary and historical topics authored by Polish scholars and writers. Translations of foreign literature and articles from the Western press appeared as well. *Around the World* had a strong cosmopolitan flavor. After 1956, the magazine limited its coverage of the Third World and increasingly turned to entertainment news, including reports on rock 'n' roll and Western movie stars, signaling a further departure from Cold War political coverage.[21] *Radar* specialized in presenting "diverse problems of the contemporary young generation" in Poland and other countries.[22] *Filipinka* specifically was focused on problems faced by teenage girls, from conflicts with parents and romantic relationships to hygiene and fashion. *ITD* presented issues relevant to the student community, for example living conditions, study habits, university programs, and student artistic activities. But *ITD* also included more general reportage on social problems and articles dealing with international developments in literature, art, and science. All of the publications strove to reflect a wide variety of interests that young people in socialist countries were supposed to cultivate. In 1962, fifteen-year-old Kinga from Szczecin, speaking on behalf of female readers of *Filipinka*, expressed this desire this way: "we are interested in everything, from the newest plane

Fig. 3.1 Cover of *Radar*, January 1968, with photo of Brigitte Bardot and personal greetings to Polish readers signed by her. Warsaw Public Library—Central Library of Mazovian Voivodeship, Warsaw.

models to handsome male actors, as well as books, sports, theater, politics, and many other things."[23]

The youth magazines actively constructed the broader youth culture in Poland. Most notably, progressive journalists, including former student "radicals" from the time of the Thaw, for example Stefan Bratkowski, made rock 'n' roll an important part of the youth magazines. Texts and scores of English and Polish-language popular songs were published in *Radar* and

Tak tańczy się twista
Ciąg dalszy na str. 16

DWUTYGODNIK ● NR 4 (119)
18 LUTEGO 1962 R. CENA 2 ZŁ

Fig. 3.2 Cover of *Filipinka*, 18 February 1962. "This is how to dance the twist." Warsaw Public Library—Central Library of Mazovian Voivodeship, Warsaw.

Around the World. In January 1960, editors at *Around the World* organized a public performance of big beat bands for the press at a café in Warsaw to familiarize them with the new music and style. "More guests arrived than we expected," Stefan Bratkowski and Wojciech Giełżyński reported. After initial reservations, the audience responded warmly once the bands started playing and asked for more.[24]

As such, these magazines were part of the contemporary pan-European explosion of youth-oriented media. In West Germany, the hugely popular

Bravo began publishing for young audiences in August 1956. Calling itself "The Journal of the Young Heart," it featured entertainment news, pop music, movie stars, advice on relationships, and sex education. The more intellectually oriented *Twen* followed in 1959.[25] *Salut les Copains*, which began publishing in 1962, quickly became a major platform for young French readers to use their consumption of pop music to connect with fellow youth.[26] By the second half of the 1960s, a plethora of independent youth magazines had swept through Western Europe and the United States, with the Italian *Mondo Beat* leading the way in combining "the generational, lifestyle, sexual, cultural, and political revolt like no other conduit in Italy or elsewhere."[27] Both commercial and underground youth publications often generated public outcry and prompted interventions from censors for crossing lines of traditional morality.[28]

In Poland, the Party-state was a constant force with which youth magazines had to reckon. The Party Press Bureau repeatedly reminded editorial boards that "the mass orientation" of youth magazines did not mean "'freedom' from ideological-educational and political tasks." The primary goal of youth publications, in the Bureau's view, was to bring young people "closer to socialist ideology, to build trust in the Party, the system; to awaken patriotism and internationalism."[29] But the Press Bureau also advised caution in packaging such ideological messages and encouraged editors to create "new forms of political-social didactics."[30]

While curbing politically undesirable content, the Press Bureau, ironically, also looked to shield Polish audiences from explicitly ideological material. A surviving document on the 1957 launch of a Polish-language illustrated magazine devoted to social and cultural issues in the Soviet Union titled *Kraj Rad* (The Country of Councils) provides a glimpse of the intricate craft of promoting socialist ideology by underplaying it. The new magazine featured images and translations of articles from the contemporary Soviet press. Yet after examining the first issue of the periodical, the Press Bureau chastised the editorial board for being too faithful to the Soviet originals and for overlooking the fact that "the Polish reader recoils from articles and reports that inevitably conclude with propaganda slogans."[31] In publishing *Kraj Rad*, the Press Bureau contended, one had to take into consideration "the psyche of society as far as the attitude toward the Soviet Union goes." Editors were advised to write articles "in a special manner in terms of the style, form, and the selection of facts" rather than just offering "reprints from the Soviet press." The report recommended modeling *Kraj*

Rad after the Polish popular press by featuring "material that entertains," "clips of information," sports, humor, readers' surveys, and "competitions with awards."[32]

Such recommendations encouraged youth magazines to deploy new terms that softened the word "ideology." In published articles and internal discussions, the Polish adjective *ideologiczny* (ideological) was often replaced with *ideowy*, which meant "faithful to ideals" or "principled" (in contrast to pragmatic or financial interests). The term had strong positive connotations. An even more innovative variation on this theme was a combination: *ideowo-moralny*, which could be translated into "faithful to ideals and full of moral values," collapsing political ideology and personal morality.[33]

Although instructions from the Press Bureau encouraged coverage of the socialist camp, youth magazines reinforced the notion that the West was the core of youth culture. Reports from the Soviet Union and other Eastern European countries were few and far between. Youth magazines usually turned to Western Europe and the United States for foreign material. Articles included tourist brochure–like pieces on cultural attractions such as the Louvre, technological trends such as the car culture in America, and brief commentary on political events. The material was typically presented in a colorful and witty language that distinguished its tone from that of the dry and propagandistic daily newspapers.[34]

Editors made efforts to familiarize their readers with the postcolonial world. In addition to *Around the World*, other youth magazines presented the Third World mostly in the form of reportage, color photographs, travel reports, and coverage of official state visits. *Radar* ran a column titled *penpal pix*, which featured photographs, interests, and mailing addresses of young people from Africa and Asia who wanted to correspond with their Polish counterparts. Polish professionals, for example medical doctors who had already worked in Third World countries, authored some of the articles.[35] The language of this coverage shifted from seeking parallels between Western colonialism and the Nazi occupation of Poland—dominant in the mid-1950s—to highlighting the apotheosis of a modernization based on a distinct anticapitalist and antiimperialist model. As the youth magazines portrayed it, the postcolonial world was an essentially European project of modernity in which Poles were to play an important part.

Popular articles presented postcolonial leaders and peoples first and foremost as enthusiastic admirers of Poland. Commentators never missed the opportunity to highlight any special recognition such leaders allegedly bestowed on Poles. When Polish prime minister Józef Cyrankiewicz and his wife, Nina Andrycz, visited Burma, Cambodia, and India in April 1957, *Around the World* featured a series of reports with color photographs that depicted the couple being followed by cheering crowds waving Polish flags. In Phnom Penh, balloons went up in the air as Cyrankiewicz was passing by in his car.[36] One photograph showed Nina Andrycz, a recognized Polish actress, giving out an autograph to a supposed Indian fan. "Everywhere, in meetings with politicians, scientists, and workers," the report stated, "the Polish delegation was greeted and hosted wholeheartedly." The president of India, Jawaharlal Nehru, explained the reasons for such ovations: "we are greeting [the Polish prime minister] so wholeheartedly, because he is the prime minister of a country which loves [national] independence as much as we do."[37] According to journalistic reports, Poland embodied a successful case of noncapitalist modernization, while also sharing with the postcolonial world the historical experience of fighting for independence against empires. As such, Poland was uniquely positioned to help lead the Global South out of colonial oppression and poverty.[38]

References to national liberation dominated articles and images about revolutionary Cuba. In December 1962, the cover of the student magazine *ITD* featured a gorgeous young woman dressed in the uniform of the Brigadas Conrado Benitez, the literacy brigades that were part of the Cuban literacy campaign launched by Fidel Castro's revolutionary government in 1961. This blonde "Cuban girl" was said to "carry the torch of education to the nation."[39] The phrase "the torch of education" (*kaganek oświaty*) carried strong nationalist connotations, as it was typically used in reference to the female Polish teachers who in the nineteenth century went to the countryside to educate peasant children in Polish language and culture.

Exotic female beauties occupied a prominent place in a personal report on the Cuban Missile Crisis penned by the Polish actress Beata Tyszkiewicz in *Around the World*. In October 1962, she and her husband, Andrzej Wajda, found themselves in Havana attending an international film festival. Her descriptions of political tensions were interwoven with those of Cuban women. "Mobilized [young people] marched through the city, including the most beautiful girls," she wrote. "They were dressed in dark green uniforms, with blouses tucked into tight, laced pants pulled up high . . . which, [it] seems to me, was the absolute necessity of fashion. On their heads, they wore flattering berets, and at their sides they carried menacing weapons intricately encrusted with what looked like mother of

Ta kubańska dziewczyna jest jedną z wielu tysięcy młodych, którzy niosą narodowi kaganek oświaty. I w przenośni i dosłownie. Bowiem symbolem brygad studenckich zwalczających analfabetyzm na Kubie jest właśnie zapalony kaganek oliwny. Gigantyczna akcja podjęta na osobiste wezwanie Fidela Castro przyniosła nadspodziewane rezultaty. Kuba jest pierwszym krajem Ameryki łacińskiej, w którym smutne zjawisko analfabetyzmu dziś należy już do przeszłości. fot. CAF

Fig. 3.3 Cover of *ITD*, 9 December 1962. "The Cuban girl." Photo by Henryk Grzęda. National Library, Warsaw. Courtesy of Polish Press Agency.

pearl."[40] On the pages of youth magazines, international politics and Cold War tensions became a spectacle.

Around the World and *ITD* often featured collages, in which news about elections, wars, and decolonization sat side by side with photographs and gossip about Western celebrities. In a 1962 issue of *ITD*, two pictures of Brigitte Bardot in a swimsuit appeared next to a note on a visit of Polish youth activists to the United States, a photograph and a note on the first elections in independent Algeria, and pictures of local folk celebrations in a mining region in southern Poland. A short note explained that the French actress had stopped wearing her bikini due to a waterskiing incident in which she had fallen and lost her bra. To the right of that story, and below the short note titled "The USA is renewing [nuclear] testing at high altitudes," were three photographs of attractive women fashioning themselves after the main female character in the newly released film *Lolita*. A note next to the pictures informed the readers about a new fashion trend in the West, the "baby bomb": women styling themselves to combine the features of "a very young girl" with those of "a mature woman." The inspiration came from *Lolita*, based on Nabokov's book "about a teenage girl who falls in love with an older man."[41]

Such collages featured not only images and texts but also concepts borrowed from American and Western European media. The pairing of the atomic bomb with a sex-bomb, that is, "a sexy woman outside the home," was common in the American visual culture of the Cold War era.[42] The perception of female sexuality as explosive dated back to the 1930s and had continued during the war, when American pilots had named their bombers after their sweethearts or ornamented planes with erotic images of pinup girls. In the postwar era, as historian Elaine Tyler May has written, the destructive

Fig. 3.4 Collage of political and entertainment news, *ITD*, 23 September 1962. National Library, Warsaw.

force of a bombshell needed to be tamed in the same way as the fears of the "atomic age": by channeling female sexuality into marriage and family.[43] Since that social context did not exist in Poland at the time, sex-bombs functioned as tantalizing elements of Western popular culture incorporated into mass culture under socialism.

Collages that presented a mix of themes, places, and modes of thinking that transcended Cold War divisions were not unique to Poland. For example, the legendary Soviet film periodical the *Soviet Screen* positioned Soviet and foreign cinema on the same page, inviting readers to participate in the global mass media culture. Soviet publications, however, were sure to supply "standard ideological messages," in which political "camps: capitalist and socialist, reactionary and progressive," were clearly identified.[44] The editors of youth magazines in Poland rarely provided such maps. Instead, Polish readers were encouraged to think of themselves as part of the global audience, while their exact ideological location within that audience remained ambiguous.

It was this kind of apolitics—projecting images and texts devoid of an explicit commentary—that aggravated the Press Bureau. In its periodic evaluations of youth magazines, the Bureau relentlessly criticized editorial boards for their alleged pro-Western orientation and weak commitment to the political and moral education of young readers. In 1966, the editors of *ITD* were accused of "avoiding ideological, worldviews-related topics" and "lack of courage and consistency in fulfilling . . . tasks of a political nature." The Bureau reprimanded the editors specifically for featuring collages of political and entertainment news, since such a "mini-chronicle" was thought to make students unlikely to read the daily press.[45]

The most severe criticism was reserved for *Around the World*. In 1959, the magazine was accused of relying on "superficial sensation" and uncritical promotion of "Western literature, art, and entertainment."[46] While Western material was served "on an elegant plate," the material on Poland or the socialist camp "is done in a colorless and lame manner." The unattractive presentation of such material was exacerbated by the editors' alleged efforts to "seek out some sorts of absurdities in the [socialist] part of the world."[47] The substantial coverage of the Third World did not satisfy the Bureau either. Reports from Africa, Asia, and Latin America, according to the Party reviewers, were "guilty of sugar-coating reminiscent of what English and French tourists wearing cork tropical helmets used to put in their travelogues."[48] According to the Bureau, the editors of *Around the World* were preoccupied "too

much ... with 'sensing' readers' tastes, while thinking too little about the pedagogical effects of their work."[49]

Despite constant attack from the Press Bureau, youth magazines continued to flourish throughout the 1960s with no substantial changes in
content, demonstrating the limits of Party-state control. In response to criticism, editors usually defended their standing as "apolitical." The Bureau
complained to the Central Committee that the editorial board of *Around the
World* "received criticism of the magazine with considerable resistance." The
editors were reported to oppose any "radical changes in the conception of the
magazine" and agreed only to a gradual modification "to track in more detail
the reaction of the readers." Moreover, in their rebuttal, the editors reminded
the Bureau that "magazines of this type cannot and should not engage in agi-
tation in a direct and imposing manner, but should only indirectly influence
ideological, ethical, and political outlooks of youth."[50] Such exchanges suggest that the editors had a strong understanding of popular culture as being
shaped by the West and were not willing to give up that notion to please the
Bureau. It is possible that members of the Bureau shared that notion but nevertheless felt compelled to show their vigilance and efforts to enforce the
proper ideological line to the Party higher-ups.

Several factors prevented Party leaders from enforcing strict control over
youth publications. One was the structural disconnect between the Press
Bureau and the censors, who interacted with editors on a day-to-day basis.
The task of censors, however, was to control the political content, which
often meant watching for specific terms and phrases. Censors had no authority to enforce a conceptual orientation of the magazine. Further com-
plicating matters, guidelines for censorship kept changing, depending on
circumstances and official policy. The outcome of these negotiations between
editors and censors depended on many factors: the status of the editor-in-
chief; the position of the publication's "patron" and his faction within the
Party; the size of readership (local papers had more freedom); and the nature of the publication ("cultural" content was typically considered less political by definition).[51] In addition, former editors and journalists have often
pointed to the "human factor" in their interactions with censors. In reflecting
on his editorial experience, Sławomir Tabkowski put it simply: it mattered
"whether [the censor] was a boor or an ... educated person."[52] Ultimately,
Party officials were unwilling to impose a stricter line on youth magazines.
Most likely, they did not consider cultural content to be a serious political
threat.

Citizens of the World

Already during the Thaw, participating in the international youth culture was considered to be an essential part of a young person's identity. When young people tuned into foreign radio stations, wore blue jeans, or read about leisure activities of African teenagers in *Radar*, they did so because being young meant engagement with the wider world. In the mid-1960s, Polish music journalist Wojciech Mann, like many of his fellow teenagers at the time, sat by the radio armed with a thick notebook: "I . . . followed the movements of song titles [on the Radio Luxembourg Top Twenty] with the same diligence that one follows the movements on the stock market today," he recalled in 2010. "Thanks to this magic buzzing [radio] station," Mann continued, "I felt myself to be a citizen of the world."[53]

Imagine how Mann and his friends must have felt when they learned that the Rolling Stones were scheduled to arrive in Warsaw in April 1967. Mann remembered: "it was as if today, a spaceship had landed at one of the main squares in Warsaw, and travelers from a different galaxy announced that they had just decided to make Warsaw the capital of the universe." For many young people, the Rolling Stones' concert was "an unearthly experience." Like listening to Radio Luxembourg, attending the concert was not just about songs as cultural products to be consumed. As Mann explained, it was about "fulfilling dreams, touching the wide world, seeing, sensing, feeling, hearing, and remembering."[54]

Youth magazines served the similar purpose of allowing their readers to "touch the wide world." The publications enjoyed tremendous popularity. In the early 1960s, *Around the World* sold 450,000 copies per issue, *Filipinka* 250,000, and *Radar* and *ITD* 60,000 each.[55] These numbers, however, do not reflect the full readership. The number of copies published was a result of state decisions, including the level of paper supply (always in shortage) rather than the readers' demand. Sociological studies and personal testimonies show that popular demand far surpassed the number of copies available. Youth magazines commanded extensive readership in all parts of Poland and among all social groups. Copies of *Around the World*, *Radar*, *Filipinka*, and other magazines were available in public libraries and reading rooms not only in large urban centers like Warsaw and Kraków but also in small towns and villages. In 1966, sociological research on small towns in Warsaw province found that *Around the World* was the second (after the women's weekly *Girlfriend*) most widely read periodical among locals regardless of age.[56]

Youth magazines were a hot item on newsstands. If one was lucky enough to fetch a copy, it circulated among friends, neighbors, and relatives. Getting one's hands on these magazines, however, required sacrifices. Sławomir Tabkowski, who was a teenager in Kraków in the mid-1950s, woke up each Sunday at 6:30 AM "to race to the newsstand in order to stand in line to get *Around the World*."[57] Tomasz Tłuczkiewicz in Wrocław was an avid reader of the magazine *Jazz*, which began publishing in 1956. He remembered a monthly ritual of fetching and reading the magazine: "this anticipation for *Jazz*, and then hunting for *Jazz* at the newsstand, and then reading from cover to cover, in both directions, multiple times. This was a powerful experience."[58] The enormous popularity of *Filipinka* resulted in the creation of shops, cafés, and clubs that adopted the name of the magazine. In 1959, nine young women in the city of Szczecin formed a vocal choir, called Filipinki, that gained nationwide recognition.[59]

Once procured, youth magazines served multiple purposes. Some people bought them for a specific item, such as a photograph of a favorite rock star or guitar chords for the latest song. Magazines facilitated a behavior typical of fans, in which young people "cut out every photograph of their idol they could put their hands on, wrote down every piece of news about the artist they could hear." Commentators found it troubling that young people often had no respect for public property as they indulged in secretly extracting pictures from the periodicals they found in bookstores, libraries, and reading rooms.[60] There were also different ways of reading the magazines. While some like Tomasz studied every page of *Jazz*, "from cover to cover, in both directions, multiple times," others read more selectively or looked at images. There is little evidence that young people were susceptible to the carefully packaged ideological messages the Press Bureau encouraged. On the contrary, they were savvy, reading magazines for the content they wanted.

Like Radio Luxembourg, youth magazines helped one feel oneself to be "a citizen of the world." According to Sławomir Tabkowski, *Around the World* "was the first youth magazine in Poland that . . . showed the world; it told us that there was something beyond the socialist countries."[61] In the words of Andrzej Sadowski, a sociology student at Warsaw University, *Around the World* "introduced the spirit of worldliness."[62] For Alicja Imlay in Wrocław, *Radar* was the magazine "for those who wanted to see more of the world, not necessarily from here, but in general."[63] In that sense, consuming popular culture, including fragments of sounds and images from other parts of the world, was part of constructing "the normal self."[64]

Fig. 3.5 The People's House under the patronage of the Rural Youth
Association. Young women reading popular magazines in the
reading room. Kozłowa Góra, near Piekary Śląskie, 1960s. Photo by
Kazimierz Seko.
Seko_170_02. Courtesy of KARTA Center Foundation.

The Polish youth magazines also acted us windows for the world onto
Poland. After 1956, Western scholars, journalists, artists, and other travelers
considered the country to be more open and less repressive than others in
the Eastern bloc. Poles liked to talk about their homeland as "the merriest
barrack in the camp" and flaunted their success in not conforming to ideological dogmatism and forced isolation.[65] They were proud to be transmitters
of Western trends to other places in the bloc. They knew that intellectuals in
the Soviet Union often learned Polish in order to read Polish newspapers,
periodicals, and academic journals. They were also proud that Soviet citizens
in neighboring Ukraine, Lithuania, and Belarus regularly watched Polish television for more reliable news and Western productions that were nowhere
to be found on Soviet channels.[66]

The idea of "openness" was also an internal construction directed at Western audiences, an endeavor in which the Polish state actively participated. When the International Book Fair took place in Warsaw in May 1962, Western correspondents were pleasantly surprised that "'the weight' of Eastern and Western books exhibited in Warsaw was almost equal."[67] Among foreign publishers, the biggest exhibition was from France, followed by West Germany, Italy, and the United States. State censors, who inspected the site at night, reportedly confiscated twenty-four books but were quick to return them on protests from the publishers.[68] The Fair exposed Polish flexibility in contrast to other countries in the bloc. A Swedish correspondent noted a poster displayed by the East German exhibitors that announced, "in bad Polish," "East German youth 'rejects the acceptance of the literary trash smuggled in from the West.'" The correspondent found himself amused as he passed by copies of published Polish translations of "trashy" authors rejected by East Germans, for example "Theodor Plievier or Graham Greene and not excluding Francoise Sagan."[69]

The image of Poland's exceptional openness was reinforced by the Polish mass media. "If one did not know or could forget for a moment that Poland is a Communist country," one Western reporter contended, "one would, upon reading a few press dispatches about Poland's participation in international life, get the impression that it is a normal European country with no restrictions or limitations on a free exchange of ideas and men."[70] Every international event, especially the ones in which Poles participated, was broadcast on the Polish radio numerous times as part of the daily news. In August 1965, listeners received updates on the 15th Conference of the International Federation of Youth Hostels and an international youth rally taking place in Kraków. They also learned that a Polish student satirical theater and jazz band had set off for Marseille to participate in an international student culture festival, while another student theater headed to a cultural festival in Istanbul. Some eighty cars from sixteen different countries set off from the picturesque Polish town of Zakopane through the Tatra Mountains to Monte Carlo on the "Polish rally," which involved "58 grueling hours of continuous driving over 3,189 kilometers of hilly, winding roads."[71]

Youth magazines took part in creating "Poland for export."[72] Starting in 1959, an English-language edition of *Radar* was being published every two months with the goal of "propagating the work and achievements of Polish youth and Polish youth organizations."[73] After just the first issue, the Press Bureau was happy to report that "the feedback . . . was very lively." The editors received 3,000 letters from foreign readers and more than 200 requests for subscriptions, "all in hard currency." The most requests came from Indonesia (100), England (25), and China (20).[74] After the second issue, the number of readers' letters doubled. Foreign readers (or perhaps their currency) were so valuable that when the state publishing house experienced a shortage of paper in the summer of 1960, it reduced the number of copies for the Polish edition of *Radar* in order to print enough copies of the English-language one.[75]

Already in 1954, a new illustrated monthly, *Poland,* had begun publishing in English and Russian. By 1962, additional editions of *Poland,* titled the *Polish Review,* were being created for African and Asian audiences. According to the Press Bureau, the Russian-language edition was especially popular among young people in the Soviet Union. Editors received numerous letters from Soviet readers, who asked them to include more information on such themes as "Polish art, literature, and the scout organization."[76] Occasionally, young people in Poland could experience how their youth culture reflected back on them from the West. On the night of October 31, 1967, millions of young Poles tuned in to Radio Luxembourg to hear a live performance by the Blue and Blacks. This time, the purpose was not to catch the latest American or British hit but to hear one of their own. It was the first band to perform from behind the Iron Curtain, in a special segment titled "Beat Session Made in Poland."[77]

* * *

Rather than engaging in explicit political propaganda, the youth magazines marketed socialism for the Poles and marketed Poland for others. The products themselves were living proof of the socialist system's ability to provide entertainment and reading material attractive to young people. The robust public affirmation of mass culture and the flourishing of the youth magazines came at a time when the Party was launching an ideological offensive against post-Thaw liberalization in literature and the arts. While young people were getting updated news on fashion, leisure, and rock 'n' roll, the Party plenary meeting in July 1963 called for restricting the autonomy of cultural and intellectual institutions, personnel changes on editorial boards, and a return to "ideological goals" in cultural policy. The actual effects of this decision were mitigated by protests from intellectuals and artists, but nevertheless this was an attempt to crack down on cultural pluralism.[78]

The two developments might appear to be in conflict, but it is possible to see them as working in tandem. The plenary meeting indicated that the

Thaw-era cultural liberalization required rechanneling. The support for universal mass culture signaled that the idea of "freedom" was primarily delegated to the seemingly apolitical space of leisure and entertainment. Communist regimes often implemented such a strategy as part of "normalization" after a political upheaval, as occurred in Czechoslovakia after Prague Spring. There is little evidence, however, to suggest that the youth magazines in Poland helped to "normalize" society by redirecting their readers' energy from political engagement to apolitical leisure. On the contrary, the youth magazines helped produce a new understanding of the self and the individual's relationship with the modern world that could hardly be sustained by the idea of a disciplined socialist citizen.

4

Bohemians and Discontents

The Making of a Student Community

University students were among the most avid readers of the youth magazines and other periodicals. This interest in the popular press only seemed to confirm long-standing perceptions that students, like other young people in the post-Thaw Poland, had shifted their interests from politics to personal growth and consumption. According to dominant historical interpretations, they would only be politically awakened by the regime's attack on the Warsaw students' demonstration in March 1968.[1] Such interpretations, however, mask the complexity and engagements of the student community. This chapter shifts the characterization of students as a uniform group waiting to be politically awakened to one made up of a diverse population in search of a voice in an era of domestic and global transformations. The protests of 1968 were a powerful expression of that voice, albeit not the only one.[2]

Students' self-expression was inspired, to a large extent, by the transformations of everyday life that were entangled with individual understandings of political subjectivity. In this context, mass culture and consumption could not be seen solely as taking students away from political engagement. As many scholars have suggested, in post-1945 Europe, elements of consumerism became "part of attempts at democratic self-invention from below."[3] In Poland, these elements became an integral part of student politics, which took place not only in lecture halls and on the streets but also in student clubs, dormitories, and private social gatherings.

In postwar Poland, students were making a new community as they came out of diverse social backgrounds; they were not drawn predominantly from the urban and landowning elite families who had traditionally dominated higher education institutions. The democratization of higher education was not only a result of communist policies that aimed to elevate the lower classes but also a part of a global opening of universities to a wider spectrum of society. Cold War mobilization of learning and science also played a pivotal role in catapulting universities to the forefront of intellectual and political

Imagining the World from Behind the Iron Curtain. Malgorzata Fidelis, Oxford University Press. © Oxford University Press 2022. DOI: 10.1093/oso/9780197643402.003.0005

life worldwide. Student enrollment grew in such diverse countries as Great Britain, the United States, Greece, Japan, and Mexico.[4]

The new demographic profile of students produced new tensions and hierarchies in the academic environment in Poland. On the one hand the student community became more inclusive and egalitarian. On the other, social diversity created divisive relationships. Some male students, for example, struggled to accept women as their intellectual equals; urban youth often looked down on students from rural backgrounds.

All students, regardless of their social origin, enjoyed privileges as an elite in the making. The Polish state granted them more cultural and intellectual autonomy than other groups. For example, students had access to a wider variety of publications, through university libraries. They learned foreign languages and could more easily travel abroad as part of the student tourist bureau Almatur, created in 1956. Students who attended prestigious institutions such as Warsaw University had an opportunity to befriend sons and daughters of high-ranking Party officials, who then provided access to more restricted products. One of my interviewees, Adam Mazurek, remembered watching American Western films, unavailable to the wider public, at the Party School, which was administered by the Central Committee of the Party, because one of his friends at the university was a son of the School's director.[5]

In the new spaces and forms of sociability that Polish students created, a new kind of self-expression emerged that was embedded in everyday practices, from student clubs and jazz performances to intellectual and political discussions. Students had greater access to knowledge about the world both because of their studies and because of the predominantly urban milieux in which the universities were located. In the process, students created an imagined community of young elites who had been negotiating the meaning of socialism, democracy, and the world long before taking to the streets in March 1968. This is not to suggest a causal relationship between the changes in everyday practices and an open political rebellion but to understand the cultural conditions that made the student protests of 1968 possible, albeit not inevitable.

The Making of a Student Community

Full-time university students made up a relatively small subset of the Polish population. In 1966, their number stood at 165,609.[6] Out of these, the largest number (close to 25 percent) studied in Warsaw, followed by Kraków and Wrocław, with 17 and 11 percent, respectively. Other academic centers included Poznań, Katowice, Gdańsk, and Łódź, as well as smaller cities such as Białystok, Lublin, and Opole.[7] Although the possibilities for acquiring higher education significantly expanded after the war, getting an academic degree was hardly an easy task. Admission to the university required one to pass a high-school exit examination (*matura*) with high grades and then to pass competitive entrance exams. One's chances of admission were still influenced by social background, family traditions, and the quality of pre-university schooling available in one's place of origin.

Once admitted, students stood out as distinctively recognizable in the urban environment. Because of the structure of Polish education and the age limit for university entrance, they typically fell between the ages of eighteen and twenty-eight. Their appearance and dress were often arresting, as they tended to be the first to display the latest fashions, for example men wearing long hair and women wearing miniskirts. Students were also a transient community, gathered together only for the duration of university studies, which typically extended for five years and ended with a master's degree. While the transitory status and competitive nature of higher education measured by periodic exams might not have created strong bonds, it could reinforce a sense of exceptionalism: the extension of a seemingly carefree youth and a prospect of joining the professional and intellectual elite.

The postwar expansion of education led to the opening of new schools and dormitories as well as the creation of student clubs and student festivals. A new official term, "Student Culture," emerged at the time to denote "cultural activity of youth during university studies."[8] Cities became hotspots for such events as "Days of Student Culture," Student Theater, jazz festivals, and Juvenalia. The latter is a traditional student holiday celebrated in May, when students put on costumes, play pranks and games, and stage open-air performances. Other city residents often came out to watch the performances. In this way, Student Culture became an important element of the urban landscape.

In the eyes of the state, universities served as laboratories for future leaders. Universities were expected to equip students with "expert knowledge" while also shaping "certain ethical norms" and preparing young people for "sociopolitical engagement."[9] Unlike universities in other countries of the Eastern bloc and Soviet Union, Polish universities remained relatively autonomous and more entrenched in the traditional Polish intellectual culture transmitted by the interwar professoriate.[10] This entailed a commitment to the Western liberal model of intellectual inquiry and, to some extent, to broadly understood leftist values of equality and social justice.[11] Moreover, ideological training for students was limited when the Party eliminated obligatory Marxist-Leninist courses. After 1956, Marxism was taught in a broader context, typically as part of required courses in philosophy and political economy.[12]

The relative intellectual autonomy carried over to other student endeavors such as the official ZSP. Although still responsible for the ideological shaping of the student community, the ZSP occupied a vague terrain between formal political allegiance and cultural autonomy. It left its most enduring mark in the realm of cultural and artistic patronage.

Between the Metropole and the Dormitory

The official principle of equality and the influx of students from a variety of social backgrounds helped make the academic environment more egalitarian than ever before. In the 1960s, unlike the interwar period, Polish and Jewish identities ceased to be one of the main dividing lines in Polish universities.[13] Individuals from minority groups were present, but between the end of the war and 1968 stigmatization based on ethnic origin was rare. The majority of Jewish students in the early 1960s self-identified as Poles, even if some of them participated in Jewish cultural activities such as those offered by the Socio-Cultural Association of Jews in Poland (Towarzystwo Społeczno-Kulturalne Żydów w Polsce; TSKŻ). Both Jewish and non-Jewish Warsaw residents regularly attended dance parties organized by the popular student club Babel under the patronage of the TSKŻ.[14]

According to many former students, Jewishness was rarely a topic of conversation. Take Ewa from Warsaw, who was told by her parents about their Jewish background when she was in elementary school. "Information regarding our ancestry was exciting and had an air of exoticism," she remembered in 2008. "I imagined myself as a Thai princess or a descendant of Chinese mandarin. But when I announced this at school, no one seemed to care. Many of my girlfriends probably did not even realize they too could be Jewish. Because back then, at the beginning of the 1960s, like in my household, people did not talk about being Jewish in private homes."[15] Ewa's account is representative of many but not all Jewish Poles from the urban

intelligentsia. In interviews and other personal testimonies gathered predominantly since the 1980s, they stress the weak awareness of their own religious or cultural identity and generally inclusive climate within their social
circles prior to 1968.

Yet new dividing lines emerged among postwar students. Despite state
efforts to recruit young people from the working class and peasant background, the majority of students continued to come from the urban intelligentsia. In 1957, such students made up more than 60 percent of the
freshman class at Warsaw University and more than 57 percent of that class at
the Jagiellonian University in Kraków.[16]

The influx of students from outside such metropolitan areas as Warsaw
and Kraków amplified differences between those from the "center" and those
coming from the "periphery." On their arrival in the city, young people from
the provinces usually lived in dormitories or rented rooms, unlike the local
students who lived in their parents' households. The local students possessed
greater familiarity with the city and were often part of established social
networks. They also enjoyed greater access to contemporary youth culture;
many of them traveled abroad or owned such coveted consumer commodities as vinyl records and blue jeans. A handful boasted Italian-made scooters,
such as Lambrettas or Vespas. In contrast, out-of-towners often faced social isolation and possessed fewer material status symbols. The social division was such that students from the city rarely got involved in romantic
relationships with their counterparts who lived in the dorms.[17]

Personal testimonies suggest that students from rural backgrounds had
to reckon with significant prejudice against them as culturally "backward."
While studying at the university in Łódź, one young woman remembered
hearing her female urban friends describe rural young women as "these
hicks from the village."[18] Another female student, Józefa, experienced her
initial marginalization early, during the summer before her freshman year,
when she participated in the student work brigades at a state farm in Lower
Silesia. She found that the urban students she met "made fun of farm work,
pretended to be adults at all cost, smoked and drank, and made love." When
she became friends with a few other rural young women, who also felt intimidated by the urban youths, their social circle was soon dubbed the "virgins"
and subjected to teasing.[19]

While at the university, rural youth faced a plethora of challenges, from
adjusting to city life to catching up to the level of academic knowledge possessed by their urban counterparts. Andrzej Sadowski, who came from

a small village in eastern Poland to study sociology at Warsaw University, found it difficult to adapt to "the noise, the daily commute, and the crowded buses." Most of his new peers were from Warsaw, and he noticed the difference in their speech and level of erudition. At first, he rarely participated in class discussions. "I always had some sort of a mental block," he explained. "Am I worthy of engaging with others ... Do I have anything to say at all?"[20]

Social dynamics at the universities were sometimes influenced by the presence of foreign students. At the time, Poland hosted only a handful of international students. The 1,806 foreigners who studied in Poland in the academic year 1966–1967 came from seventy-six countries. The majority (721) came from socialist countries, while 511 were from Africa, 347 from Asia, 82 from Latin America, and 143 from "other capitalist countries."[21] Foreigners usually were not integrated into student culture to the same extent as their Polish counterparts. Racist attitudes among Polish students were not uncommon, and they most often found their expression in dating culture, a phenomenon that was also rampant at Soviet universities.[22] Female students who lived in the dormitories faced the greatest stigma if they befriended male students of a different skin color. According to contemporary sociological research, traditional assumptions about gender roles were more common among dormitory residents than among urban students. As one young woman stated, "a female student from the dormitory, who decides to go on a date with a foreign student automatically closes the door to dating a Polish man." An African student complained that he once tried to invite a young woman from the dormitory on a date. She refused, explaining that her Polish male colleagues would call her "a dirty whore."[23]

The presence of students from the postcolonial world did not seem to have a significant impact on local students' accepting racial diversity or to open them to new perspectives on the developing world. The small number of foreign students and their relative isolation contributed to the weakness of crosscultural communication. In personal memories, students from the postcolonial world rarely appear, but when they do they are usually remembered for their exotic looks and behavior. In one memoir, an African student in Wrocław, Kaba, was warmly recalled as "the most colorfully and fashionably dressed, fawned over by the girls." Moreover, interaction with African students such as Kaba could reinforce the alleged higher civilizational status of Poland. As Kaba prepared to return to his native country after graduation, he was remembered for crying and confessing to his Polish friend that he did not want to go back "to that savage place."[24]

The Challenge of the Female Student

The mass entry of women into higher education presented a distinct challenge to the traditional university culture. The proportion of women in the student body grew from 35 percent in 1960–1961 to 42 percent, or close to 135,500 students, in 1969–1970.[25] The social and cultural impact of the changing gender ratio in higher education should not be underestimated. Women claimed access to the most advanced degrees and most prestigious professions, which had traditionally been reserved for male elites. Women were also highly visible in the urban environment. Educated, independent, and often dressed according to the latest fashion, they embodied both women's emancipation and youth culture.

In a socialist society where women's right to education and work could not be questioned in official venues, a variety of reactions to female students

Fig. 4.1 Female students preparing for exams, Warsaw University, April 1964. Photo by Tadeusz Uchymiak. Courtesy of Polish Press Agency.

often found expression in popular culture. Youth and student magazines tried to neutralize any fears that educated young women would pay less attention to their looks or challenge other feminine norms. The student magazine *ITD* was a case in point. It celebrated female students as eroticized beauties who combined physical attractiveness with intellectual qualities. Although intended for all students, the content of *ITD* was geared toward male readers. From its launch, almost every issue featured a photograph of an attractive female student on the front cover. The image was typically accompanied by a brief statement giving the woman's name, her school affiliation, and a justification for her appearance on the cover. The short introduction often referred to these woman literally as "the cover" and ensured the reader of the attractive content of the issue. "Ewa Strzelecka," one introductory statement read, "a female student at Warsaw University, invites you to read this issue. It is interesting!"[26] In other cases, cover girls were presented as winners of the contest for "the nicest female student" in a particular city.[27] As such covers suggested, the magazine became a feminized "commodity" for the male reader to acquire and explore. While reaffirming healthy heterosexual male desire, cover girls reminded everyone that beauty and docility were fundamental to proper femininity and that these qualities would not change as a result of women's intellectual pursuits.

The editors of *ITD* invited readers to participate in the beauty culture the magazine promoted. A series of photographic contests titled "My Girl," begun in 1961, called on male readers to take pictures of their girlfriends and submit them to the magazine. The editors would then publish these photographs inside, but the winning picture would be placed on the front cover of the magazine every two months, earning the winner a cash honorarium. Contest participants were asked to send a detailed technical description of the photo, including the level of light, aperture, and brand of the film as a way of "exchanging information" with other men. Editors suggested possible poses for the young woman: "the girl is studying, combing her hair, darning panty hose, crying, laughing." One could also photograph "the spring hairstyle of my girlfriend," "the girl for winter," and "the girl for vacation."[28] The contest rested on the notion of gender hierarchy, in which the man functioned as a technologically savvy creator of art and the woman as an attractive object.

While celebrating educated beauties, student magazines were only slightly less eager to join other publications in chastising female students for their alleged sexual transgressions and consumer indulgences. It was not uncommon for the press to write about all-female dormitories as "a comfortable place for

Fig. 4.2 Cover of *ITD*, 19 January 1964. "Our cover invites you to read this issue ' from end to end.' " Photo by Władysław Pawelec. Warsaw University Library, Warsaw. Courtesy of Aleksandra Pawelec.

trysts" or to allege that some female students performed sexual favors in exchange "for go-go boots."[29] Far from affirming women in higher education, the beauty culture promoted by the popular press forced on female students an unresolvable double bind: if they heeded the message that they were most acceptable as proper educated beauties and presented a consumerist, objectified femininity, they opened themselves to the innuendoes that they were using their status as students only to pursue sexual and consumer pleasures.

Female students found themselves subject to new social rules in their everyday lives. When female freshmen from the provinces came to live in a dormitory, they often found that they had to adjust to gendered rituals such as dating. In all-female dormitories, boyfriends often visited on Sundays, and single young women customarily were expected to leave the shared bedrooms so their dating roommates could have privacy. "Characteristic to the female dormitory on visitation days," one sociologist noted in his study of a dormitory complex in Łódź, "is the sight of girls sitting in the hallway by heaters (in the wintertime), [or] in the kitchen or study rooms."[30]

Coeducational dormitories offered a friendlier environment, but here, too, social rules disadvantaged young women. Going to a dance party at a dormitory club, for example, was a stressful experience for many young women. Dance parties—a popular way for male and female students to meet and start a romantic relationship—assigned the initiative entirely to men. One female student thought of dances as "humiliating for women, if a guy comes over and checks her out. He often gives such a condescending look that the girls would feel as if they were a commodity at an open auction."[31]

A woman could, of course, forgo dance parties, but such decisions could result in her social marginalization. As dormitory residents agreed, dating was an important "part of adaptation to the new environment during the freshman year."[32] If a woman did not date, "she would not have a social circle."[33] Such "social circles" held a special importance for dormitory residents. As newcomers to the city and the university, finding trusted friends (and possibly a husband of an established social status) was "like finding a new family after leaving your own."[34]

The Magic of the Place

In the evenings, Mokotowska Street, close to Warsaw city center, filled with the buzz of scooters and the laughter of young people. They were gathering by the three-story nineteenth-century building where the student club Hybrydy (Hybrids) was located. The club, which had opened in February 1957, featured no fewer than ten halls, including several dance rooms, four bars, a billiards room, a room for playing bridge, and a theater.[35] One Polish reporter compared Mokotowska Street to the Kungsgatan in Stockholm, where scores of Swedish youths "dressed in leather jackets, blue jeans, and high-heeled boots" visited night clubs and movie theaters, the only difference being "the lack of advertisements on Mokotowska."[36]

Hybrydy and other student clubs have been remembered as unique bohe-mian places where one could find freedoms and pleasures unimaginable in other areas of Polish life. Such romanticizing of the student clubs dominates the collective memory of former participants, making it difficult to separate the social reality of the club from the myth-making.[37] Originating during the Thaw as spaces for free discussion and artistic experimentation, the stu-dent clubs under the patronage of the ZSP numbered almost 250 between 1956 and 1976.[38] Alongside Hybrydy, the best known clubs were Stodoła (The Barn) in Warsaw; Pod Jaszczurami (Under the Lizards) and Piwnica pod Baranami (Basement under the Sheep) in Kraków; Żak (medieval Polish term for "student") in Gdańsk; and Pałacyk (Little Palace) in Wrocław. After the Thaw, clubs were geared toward educational leisure and entertainment rather than political discussions. As the ZSP declared in 1957, the main goal of the student clubs was to create "intelligent and thoughtful consumers" as well as to cultivate "creative ambitions."[39]

Going to the club became an important formative experience for many students and young artists. Consider the student club Pałacyk in Wrocław, which opened in 1959 in the nineteenth-century aristocratic residence of Gustav Von Bess. Club participants described Pałacyk as "a magical place."[40] By the early 1960s, it had become the home of the avant-garde theater Kalambur and several jazz groups. It hosted reg-ular jam sessions, art exhibitions, meetings with prominent artists and intellectuals, and Saturday night parties. In Kraków, the student club Pod Jaszczurami offered a rich weekly schedule. Each day featured a meeting with representatives of specific arts and professions such as theater people, filmmakers, musicians, journalists, and athletes. Saturday was reserved for parties, while Sunday morning hosted a "literary breakfast with poets, novelists and dramaturges."[41] Leaders of the ZSP insisted on dis-associating the clubs from the idea of "mass culture" and instead making "elite culture" more widespread and accessible.[42] Hybrydy, Pałacyk, Pod Jaszczurami, and countless other student clubs attracted a variety of urban intelligentsia of all ages. While students remained the most numerous participants, faculty members, intellectuals, and professionals attended many events at the clubs.[43]

Most former students remember clubs as places where they experienced new feelings and sensations. Wiesław Misiek associated Pałacyk "with huge crowds at the entrance, stale air inside, and an indescribable atmosphere that I will remember forever."[44] Jan Miodek, who entered Wrocław University in 1963, was too shy to visit the club during his freshman year. When he finally decided to go to a Saturday night party, he was entranced: "I never heard more beautiful instruments than those of the Pakulski jazz band."[45]

No wonder some individuals made efforts to maintain their formal student status just to be able to regularly attend the clubs. "I repeated my third year of studying law at least five times," Bogumił Paszkiewicz remembered in 2018, "not to finish but to maintain my status as a student." He explained: "this was a way of life. Classes in the morning, and hitting the clubs in the evening. . . . I would return at 6 in the morning to the basement I was renting out. The janitor greeted me: 'It's the student's bedtime.' "[46]

Mythologizing student clubs became an important part of the collective memory of the intelligentsia. Such memories no doubt intensified with the encroachment of commercial culture on post-1989 Poland and the decline of cultural and artistic life at the clubs. Yet the tendency to see the clubs as "magical places" was part of students' imagination from the very beginning, and it had much to do with these places' symbolic proximity to the outside world.

Fig. 4.3 Student Club in Łódź, February 1960. Photo by Romuald Broniarek. Broniarek 142-05. Courtesy of KARTA Center Foundation.

Like reading popular magazines, a visit to the club could become a substitute for traveling to the West. Former student Jurek Lukierski from Wrocław remembered: "at the same time as [in] Paris and New York, the twist and bossa nova were making the rounds in student clubs." One could also acquire rare cultural products at the club. Lukierski continued: "this was the place where one could exchange vinyl records of Louis Armstrong for the chaotic jazz of Charlie Mingus." In students' imagination, the clubs existed almost in a different time zone, away from "the brutalist model of studying in communist Poland" and closer to the diverse and exciting world.[47]

The clubs were magnets for foreign visitors. When renowned American physicist and future Nobel Prize laureate Richard Feynman arrived in Poland in July 1962 to attend a conference in Jabłonna near Warsaw, he was curious to see the night life of Poland's capital. A young graduate student, Marek Demiański, took him to Hybrydy. "The security guards had no clue who Feynman was," Demiański remembered in 2007, "but the American passport and a few dollars did the trick—we got inside in no time at all."[48] Soon, Feynman made friends with the Polish band. The next thing Demiański saw was the scientist playing the drums with the band and teaching the club guests samba steps.

Student clubs created bonds of solidarity among participants based on common cultural consumption and aesthetic choices. But these clubs also marked new hierarchies among students. Those who did not find the activities offered by the club attractive could feel alienated. Despite the popularity of the clubs, sociology student Jolanta Wachowicz-Makowska was not fond of them. She sometimes went to Hybrydy but confessed that she did not find the place pleasurable. "They must have never opened the windows in that place," she recalled in 2007, "because the stuffiness was exceptionally irritating as was the 'lax' atmosphere." She abhorred the drinking culture at the club. "People drank straight from the bottle, often excessively," she remarked. "Admittedly, drunks and belligerents were thrown out, but those who were on the verge of absolute drunkenness were allowed to stay and set the mood."[49] Jolanta and her social circle preferred to spend their free time in other ways.

Although many students found the clubs liberating, gender and class hierarchies informed the new socializing spaces and might have been a factor in distancing young women like Jolanta from the club culture. In personal testimonies, women who attended the clubs, many of them participants in the Student Theater or musical groups, tended to be remembered for their exceptional beauty rather than their intelligence or other qualities. In the words of one male club regular, the young women at the club "were a bonus, an ornament." Rather, the main goal of going to the club was "to meet up with friends . . . drink booze [napić się gorzały], to talk, to dance, and to sing."[50] Other men remembered females primarily as objects of desire. Some male students jokingly admitted that they attended the club mainly for an opportunity to meet women, a goal that was not always fulfilled.[51]

Above all, student clubs such as Pałacyk and Hybrydy provided opportunities for men to reinvigorate their masculinity, now increasingly embedded in a distinct consumer style and artistic taste. Nowhere was this more visible than in playing and listening to jazz, a quintessential club activity. Even though jazz had become part of the official culture during the Thaw, it retained a flavor of rebellion in the years to come.[52] Political and intellectual elites considered jazz to be more ambitious and intellectually stimulating than popular music. The monthly *Jazz* announced that "jazz is not a fashion, but an era in music."[53] The magazine, which began publishing in 1956, promoted jazz knowledge by featuring articles about the history of jazz and news on artists and styles. The editors encouraged young people to establish jazz clubs as part of student club activities, for "shaping the club participants, providing practical help to jazz bands, and organizing concerts open to the public."[54]

For many students, jazz became part of group identification and a marker of a young member of the intelligentsia with refined taste and an attitude of distancing from state-sponsored mass culture, most visibly exemplified by the big beat. Tomasz Tłuczkiewicz, who studied at the Wrocław Polytechnic, was drawn to jazz for its "alternative bite." Like other male jazz fans in the early 1960s, Tomasz distinguished himself by his sartorial choices: a crew cut, horn-rimmed glasses, and a goatee. He wore tweed, rather than a regular blazer, and a popped collar with a tie. Such outfits were hardly available in Polish stores and often had to be made from scratch. Tomasz was lucky to have a mother who liked to sew. "Although I was a grown man, a regular at night clubs," he remembered with irony in 2013, "my suits and shirts were made by my mom."[55] Others relied on private tailors or local *komis* stores (secondhand stores with Western clothes).

The contemporary press, including youth magazines, presented jazz as an almost inherently masculine activity associated with men's allegedly superior intellect. Music critic and journalist Roman Waschko estimated that as many as 85 percent of jazz fans were men, while women usually became interested in jazz because of their boyfriends.[56] According to Waschko, not jazz but rock 'n' roll attracted young women, who allegedly followed it "with a fanatical disposition." Their interest in rock 'n' roll was not because of the music but because they found the male performers erotically appealing.[57] Such writings divided youth culture in stereotypical gendered terms: ambitious and intellectual forms of art attracted young men, young women succumbed to emotions and easy consumption.

Student clubs nevertheless provided new opportunities for young women to develop their places in the student community. Clubs facilitated female performers, and many future female vocalists and actresses began their professional careers there. One such artist was Urszula Dudziak, who eventually became a professional jazz vocalist. She discovered jazz as a teenager in the early 1960s with the help of her older brother, Leszek, a regular at Pałacyk. A bassist and percussionist, Leszek put on a jazz record to demonstrate to his younger sister "what great music this is!" She remembered in 2011: "as soon as I heard the music, I went crazy."[58] Shortly afterward, she found herself singing jazz at the Pałacyk. Like Tomasz, she wanted to dress the part of a jazz performer and had to rely on the sewing skills of her mother. "I begged my mother," she recalled, "to sew me a bell-shaped skirt out of the most fashionable, thick blue cotton." She then matched the skirt with a boatneck blouse, stockings, and ballerina pumps, all in black.[59]

For young people like Tomasz and Urszula, the club facilitated personal autonomy and artistic expression. Although such experiences were not uniform, the clubs symbolized the distinct freedoms available to students in Polish society. Even if not all students attended clubs, they had access to this unique space where one could experience connection to the world through sounds and sensations and act more freely than in other places.

Seeking Contradictions?

While the clubs could make students feel closer to the world, the interactions that took place with global trends there were mainly through leisure and consumption rather than political ideas. Meanwhile, universities remained hotbeds of multiple visions of democratic socialism, increasingly embedded in students' observation of international politics. Historian Andrzej Friszke points to "the hunger for ideological literature" among intellectuals and students in the early 1960s, who turned to a variety of writings that challenged the Soviet version of socialism. These included contemporary

Trotskyites, early Eurocommunists such as Palmiro Togliatti, and Maoists, among others.[60]

When sociologist Stefan Nowak and his team examined political attitudes among Warsaw students in 1958, they found that two-thirds of them supported a generally defined socialism and thought of it as the way of the future for the world.[61] These students' understanding of socialism, however, was not uniform or necessarily accurate. When asked to give examples of countries they considered "to be the closest to what you understand as socialism," Yugoslavia topped the list, followed by the Soviet Union, Poland, Sweden, and China. But the top ten also included the United States and Switzerland, in seventh and eighth positions, respectively. Respondents claimed that they considered these two countries "socialist" because of their high standard of living.[62]

Perhaps the most intriguing finding was that some students believed that the West would achieve socialism sooner than Poland and the Eastern bloc. In the words of one respondent, "the pursuit of equality and freedom is common to all people," but "unfortunately, we have less chance for socialism than the West. We did not go down the main road, but rather the side streets." According to this statement, the West was on the correct path to socialism because "the freedoms of human beings and their influence on the fate of their country are expanding," whereas in Poland "the very essence of the system [is] aimed at . . . the subordination of the human being to the rulers, the raison d'être."[63] Many students believed that socialism was tantamount to the citizens' full participation in the political process. Almost all these students rejected one-party dictatorship and supported "a multiparty system" as part of genuine socialism.[64]

Little wonder that not all students found the cultural autonomy of clubs sufficient. Some turned to new opportunities for intellectual engagement created by the Catholic Church, which acquired institutional autonomy from the state.[65] During the Thaw, liberal Catholics created a network, the Clubs of Catholic Intelligentsia, that proved appealing to some young people. By 1959 in Kraków, for example, the youth section of the Catholic Intelligentsia Club, under the patronage of local Jesuits, recruited as many as 300 members.[66] Not all of them were devout Catholics. In general, students tended to be more secular than other social groups in Poland. In 1958, according to sociologist Anna Pawełczyńska, 30 percent of students in Warsaw identified themselves as either atheist or agnostic. At the same time, among the 70 percent who described themselves as "believers," one-third practiced on an irregular basis. In addition, students displayed a high degree of tolerance toward others' thinking about religion. Pawełczyńska wrote: "most of the respondents were completely indifferent toward the religious beliefs of other people, and practically no one harbored aggressive attitudes toward people of different worldviews from their own."[67] In fact, many secular leftist students considered the intellectual environment created by liberal Catholics to be particularly attuned to the ideas of the Thaw, including democratization and social equality. Both groups engaged in a productive dialogue.[68]

Over the course of the 1960s, the Church became especially active in attracting young people through a mixture of traditional and newer forms of worship. These initiatives, to some extent, came from the reforms of Vatican II and the impetus for making Catholicism more compatible with the modern world. But the Church in Poland was additionally motivated by fast-moving secularization and competition with the state for the hearts and souls of the younger generation. In the late 1960s the Church began organizing regular summer retreats for secondary school students, which later would become the basis for the Light and Life Movement (Ruch Światło-Życie) popularly known as the Oasis (Oaza). While in 1969, 1,500 young people participated in the Oasis summer retreats, that figure had risen to 30,000 by the end of the 1970s, and to 77,000 by 1985.[69]

The most troublesome members of society for the Party were the young people who continued the Thaw-era search for leftist ideas alternative to the ones professed by the regime. In this, Warsaw University led the way. In 1962, Karol Modzelewski, a doctoral student of medieval history who had been active in the Thaw movement, formed the Political Discussion Club. In creating the club, he was inspired by his recent encounter with the contemporary Italian Left as a research fellow of the Giorgio Cini Foundation. After witnessing open discussions at Italian universities and a strike by leftist students in Venice, he hoped to bring some of that intellectual dynamism to his home institution.[70] At first, the ZMS agreed to support the initiative.

The open meetings of the Political Discussion Club proved attractive to young people craving intellectual and political engagement. Some of the most eager followers of Modzelewski turned out to be high school students under the leadership of Adam Michnik. Like Modzelewski, Michnik found the idea of a political discussion club attractive and in 1962 he formed the Club of Seekers of Contradictions (also at first supported by ZMS), which gathered students from Warsaw's elite secondary schools. The teenagers often joined Modzelewski's club, where they read and discussed works by Polish and international authors such as Trotsky, Milovan Djilas, Włodzimierz Brus, and Robert Conquest.[71] They took interest in leftist student activism in the West, especially in France.[72] It was not uncommon for the discussions to turn into an open critique of the communist system in the Eastern bloc as contradictory to Marx' original writings. By the end of the academic year in 1963, the Party had officially disbanded both Modzelewski's and Michnik's clubs.[73]

Yet Modzelewski's initiative had a snowball effect, as many students continued political discussions in small unofficial circles. A few years later, when former members of Michnik's club entered Warsaw University, they formed a loosely organized group, soon known as the Commandos (Komandosi). The name of the group came from the tactics they employed: like a specialized military unit, they suddenly appeared at lectures and official meetings with the purpose of taking over the floor. Challenging the state's Marxist-Leninist orthodoxy, Commandos forcefully voiced alternative interpretations of leftist politics.[74]

The Commandos blended political engagement with a more relaxed form of socializing. According to female Commando Paula Sawicka, the club was to a large extent "a social group with small parties at the core." Although, as many acknowledged, a lot of drinking and smoking was going on, "these were not purely fun meetings," she insisted. "There was always an intellectual strand to it."[75] For Barbara Toruńczyk, joining the Commandos was a way to rebel against the state-endorsed turn toward consumerism after 1956. She remembered in 2008: "we did not want to hoard wealth, collect furniture and paintings; we did not aspire to have a TV or a car; we abhorred the rat race for positions of power and prestige." Instead, as she claimed, "we practiced hitchhiking and free love. We wanted total freedom. Life should be an adventure and a pursuit of new experiences."[76] Accordingly, the Commandos functioned apart from, but also parallel to, the student clubs such as Hybrydy or Pałacyk. Many of them felt alienated from what they saw as the "mass student culture" exemplified by the entertainment-oriented student clubs and attended them only sporadically for such events as student song festivals or "an interesting discussion."[77]

"Free love" and "total freedom" for Polish students did not necessarily have the same meaning as they did for those in the midst of the "sexual revolution" in Western leftist circles. For the latter, sexual freedom was often synonymous with a political rebellion against all forms of bourgeois oppression.[78] In contrast, young Poles rarely articulated the need for sexual liberation in public the way their West German or French counterparts did. An open challenge

cy, redistribution of national wealth in different coun-
ice and income inequality in socialist countries. No one
e on the same level about these topics!"[83]

alone in finding empowerment through leftist student
ducated woman. Many former female students recall
participating in nonconformist student circles even if
with the traditional "division of roles," such as letting
k up on political issues more often than they did.[84] Still,
mandos provided new opportunities for young women
participants in a meaningful intellectual community,
d not always find in their formal university studies. In
th elements of consumer culture, Polish students dem-
wo were not necessarily mutually exclusive. They dem-
Children of Marx and Coca-Cola"—to use Jean-Luc
n of French youth at the time—had a distinct presence
tain.

* * *

the sixties, students in Poland were a community in flux.
men who entered institutions of higher education from a
ckgrounds found themselves confronting and negotiating
s in academic centers and varied material statuses. But as
ng elite in the making—they also searched for their own
at was preoccupied with young people as the embodiment
he future.
bs that emerged to facilitate young people's aspirations
as tangible markers of a distinct student status, where
experiment with music, art, and sociability. In a way, they
of students' "freedom," which was more extensive and more
n the opportunities granted to other groups. Although of-
pes of activities, both student clubs such as Hybrydy and
uch as the Commandos shared common characteristics.
at they saw as state-supported "mass entertainment" and
itious and independent expressions of student subjectivity,
art or alternative Marxism.
status of students, however, left them in a vulnerable posi-
times of political crises. Periodic media attacks on students
ented and hedonistic revealed distrust on the part of the

gender equality and
of dominant norms.
tion in an interview i
mores were rather na
so why would one wa
the Commandos and
they practiced it.

The link between po
the West when a powe
to challenge the male-
to historian Dagmar H
eagerly in the new oppo
available by the pill and
illusioned with their ma
and their unwillingness t
Their feminist politics "b
flict over sexual relations

Although a public fer
circles at the time, the Co
over gender and class. Per
erosexual masculine perf
tity. In the 1980s, Michni
[Modzelewski]." Michnik
admired him. Unconsciou
Michnik suggests, the Cor
in claims to intellectual sup
like-minded men, and eroti

A mixture of gender and
mony from former female s
started attending Command
better," she remembered in
the Adriatic Sea, Moscow, an
array of drinks I never heard
flirt, how to wear a sweater to
And we lived modestly."[82] M
their gatherings an eye-openi
covered completely new ways

socialist state toward the elite in the making. The Commandos, in particular, took the students' autonomy to new levels by creating their own social and consumer styles, and combining them with the explicitly political language that challenged the ruling Party monopoly on defining Marxism. By the mid-1960s, the Commandos and their supporters had emerged as formidable competitors of the state in defining not only socialism at home but also transnational engagements in an era of global upheaval from below.

5

Tensions of Transnationalism

Youth Rebellion, State Backlash, and 1968

The morning of Friday, March 8, 1968, began quietly in Warsaw. Spring was
in the air even as patches of snow were still melting on the ground. March 8
was International Women's Day, an important holiday in the Eastern bloc.
Some women were more nicely dressed than usual, expecting customary
celebrations and small gifts at their workplaces. But this was shaping up as anything but a typical Women's Day. At the main campus of Warsaw University,
on Krakowskie Przedmieście, a peaceful student rally was planned. These
young people were to gather to demand civic freedoms and to protest the
expulsion of two students from the university. The rally started at noon, and
within a few minutes seven tour buses had arrived at the campus entrance.
As the passengers disembarked, it became clear that these were not tourists
arriving to explore historical sights of the Polish capital but stern-looking
middle-aged men in civilian clothes armed with clubs. Party officials had
recruited them from factories and offices to help suppress the student demonstration. At a quarter past noon the men began their attack.

The students' demonstration in Warsaw initiated a chain of events known
in Polish historical narratives as "March 1968" or simply "March" (Marzec).
The violent state action against unarmed students generated massive
protests by young people all over Poland that lasted for nearly two months.[1]
In response, the communist regime not only dispatched police and armed
civilians to quell street demonstrations but also launched a powerful antisemitic campaign. Party officials and the media denounced protestors as
Zionists, imperialists, and Marxist revisionists who wanted to overthrow
socialism and the Polish state. In the wake of this campaign, approximately
15,000 Polish Jews emigrated.[2]

Encompassing both youth unrest and the state's antisemitic response,
"March" significantly transformed the Polish political and intellectual
landscape. The willful embrace of racist, right-wing nationalism by ruling
communists shocked the leftist intelligentsia, many of whom abandoned

Imagining the World from Behind the Iron Curtain. Malgorzata Fidelis, Oxford University Press. © Oxford University Press
2022. DOI: 10.1093/oso/9780197643402.003.0006

their faith in the possibility of reforming state socialism and turned to anti-communist political opposition. The crushing of Prague Spring by Warsaw Pact forces in August 1968 only solidified their position.

Unsurprisingly, conventional Polish narratives of 1968 are deeply entrenched in the domestic context. After 1968, as Adam Michnik, a central figure of the student movement, put it, "we were no longer Marxist dissidents but members of the antitotalitarian opposition."[3] According to such dominant interpretations, student demonstrations belonged to the sequence of "Polish months": the periodic revolts of Polish society against the communist regime that started in June 1956 with the workers' uprising in Poznań against the Stalinist regime and culminated in the emergence of the Solidarity movement in August 1980.[4]

Rather than replicating this standard nation-centered narrative, this chapter repositions 1968 in Poland as an integral part of global 1968. It shows Polish students not simply as protestors against a "totalitarian" regime but as active participants in contemporary global leftist politics. Those politics involved turning away from the state as a potential vehicle for a socialist transformation, reformulating ideas of justice and solidarity, and engaging in leftist conversations across borders. The state's violence against the protestors only confirmed the threat of the leftist challenge from below by exposing the deep insecurity of the ostensibly socialist regime with regard to its own ideological commitments and claims to legitimacy.

Historians of the "European 1968" explain the ubiquity of the protests in such different contexts as Western European democracies, Eastern European communisms, and southern European military dictatorships by highlighting "common causes" and inspirations, including shared desires for "participatory democracy," generational conflict, and antifascist legacies of the interwar era.[5] In much of this literature, Eastern Europe stands out as the least theoretically integrated into scholars' understanding of 1968. Existing work on student protests in places such as Prague, Warsaw, or Belgrade usually focuses on domestic political narratives, while the comparative angle tends to highlight differences, similarities, and points of contestation between Eastern European and Western European student movements.[6] The recurring theme has been that Western activists had little understanding of Eastern European concerns. The very fact, however, that tensions existed and were often passionately articulated testifies to the Eastern European students' intense identification with the transnational community of rebels.[7] The framework of the global sixties helps to better explain these transnational dynamics and to highlight the influence of the postcolonial world on shaping them.

The Polish protestors sought to insert themselves into global conversations prior to and during 1968 by linking their activism to historical and contemporary leftist movements. In March 1968, young rebels employed global protest strategies such as rallies, sit-ins, singing and writing songs, and satire, while also evoking the ideas of solidarity and authenticity that were inherent in student demonstrations worldwide. This chapter looks at how contemporary actors in a specific locality, Poland, understood transnational connections.[8] Seen through their eyes, transnationalism in Eastern Europe has quite a different meaning from the more familiar tale of global leftist solidarity developed across the First World and the Third World.[9]

A closer look at the Polish student revolt of March 1968 suggests that what scholars have identified as the "global consciousness," or the tendency of leftist activists in the sixties to interpret local events "through a larger transnational lens,"[10] was particularly challenging for young rebels in the Eastern bloc due to their geopolitical position outside the capitalist world and within the Soviet imperial project. Indeed, the Polish student movement employed limited references to contemporary international political events, for example anticolonial movements, that permeated the rhetoric of French and German protestors. Yet transnationalism mattered in a different way. The attempt to project a proper leftist vision of transnational commitments was a critical element of legitimizing one's agenda, and it resulted in long-term consequences for Polish politics and society.

When young Polish rebels tried to take on both American imperialism in the Global South and Soviet domination at home, they moved beyond the Cold War divide. But sustaining such commitment proved unworkable in an environment in which the communist state held a virtual monopoly over the public representation of antiimperialism and the Polish national identity. At the same time, the reluctance of many leftist activists to acknowledge their own privileged position as Europeans vis-à-vis the postcolonial world further undercut their global impulses.

When Polish students did evoke anticolonial struggles, they most frequently referred to two events that affected leftist movements everywhere: the Cuban Revolution and the Vietnam War. Moreover, they tried to create a narrative that competed with the official reading of these events promoted by the communist state. However, the communist state could also use the transnational imagination to undermine students. As the Polish state's crackdown on student protestors demonstrated, the political establishment effectively deployed and weaponized the transnational imagination to stigmatize youth rebellion as foreign infiltration. For the communist regime, the international event that proved particularly useful in suppressing the leftist challenge from below turned out to be the Six-Day War in June 1967. This war between Israel (supported by the United States) and a coalition of Arab countries (backed by the Soviet Union) helped the Polish state revive antisemitic tropes and deploy them against the protestors. Amplified by the exigencies of the Global Cold War, the antisemitic campaign not only helped suppress the student movement but also solidified a racialized understanding of the "Polish nation" that had lasting political consequences.

Exploring the Polish case suggests that the Global South may offer a more meaningful point of reference for Eastern Europe than previously thought. When placed in global perspective, the student protests were not always defined by a bipolar clash between conservative governments and radical youth, as in Western Europe or the United States. Rather, 1968 often entailed a fierce competition over who represented true antiimperialism and the liberation of "the people." In the Eastern bloc and parts of the Global South, leftist students confronted regimes that already claimed to govern on behalf of a revolution and on the basis of antiimperialism. In newly decolonized states such as Tunisia or Senegal, anticolonial governments responded to student rebels by stigmatizing them as not genuine revolutionaries but rather "practitioners of neo-imperial mimicry, merely copycats of the decadent protest movement that was challenging their former French colonial oppressors at that time."[11] In Poland, questions of who represented true socialist values and who was an impostor in the service of one of the global superpowers were critical to the protests and their aftermath. Through their conflicts, both the protesting students and the state created discourses about proper and improper transnational solidarity that they projected onto themselves and onto the other side.

Competing Antiimperialisms

For at least two years before the March demonstrations, the Commandos and other informal student groups were active in the halls of Warsaw University, challenging the dominant political language of the communist establishment. Adam Michnik recalled the careful planning that went into the Commandos' tactics prior to 1968, such as studying the topics of political meetings organized by official university bodies. As the Commandos prepared for one such meeting on the Soviet Union's "Pacifist External Policy," they gave themselves specific assignments to discuss historical events that contradicted this "pacifist" policy. Talking points included the attack on Finland in 1939, the massacre of Polish officers by the NKVD in Katyń in 1940, and the Soviet invasion of Hungary in 1956.[12] The speaker at one such meeting was Walery Namiotkiewicz, who served as secretary to the head of the Party, Władysław Gomułka. Michnik recounted:

> We would come and sit all around the room. He [Namiotkiewicz] made a speech reminding us that the Soviet Union had been fighting for peace for fifty years. Then my friend Józek got up and asked, "Is this peace a room with a kitchen?"[13] And he answered, "This is a provocation. You are not qualified to discuss this subject." So I got up and yelled, "Yes we are! Yes we are! You have to listen!" He answered, "Contradiction does not scare the party!" And I continued, "That remains to be seen!" [and] an uproar ensued: Janek spoke about Hungary, Józek about Finland, Stefan about Yugoslavia, and, at the end, I quoted Fidel Castro . . . who said that the peaceful coexistence Moscow fought for consisted in keeping the bombs from falling on Moscow or Washington. But they could fall on Vietnam. "How do you feel, as members of the Communist Party, knowing that bombs fall on Vietnam every day? You don't do anything, and you don't want to do anything!" Walery Namiotkiewicz couldn't tell if I was pro or anti-Soviet. In his place, I wouldn't have known either![14]

In telling this story to Daniel Cohn-Bendit in 1987, Michnik intended not only to make an impression on the icon of the French May but also to underscore that the Commandos, like their Western counterparts, framed their arguments in a global setting. By placing Poles and Hungarians next to Cubans and Vietnamese as victims of the same Cold War confrontation between the two superpowers, the Commandos undermined the state's sole power to define world affairs. Yet their arguments were primarily rhetorical. Young Polish leftists evoked the Third World to draw attention to themselves as victims of Soviet imperial conquest rather than to forge meaningful connections with anticolonial movements or to understand those movements on their own terms. At the same time, references to revolutionary heroes like Castro enhanced the Commandos' performance of masculine defiance.

As the Commandos' actions demonstrated, leftist students competed with their own state to speak about Poland's place on the global stage. Young people assimilated the images of the West and the Global South that were available to them through the popular press in a variety of ways, but they also developed their own modes of connecting to the outside world.

Taking advantage of the expanded travel opportunities after the Thaw, some Commandos went to Western Europe before they started their activities at home. At the age of seventeen, Irena Grudzińska toured Austria, France, and Italy with her father, who was on a business trip. "In Paris, I had my first taste of Coca-Cola," she recalled in an interview in 2013. The drink was served in a small, elegant, frosted glass with ice: "It was like a taste of freedom to me." Grudzińska also bought her first pair of blue jeans at the Galeries Lafayette.[15]

Other Commandos went to the West without parental supervision and with an explicit political agenda in mind. Michnik left Poland for three months shortly after graduating from high school in 1964: "I met a lot of people, read a lot of books, talked with Polish émigrés, Italian Communists, French Trotskyists. I returned with the firm intention of doing something."[16] Two years later, Barbara Toruńczyk relied on an international network of the Old and New Left to travel to Germany and France. Her journey was facilitated, in part, by her father's comrades-in-arms, veterans of the International Brigades of the Spanish Civil War who lived in the West. Toruńczyk first went to Munich to meet with the Polish section of Radio Free Europe.[17] She then traveled to Paris, where she visited with Jerzy Giedroyc, the émigré intellectual and editor of the Polish-language literary periodical *Kultura*, and with activists in the interwar Polish Socialist Party. While in France, she got in touch with Amnesty International as well as French students and leftist organizations.[18]

Such personal experiences, in addition to media images and an occasional interaction with foreign students, inspired the Polish students' search for an alternative Marxism. They also sought to insert their voices into the global leftist debates by drawing attention to the distinct circumstances of Soviet-dominated Eastern Europe.

An opportunity to formulate an alternative vision of leftist politics emerged in 1964, when Jacek Kuroń and Karol Modzelewski penned the *Open Letter to the Party*.[19] At the time, thirty-year-old Kuroń worked for the national headquarters of the Polish Scout Association. Three years Kuroń's junior, Modzelewski was already known for organizing the short-lived Polish Discussion Club in 1962. Both had been active in the upheaval of the Thaw.

The *Letter*, which quickly made its way to the Commandos and other young rebels, repudiated the Soviet and Eastern European regimes as oligarchies that ruled over disempowered populations with the help of expansive and oppressive bureaucracies. Although the nearly 100 pages of the *Letter* primarily focused on Eastern European political and economic problems, the authors recognized the need to rethink international leftist solidarity in light of decolonization. In the chapter "The International Problems of the Revolution," they put forward a vision of a global workers' uprising driven by the entangled forces of Eastern European rebellions against Stalinism and anticolonial revolutions in the Third World. The authors identified the Cold War division as a product of cooperation between Western "imperialists" and Soviets that was directed toward suppressing genuine democratic movements from below. They believed that the powerful rebellions in the East-South "periphery" produced conditions ripe for another socialist revolution and the ascendance of a genuine workers' democracy. They wrote:

> The liberation of a large group of countries from capitalist domination was—and still is—a factor favoring revolutionary struggle against imperialism. . . . However, the colonial revolution is getting out of control. More than once, revolutions in the colonial world have been successfully organized and led by groups outside the official Communist parties—as in Cuba and Algeria, for example. The international bureaucracy's ability to control the world communist movement is also undergoing a crisis, which must inevitably worsen. It is not by chance that the emergence of this crisis coincided with the beginning of the crisis in our camp and with the first anti-bureaucratic revolutions in Poland and Hungary.[20]

Scholars have debated whether the *Letter* truly called for a new socialist revolution or was a rhetorical device intended to challenge the ideological monopoly of the ruling communists.[21] Regardless of its purpose, one of the document's most significant elements was its challenge to the state's vision of internationalism. In the *Letter*, Polish leftists imagined alternative connections to the Global South in direct defiance of the anticolonial model advanced by the state that was still hierarchical and in which Poland assumed the role of the "modernizer." Kuroń and Modzelewski would have none of that. Instead, they called for Eastern European and anticolonial rebels to launch a common front against the Cold War order.

On March 18, 1965, Kuroń and Modzelewski submitted a typed copy of the *Letter* to the Party chapter at Warsaw University and another to the ZMS. They distributed the remaining copies among friends who later arranged to

spoke about democracy, redistribution of national wealth in different countries, about social justice and income inequality in socialist countries. No one had ever spoken to me on the same level about these topics!"[83]

Małgosia was not alone in finding empowerment through leftist student circles as a young educated woman. Many former female students recall "feeling equal" while participating in nonconformist student circles even if they often complied with the traditional "division of roles," such as letting their boyfriends speak up on political issues more often than they did.[84] Still, groups like the Commandos provided new opportunities for young women to be recognized as participants in a meaningful intellectual community, something they could not always find in their formal university studies. In blending politics with elements of consumer culture, Polish students demonstrated that the two were not necessarily mutually exclusive. They demonstrated that "the Children of Marx and Coca-Cola"—to use Jean-Luc Godard's description of French youth at the time—had a distinct presence behind the Iron Curtain.

* * *

At the threshold of the sixties, students in Poland were a community in flux. Young women and men who entered institutions of higher education from a variety of social backgrounds found themselves confronting and negotiating diverse experiences in academic centers and varied material statuses. But as students—the young elite in the making—they also searched for their own voice in a world that was preoccupied with young people as the embodiment of modernity and the future.

The student clubs that emerged to facilitate young people's aspirations for leisure served as tangible markers of a distinct student status, where participants could experiment with music, art, and sociability. In a way, they became symbolic of students' "freedom," which was more extensive and more transnational than the opportunities granted to other groups. Although offering different types of activities, both student clubs such as Hybrydy and political groups such as the Commandos shared common characteristics. Both rejected what they saw as state-supported "mass entertainment" and sought more ambitious and independent expressions of student subjectivity, whether through art or alternative Marxism.

The privileged status of students, however, left them in a vulnerable position, especially at times of political crises. Periodic media attacks on students as consumer-oriented and hedonistic revealed distrust on the part of the to bourgeois morality made little sense in a nonbourgeois society where gender equality and a tacit acceptance of premarital sex were already part of dominant norms. Former student Maciej Kozłowski articulated this position in an interview in 2013: "despite the Church and all that, relaxed sexual mores were rather natural within the social circles with which I interacted, so why would one want to make a revolution about that?"[79] Consequently, the Commandos and others rarely theorized about "sexual liberation" even if they practiced it.

The link between politics and sexuality became even more pronounced in the West when a powerful feminist movement emerged from the New Left to challenge the male-dominated concepts of sexual liberation. According to historian Dagmar Herzog, young leftist women "had initially participated eagerly in the new opportunities for promiscuity and experimentation made available by the pill and the sexual revolution." Soon, however, they grew disillusioned with their male partners' disdain for women's intellectual abilities and their unwillingness to share the burden of childcare and household labor. Their feminist politics "became enmeshed with and articulated through conflict over sexual relations."[80]

Although a public feminist critique did not emerge from Polish leftist circles at the time, the Commandos and other groups did not avoid tensions over gender and class. Personal testimonies speak to the importance of a heterosexual masculine performance as an element of the Commandos' identity. In the 1980s, Michnik admitted that he liked "being seen with Karol [Modzelewski]." Michnik continued: "students appreciated him, women admired him. Unconsciously, I wanted some of it to rub off on me."[81] As Michnik suggests, the Commando masculine performance was embedded in claims to intellectual superiority, defiance of authority, bonding with other like-minded men, and erotic appeal to women.

A mixture of gender and class tensions can be found in a personal testimony from former female student Malgosia Tal, who felt awkward when she started attending Commandos' parties. "They were more well off and dressed better," she remembered in 2008. "Many traveled internationally (they saw the Adriatic Sea, Moscow, and Paris). They had fancy apartments . . . and the array of drinks I never heard of; Vermouth was one. The girls knew how to flirt, how to wear a sweater to accent their figure. I did not have such sweaters. And we lived modestly."[82] Małgosia eventually found her participation in their gatherings an eye-opening intellectual experience. "At the club I discovered completely new ways of thinking," she remembered. "Because they

socialist state toward the elite in the making. The Commandos, in particular, took the students' autonomy to new levels by creating their own social
and consumer styles, and combining them with the explicitly political language that challenged the ruling Party monopoly on defining Marxism. By
the mid-1960s, the Commandos and their supporters had emerged as formidable competitors of the state in defining not only socialism at home but also
transnational engagements in an era of global upheaval from below.

5

Tensions of Transnationalism

Youth Rebellion, State Backlash, and 1968

The morning of Friday, March 8, 1968, began quietly in Warsaw. Spring was in the air even as patches of snow were still melting on the ground. March 8 was International Women's Day, an important holiday in the Eastern bloc. Some women were more nicely dressed than usual, expecting customary celebrations and small gifts at their workplaces. But this was shaping up as anything but a typical Women's Day. At the main campus of Warsaw University, on Krakowskie Przedmieście, a peaceful student rally was planned. These young people were to gather to demand civic freedoms and to protest the expulsion of two students from the university. The rally started at noon, and within a few minutes seven tour buses had arrived at the campus entrance. As the passengers disembarked, it became clear that these were not tourists arriving to explore historical sights of the Polish capital but stern-looking middle-aged men in civilian clothes armed with clubs. Party officials had recruited them from factories and offices to help suppress the student demonstration. At a quarter past noon the men began their attack.

The students' demonstration in Warsaw initiated a chain of events known in Polish historical narratives as "March 1968" or simply "March" (Marzec). The violent state action against unarmed students generated massive protests by young people all over Poland that lasted for nearly two months.[1] In response, the communist regime not only dispatched police and armed civilians to quell street demonstrations but also launched a powerful antisemitic campaign. Party officials and the media denounced protestors as Zionists, imperialists, and Marxist revisionists who wanted to overthrow socialism and the Polish state. In the wake of this campaign, approximately 15,000 Polish Jews emigrated.[2]

Encompassing both youth unrest and the state's antisemitic response, "March" significantly transformed the Polish political and intellectual landscape. The willful embrace of racist, right-wing nationalism by ruling communists shocked the leftist intelligentsia, many of whom abandoned

Imagining the World from Behind the Iron Curtain. Małgorzata Fidelis, Oxford University Press. © Oxford University Press 2022. DOI: 10.1093/oso/9780197643402.003.0006

their faith in the possibility of reforming state socialism and turned to anti-communist political opposition. The crushing of Prague Spring by Warsaw Pact forces in August 1968 only solidified their position.

Unsurprisingly, conventional Polish narratives of 1968 are deeply entrenched in the domestic context. After 1968, as Adam Michnik, a central figure of the student movement, put it, "we were no longer Marxist dissidents but members of the antitotalitarian opposition."[3] According to such dominant interpretations, student demonstrations belonged to the sequence of "Polish months": the periodic revolts of Polish society against the communist regime that started in June 1956 with the workers' uprising in Poznań against the Stalinist regime and culminated in the emergence of the Solidarity movement in August 1980.[4]

Rather than replicating this standard nation-centered narrative, this chapter repositions 1968 in Poland as an integral part of global 1968. It shows Polish students not simply as protestors against a "totalitarian" regime but as active participants in contemporary global leftist politics. Those politics involved turning away from the state as a potential vehicle for a socialist transformation, reformulating ideas of justice and solidarity, and engaging in leftist conversations across borders. The state's violence against the protestors only confirmed the threat of the leftist challenge from below by exposing the deep insecurity of the ostensibly socialist regime with regard to its own ideological commitments and claims to legitimacy.

Historians of the "European 1968" explain the ubiquity of the protests in such different contexts as Western European democracies, Eastern European communisms, and southern European military dictatorships by highlighting "common causes" and inspirations, including shared desires for "participatory democracy," generational conflict, and antifascist legacies of the interwar era.[5] In much of this literature, Eastern Europe stands out as the least theoretically integrated into scholars' understanding of 1968. Existing work on student protests in places such as Prague, Warsaw, or Belgrade usually focuses on domestic political narratives, while the comparative angle tends to highlight differences, similarities, and points of contestation between Eastern European and Western European student movements.[6] The recurring theme has been that Western activists had little understanding of Eastern European concerns. The very fact, however, that tensions existed and were often passionately articulated testifies to the Eastern European students' intense identification with the transnational community of rebels.[7] The framework of the global sixties helps to better explain these transnational dynamics and to highlight the influence of the postcolonial world on shaping them.

The Polish protestors sought to insert themselves into global conversations prior to and during 1968 by linking their activism to historical and contemporary leftist movements. In March 1968, young rebels employed global protest strategies such as rallies, sit-ins, singing and writing songs, and satire, while also evoking the ideas of solidarity and authenticity that were inherent in student demonstrations worldwide. This chapter looks at how contemporary actors in a specific locality, Poland, understood transnational connections.[8] Seen through their eyes, transnationalism in Eastern Europe has quite a different meaning from the more familiar tale of global leftist solidarity developed across the First World and the Third World.[9]

A closer look at the Polish student revolt of March 1968 suggests that what scholars have identified as the "global consciousness," or the tendency of leftist activists in the sixties to interpret local events "through a larger transnational lens,"[10] was particularly challenging for young rebels in the Eastern bloc due to their geopolitical position outside the capitalist world and within the Soviet imperial project. Indeed, the Polish student movement employed limited references to contemporary international political events, for example anticolonial movements, that permeated the rhetoric of French and German protestors. Yet transnationalism mattered in a different way. The attempt to project a proper leftist vision of transnational commitments was a critical element of legitimizing one's agenda, and it resulted in long-term consequences for Polish politics and society.

When young Polish rebels tried to take on both American imperialism in the Global South and Soviet domination at home, they moved beyond the Cold War divide. But sustaining such commitment proved unworkable in an environment in which the communist state held a virtual monopoly over the public representation of antiimperialism and the Polish national identity. At the same time, the reluctance of many leftist activists to acknowledge their own privileged position as Europeans vis-à-vis the postcolonial world further undercut their global impulses.

When Polish students did evoke anticolonial struggles, they most frequently referred to two events that affected leftist movements everywhere: the Cuban Revolution and the Vietnam War. Moreover, they tried to create a narrative that competed with the official reading of these events promoted by the communist state. However, the communist state could also use the transnational imagination to undermine students. As the Polish state's crackdown on student protestors demonstrated, the political establishment effectively deployed and weaponized the transnational imagination to stigmatize youth rebellion as foreign infiltration. For the communist regime, the international event that proved particularly useful in suppressing the leftist challenge from below turned out to be the Six-Day War in June 1967. This war between Israel (supported by the United States) and a coalition of Arab countries (backed by the Soviet Union) helped the Polish state revive antisemitic tropes and deploy them against the protestors. Amplified by the exigencies of the Global Cold War, the antisemitic campaign not only helped suppress the student movement but also solidified a racialized understanding of the "Polish nation" that had lasting political consequences.

Exploring the Polish case suggests that the Global South may offer a more meaningful point of reference for Eastern Europe than previously thought. When placed in global perspective, the student protests were not always defined by a bipolar clash between conservative governments and radical youth, as in Western Europe or the United States. Rather, 1968 often entailed a fierce competition over who represented true antiimperialism and the liberation of "the people." In the Eastern bloc and parts of the Global South, leftist students confronted regimes that already claimed to govern on behalf of a revolution and on the basis of antiimperialism. In newly decolonized states such as Tunisia or Senegal, anticolonial governments responded to student rebels by stigmatizing them as not genuine revolutionaries but rather "practitioners of neo-imperial mimicry, merely copycats of the decadent protest movement that was challenging their former French colonial oppressors at that time."[11] In Poland, questions of who represented true socialist values and who was an impostor in the service of one of the global superpowers were critical to the protests and their aftermath. Through their conflicts, both the protesting students and the state created discourses about proper and improper transnational solidarity that they projected onto themselves and onto the other side.

Competing Antiimperialisms

For at least two years before the March demonstrations, the Commandos and other informal student groups were active in the halls of Warsaw University, challenging the dominant political language of the communist establishment. Adam Michnik recalled the careful planning that went into the Commandos' tactics prior to 1968, such as studying the topics of political meetings organized by official university bodies. As the Commandos prepared for one such meeting on the Soviet Union's "Pacifist External Policy," they gave themselves specific assignments to discuss historical events that contradicted this "pacifist" policy. Talking points included the attack on Finland in 1939, the massacre of Polish officers by the NKVD in Katyń in 1940, and the Soviet invasion of Hungary in 1956.[12] The speaker at one such meeting was Walery Namiotkiewicz, who served as secretary to the head of the Party, Władysław Gomułka. Michnik recounted:

> We would come and sit all around the room. He [Namiotkiewicz] made a speech reminding us that the Soviet Union had been fighting for peace for fifty years. Then my friend Józek got up and asked, "Is this peace a room with a kitchen?"[13] And he answered, "This is a provocation. You are not qualified to discuss this subject." So I got up and yelled, "Yes we are! Yes we are! You have to listen!" He answered, "Contradiction does not scare the party!" And I continued, "That remains to be seen!" [and] an uproar ensued: Janek spoke about Hungary, Józek about Finland, Stefan about Yugoslavia, and, at the end, I quoted Fidel Castro . . . who said that the peaceful coexistence Moscow fought for consisted in keeping the bombs from falling on Moscow or Washington. But they could fall on Vietnam. "How do you feel, as members of the Communist Party, knowing that bombs fall on Vietnam every day? You don't do anything, and you don't want to do anything!" Walery Namiotkiewicz couldn't tell if I was pro or anti-Soviet. In his place, I wouldn't have known either![14]

In telling this story to Daniel Cohn-Bendit in 1987, Michnik intended not only to make an impression on the icon of the French May but also to underscore that the Commandos, like their Western counterparts, framed their arguments in a global setting. By placing Poles and Hungarians next to Cubans and Vietnamese as victims of the same Cold War confrontation between the two superpowers, the Commandos undermined the state's sole power to define world affairs. Yet their arguments were primarily rhetorical. Young Polish leftists evoked the Third World to draw attention to themselves as victims of Soviet imperial conquest rather than to forge meaningful connections with anticolonial movements or to understand those movements on their own terms. At the same time, references to revolutionary heroes like Castro enhanced the Commandos' performance of masculine defiance.

As the Commandos' actions demonstrated, leftist students competed with their own state to speak about Poland's place on the global stage. Young people assimilated the images of the West and the Global South that were available to them through the popular press in a variety of ways, but they also developed their own modes of connecting to the outside world.

Taking advantage of the expanded travel opportunities after the Thaw, some Commandos went to Western Europe before they started their activities at home. At the age of seventeen, Irena Grudzińska toured Austria, France, and Italy with her father, who was on a business trip. "In Paris, I had my first taste of Coca-Cola," she recalled in an interview in 2013. The drink was served in a small, elegant, frosted glass with ice: "It was like a taste of freedom to me." Grudzińska also bought her first pair of blue jeans at the Galeries Lafayette.[15]

Other Commandos went to the West without parental supervision and with an explicit political agenda in mind. Michnik left Poland for three months shortly after graduating from high school in 1964: "I met a lot of people, read a lot of books, talked with Polish émigrés, Italian Communists, French Trotskyists. I returned with the firm intention of doing something."[16] Two years later, Barbara Toruńczyk relied on an international network of the Old and New Left to travel to Germany and France. Her journey was facilitated, in part, by her father's comrades-in-arms, veterans of the International Brigades of the Spanish Civil War who lived in the West. Toruńczyk first went to Munich to meet with the Polish section of Radio Free Europe.[17] She then traveled to Paris, where she visited with Jerzy Giedroyc, the émigré intellectual and editor of the Polish-language literary periodical *Kultura*, and with activists in the interwar Polish Socialist Party. While in France, she got in touch with Amnesty International as well as French students and leftist organizations.[18]

Such personal experiences, in addition to media images and an occasional interaction with foreign students, inspired the Polish students' search for an alternative Marxism. They also sought to insert their voices into the global leftist debates by drawing attention to the distinct circumstances of Soviet-dominated Eastern Europe.

An opportunity to formulate an alternative vision of leftist politics emerged in 1964, when Jacek Kuroń and Karol Modzelewski penned the *Open Letter to the Party*.[19] At the time, thirty-year-old Kuroń worked for the national headquarters of the Polish Scout Association. Three years Kuroń's junior, Modzelewski was already known for organizing the short-lived Polish Discussion Club in 1962. Both had been active in the upheaval of the Thaw.

The *Letter*, which quickly made its way to the Commandos and other young rebels, repudiated the Soviet and Eastern European regimes as oligarchies that ruled over disempowered populations with the help of expansive and oppressive bureaucracies. Although the nearly 100 pages of the *Letter* primarily focused on Eastern European political and economic problems, the authors recognized the need to rethink international leftist solidarity in light of decolonization. In the chapter "The International Problems of the Revolution," they put forward a vision of a global workers' uprising driven by the entangled forces of Eastern European rebellions against Stalinism and anticolonial revolutions in the Third World. The authors identified the Cold War division as a product of cooperation between Western "imperialists" and Soviets that was directed toward suppressing genuine democratic movements from below. They believed that the powerful rebellions in the East-South "periphery" produced conditions ripe for another socialist revolution and the ascendance of a genuine workers' democracy. They wrote:

> The liberation of a large group of countries from capitalist domination was—and still is—a factor favoring revolutionary struggle against imperialism. . . . However, the colonial revolution is getting out of control. More than once, revolutions in the colonial world have been successfully organized and led by groups outside the official Communist parties—as in Cuba and Algeria, for example. The international bureaucracy's ability to control the world communist movement is also undergoing a crisis, which must inevitably worsen. It is not by chance that the emergence of this crisis coincided with the beginning of the crisis in our camp and with the first antibureaucratic revolutions in Poland and Hungary.[20]

Scholars have debated whether the *Letter* truly called for a new socialist revolution or was a rhetorical device intended to challenge the ideological monopoly of the ruling communists.[21] Regardless of its purpose, one of the document's most significant elements was its challenge to the state's vision of internationalism. In the *Letter*, Polish leftists imagined alternative connections to the Global South in direct defiance of the anticolonial model advanced by the state that was still hierarchical and in which Poland assumed the role of the "modernizer." Kuroń and Modzelewski would have none of that. Instead, they called for Eastern European and anticolonial rebels to launch a common front against the Cold War order.

On March 18, 1965, Kuroń and Modzelewski submitted a typed copy of the *Letter* to the Party chapter at Warsaw University and another to the ZMS. They distributed the remaining copies among friends who later arranged to smuggle them out of the country. The next day, both authors were arrested. The trial of Kuroń and Modzelewski for disseminating the *Letter* was one of the most internationally publicized political trials in post-Stalinist Poland. In 1966, Kuroń was sentenced to three years in prison and Modzelewski to three and half.[22]

Meanwhile, the *Letter* became part of the international circulation of New Left ideas. The Paris-based *Kultura* printed the original Polish version in August 1966. Shortly thereafter, RFE broadcast the text to Polish audiences. The same year, French Trotskyites published the document in French. The Italian translation came out in 1967, followed by the Czech and English versions in 1968, and the German, Swedish, and Japanese translations a year later.[23] Polish historian Andrzej Paczkowski, who found himself in Paris on a research scholarship during the French May, recalled seeing pages from the *Letter* displayed on walls in student dormitories.[24]

The ideas of alternative transnational solidarities soon faced a new challenge. By the second half of the 1960s, the Vietnam War had become the most potent symbol of Cold War imperialism. Crossing national and continental borders, the antiwar movement mobilized an unprecedented global solidarity of young people. Eastern European regimes also made the Vietnam War a cornerstone of their antiimperialist and anticapitalist stance. Publicizing American atrocities became an important component of the daily political propaganda. Much like the Cuban Revolution, the spectacle of the Vietnam War held the potential to reinvigorate the revolutionary spirit at home in Poland by "providing Eastern European political elites with powerful and heroic images of peasant and worker revolutionaries defending their homeland against the greatest capitalist power."[25] Indeed, by publicly placing themselves on the side of antiwar protestors, communist states left little room for other domestic leftists to enter the conversation. Nevertheless, some young people attempted to do just that.

In 1965, another group of rebellious students at Warsaw University confronted the establishment on the issue of Vietnam. Henryk Szlajfer, a student of political economy, formed a small "Vietnam group" also known as "the Vietnamese" (Wietnamczycy). In contrast to the Commandos, who typically deployed international rhetoric to express the Polish predicament, Szlajfer and his circle directly addressed global affairs.

The "Vietnamese" organized several small demonstrations in front of the American embassy and wrote petitions to the Polish government asking it to provide aid to North Vietnam. "Our thinking was leftist," Szlajfer recalled in

2007, "but our critique grew from the fact that we felt that the Communist regimes in Eastern Europe were playing with Vietnam. That help was provided, but it was limited. The support was ambiguous. So it was rather a rebellion against this kind of hypocrisy."[26] Szlajfer also reportedly petitioned the Polish Ministry of Internal Affairs in 1965 to allow him to go to Vietnam. Two years later, he allegedly contacted the Cuban embassy to apply for a work visa to Cuba and asked a functionary in the Polish security apparatus for assistance in the matter. In neither case did the leader of the "Vietnamese" receive help from the Polish government. Rather, this unexpected solidarity with the Third World expressed by a student outside the official state structures generated anxiety and suspicion within Party-state circles.[27]

Szlajfer and his group nevertheless continued to call on the government to provide more help to North Vietnam. To this end, they declared May 1, 1966, the Day of Vietnam and attempted to include their agenda in the official May Day Parade.[28] More than 2,000 students and faculty from Warsaw University marched in the parade, many carrying the customary banners with official slogans supporting socialism. Some students, however, displayed their own banners offering an alternative conceptualization of domestic and global affairs to the one advanced by the state. In addition to domestic political demands such as "Transparency in public life is the foundation of socialist democracy" and "We want socialist democracy," participants explicitly connected Poland to historical and contemporary revolutionary movements. These included the sign "One Thousand Flowers for One Thousand Years of the Polish State." Another displayed the following list: "Spain 1939, Poland 1939, Vietnam 1962 . . . ?," which equated the fascist conquest of Europe in the 1930s with the United States' involvement in Vietnam. After the demonstration, a group of almost 200 students marched to the American embassy, where they shouted anti-American slogans such as "Hands off Vietnam" and "Americans go home." They also collected money to help Vietnam.[29]

Not every participant, however, understood Vietnam Day in the same way, and some felt ambivalent about the demonstration. Most of the participating Commandos dispersed before the group reached the American embassy. Teresa Bogucka and Wiktor Górecki stayed with the demonstration, but as Górecki recalled in 2009: "I felt . . . an impropriety and inauthenticity of this demonstration. It was as if we wanted to beat the regime at their own game of anti-American slogans."[30]

Nevertheless, the Commandos soon staged their own Vietnam-related event. On October 27, 1967, students from Warsaw University distributed

a leaflet calling for an International Week of Solidarity with Vietnam. The leaflet opened with a list of cities in which young people had demonstrated against the Vietnam War. "Washington—140,000; Paris—100,000; West Berlin—40,000; Warsaw—?" The first sentence repudiated imperialist politics: "'This is not the first time that powerful empires have enforced the rule that intervention with tanks is required to guarantee social order." The mention of "tanks," which had been used by the Soviet Union to crush the uprisings in East Germany and Hungary in 1953 and 1956, respectively, accused the Soviets of similar behavior. The leaflet then proceeded to name the injustices inflicted on small nations by great powers, grouping together the 1938 Munich Agreement, the Hungarian Revolution of 1956, and the recent execution of Che Guevara, all of which were understood as outcomes of the same chain of developments in which reactionary forces suppressed the liberating impulses of the people. While calling for transnational solidarity with the European and American Left "that is fighting for peace and freedom in Vietnam," the leaflet also stressed the unity of social and national struggle: "by fighting for a sovereign and socialist Vietnam we are fighting for a sovereign and socialist Poland."[31]

Equating social and national liberation was a centerpiece of Gomułka's regime, which aimed at nationalizing Polish communism. The term "sovereignty," however, was not part of the official vocabulary, as it might have invited questions about Soviet control over Poland. By making the explicit link between anticolonial struggle and Polish sovereignty, therefore, the Commandos disrupted the state's hegemonic discourse. Although the leaflet offered no rethinking of the postcolonial world beyond affinity based on a shared commitment to antiimperialism, it still envisioned Polish struggles as part of the global movement against Cold War superpower domination.

1968

It was the suppression of a cultural event that sparked the student demonstration in Warsaw in March 1968: a Party-state ban on further performances at the National Theater in Warsaw of the play The Forefathers' Eve (Dziady), written by the national Romantic poet Adam Mickiewicz in the first half of the nineteenth century. The play evoked plenty of parallels through its depiction of young Polish student-revolutionaries fighting for national independence against the Russian empire following the partitions of Poland

in the late eighteenth century. Although this production of *The Forefathers' Eve* was part of a series of artistic events organized to celebrate the fiftieth anniversary of the Russian Revolution, Party-state leaders believed that the play was generating anti-Soviet sentiments. During performances, the audience were reportedly applauding statements made by the actors that repudiated the Russian empire. In the popular mind, as communist leaders well knew, "Russian" and "Soviet" were not clearly differentiated, and Poland's fate after 1945 was often interpreted as a continuation of age-old Russian expansionism.

The last performance of the play, attended by 3,000 people (there were only 900 seats in the theater), was scheduled for January 30, 1968. Varsovians flocked to the theater to protest the state's ban. A peaceful demonstration in support of cultural freedom followed. Afterward, Michnik and Szlajfer, who had participated in the protest, met with the French correspondent of *Le Monde*, Bernard Marguerite, to provide him with their account of events; RFE then broadcast news about the demonstration back to Poland. As a result, Michnik and Szlajfer were expelled from Warsaw University. The Commandos decided to schedule a rally for March 8 to protest what they saw as the violation of the constitution of the People's Republic of Poland by its very government. Soon, leaflets announcing the gathering "in defense of democratic freedoms" appeared around the university.[32]

The day of the rally was just like any other. Students attended lectures and seminars; some took tests and exams. Shortly before noon, as former student Anna Dodziuk recalled, "groups of people came from all sides of the street. Many girls held flowers in their hands, the ones they got for Women's Day." For Anna this was "my first experience of social unrest," and she felt exhilarated to see "so many people who thought in a similar way and were ready to take a risk."[33] Just as the clock struck noon, a female student named Irena Lasota read this resolution: "we, the students of the Warsaw University, gathered at a rally on this day of March 8, 1968, announce: we will not allow anyone to trample the Constitution of the People's Poland. Repressions against students who protested against the shameful decision to ban the performance of *The Forefathers' Eve* at the National Theater constitute an open violation of article 71 of the Constitution.[34] We will not allow anyone to take away from us the right to defend the democratic and independence-oriented traditions of the Polish Nation."[35] The resolution also demanded the immediate reinstatement of Michnik and Szlajfer.

Fig. 5.1 Student rally, Warsaw University, March 8, 1968. Photo taken from a window of the Academy of Fine Artis, opposite the university. Photo by Krzysztof Burnatowicz. Burnatowicz_039. Courtesy of KARTA Center Foundation.

The gathered students applauded the resolution and then sang the national anthem. Since singing the national anthem was usually done only at official state events, this act indicated that the students were appropriating national symbols for their own use. They were making it clear to the Party-state that they were acting not just as students but as representatives of the nation and defenders of citizens' rights. It was at that moment that, as one student recalled, "suddenly the main gate . . . opened wide. Slowly, the buses pulled in, each with a sign that read 'sight-seeing tour.' "[36] Groups of men in civilian clothes, some of them wearing red armbands, disembarked. The "tourists" hid clubs under their sleeves. In official messages, the Party-state would later call these men "workers' activists."[37]

After about an hour of relentless beatings, the attackers pushed demonstrators to the end of the main plaza where the university administration was located. When the vice-provost appeared on the balcony and called on the students to disband, the protestors gradually dispersed, while the attackers returned to their buses. The worst, however, was yet to come. The moment these "workers' activists" (the men who had beaten the students) left the campus, a battalion of riot police entered the main plaza, and the "tour" buses turned around. The students found themselves once again under attack, this time by both the professionally trained riot police and the "workers' activists" with their clubs.

Although both male and female students became targets of physical violence, eyewitnesses' accounts often noted the attackers' inclination to beat females. Teresa Bochwic recalled: " 'workers' grabbed me by my hands and tried to twist my arms. My friends were holding me by my jacket and my neck and tried to pull me away."[38] Doctoral student Krystyna Starczewska was hit in the face, she was thrown to the ground, and her feet were stomped on. The attackers taunted her: "where are you going, you Żydówa?"[39]

The targeting of female students revealed a strong antifeminist current in the conservative reactions to youth unrest, common in other parts of the world as well.[40] Early press reports on the March 8 rally singled out females for joining the demonstrations, only to cheer on the young men. "Dżery [Jerry], pass me a Coca-Cola," one female student reportedly demanded of a male protestor, "because our nasty stuff is not worth a thing."[41] Female students were denigrated not only as decadent and consumerist-oriented but also as contemptuous of all things Polish, including domestically produced drinks.

Students, too, tried to instrumentalize gendered images to their advantage, but in a different way. By selecting March 8 as the day of the rally, the Commandos had hoped to avoid state brutality.[42] After all, the communist regime ostentatiously celebrated International Women's Day, issuing public calls for courtesy toward women and the appreciation of their roles in society. Indeed, several days prior to March 8, on learning about the plans for the rally, security functionaries had apprehended most of the male Commandos but not their female colleagues.

Shortly after the rally was suppressed, one of the most effective mobilizers of nationwide solidarity of young people with the Warsaw students proved to be a spreading rumor that a female student had been killed during the demonstrations.[43] Images of gendered violence were intended to elicit an emotional response. But in spreading the rumor (which many no doubt genuinely believed), students and their allies, to stir up political action, relied on the powerful sentimental stereotypes of women as weak and men as their chivalric protectors. Despite the prominence of female students in the protests, the storytelling by both the state and the students tended to deny these women political subjectivity.

The state-led attack on the peaceful gathering at Warsaw University generated an unexpected wave of protests. The next day, students from the School of Fine Arts and the Warsaw Polytechnic marched through the streets in support of their fellow students. Street demonstrations and sit-ins continued in Warsaw through the following week. Demonstrators were often joined by passersby and by other youths who broke windows, demolished stores and other enterprises, and capsized several militia vehicles.[44]

News of the Warsaw student demonstrations quickly spread to other parts of Poland through personal accounts, leaflets, and an RFE broadcast; the Polish media at first did not disseminate much information. The next day in Kraków, a group of 400–500 students gathered in the old town and marched to the main campus of Jagiellonian University. They put forward a resolution in which they called for *The Forefathers' Eve* to be returned to the stage and for Michnik and Szlajfer to be reinstated. In Kraków, students also condemned the state's suppression of the student demonstration in Warsaw, called for censorship to be lifted, and demanded the expansion of university autonomy.[45] A few days later in Wrocław, as many as 900 students marched from the city center to Wrocław University's historic Aula Leopoldina (the main university auditorium decorated in an Italian Baroque style), where they condemned the beatings of the Warsaw students and demanded freedom of the press.[46] Protests in other cities, including Poznań, Gdańsk, Łódź, Katowice, and Opole, followed a similar trajectory, starting with rallies and the writing of resolutions. When university administrators and political officials ignored the students' demands, they took to the streets. In all of these places, the state dispatched units of riot police, voluntary militias, and sometimes regular workers to beat demonstrators.

False reporting on the demonstrations, in which the press smeared students as "hooligans" and "Zionists," simultaneously contributed to student outrage and became a topic of biting satire. Warsaw student Natan Tenenbaum parodied the official coverage of the protests in a poem whose opening lines ridiculed the state's portrayal of students as agents of foreign governments: "Renowned were the times, renowned were the capers / how it all went down you will read in the papers. / For Wyszyński and Kuroń it did not take long / to sell Poland to the Jews for cash from Mao Zedong."[47] Calls for truth telling and the accusation that "the press is lying" soon came to the forefront of the nationwide protests.

Rallies, marches, and sit-ins became important communal experiences that strengthened student solidarity. Participants gave passionate speeches and sang songs, often switching between the Polish national anthem and "The Internationale." Lena, who participated in a sit-in at Wrocław University, recalled that the opening phrase of "The Internationale"—"arise ye workers from the slumbers / Arise ye prisoners of war"—had a particular meaning. "It sounds funny today," she reflected in an interview in 2008, "but we did sing it with conviction! We had a very sincere sense that it was we who were the oppressed and the imprisoned."[48]

As the struggle spread beyond Warsaw, the demonstrations became more playful and informed by elements of global youth culture. Guitar-playing, singing, and bridge were indispensable elements of rallies and sit-ins; so, too, were meeting new people and collaborating on exciting projects together. At a Wrocław Polytechnic sit-in, Tomasz Tłuczkiewicz, a student and a jazz fan, started talking with two young musicians, Romuald Piasecki and Roman Runowicz, and they decided to form a band. Soon afterward, Romuald and Roman would be one of the first bands in Poland to play psychedelic rock music and stage live shows using colored lights and smoke. As Tomasz recalled, he noticed Romuald and Roman during the sit-in because the three of them were the only ones in the crowd with long hair. Men wearing long hair was not common in Poland at the time and indicated an identification with a relatively new countercultural movement: the hippies.[49]

Wrocław was also the site of the last street demonstration during the spring of 1968, when a group of Wrocław Polytechnic students joined the official May Day parade. Carrying signs with slogans such as "Free the arrested students!" and "The press is lying," they mixed with the official parade, marching in front of Wrocław dignitaries and a visiting Soviet general. The students circulated the banners among themselves to make it difficult for the militia to see who was carrying them. The crowd found it amusing when the Soviet general, who could not read or understand the signs, enthusiastically clapped at the marching students.[50]

Secondary school students and young workers joined the street demonstrations and staged protests of their own. The upheaval also extended beyond large cities into small towns and even some villages. Interestingly, demonstrations staged by teenagers or young workers in smaller cities and towns were sometimes more radical, as they included explicit calls for the overthrow of the government. Such radical protests took place, for example, in the city of Tarnów in southern Poland, which had no university. On March 13, a group of young people gathered in the city center shouting: "away with

Gomułka, away with the government, long live youth!" A week later, a crowd of 1,500 people, mostly young male workers, marched through the city center displaying such slogans as "The press is lying!" They also burned newspapers and threw stones at the militiamen. Riot police used clubs and tear gas against the protestors, but similar street demonstrations erupted again on March 22 and March 23.[51] Street fights between teenagers and militia units broke out in the city of Radom, in central Poland. Young people shouted: "we are in solidarity with Warsaw students!" And in Sandomierz, a large sign—"Bravo Students"—was hung on the wall of the city hall.[52]

In rural areas, the student revolt triggered explicit expressions of national sentiments against Soviet domination. A bundle of leaflets found in the Białobrzegi district near the city of Kielce called for avenging Soviet crimes against Poles during World War II: "brothers! Remember our compatriots who perished in Katyń," one leaflet began. "The Russians murdered them, and then they nurtured freeloaders and exploiters among us. Honor to the Poles who perished in Katyń!" Another leaflet endorsed the United States' involvement in Vietnam: "we support American politics in Vietnam. Long live our American friends!" Yet another called for the creation of an anti-Soviet version of communism, possibly with help from the Chinese: "Poland had been sold to [the Russians] only for 20 years. . . . Let's follow in the footsteps of Romania and Albania."[53]

The urban/rural divide revealed important differences in the language of protest. While young elites expressed their protest in an international Marxist idiom that was particularly uncomfortable for the state, the less educated turned to nationalist tropes or the adoption of various adversaries of the Soviets as friends. In rural protests, the "us versus them" trope set Polish victims against Russian oppressors. Unlike the students' movement, this represented not a contest of ideas but a national struggle against foreign domination. As such, the rural language of protest laid bare an additional layer of ambiguity the Polish leftists faced: the struggle between an international leftist student ethos and a domestic agenda that dovetailed in global terms with the demands and desires of the Right.

To make the situation even more confusing, the anti-Soviet slogans found in villages rarely went hand in hand with support for the young rebels in the cities. On the contrary, the security apparatus received reports from rural areas noting that, despite anti-Soviet pronouncements, "the rural milieux . . . supported actions undertaken by the state toward the Zionist elements."[54] In other words, at least some segments of the rural population, even if critical of the Soviet-supported communist regime, did not object to the antisemitic campaign conducted by the same regime.

The Establishment Responds

On March 14, 1968, Radio Warsaw informed its listeners that "West German circles inimical to Poland," including "a group of representatives of Zionist organizations in West Berlin," had staged demonstrations in solidarity with the Polish students. This was one of the first public messages from the Polish regime that linked domestic student turmoil to international leftist groups. In fact, members of the West Berlin "Extra-Parliamentary Opposition" had marched to the Polish Military Mission in Germany to deliver a protest letter addressed to Polish prime minister Józef Cyrankiewicz. Carrying red banners and portraits of Lenin and Trotsky, they had claimed to support socialism but objected to the state's violence against students, which they saw as stemming from the "excesses of bureaucracy." These West Berlin marchers had found the Polish mission's building locked and so had attached their letter to a lamppost outside.[55] The Polish broadcast, however, by classifying international student activists as "Germans" and "Jews," was appealing to a very different historical and transnational imagination from the one the Polish students were advocating.

The state's discourse on student protests operated on two main levels. First, it repudiated the demonstrators as alien to the Polish national community. The language of antisemitism was key to discrediting the transnational connections students had come to symbolize, whether through cultural styles or the search for alternative Marxisms. Second, the state projected a vision of "internationalism" as cooperation between socialist states and state-sponsored organizations and support for communist movements abroad and presented as illegitimate and unacceptable any alternative vision of cooperation involving other international networks that might have emerged outside the state.

The antisemitic campaign in Poland has been explained in scholarly and popular narratives as primarily an outcome of internal conflicts within the communist leadership. According to these accounts, the right-wing nationalist faction of the Polish United Workers' Party, under the name "Partisans," led by Mieczysław Moczar, was responsible for launching the antisemitic purges in the Party and society. The Partisans had been working extreme

munism but also went deeper to advance, in the words of Polish lit-
holar Maria Janion, a "dehumanization of the Jews" as a corollary to
treme exaltation of sanctified Poles [nieprawdopodobne wywyższanie
ch Polaków]."[60] To call someone a Jew—as the male civilians did while
ng the students at Warsaw University—carried a potent meaning be-
d an ethnic or religious designation. For Polish nationalists, assigning
vishness to a person was the ultimate way to humiliate and debase that
erson.

In March 1968, stigmatizing protestors as "Jews" offered nationalists an
opportunity to revive the ethnonationalism and antisemitism of the interwar
era. Added to this were new elements of the state's nationalist discourse that
were grounded in the interplay between the domestic and international imagery of the Global Cold War.

The trigger for the antisemitic campaign in Poland occurred less than a
year before the student demonstrations and thousands of miles away. The
Six-Day War in June 1967 stunned the world: in a swift military action, the
tiny Israeli army, claiming self-defense, defeated a coalition of Arab countries that were heavily armed by the Soviets. The Six-Day War captured the
popular imagination of many Poles, generating, in the words of contemporary writer Marek Nowakowski, "feelings of camaraderie with this small
nation situated on a strip of land, put to the test by bloody wars and bloodthirsty neighbors."[61] Such admiration for Israel was not uncommon in other
parts of the world at the time.[62] In Poland, however, the popular support for
Israel exposed a rift between the regime and society. While the state equated
Israel with American imperialism, for many Poles the Israeli victory became
a symbolic revenge for the Soviet conquest of Poland during World War II,
best captured by the contemporary popular saying "Our Jews beat Russian
Arabs."[63] The feeling cut across social and political lines. Nowakowski
observed: "How elated was the carpenter from a local shop on my street,
and the watchman, and the snitch, and the bootlicker; how excited was my
friend's boss at the factory where he works, though he was a careerist and an
anti-Semite."[64]

The possibility of significant societal support for Israel irritated communist leaders, who had their own history of distrust toward their "Jewish
comrades." Already in June 1967, Gomułka severed diplomatic relations
with the State of Israel (together with the Soviet Union and other countries
in the Eastern bloc) and closed down a number of Jewish cultural and educational institutions.[65] In addition, he gave the public the go-ahead to expose

nationalism into the agenda of the rulin⌐
but only in 1968 convinced First Secretary ⌐
a potent political tool.[56] Recently, scholars hav⌐
by arguing that the antisemitic campaign had m⌐
volved not only the Party leadership but also the Ch⌐

The nationalist public discourse became especi⌐
during the celebrations of the "Millennium"—1,000 ye⌐
founding of the Polish medieval state. In that year, Prin⌐
ried Dobrawa, a daughter of the Duke of Bohemia, sealin⌐
Polish alliance and marking Mieszko's adoption of Christiani⌐
and the lands under his rule. The preparations for the Millenni⌐
early and involved a competition between the communist state⌐
Church over the definition of the Polish nation. What the state referre⌐
"One Thousand Years of the Polish State" the Church called the "Baptis⌐
Poland." According to literary scholar Tomasz Żukowski, both the state an⌐
the Church claimed to represent "the mythical essence of the nation while⌐
placing themselves at the center of that nation's past and present, as the embodiment of its interests and desires." Whether allied with communism or
Catholicism, both projected "an increasingly exclusionary and closed" understanding of the national community.[58]

Consequently, the antisemitic campaign, although instigated from above,
acquired its own social dynamics that had less to do with power struggles
within the Party-state leadership and more to do with contested notions of
national identity, social grievances (including those of lower-ranking Party
members), and cultural anxieties generated by a generational change. The
Partisans represented those kinds of emotions from below while also manipulating them to their advantage.

Moczar and his associates built on the ethnonationalism and antisemitism professed by the National Democratic Party (Endecja), which had been
especially influential in the interwar period.[59] Although Roman Dmowski,
Endecja's founder in the late nineteenth century, had promoted the modern
racialized concept of the "nation" along the lines of integral nationalism, by
the early twentieth century, Polish nationalists had successfully harnessed
Catholicism in an effort to connect with the "common people." Consequently,
being Catholic and being Polish were not separate identities. Indeed, right-
wing nationalists and their followers understood Polishness to be imbued
with almost mystical qualities. In interwar Poland, popular antisemitism not
only associated Jews with modern ideologies including liberalism, socialism,

nationalism into the agenda of the ruling regime for several years already but only in 1968 convinced First Secretary Gomułka to use antisemitism as a potent political tool.[56] Recently, scholars have begun to challenge this view by arguing that the antisemitic campaign had more complex origins that involved not only the Party leadership but also the Church and other players.[57]

The nationalist public discourse became especially pervasive in 1966 during the celebrations of the "Millennium"—1,000 years since the official founding of the Polish medieval state. In that year, Prince Mieszko I married Dobrawa, a daughter of the Duke of Bohemia, sealing a Bohemian-Polish alliance and marking Mieszko's adoption of Christianity for himself and the lands under his rule. The preparations for the Millennium started early and involved a competition between the communist state and the Church over the definition of the Polish nation. What the state referred to as "One Thousand Years of the Polish State" the Church called the "Baptism of Poland." According to literary scholar Tomasz Żukowski, both the state and the Church claimed to represent "the mythical essence of the nation while placing themselves at the center of that nation's past and present, as the embodiment of its interests and desires." Whether allied with communism or Catholicism, both projected "an increasingly exclusionary and closed" understanding of the national community.[58]

Consequently, the antisemitic campaign, although instigated from above, acquired its own social dynamics that had less to do with power struggles within the Party-state leadership and more to do with contested notions of national identity, social grievances (including those of lower-ranking Party members), and cultural anxieties generated by a generational change. The Partisans represented those kinds of emotions from below while also manipulating them to their advantage.

Moczar and his associates built on the ethnonationalism and antisemitism professed by the National Democratic Party (Endecja), which had been especially influential in the interwar period.[59] Although Roman Dmowski, Endecja's founder in the late nineteenth century, had promoted the modern racialized concept of the "nation" along the lines of integral nationalism, by the early twentieth century, Polish nationalists had successfully harnessed Catholicism in an effort to connect with the "common people." Consequently, being Catholic and being Polish were not separate identities. Indeed, right-wing nationalists and their followers understood Polishness to be imbued with almost mystical qualities. In interwar Poland, popular antisemitism not only associated Jews with modern ideologies including liberalism, socialism, and communism but also went deeper to advance, in the words of Polish literary scholar Maria Janion, a "dehumanization of the Jews" as a corollary to "the extreme exaltation of sanctified Poles [nieprawdopodobne wywyższanie świętych Polaków]."[60] To call someone a Jew—as the male civilians did while beating the students at Warsaw University—carried a potent meaning beyond an ethnic or religious designation. For Polish nationalists, assigning Jewishness to a person was the ultimate way to humiliate and debase that person.

In March 1968, stigmatizing protestors as "Jews" offered nationalists an opportunity to revive the ethnonationalism and antisemitism of the interwar era. Added to this were new elements of the state's nationalist discourse that were grounded in the interplay between the domestic and international imagery of the Global Cold War.

The trigger for the antisemitic campaign in Poland occurred less than a year before the student demonstrations and thousands of miles away. The Six-Day War in June 1967 stunned the world: in a swift military action, the tiny Israeli army, claiming self-defense, defeated a coalition of Arab countries that were heavily armed by the Soviets. The Six-Day War captured the popular imagination of many Poles, generating, in the words of contemporary writer Marek Nowakowski, "feelings of camaraderie with this small nation situated on a strip of land, put to the test by bloody wars and bloodthirsty neighbors."[61] Such admiration for Israel was not uncommon in other parts of the world at the time.[62] In Poland, however, the popular support for Israel exposed a rift between the regime and society. While the state equated Israel with American imperialism, for many Poles the Israeli victory became a symbolic revenge for the Soviet conquest of Poland during World War II, best captured by the contemporary popular saying "Our Jews beat Russian Arabs."[63] The feeling cut across social and political lines. Nowakowski observed: "How elated was the carpenter from a local shop on my street, and the watchman, and the snitch, and the bootlicker; how excited was my friend's boss at the factory where he works, though he was a careerist and an anti-Semite."[64]

The possibility of significant societal support for Israel irritated communist leaders, who had their own history of distrust toward their "Jewish comrades." Already in June 1967, Gomułka severed diplomatic relations with the State of Israel (together with the Soviet Union and other countries in the Eastern bloc) and closed down a number of Jewish cultural and educational institutions.[65] In addition, he gave the public the go-ahead to expose

"Zionists."[66] Such populist nationalism resonated with large segments of society and, more important, with rank-and-file Party members who were encouraged to overthrow "Zionist" supervisors in local Party chapters and workplaces. The student demonstrations offered an opportunity to escalate this campaign.

In March 1968, politicians and eager journalists denounced protesting students and their supporters as Zionists, capitalists, imperialists, liberals, leftists, and Stalinists. Henryk Szlajfer, the leader of the "Vietnam group," was reported to have visited the Israeli embassy in June 1967 to express his solidarity with Israel and congratulate diplomatic personnel on the "successes of the Israeli troops."[67] A leaflet distributed in Warsaw a few days after the March 8 rally, signed by the Voluntary Reserve of the Citizens' Militia, listed the names of alleged student leaders followed by short notes on their Jewish origins, consumer indulgences, and foreign attachments. Michnik was described as "the son of Ozjasz Szechter . . . the regular and distinguished informer of the Radio Freies Europa."[68] Irena Grudzińska, "the most beautiful in the group," was "a regular client of komis [secondhand stores with Western clothes]." According to the leaflet, student leaders were "the flower of banana youth . . . without a care in the world about self sustenance. Dressed sharply, having their own cars, and traveling the world; when all of this activity tires them out, they rest in Western resorts."[69] The state's attack on students entailed a full-scale assault on expressions of global consciousness, including imagined consumer choices and transnational mobility.

The antisemitic campaign unleashed racialized and gendered language that representatives of Party-state institutions and ordinary people alike freely deployed to intimidate others in public and private settings. When philosophy student Beata Dąbrowska found herself under arrest for participating in protests, she was addressed by her interrogators as "the girlfriend of that curly-haired Jew." Security officials dismissed her as an independent actor because she was a woman; as such, they acted as though they believed that her actions derived merely from her intimate relationship with a Jewish man. In a letter of complaint she wrote to First Secretary Gomułka in 1968, she recounted the humiliating remarks she had been subjected to during the interrogation: "A Polish lady can go ahead and flirt with a Jew," she was told, "but a lasting relationship should not happen. . . . After all, you, madam, are a pure-blooded Aryan woman." Furthermore, the interrogators denigrated female sexuality in racist terms: "we understand that some women are aroused by other races. For example, some like blacks, and others like Jews."[70] Such verbal abuse suggested that female protestors, although considered less important than men, posed an additional threat to Polish masculinity because they allegedly directed their sexual desire at the racial "other": Jews and blacks.[71]

As in the case of consumerist preferences and lifestyle, Party-state leaders had no doubt that young Poles took inspiration from their foreign counterparts in conducting their demonstrations. The press used a new category, "bourgeois Marxology," to discredit student protestors as not really leftist but just hedonist and elitist. Campus rebellions in Western Europe and the United States, many commentators claimed, were staged by infantile young people duped by New Left intellectuals. In response, Party officials called for mobilizing all pedagogical and intellectual resources against the "bourgeois Marxology" that aimed at "the degradation of the theoretical concepts of communism in the eyes of society."[72]

The quest to enforce a proper understanding of patriotism and internationalism in an era of global upheaval became the paramount concern. Many commentators labeled students "cosmopolitans," evoking a term that had first entered public discussions in Poland in the early 1800s to denote Western liberal influences and progressive outlooks. For nineteenth-century conservatives, cosmopolitanism had quickly become associated with unpatriotic attitudes.[73] More important, "cosmopolitanism" acquired a new meaning under Stalinism, functioning as a code word for Jewishness during the antisemitic purges in the Soviet Union and Czechoslovakia. After the March 1968 rebellion, "cosmopolitanism" reentered public discourse as a powerful way to condemn any transnational ideas that departed from the official version of "internationalism," understood as "the shared position of all socialist states in relation to their main foe, imperialism."[74]

Cosmopolitanism effectively conflated "deviant internationalism" with non-Polish identity without using an explicitly antisemitic vocabulary.[75] As such, the term opened a new way for nationalist and racialized discourses to become morally and ideologically permissible under communism. State propaganda made a clear distinction between the privileged "cosmopolitans," with ties to the outside world, and the "common people," whose lack of such connections testified to their genuine Polishness.[76]

Nationalism was declared to be the foundation of healthy internationalism and, more important, an indispensable expression of one's humanity. Krzysztof Gawlikowski, a contributor to *ITD*, wrote that "the individual gains humanity only through participation in the nation and through absorbing its achievements. By becoming a Pole, a Frenchman, or a German—only then could one become a human being. This is because both the language—the foundation on which the individual psyche can be formed—and culture can only have a national form." Gawlikowski supported solidarity with "the beaten and persecuted, regardless of their nationality, with the struggle for freedom and justice anywhere it takes place," but nevertheless "true internationalism is grounded in patriotism. . . . Can one love humanity if one is not capable of loving one's nation?"[77]

As this article illustrates, Party-state actors called for clear national boundaries and nationalized individuals as a precondition for international solidarity. Such solidarity could not occur as a spontaneous action from below and could not come from individuals whose national "loyalties," as in the case of students like Szlajfer, were in question. In this way, Gawlikowski and others inadvertently exposed just how powerful the leftist students' challenge was to the communist establishment. The Party leaders abandoned socialist argumentation and felt they had no choice but to cling to ethnonationalism and antisemitism as a last-ditch effort to save themselves.

In the wake of March 1968, more than 3,000 students were expelled from institutions of higher education. Hundreds of young people were arrested.[78] Some students were subjected to forced military conscription in special units in which they served at least one year but were not given weapons.[79] Intellectuals who supported students were subjected to repression as well. Some, like Kuroń and Modzelewski, landed in prison; others were demoted from their professional posts.[80]

The state effectively pressured thousands of Poles with Jewish origins to emigrate. First, the communist regime lifted restrictions on foreign travel for those who "considered Israel their fatherland."[81] Such a declaration could not come from a non-Jewish Pole, as the state required applicants to present evidence of their Jewish ancestry. Second, dismissals from work produced an economic motive for leaving. Such dismissals affected not only high-profile professionals at universities and state institutions but also regular employees in workplaces such as schools, hospitals, and factories. Mere suspicion of pro-Israeli sympathies could be enough for someone to lose a job.[82] Furthermore, pressure from neighbors, media attacks, and a general climate of hostility contributed to Polish Jews' decision to emigrate.[83] Finally, the post-March emigrants were granted so-called travel documents instead of a regular passport, which effectively stripped them of Polish citizenship and the right to return.[84]

At his trial, Adam Michnik was also encouraged to emigrate. "The judges were forever repeating that I was Jewish and that I should leave Poland," he recalled. " 'Mr. Michnik,' they would say, 'why don't you leave for Tel-Aviv?' And I would answer that I would love to go, but only if they went to Moscow first."[85] Michnik was sentenced to five years in prison but was released after eighteen months and then was assigned to do manual labor for two years at the Rosa Luxemburg electric bulb factory in Warsaw.[86]

* * *

Global 1968 involved a fierce battle over a transnational imagination that informed the dynamics of the sixties movements and countermovements. Through the 1960s, young activists in Poland, like other "new" leftists, attempted to position themselves and others on a global map of oppression and liberation, in defiance of Cold War divisions. They saw the value of such a maneuver both as tactical and as a substantive part of their leftist identity. Time and again, however, they found that developing such a stance was immensely difficult. This was because the ruling communists already owned so much of the antiimperialist ideological terrain and because of the activists' own blind spots, especially their own Eurocentric leanings, which made it hard for them to see the postcolonial world as anything more than a metaphor for their own geopolitical position.

The antisemitic campaign the Party-state launched against the student protestors wiped out any possible political effect that grassroots ideas of transnational solidarity might have had, including the ideas held by the activists who had sought affinities between Polish struggles for "genuine" socialism and the anticolonial rebellions in the Third World. The students who sang the national anthem alongside "The Internationale" in March 1968 could still imagine their cause to be entwined with Third World solidarity. After 1968, this was no longer possible. The state's attack on the students strengthened the exclusionary vision of the Polish nation and elevated nationalist discourse as the foremost legitimizing tool for future political activism. Although leftist students and intellectuals rejected exclusionary nationalism, they nevertheless turned to the "nation" in formulating their anticommunist ideas in the 1970s and 1980s.

These leftists' post-1968 disengagement from international leftist conversations was a significant departure not only from these activists' earlier aspirations but also from the history of Polish Marxism. Since the beginning of Marxist-inspired movements in the Polish lands, their adherents had seen themselves as part of a pan-European community, seeking allies across the continent and actively shaping debates about such vital concepts as class, nation, antiimperialism, and revolution.[87] After 1968, Polish leftists showed little interest in the wide variety of sixties' movements or their embrace of such causes as environmentalism, feminism, or gay rights. Instead, they became preoccupied with forging an effective front against the communist regime. In so doing, they turned to the Catholic Church and other domestic oppositional groups, including "right-wing sympathizers of the Endecja."[88]

According to the dominant postdissident narrative, the Polish '68-ers eventually emerged victorious, as they played key roles in overthrowing communism two decades later. But the Party-state actors who conducted the antisemitic campaign had their own peculiar victory in the way they shaped the trajectory of opposition movements. The long-term impact of the state's backlash against the students could be discerned in the nationalist and Catholic bent of the Solidarity movement. Although deeply entrenched in universal ideas of social justice, the Solidarity leaders of the 1980s were notable for their distance from leftist international organizations.[89]

This is not to say that the search for alternative transnationalism ended in Poland in 1968. It continued in countercultural circles, including the hippie movement that blossomed in the early 1970s. But such interests became the purview of artistic, psychotherapeutic, and academic circles.[90] Political dissidents, by contrast, used transnational ideas and movements, such as the human rights movement, mainly to draw Western attention to the Polish "cause."

By the 1980s, former Commandos had begun to position themselves in the new anti-Marxist political landscape. In 1987, Michnik told Cohn-Bendit that the Vietnam leaflet the Commandos had circulated twenty years earlier had been a mistake: "the first tract we distributed at the university was about Vietnam," he recalled, "and in it we put the American invasion of Vietnam and the Soviet intervention in Hungary at the same level. But the two are not comparable: Vietnam was a war against totalitarianism, and Hungary was a war against freedom. Or at least that's my opinion."[91] Michnik accused the Western New Left of standing up only for those who suffered from capitalist but not communist oppression.[92] He was right in identifying the blind spots of many Western leftists, but such statements also revealed a lack of understanding of colonial politics and the narrow Eurocentric lens through which many Eastern European dissidents assessed global affairs post-1968. In the language of those like Michnik, the Global South became no longer even a metaphor for their own geopolitical position but merely a competitor for Western attention.

Polish leftists' limited interest in the Global South, post-1968, went hand in hand with a lack of critical engagement with contemporary capitalism as an economic and social system. These attitudes shaped the transition to liberal democracy after 1989 and contributed to both the heightened nationalism of the postcommunist era in Poland and the embrace of neoliberal capitalism as the only model of global connectivity worth emulating. In that sense, the protests of 1968 set the stage for transnational tensions that Poland confronted after the fall of communism, as a young democracy again struggling to make sense of global engagement and Polish identity.

6

The Counterculture

Hippies, Artists, and Other Subversives

When Tomasz Tłuczkiewicz found two other kindred spirits in musicians Romuald and Roman because of their long hair at a sit-in at Wrocław Polytechnic in March 1968, it was clear that the stylistic hallmarks of hippies had not yet become mainstream among Polish students. A year later, however, Tomasz and others could count on meeting more and more of these "long-haired" men and women on Polish streets and country roads. In 1969, the estimated number of hippies in Poland stood at 1,000. Most were between the ages of fifteen and twenty-five. If one counted young people who adopted select hippie lifestyles and fashions or were in and out of the movement (so-called Sunday hippies) the number was significantly higher.[1] As elsewhere, Polish hippies openly demonstrated their support for pacifism, love, friendship, and respect for the natural environment. They dressed and behaved in ways that challenged societal conventions by wearing colorful clothes (often handmade), hats, bead necklaces, and religious accessories. They experimented with drugs and practiced what they called "free love."

In Western narratives, counterculture has been typically associated with middle-class youth rebelling against dominant middle-class norms in the conditions of "advanced capitalism." This is how Theodore Roszak understood the term "counter culture" when he first coined it in 1969.[2] Such definitions, however, are less helpful when examining counterculture in communist societies. Soviet hippies, for example, practiced an alternative emotional style that "stood in contrast to the highly regulated emotional practices sanctioned by the Soviet official culture."[3] The hippie phenomenon was also characterized in communist and capitalist countries by "the changing cultures of subjectivity" that crossed geopolitical boundaries.[4] These subjectivities were driven by a deep transnational desire for authenticity that was expressed in emotional and bodily ways.[5]

Imagining the World from Behind the Iron Curtain. Malgorzata Fidelis, Oxford University Press. © Oxford University Press 2022. DOI: 10.1093/oso/9780197643402.003.0007

This chapter takes up the hippies' search for an authentic subjectivity as it was expressed in postwar Polish society. The hippie counterculture was, in essence, a project of personal and communal self-creation against hegemonic ideologies of nation, state, religion, and patriarchy, among others. While the existing scholarship on Polish hippies has privileged the state's perspective on them, this chapter examines how the hippies themselves understood their beliefs and practices.[6] Supplementing memoirs and interviews, which form the core of the analysis, are documents, including those of the security apparatus, that demonstrate the broader implications of pursuing an alternative lifestyle in a state socialist context.[7]

The bulk of this analysis focuses on the early phase of the hippie movement in Poland, between 1966 and 1971, the most idealized and "innocent" time in hippies' personal memories. By the early 1970s, according to those memories, some young people who joined the hippies did so primarily for access to drugs rather than countercultural identification. By that time, the militia and the security apparatus were targeting hippie communities primarily on the account of drug possession rather than lifestyle or suspected political agenda, as had been the case before. In popular perceptions, the movement later on became associated with youth delinquency, drug addiction, and often crime.

At the same time, the romanticized and liberational legacy of the hippies persisted and imprinted on mainstream culture in surprising ways given the authoritarian nature of the state. By the early 1970s, large circles of young people had adopted elements of hippie philosophy and lifestyle. They rarely identified themselves as members of the hippie community but rather spoke about *hipisowanie*, a colloquial term that could be translated as "hippie-ness." Counterculture also became part of state-sponsored internationalism as exemplified in the International Festival of Student Theater Festivals (Międzynarodowy Festiwal Festiwali Teatrów Studenckich), held in Wrocław every two years after 1967.[8]

Are We Hippies?

Where did Polish hippies come from? Evidence suggests that long-haired men in colorful clothes appeared on Polish streets at least a year before the name "hippie" entered Polish vocabulary. They tended to congregate in city centers, usually near the international press clubs popularly known as the

Empiks.[9] One of the first articles on these new gatherings was published in the youth periodical *New Village* in September 1966. The author, who signed himself "Your Andrzej," was a regular columnist in charge of responding to readers' letters. As the editors received more and more questions from readers regarding the long-haired men, Andrzej felt compelled to discuss the subject. He wrote: "they walk with greasy locks of hair coming down to their shoulders. That is the required fashion of today's youth. Thus far we have not seen those styles; we had *bikiniarze* [zoot-suiters] with their hair slicked back, we had those who got haircuts like Fanfan;[10] we had bearded 'existentialists'; finally, there were the wannabe Beatles, who had bangs on their foreheads. But the most up-to-date and fashionable comb themselves to look like Jesus Christ from cheap imitation prints; the girls call them beatniks [bitnicy].[11] Older generations call them cross-dressers [obojniacy]."[12] This text discredited the new movement in aesthetic terms. The long-haired men stood for ugliness and disregard for modern hygiene: their hair was ungroomed and unwashed. They failed to offer anything new but belonged to the predictable cycle of life in which the young generation fell for superficial fashions. Moreover, the long-haired men were associated with kitsch ("Jesus Christ from cheap imitation prints") and the supposed lack of sexual attractiveness was seen as androgyny. They were not a "problem" but a developmental phase that would eventually pass.

Rather than fading away, however, the movement grew. Just a year later, the Polish press recognized the hippies as a new global phenomenon. In December 1967, the Polish magazine *Forum* published a translation of three articles, from the French magazines *Candide*, *Elle*, and *Réalité*, about American hippies.[13] Although the texts depicted them in a negative light as drug users and social misfits, the articles generated enthusiastic responses from young readers. The long-haired men from the Polish streets also acquired a name of their own: the hippies (*hipisi*). Some young people used the publication as a manual for becoming a "true" hippie. For Prophet, who came from a small village near Bochnia in southern Poland, the slogan "Make Love Not War," discussed in the articles, proved particularly intriguing. From then on, he and his friends wrote the phrase, translated into Polish as *Czyń miłość nie wojnę*, on the fabric of their clothes. More important, as Prophet remembered, "after reading the article, we became more courageous. Now we knew that we were not alone." He and other Polish hippies felt legitimized as part of a global movement. Prophet remembered a strong feeling of a special mission: "I was convinced that we were going to change the world."[14]

Fig. 6.1 Hippies at Victory Square, Warsaw, November 1969. Photo by Tadeusz Zagoździński. Courtesy of Polish Press Agency.

There was no single path for becoming a hippie. Milo Kurtis, born in Warsaw in 1951, had felt "different" in Polish society from early on. His parents, who were Greek communists, had come to Poland two years earlier as refugees after the Greek Civil War; his father eventually became a professor at Warsaw University. Milo experienced his difference in a brutal way while still in elementary school. Coming from a Greek communist family, he did not attend the Catholic religion classes taught in postwar Polish schools between 1945 and 1961.[15] "And because I had dark hair," Milo remembered in 2013, "[boys] beat me up after school." His schoolmates thought he was Jewish: "I did not attend religious instruction," he explained, "so they figured I must be Jewish." It is not clear how the school administration reacted to the situation, but Milo's parents responded by enrolling their son in a boxing club for youth so he could defend himself.[16]

As a teenager in the mid-1960s, Milo finally found the circle of friends he had yearned for. As he walked one afternoon through the Old Town in

Warsaw, he saw a group of "strange-looking guys with long hair." As it turned out, these were some of the first hippies, who nicknamed themselves Turk, Baluba, and Crocodile. "I was ecstatic," Milo remembered, "because they were weirdos. So I approached them, because all my life I was a weirdo, and suddenly I see these kindred souls."[17]

Jerzy Illg from the city of Katowice in industrial Upper Silesia felt estranged from his surroundings because of what he saw as limits on one's self-expression. "I did not fit into those existing categories they had for young people at that time," Jerzy remembered in an interview in 2011. "These two colors," he continued, "you could be either red or grey. You either put on the red tie of a communist activist or you live a grey life." Jerzy wanted to be "multicolored."[18] Accordingly, one of his first acts of rebellion was to acquire a piece of bright-colored white fabric with orange and blue flowers on it, originally intended for making curtains. He then persuaded a respected tailor in Katowice to turn the fabric into bell bottoms. This new outfit, complete with a large Orthodox cross on a silver chain worn across his chest, caused a sensation on the streets. In accordance with the hippies' custom, Jerzy took the

Fig. 6.2 Two hippies: Chlorek and Jaegger, 1969. Chlorek was a technical assistant for rock bands; Jaegger was a blue-collar worker from Szczecin. The wall behind them features a collage of photos, mainly of inspirational international figures, including President John F. Kennedy and Martin Luther King (left) and jazz musician Miles Davis (right). Kamil Sipowicz, *Hipisi w PRL-u* (Warsaw: Baobab, 2008), 99. Courtesy of Kamil Sipowicz.

nickname Missionary (Misjonarz). As female hippie and rock singer Kora explained many years later, "we felt [ourselves] to be new people with new ideas, attitudes, worldviews, so we took new names."[19]

Alicja Imlay came from a place that was already "different" from other parts of Poland. She was among the first Polish babies born in Wrocław, a city that had been transferred from Germany to Poland in 1945. Wrocław proved to be a fertile ground for unconventional choices. Nearly all the residents came from somewhere else, since the majority of the interwar German population had been expelled after the war. As a result of territorial shifts, Wrocław became a destination for many Poles from the former eastern Poland or what became the Soviet republics of Ukraine, Belarus, and Lithuania. They were joined by thousands of Poles who arrived from central Poland in search of better opportunities in the newly acquired Western Territories. Ukrainians and Lemkos were also there, as the Polish authorities deported these groups from southeastern Poland in retaliation for their real and imagined support of the Ukrainian nationalist underground.[20] Finally, postwar Wrocław had a considerable Jewish community, as the region attracted Holocaust survivors who sought to rebuild their lives in a new place that "reminded them of neither Germany not Poland."[21]

Indeed, the memory of war was fresh in Wrocław as the first postwar generation came of age. Alicja remembered riding on a tram and seeing "ruins that were three stories high."[22] For some, Wrocław seemed like the Wild West: dynamic, dangerous, and unruly. To others, Wrocław resembled New York City with its mixture of people and cosmopolitan outlooks.[23] By the 1960s, the city had become the site of international festivals that attracted young people from many parts of the world, including the annual Jazz on the Odra festival and the biannual international festivals of avant-garde theater. Many Wroclavians thus felt a special connection to the global youth culture. Alicja and her friends flocked to the student club Pałacyk, festivals, and other cultural events. "There was constantly something going on, every day," Alicja remembered in 2013. "One was afraid to go to sleep so as not to miss anything exciting."[24]

No wonder becoming a "flower child" came almost naturally to Alicja. She was inspired by the Flowers Holiday held annually in Wrocław on July 22 as part of the celebrations for the Lublin Manifesto, a foundational document that established the People's Poland in 1944. On that day in the mid-1960s, Alicja recalled, she bought fresh red, orange, and yellow marigolds and attached them to her red miniskirt, a new and almost revolutionary garment for young women. Then she went to the street to take part in the celebrations. Alicja's story illustrated the potential for official culture, in this case the Flower Holiday, to contribute to the emergent counterculture.

Ethnographic research in the Pomerania region in northwestern Poland has demonstrated that hippie groups were formed not only in Warsaw, Kraków, and Wrocław but also in smaller cities and towns such as Toruń, Bydgoszcz, Grudziądz, Włocławek, and Ciechocinek. In addition, groups of two or three hippies could be found in the small Pomeranian towns of Wąrzeźno, Chełmża, and Brodnica.[25] Hippies came from a variety of social backgrounds. In 1971, the security apparatus estimated that half the hippies came from "well-situated" white-collar families, while those from working-class backgrounds made up a significant 30 percent. While many were university students, others had dropped out of school or worked in blue-collar jobs.[26] Almost every young person knew a hippie in their locality. Poet Irena Groblewska, who grew up in the town of Szczecinek in northern Poland, remembered two brothers by the name of Zawadzki who "had the courage to be true hippies . . . to grow long hair." The Zawadzki brothers attached peace signs to their clothes, listened to the Beatles and the Rolling Stones, and made sure to put Radio Luxembourg on a loudspeaker for the whole neighborhood to hear. Young people from the neighborhood looked up to them.[27]

"Leaving the Nation"

It may be tempting to see counterculture at least as a partial outgrowth of the suppression of student protests in March 1968 and the Warsaw Pact invasion of Czechoslovakia, involving Polish troops, in August. Such a causal relationship has been noted for other places where student demonstrations had been suppressed, such as Mexico City.[28] Such a relationship, however, is more difficult to argue for the Polish hippies. The effects of the suppression of the 1968 rebellions in Poland are more visible in the literary and artistic world than the hippie counterculture. For many young Polish artists and writers, the invasion of Czechoslovakia provided "the impulse to take a principled stand" and ushered in a new wave of politicized work.[29] For the hippies, 1968 was their first "summer of love," the beginning of nationwide rallies and expansion of the movement.[30] By August the hippie philosophy was already in place. The hippies at the Polish-Czechoslovak border on August 21 responded to the invasion of Czechoslovakia by juxtaposing their celebration of peace and love against the display of military might. They played guitar, danced, and gave out flowers.

This does not mean that there was no interaction or mutual influence between different strands of dissent. Hippies, artists, and former Commandos socialized together and exchanged ideas, often to discover their differences. Tomasz Rodowicz, an experimental theater actor and musician, remembered a gathering at an apartment in the Mokotów district of Warsaw in the early 1970s where leftist rebels Jacek Kuroń and Seweryn Blumsztajn mingled with the countercultural crowd. Tomasz recounted in 2008: "they [Kuroń and Blumsztajn] as usual were in a heated discussion, and we turned on some music and started dancing. We were jealous of their bravery and the importance of the cause they were fighting for, and they were jealous of our happiness, carefree lifestyle, and refusal to accept adulthood. We knew each other from many meetings, but at that time this was a clash of two different countercultural worlds. One with the loaded gun in hand and the other with a flower in the mouth. Blumsztajn even tried to dance with us."[31] The confrontation between political dissidents and countercultural rebels revealed different sensibilities and understandings of "freedom," which for former Commandos was tied to political action.

As British historian Arthur Marwick once observed, writing about the hippies within any particular country was somewhat contradictory since "in some ways, the hippies were the most international of all the phenomena associated with the sixties."[32] Polish hippies distanced themselves from national identity. In a short document from 1971, *How to Become Free*, Prophet called for "leaving the nation so as to sever its ownership over yourself because of the language [or because of] blood, race, or borders."[33] Rather, the hippies insisted on defining themselves as "the other" or "the oppressed people" ostracized by nearly everyone.[34]

Polish hippies expressed their distance from pervasive national categories by using transnational symbols of their core values. One of the best illustrations of this practice was the public use of the peace symbol. In March 1971, a group of young people, identified by the security apparatus as hippies, painted three large peace symbols on two public buildings in Warsaw. One of them was at the base of the monument to the Soviet revolutionary hero of Polish origin Feliks Dzierżyński; the other two were on the walls of the church of the Holy Cross on Krakowskie Przedmieście. One of the peace symbols on the church walls was accompanied by an equally large graffito of the word WOLNOŚĆ (freedom).[35] The public use of the peace symbol not only challenged the existing hegemonies of the state and church but also proposed an alternative internationalism embedded in pacifism.

Hippies drew on other transnational inspirations. Irena Groblewska remembered posters of Angela Davis and Jimi Hendrix that young people put up in their rooms, some of them copied by hand from printed ones.[36] A handwritten Polish translation of Ginsberg's poem "Howl" circulated and was read aloud at hippie gatherings. Some hippies adopted elements of their outfits from the global icons of dissent. Mieciu Banaszak from Gniezno has been remembered for wearing "sweaters that he made himself," complete with "bead necklaces . . . and a goatee like Ho Chi Minh."[37] Others carried the "Little Red Book" of quotations from Mao Tse Tung with them, as well as pins and shirts bearing Mao's image.[38] These were rarely signs of ideological identifications and most often were emblems that connected the Polish hippies to the imagined global community of dissent.[39]

Eastern philosophies and religions played an important role in hippie communities and later became a major influence on new directions in theater, music, and humanistic psychotherapy.[40] By the early 1970s, brochures about Zen and other types of Buddhism were being printed in private homes and distributed among friends.[41] For some, Eastern philosophies provided a way to avoid the fetishizing of the West that was rampant in Polish mainstream youth culture. Musician Jacek Ostaszewski turned to oriental music and philosophy to get away from the Eurocentric perspective or what he called "euro-chauvinism" (euroszowinism).[42]

A handful of foreigners could be found among the hippies in Poland. The country was hardly a destination like Nepal or Mexico where international countercultural tourism flourished, but nevertheless some hippies from abroad were present.[43] Most of them found themselves in Poland as exchange students, visiting artists, or tourists. A security apparatus document from 1969 listed ten foreign hippies, who "maintained contacts" with the hippies in Kraków. These included a diverse mix: one person from Venezuela, France, Italy, India, and Scandinavia each and five from Czechoslovakia.[44] During the same year, small groups of hippies traveled to Poland from Canada, Great Britain, Sweden, and Denmark.[45] In Warsaw, a few American students, some of them of Polish origin, could be found among the hippies, and in November 1968, a cultural attaché from the American embassy invited a group of Warsaw hippies to a party at his residence.[46]

In April 1965, American beat poet and hippie icon Allen Ginsberg visited Warsaw and Kraków. His journey to the communist world had started
in Cuba in January 1965, where he had got into conflicts with the authorities over freedom of expression, homosexual rights, and drugs. He then
went to Czechoslovakia, the Soviet Union, and Poland and then back to
Czechoslovakia.[47] At the time, his poetry and social activism were little
known in Poland. Literary magazines and sometimes popular periodicals
wrote about the beat generation, but they considered Jack Kerouac to be the
most prominent representative of the Beats. Yet in April 1965, when word
spread that "the beatnik" was in Warsaw, artists, writers, and poets rushed to
invite him to local cafés and their apartments.[48]

According to Ginsberg's diary, he spent most of his time in Warsaw
roaming the streets alone during the day, drinking vodka with the Polish
artistic "Bohemians" in the evening, and periodically showing up at the
militia headquarters to extend his visa and collect a per diem from the
Ministry of Culture.[49] His appearance as he walked through the streets of
Warsaw and Kraków caused a sensation among passersby, revealing just
how unique the long-haired men in unkempt clothing were in 1965 and
what a shock it must have been to see more of them within just a few years.
"Intense solitude on the walk, hours & hours, and young people staring
at me contemptuous or giggling at my rare hairy appearance," Ginsberg
jotted down.[50]

Although few Polish hippies met Ginsberg in person, the very fact of his
visit to Poland figures prominently in the memory of Polish hippies as a remarkable moment of proximity to global counterculture. According to one
story, Ginsberg placed his autograph on a kitchen wall in an apartment he
visited in Kraków. The apartment's owner, artist Krzysztof Niemczyk, later
remembered "processions" of hippies invading his residence to "worship" the
autograph and "kiss it in ecstasy."[51] In 1967, "Howl" was unofficially translated into Polish. Jerzy Illg remembered communal readings of the poem at
hippie rallies together with 1 Corinthians 1. "We saw no contradiction between the two," Jerzy commented in 2008.[52]

Polish hippies' transnational identification stimulated a reimagining of
domestic culture. Catholicism, in particular, did not remain untouched by
the hippie movement. Those young Catholics who were searching for mys-
ticism and a nontraditional way of worship found the hippie philosophy inspiring. More and more young Catholics sang prayers, played guitars, and
sometimes formed communes or summer retreats in the wilderness. In

January 1968, the first Catholic folk mass in Poland, composed by renowned female composer Katarzyna Gartner, was performed by the Red and Blacks at a small church in Podkowa Leśna near Warsaw. A year later, the same mass made it to the main cathedral in Kraków.[53] Catholic ministries for university students, swelling in ranks by the early 1970s, often stood at the forefront of the new movements in worship.[54]

Although the institutional church remained deeply ambivalent toward the hippies and the hippie-inspired Catholic youth, a number of priests, for example Father Adam Boniecki in Kraków and Father Konrad Hejmo in Poznań, regularly met with the hippies and conducted pastoral work among them.[55] Such priests also facilitated the exchange between the hippies and other Catholics to discuss philosophical and moral issues. One such meeting took place at the Dominican Church in Poznań in October 1969 when a group of hippies were invited to discuss their beliefs and practices. According to the reports of the security apparatus, close to 700 people, most of them young, attended the event.[56] Two years later, in October 1971, a funeral mass for Jimi Hendrix's soul was celebrated at the St. Anne Church in Warsaw. The mass was attended by an estimated 1,500 people, predominantly between the ages of thirteen and twenty-five. The mass had been advertised all over the city with the following text: "People! When gods leave us don't cry! Don't shed any tears for human beings who are free. . . . Come to the church of St. Anne on Monday, the 4th, at 20:30, and you will find out that HENDRIX and JOPLIN are GODS too!" In the top left corner of the poster was a stylized drawing of a human hand with the index and middle fingers spread apart in the shape of the letter V—a hippie symbol commonly used alongside the peace sign.[57]

Despite their rejection of conventional political identifications, the hippies could not entirely extract themselves from politics. According to the security apparatus, in March 1968, some hippies supported student demonstrations and helped spread information about the Warsaw protests to other cities.[58] More often, however, the hippies responded to political events in unconventional and creative ways that reaffirmed their core values. In March 1968, for example, Prophet painted a series of Stars of David on his clothes as a response to the state-driven antisemitic campaign. He was put under arrest.[59] In December 1970, on learning that workers' demonstrations had erupted on the Baltic coast, a group of hippies in Warsaw boarded a night train bound for Gdańsk. They had no specific political agenda but wanted to participate in an event that questioned the status quo.[60] Some hippies aimed actions

at ethical and political messages using historical references to human trag-
edies of global significance. In August 1970, close to 200 hippies gathered
in Oświęcim (Auschwitz), where they arranged flowers in the shape of the
peace symbol at the site of the former Nazi concentration camp. According
to one of the participants, the hippies gathered there on the anniversary of
the bombing of Hiroshima with the intention to show "that pacifism exists."[61]
Although no explicit references to the Holocaust were made in the testimony, the choice of the meeting place suggested that the hippies symbolically
connected the Nazi genocide to the American bombing of Hiroshima so as
to highlight their opposition to war and violence, regardless of the place or
context.

Living Free

Once self-defined hippies found "kindred souls," they sometimes formed
communes. Ironically, creating "communes" under communism was an
arduous task. First, communes were illegal. The state promoted family
apartments as the most desirable form of residence, while every person
also had to be officially "registered" (*zameldowany*) at a particular address.
Second, the endemic shortage of housing limited available space. And
even if one found a suitable dwelling, the cost of renting or buying was relatively high. Yet the hippies managed to form a network of communes, or
hip-huts (*hip-chaty*), all over Poland, in urban and rural settings. Although
most hippies did not live in communes but rather with their parents, these
dwellings played a critical role in shaping hippie values and practices.
Communes cemented bonds among hippies and created a network of trusted
friends. On the practical level, communes served as temporary shelters for
those who found themselves homeless or were on the move.

Consider the now legendary commune at Cyganeczki Street in Warsaw,
which prioritized artistic creativity. Baluba discovered the building, an elegant villa, in 1970, but he had no money to pay for it. That help came from
Marysia, a Polish-British student attending the Academy of Fine Arts in
Warsaw. She convinced her relatively well-to-do parents, who lived in
England, to pay the monthly rent of 6,000 Polish zloty, which was the equivalent of approximately three average monthly salaries in Poland at the time.
The commune soon became a major gathering point for hippies, artists,
professionals, and other practitioners of countercultural lifestyles. Wojciech

Eichelberger, a pioneer in new techniques in psychotherapy, often visited the commune. Some of the former Commandos did as well.[62]

Personal testimonies suggest that many communes functioned as extended families. Some apartment and rural communes were run by older women, in many cases mothers and grandmothers of hippies. These were "open houses," where female owners welcomed visitors, offered homemade food, and let people stay as long as they wished. According to Alicja, one could find many such communes in Wrocław. These places were not permanent; rather, "someone lived there, someone visited, someone was a couch surfer in someone's home."[63] In Ożarów in central Poland, interwar female communist Dorota Szumowska welcomed hippies. Eccentric even by hippie standards, she lived with two goats, two dogs, and a cat under one roof.[64]

Fig. 6.3 "A visit with the hippies in Ożarów," 1968. Photo by Eustachy Kossakowski, 1347. Courtesy of Museum of Modern Art in Warsaw.

Another female patron of hippies in Warsaw was writer Stanisława Zakrzewska, whose daughter, Wilga, was a hippie. Zakrzewska welcomed hippies into her apartment and was reported to have hosted a wedding for her daughter to another hippie as "the first wedding in the Alan [sic] Ginsberg commune."[65] As a writer and member of the official Association of Polish Writers, Zakrzewska invited journalists and writers to her apartment to meet with the hippies. In June 1970, she tried to publish an article, "The Tragic Flowers," in which she called for helping the hippies rather than "measuring their value by the length of their hair." She used the language of the state and the ethos of inclusion in making this appeal: "give them the rights to citizenship, the right to dignity. Undo their status of infamy and the libel being written about them! Give them a place in the world and protect them from assault by hooligans, give them the opportunity to work and study. Let them do what they do best."[66] The manuscript never made it to the press; the security apparatus was quick to confiscate it.[67]

Like their counterparts elsewhere in the world, many Polish hippies yearned to get away from urban civilization. A group of hippies who had been gathering by the Barbara Bar in Wrocław found a suitable place in Kopaniec in the Sudety Mountains south of the city. The cottage was located in a remote place, almost a mile from the closest grocery store or a bus stop. "Everyone who visited us was enchanted with the beauty of our place," one of the commune founders, Zappa, remembered in 2008.[68]

After the initial excitement of joining a commune came the challenges of acquiring basic necessities such as food and fuel. In Kopaniec and other rural communes, hippies took on temporary jobs such as tree logging or helping locals in farm work. Surviving the winter outside the city proved to be particularly difficult. In Kopaniec, harmonious living was tested when the cold weather arrived. "The commune shrank to three people," Zappa remembered. "We worked as loggers; after coming back from work, we ate supper, and tired, after a hard day's work, we went to our rooms." Such hardships made some hippies question their own way of life. "I slowly realized," Zappa continued, "that hippies could only practice their philosophy if they leeched from society, the same society that hippies fundamentally rejected and ridiculed."[69]

Like communes, being on the road, especially during summer, was an important element of hippie lifestyle. Kerouac's *On the Road* was available to few young people in Poland, but many learned about this foundational text of the hippie movement from the popular press or by word of mouth.[70]

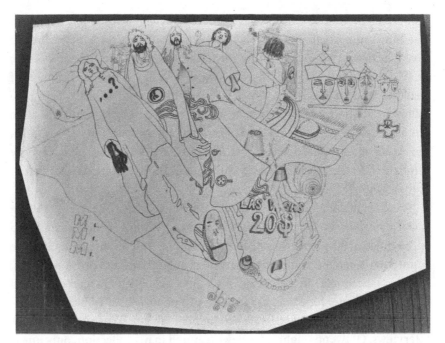

Fig. 6.4 Contemporary drawing of the commune in Kopaniec, c. 1972. Drawing by Jurek Zamoyski. Courtesy of Jurek Zamoyski.

The state-sponsored program of hitchhiking proved to be helpful in providing opportunities for mobility. The program was instituted in 1957. Youth magazines such as *Around the World* took to popularizing the hitchhiking movement as an inexpensive way for young people to spend their summer vacations. The state then offered hitchhikers special booklets that drivers who picked them up could mark with a stamp. Although most hippies made a point of not using the booklets, they benefited from the widespread awareness of hitchhiking and the willingness of many drivers to transport them.[71]

While on the road, hippies developed their own geography. Attractive places of nature held a special status in their community. In the early 1970s, the picturesque landscape and the abundant forest of the Bieszczady Mountains became a popular place for establishing communes. Hippies also marked their presence in the country by organizing rallies in different places in Poland. The first such rally took place in July 1968 in Mielno, followed by the one in Duszniki on the day of the Warsaw Pact invasion of Czechoslovakia. There were two other rallies the same year: one in Kazimierz on the Vistula in September, and one in Święty Krzyż and Chęciny in the Świętokrzyskie

Mountains in October. Each rally gathered anywhere from several dozen to a hundred participants. Starting in 1970, hippies held regular rallies in Ruciane Nida and Ostróda on the Mazurian Lakes in northeastern Poland. In 1971, the hippies for the first time gathered at the Catholic sanctuary of Jasna Góra in Częstochowa, which later became a regular place for hippie rallies. In addition, a number of state-sponsored events were known for large hippie attendance. These included the annual Polish Song Festival in Opole, the Academic Youth Creative Arts Festival FAMA (Festiwal Artystyczny Młodzieży Akademickiej) in Świnoujście, and the International Festival of Student Theater Festivals in Wrocław.[72]

No attempt at living free would be complete without shedding existing social conventions, including traditional gender roles. Females made up approximately 30 percent of all Polish hippies.[73] In contrast to their male counterparts, female hippies have given few interviews, and only one, Kora, an icon of the hippie movement and rock star, has published a memoir. Kamil Sipowicz, a former hippie and the author of a popular 2008 book on the history of Polish hippies, said that he had found it difficult to recruit women for interviews. Of twenty-eight interviews featured in his collection, only one is with a woman, Kora.[74] Sipowicz explained that hierarchies inevitably developed in hippie communities. "Men dominated in an ideological sense," he remarked. "There were girls, but the hippie gurus were the guys." Sipowicz

Fig. 6.5 Hippie rally in Duszniki, Karkonosze Mountains, August 21, 1968. Photo by Jacek Szmuc. Courtesy of Jacek Szmuc.

concluded: "alas, the patriarchal social model was being replicated."[75] Milo Kurtis pointed to the impact of differences in socialization of males and females. He recognized that becoming a hippie required more courage from the young woman, as the traditional society made it particularly difficult for women to transgress social norms. If a woman joined the movement, Milo stated, "she had to be truly assertive."[76]

Women's later reluctance to speak about their hippie experiences could stem from many factors, including the social stigma attached to female hippies. In popular perceptions and state propaganda, female hippies were associated with loose morals and sexual availability. The contemporary press often depicted the hippie movement as particularly dangerous for young women. In those narratives, male hippies supposedly had formed their movement primarily in order to glorify sexual promiscuity and take advantage of young women.[77]

The few available testimonies from female hippies suggest that many women, like their male counterparts, found the hippie community a source of empowerment. Kora, who first joined the hippies in Kraków in the late 1960s, remembered her experiences as "an intense time. Thoughts and ideas spiraled around us. A great fusion of theater, literature, psychology. And my youth."[78] Another female hippie, Magdalena, was attracted not only to "the colorful and the fairytale-like [appearance of hippies]" but also to "free love, love for children, togetherness, and generosity." When interviewed in 2013, Magdalena rejected the idea that the hippie movement was male dominated. Rather, "women gave the movement character! They were the matrons. Women were strong, courageous, and they were the ones to decide to give birth!"[79] The last statement pointed to motherhood as a choice. But the testimony also suggested that traditional gender roles influenced the dynamics of the hippie community. Motherhood could be a source of empowerment, as Magdalena suggested, especially if children were raised in a communal setting. More often than not, however, hippie women remained overwhelmingly responsible for pregnancy and childcare.

Hippies practiced what they called "free relationships" or "free love," which were interpreted in many ways. For some, it meant an informal monogamous relationship; for others, it entailed multiple sexual partners. The terms typically referred to heterosexual relations, confirming the observation that the patriarchal order was replicated in hippie communities. Yet others practiced sexual abstinence. The founder of a commune near Kielce who went by the nickname Gnome, for example, stayed away from sexual activity. According to Tarzan, who temporarily lived with the commune, Gnome's life included "sleeping, eating, and reading books about Hindu philosophy, which he carried in his backpack and did not let anyone touch, as well as going on lonely forest walks. He spoke to almost no one."[80]

Likewise, Catholic communes, which drew selectively on hippie philosophy, made abstinence from sex, drugs, and alcohol one of their central principles, at least in theory. Tarzan, who found a temporary shelter with a Catholic commune in the early 1970s, was struck by the gender division they practiced, which contrasted with the communes he had seen thus far. "The girls slept separately from the boys," Tarzan reported. "I thought this segregation was absurd. After all, if I wanted to be abstinent, I could restrain myself even while sleeping with a naked girl in bed with me." When Tarzan found himself at the apartment of a female Catholic where young people came for food and shelter, he was surprised that she took it upon herself to fix a meal for her guest. "I felt a bit embarrassed," Tarzan wrote, "that someone was taking care of me. In our communes everyone helped themselves. But Maria refused my offers to help." She was also hesitant at first to let Tarzan stay overnight, but after he made it clear he respected her sexual restraint ("What do you think I am, some kind of animal?") she rolled out a mattress for him on the floor.[81]

The vision of egalitarian gender relations found in personal testimonies reveals as much as it conceals. No doubt, limited access to birth control made the experience of "free love" different for women. In addition, some hippies pointed to the persistence of a double sexual standard. Piotr, who in the early 1970s lived in a commune in the Bieszczady Mountains, remembered how difficult it was for some men, who themselves had multiple sexual partners, to accept a similar practice on the part of their female partners. In some cases, as Piotr recalled, the man would preach about the "sexual revolution" to his girlfriend "because this was what he needed at the moment." But if the woman decided to engage with multiple partners, "then suddenly it turned out that this caused wailing and gnashing of teeth [on the part of the man]."[82]

Women often paid the price of the male-oriented sexual liberation. Tarzan's experience of spending winter in a commune located in the apartment of a young mother, Halina, offers a glimpse of the persistent gender inequality that restricted the lives of female hippies, especially if they became mothers: "there is a lot of tension as some visitors with withdrawal symptoms or paranoia drop by. On top of that, Halina has a small child. If she were not taking enough tranquilizers to kill a horse, she would be finished. It was from her that I learned how to eat this poison [tranquilizers], which before I would not have touched with a ten-foot pole. . . . In the end, everyone is angry at everybody about everything. I clench my teeth, gobble dope, and wait for spring. As soon as the snow melts, I hit the road."[83] The contrast between Tarzan's freedom to move on and Halina's confinement to a stable residence is a telling one. Men were free to stay or go. Female hippies with children rarely had such a choice.

Living Dangerously

Tarzan's story about a commune in which drug addiction replaced philosophy and artistic activity reveals the dark side of the hippie movement. Living free often meant living dangerously. Drug addiction tends to be marginalized in personal narratives of the hippies, but it constituted an important dimension of the hippie experience. Tarzan, who became an addict, spoke about the toll the drugs took on the community: "I saw people become slaves to their addiction. And I saw those who died from overdosing."[84] What historian Alice Echols said about American hippies "being involved in high-risk experimentation, often with the self the site of experimentation," applied to their Polish counterparts as well.[85] In Poland, the practice was shaped by the limited access to drugs and a changing hippie philosophy.

Not all hippies used drugs, and not all the time. Those who were religiously inclined often preferred to stay away from addictive substances. Some of the first hippies rejected the idea of taking drugs for pleasure and thought it was important to take only those drugs that were believed to enhance one's perception, such as marijuana and LSD. For them, the goal was to achieve higher levels of self-understanding.[86]

Access to drugs was far more restricted than in the West. Small amounts of LSD and hashish reached Poland through foreign visitors or Poles who went abroad. But more common were homemade narcotics and pharmaceuticals. Methyl chloroform (known as *tri*), for example, could be found in a stain-removing bleach available in Polish stores. Some hippies discovered that sniffing the bleach caused hallucinations. Another popular drug was a weight-loss pill, Phenmetrazine, commonly known as Pherma, available in pharmacy stores; it contained amphetamine. Since Pherma could not be obtained over the counter, some hippies specialized in forging medical prescriptions. Others staged break-ins into pharmacies in order to steal Pherma.[87]

Those hippies who rejected pharmaceuticals and preferred marijuana often took to growing their own "grass" (*trawa*) on the balconies of their apartments or in small garden plots. The seeds were usually obtained from abroad. Neither customs control officials nor militiamen paid attention to the plants, as they did not know – according to the hippies - what marijuana was.[88] If *trawa* was not to be had, some hippies tried to make a powder out of dried bananas and smoke it. Others gathered or cultivated local mushrooms and herbs, such as sage, believed to cause hallucinations. There were also those who hoped that eating large amounts of nutmeg could help achieve a similar effect.[89]

By the early 1970s, some hippie groups turned to taking drugs as their sole activity. Tarzan's life story is emblematic of the dual nature of the hippie movement. After his initial phase of involvement, dominated by spiritualism and philosophy, he became addicted to drugs and alcohol. His addiction, unlike that of many others, ended with successful detox therapy. While producing drug addicts, the hippie movement also made the problem of drug addiction part of the public discourse and medical practice in Poland. By the early 1970s, self-help groups and other therapeutic methods had become part of the countercultural scene. One of the movement's goals was to raise public awareness of the problem and educate young people about the harmful effects of drugs. Tarzan eventually began working for Monar, a network of institutions and professionals established in the 1970s to treat drug addiction.[90]

Through the 1970s, the militia targeted hippie communities primarily on account of drug possession. State surveillance of the hippies, however, started earlier and was primarily motivated by ideological and moral factors. The hippies were suspected of spreading "alien" ideas among the youth. A security apparatus report from September 1969 depicts the movement as inauthentic and deceptive: "this imported alien strain of pseudo-philosophy and subculture, purporting to refresh the youth movement, is a potentially dangerous phenomenon, because it brings with itself the conception of nonideology, indifference, and fringe egocentrism."[91] The hippies' support for pacifism, draft dodging, and desertion were of particular concern to the state, as was the rejection of "state administration, borders, and the concepts of nation and family."[92]

From the beginning, the hippies became subject to not only state surveillance but also state violence. Hippie rallies, though often remembered in idealistic ways by the participants, were often disrupted by militia raids and beatings. In 1969, at the rally in the Świętokrzyskie Mountains, militiamen unleashed dogs and subjected the hippies to a gauntlet, a particular method of torture that had been used in 1956 against participants in the workers' uprising in Poznań.[93] In 1972, hippies were attacked by the militia in Częstochowa, the site of the Virgin Mary shrine that was thought to be safe as a place of worship. The hippies were camping just outside the Paulinian Fathers and Brothers Monastery when militia armed with clubs surrounded the place. As the beatings started, some hippies ran to the monastery's gate, which was locked at the time. As Zappa remembered, "they eventually opened the gate, but the whole action lasted for more than twenty minutes, and none of the clergy took notice of what was happening during that time."[94]

Verbal and physical attacks on the hippies rarely provoked outrage from society, as many people considered the long-haired men and women a threat to family and morality. The violence from the state often encouraged others to commit similar acts. Hippies were regularly physically attacked by local hooligans, especially by the subcultural group made up of former criminal prisoners, known as *garownicy*.[95]

Surviving documents of the security apparatus offer glimpses of the state's surveillance of the hippie community. The surveillance methods included gathering information about the movement and regularly conducting what were called "preventative-cautionary conversations" with the suspected hippies and their parents.[96] While this may sound innocent, this form of questioning young people and their parents typically involved intimidation and emotional abuse.

The handwritten personal "statements" by young people found in the security apparatus files can be emotionally challenging to read. These testimonies often focused on details from private lives that the subjects most likely were pressured to reveal. Moreover, the bulk of personal testimonies came from young women, who were usually subjected to interrogation by men.[97] Given the numerical predominance of men in the hippie movement, the large number of female testimonies raises questions. From reading the documents, one could infer that the security functionaries targeted young women, many of them still teenagers, on purpose. First, the interrogators took advantage of these women's subordinate position in society as females and the fact that they were usually subjected to more discipline from family and community than were young men. The security officers might have thought that young women would be more easily intimidated and willing to talk, especially if their parents cooperated, too. Second, since women were considered to be

less politically aware than men in the eyes of the state, the security functionaries might have assumed that female hippies were less committed to the
movement and more open to revealing its "secrets." Finally, apart from the
"rational" motivation to extract information, going after vulnerable young
females was a way for interrogators to perform and affirm their masculinity
by exercising power over people weaker than them. In that context, gender
functioned as a deliberate tool of power and a technique in the surveillance
process.

The personal statements gathered by the security apparatus follow a distinct script. They typically start with a description of the author's first encounter with the hippies. Young women usually claim to have joined the
hippies temporarily, because of a boyfriend or out of curiosity. They claim to
be uncommitted and underinformed. The testimonies typically end with a
declaration of intention to leave the hippies. Such declarations often employ
the vocabulary of the state and may have been suggested or dictated by the
interrogators. A typical concluding statement reads: "I definitely severed ties
with the hippie movement. I consider the hippie movement to be socially
harmful. In my opinion, this constantly expanding group that entices young
people could influence the rest of society in irresponsible ways."[98]

The hippies found few allies even within their own families. Parents
tended to cooperate with the militia and the security apparatus in tracking
down and apprehending their own children. In some cases, they joined the
state in perpetrating violence on the hippies. In one case from January 1970,
a young woman from Warsaw who became a hippie was confronted by her
father after returning home late in the evening. The two had an argument,
and the father hit his daughter in the head, knocking her out with a con-
cussion. The daughter was then taken to the hospital, where she stayed for
a week. There were no recorded consequences for the father. Rather, the incident was related to the security officers by the young woman's mother in a
matter-of-fact way. The mother then complained that even after that experience, her daughter still associated with the hippies and eventually ran away
from home to live in the commune ran by Zakrzewska.[99]

Breaking away from societal constraints entailed significant risks. For
some, the "high-risk experimentation, often with the self the site of experimentation," led to drug addiction and sometimes death. Those who survived
often had to live with traumatic memories of losing friends. The search for
freedom also meant a painful confrontation with the established social and
political structures, be it the communist state or traditional society.

Going Mainstream: *Hipisowanie*

By the early 1970s, the adoption of elements of hippie dress and lifestyle had become widespread, especially among students and young intelligentsia. The trend was colloquially referred to as *hipisowanie*. The growing acceptance of *hipisowanie* stemmed, in part, from political change at the highest echelons of the state. In December 1970, Władysław Gomułka was ousted from power as the result of a workers' revolt on the Baltic Coast. The new First Secretary, Edward Gierek, proved to have a more cosmopolitan outlook than his predecessor. Shortly after assuming power, he made himself known as a leader open to the West and attentive to Polish citizens' consumer needs.

At the threshold of the 1970s, long-haired young men came to be accepted as a new cohort of students and professionals who were contributing their creativity and education to the broader society. Kraków journalist Jerzy Lovell called them the "bearded ones" (*brodacze*). This new term helped bring about a reinterpretation of hippie styles in a positive light. Lovell described *brodacze*, whom he regularly saw at Kraków cafés, as "dressed in a quiet manner with a certain distinction even if their style was casual. They act in balanced and solemn ways."[100]

For many, *hipisowanie* became a personal project of self-creation. For Irena Groblewska, who described herself as an "internal hippie," taking on a hippie appearance was "a refuge from the greyness of the communist system, because there were no other ways. I walked through downtown Warsaw in long floral dresses, barefoot, with a hat on my head."[101] Krzysztof Jerzy Baranowski from Poznań spoke about his "mental engagement" with what he called "post-hippism." This involved an unconventional appearance: "I had a big, black and green sweater that I loved. I used to wear it all fall and winter. It reached my knees like a toga. . . . I also—very controversially for the time—pierced my ear."[102] Tomasz Rodowicz pointed to the significance of a hippie appearance as a sign to others. Outer looks such as colorful clothing and long hair were not "shallow" matters of fashion but enabled "easy identification" of like-minded people.[103]

For some, hippie music became an important way to express themselves. "We didn't listen to the Beatles any more," Bolesław Kuźniak remembered. "Instead, we listened to King Crimson, who had a more complex emotional and liberated depth to their music." Kuźniak considered music to be a pure form of counterculture. "Communists took over everything in Poland," he added, "but music was something they could not control; music came into being in all those places in which they did not rule."[104] Rodowicz organized psychedelic dance parties in the basement of his parents' house. Young people who gathered there used the slide projector to display colored dyes and danced to the music of King Crimson, Jimi Hendrix, and Ten Years After. Rodowicz remembered: "we sipped red wine (it was still hard to get our hands on pot), and we felt like we were on top of the world."[105] Although these interviewees expressed strong anticommunist feelings, it is significant that Kuźniak echoed the hippie desire to distance themselves from the conventional political action of the time. The goal of their cultural style was not to "get rid of communism" but "to bring about a different way of living in the world."[106]

Going International: The Student Theater Festivals

Hipisowanie acquired an unexpected institutional dimension when it became entangled with the changing landscape of the Student Theater. By the late 1960s, the Student Theater had evolved to presenting more experimental art, often combined with political undertones. Student theater groups were at the forefront of what was called "speaking one's mind," as part of the radicalization of art and culture after 1968.[107] For sociologist Elżbieta Matynia, the Student Theater became a vehicle for "performative democracy" understood as "a substitute for civil society."[108]

Matynia describes a breakthrough play, *Without Stopping for Breath* (Jednym tchem), written by a young Polish poet, Stanisław Barańczak. The play was first staged in December 1971 by the Eight Day Theater from Poznań. The play is set at a blood donation facility, where a television journalist is interviewing a worker donating blood in an effort to create a propaganda portrait of an "average" donor. Matynia describes the performance and the impact it made on the audience:

> After a while it becomes clear to the characters in the play—the nurse, the average man, the journalist, the petty bureaucrat—that they are all simply acting according to a script written for them by somebody else, somebody they do not have access to. When the incessant and clearly physically exhausting routine provokes resistance among the "average" blood donors, the rubber pipes meant for donating blood become the tools of punishment and incarceration. The actors wash their faces in a bucket of red paint

as though it is water. The protest in the blood donation center ends up in bloodshed. An innocent person is killed. Full of passion and desperation, the performance ended with a song: "It's only the word, 'no,' have it in your blood / That runs down the wall, drop by drop at dawn." At the play's end, the audience did not move, for it could hardly believe what it had just seen. No one wanted to leave a room where one could speak the unspeakable.[109]

Without Stopping for Breath was different from performances by the Thaw-era Student Theater groups, such as the Student Theater of Satirists or the Bim-Bom. The transformation of the Student Theater into an organization that expressed explicit messages about power and politics was in part a result of the increasing interaction with the international countercultural arts that took place at such settings as the International Festival of Student Theater Festivals in Wrocław. The festival was another example of cultural diplomacy in which theater groups from East and West came together to perform and socialize with each other. Although this event was officially sanctioned on both sides of the Iron Curtain, the theater groups and audiences, to a large extent, subverted the agendas of their respective governments.

Such subversion was not immediately obvious. The festival was possible, in part, because communist regimes tended to see counterculture as an exclusively Western phenomenon. For these reasons, Western European and American experimental theaters that opposed "bourgeois values," from imperialism to consumerism, were welcome in Poland and were believed to enhance the legitimacy of the socialist system. This is not to say that the Polish state supported Western counterculture. On the contrary, Polish leaders viewed it with the utmost suspicion and anxiety and as antithetical to any social, political, or moral order. Yet at least some Party-state officials believed that Western counterculture could be instrumentalized.

Although inspired by contemporary global trends, the Wrocław festival harkened back to the domestic tradition of the Thaw. Bogusław Litwiniec, the mastermind behind the event and the director of the Festival Bureau, started out as a student "radical" during the Thaw. In 1956, he cofounded Wrocław-based *Views* as part of critical journalism of the era. When the Gomułka regime shut down independent student publications a year later, he and a friend, Eugeniusz Michaluk, looked for another outlet for their creative energies. Soon, they launched a theater group in Wrocław called Kalambur. Like other Student Theater groups at the time, Kalambur was, more than an artistic group, a way of life that cherished human creative powers. Bogusław remembered: "we belonged to the group of young people who sewed their own clothes, wrote plays, even sculpted from clay. This is how our hippie philosophy took shape."[110] For him, the embrace of international counterculture was a natural outgrowth of the Thaw.

In the mid-1960s Bogusław Litwiniec won a two-year scholarship to the University of Nancy in France. His formal studies included avant-garde theater and art. He also attended performances at the World Theater Festival, one of the best known experimental theater festivals hosted by Nancy at the time.[111] He returned from France filled with new ideas. As he explained, "I could not stand knowing that half the world could not experience the idea of a theater festival like the West has. . . . I said to myself: I am going to do this better than Nancy!"[112]

In May 1967, Bogusław organized what he called the International Festival of Student Theater Festivals, involving fourteen foreign and four Polish theater groups. The festival was not a typical competition, as there were no official rankings or awards.[113] Both Polish and international press lauded the event as a success of cultural diplomacy. The Polish press praised the "first encounter" of large segments of international youth "with the achievements of our society and our culture," while foreign commentators applauded Poland's openness to progressive art and willingness to bridge Cold War divides. Encouraged by these enthusiastic responses, Polish officials agreed to hold the festival every other year.[114]

The second and third festivals, held in October 1969 and October 1971, respectively, were carefully prepared by Bogusław and his associates with assistance from local and state officials and were widely advertised nationally and internationally.[115] The Festival Council included representatives of the ZSP, the Ministry of Culture and Art, the Ministry of Foreign Affairs, and several artists and theater critics.[116] High-ranking Polish political officials in charge of culture, such as Julian Motyka and Józef Tejchma, were invited to the festival as honorary guests.[117]

A total of five Polish and sixteen foreign theater troupes participated in the second festival in October 1969. In selecting foreign theater groups, the Festival Council took into consideration not only their artistic quality but also their "left-wing views and friendly attitude toward Poland."[118] Foreign participants in 1969 included groups from Zagreb, Budapest, Bucharest, Avignon, Amsterdam, Denmark, Genoa, Bradford, and most memorable, the Bread and Puppet Theater from New York.[119] These accounted for as many as 400 artists. An equal number of critics and journalists from abroad also attended the event. Two years later, theater groups from Japan and Brazil joined the festival. For the first time, the festival audience included 60 foreign tourists, who came with the assistance of the Polish student tourist bureau, Almatur. The 1971 festival was attended by an estimated audience of 25,000.[120]

In accordance with the experimental theater formula, the festival actively engaged the audiences. Performances were usually followed by a discussion between the actors and the viewers, who could also attend theater rehearsals and film showings.[121] All participants were encouraged to act in nonconventional ways throughout the festival. The daily *Courier* printed by the organizers every morning during the festival suggested that "in the theater one should feel at home, drinking, smoking, and flirting."[122] The festival became a microcosm in which attendees could experiment with counterculture.

Fig. 6.6 International Festival of Student Theater Festivals in Wrocław. Photo by Irena Jarosińska. OK_0500_0036_0028_006. Courtesy of KARTA Center Foundation.

Internal state documents reveal surprisingly little anxiety regarding potentially undesirable Western influence on Polish youth during the festival.
Although undercover security apparatus functionaries and informants mingled with the crowd during the festival, Party-state officials primarily saw the
event as an ideological opportunity to showcase the achievements of communist Poland to Western audiences.[123] The festival offered an opportunity for
Wrocław, so recently incorporated into Poland, to be seen as genuinely Polish
by international audiences. Strategies included familiarizing foreign guests
with the "cultural achievements" of Wrocław as well as "facilitating contact
with working-class youth" and showing "the natural beauty of Lower Silesia."[124]

Locals remembered the festivals as a week of ceaseless celebrations that
"enlivened the streets" of Wrocław.[125] Young people bonded not so much
over the anticapitalist agenda of the festival, as the Party-state had hoped, as
over newly discovered shared values and ideas. Edward Chudziński, editor
of the Kraków magazine *Student*, traveled to the Wrocław festival in October
1969 together with his friends to become personally acquainted with people
from the international New Left. As he explained in an interview in 2012,
"the knowledge we had had about the New Left thus far was largely theoretical." He found the contrast between the Polish Student Theater and the
New Left artists to be stark and fascinating. When a group of Western actors came to watch a performance by the Wrocław pantomime theater Gest
(Gesture), "they could only take ten minutes of it." According to Chudziński,
the Western actors objected to the aesthetic purpose of the art displayed by
Gest. "Art?" they shouted at the Polish performers, "meanwhile when people
are dying in Vietnam and Africa, you are going to make art?"[126]

Indeed, former students, artists, hippies, and others have pointed to the
1969 festival as an eye-opening experience. In contrast to contemporary
Polish actors, their Western counterparts, in the words of director Lech
Raczak, "had the courage to show up on an undecorated stage, with no
costumes, props, or prepared dramaturgy, to speak about our times, to una-
bashedly deliver political slogans, which did not always find fertile ground in
Poland, but one could feel resonated somewhere else." The Bread and Puppet
Theater made a lasting impression on Polish participants by introducing
street theater and using puppets with no speech in their performances. Their
plays, as Raczak recalled in 2008, nevertheless "told shocking stories that
were relatable to everyone."[127]

* * *

The Polish practitioners of the counterculture searched for an alternative way of life to both communism and traditional national culture. Likewise, they distanced themselves from any anticommunist or reform movements. Eschewing geopolitics, many hippies felt themselves to be part of an international counterculture, despite condemnation from the regime, society, and often their own families. The hippie societal critique was located in the persistent attempt to assert what they understood as universal human values and to push the boundaries of social convention.

The story of the decline of hippie culture in Poland is similar to that of contemporary countercultures elsewhere. In America, the end of the idealistic counterculture community was marked by the Charles Manson murders and the violence that erupted at the rock concert at the Altamont Speedway in northern California in 1969. In Poland, the decline is believed to have taken place in the early 1970s. At that time, the earliest hippies went on to get married and have families. Some left Poland for the West. The younger hippies, at least in the eyes of the movement's pioneers, understood little of countercultural philosophy but rather were drawn to hedonism and drugs. Yet both these narratives of decline miss important parts of the counterculture's continuity. Counterculture persisted through the 1970s on both sides of the Iron Curtain, entering the mainstream through commercial endeavors or as new movements focused on environmentalism, feminism, and myriad other causes.[128] By the early 1970s in Poland, the circle of those who practiced *hipisowanie* had expanded and affected both the official culture and the emerging anti-communist opposition in unexpected ways.

7

The World in the Village

Rural Rebels in Search of Modernity

In the late 1960s, Andrzej Sadowski left his native village in eastern Poland to study sociology in Warsaw. In an interview in 2013, he remembered growing up in a world far removed from modern civilization "where everything was made by hands, even clothes and work tools were handcrafted. There was almost nothing from outside except for sugar and salt." By the time he entered the university, "farm machines appeared in our village, and this was an epoch-making event."[1] The story exemplified the experience of many young people who ventured from the village into the outside world in the 1960s. Not only the mechanization of farm work and consumer goods but also the media and youth culture brought about significant changes to rural life.

Until the mid-1960s, the majority of Poles lived in the countryside. Even as these numbers shifted toward the urban population, at the close of the 1960s as many as 16 million people still resided in the 70,000 villages scattered all over Poland, most of them inhabited by anywhere from 100 to 400 people. In addition, the so-called colonies, or individual farmhouses, located at the outskirts of the village made up about 35 percent of all rural infrastructure.[2] For all the public celebration of youth as the embodiment of modernity, villagers often grew up in conditions that bore little resemblance to anything modern. By 1968, only 20 percent of farm households were equipped with running water or a water pump inside the home, and the majority of villagers got their water from a well. Only 7 percent of farm dwellings could boast of a well-equipped modern bathroom.[3]

Such rural environments were not unique to Poland or Eastern Europe at the time but were similar to many of those in the less developed capitalist countries and the Global South. In rural Italy, for example, the most rapid modernization, including the rise of consumer culture and the exposure to modern mass media, took place between the late 1950s and the late 1960s, while villages just south of Rome continued to lack running water, electricity, and radios. This was true of countless other such places in Italy, Greece,

Imagining the World from Behind the Iron Curtain. Malgorzata Fidelis, Oxford University Press. © Oxford University Press 2022. DOI: 10.1093/oso/9780197643402.003.0008

Spain, Portugal, and parts of France such as Brittany.[4] The rural experience of the sixties, perhaps more than anything else, cut across geopolitical divides.

The rural encounter with the cultural and political upheavals of the global sixties had its own distinct characteristics. While villagers experienced cultural and technological change of massive proportions, for young rural people, becoming "global" was first and foremost about breaking free from the confines of the village and the region. In the Polish countryside, this process unfolded in ambiguous ways.

October 1956 was a turning point for the rural population. Bowing to strong peasant resistance, Gomułka, as new first secretary, dismantled the collectivization of agriculture, allowing for the return to private farming and ownership of land. This also meant that farmers, as nonstate workers, were excluded from social benefits available to the urban population, for example salaries, pensions, vacation time, and disability and medical insurance. Moreover, the state reduced but did not eliminate the burdensome tax payments and delivery quotas for agricultural products that were imposed on farmers during Stalinism. Indeed, it was not until the demise of Gomułka and the coming to power of Edward Gierek in the early 1970s that these burdens were abolished and villagers became eligible for most of the provisions of the state welfare system, including universal healthcare.

Gomułka's retreat from collectivization was designed as a temporary measure with the understanding that the village needed more time to prepare for the socialist transformation. Although most farmers were relieved by the decision, their position remained precarious. Lacking access to state benefits and burdened by excessive taxation, they occupied an ambiguous space between socialist modernity and traditional farming.

But if Poland failed to change property relations in the countryside— critical to the socialist transformation in the eyes of the state, how would the villagers become modern socialist citizens? The answer, in part, came from urban-based professionals and politicians, who encouraged intense cultural activity as the primary mode for modernizing the village. Enhancing "the intellectual-cultural level of the peasant masses," members of the Wrocław provincial Party chapter concurred in 1965, was "the key condition for socialist transformation."[5] Such transformation could not take place in isolation, as being modern required intercultural connections and knowledge about the world. Young villagers, whether in their capacity as local activists or regular residents, proved eager to challenge the traditional isolation of rural life. From technological innovation to new forms of leisure, young rural men and women brought the global sixties to the Polish countryside. In the process, they searched for their own identities as independent young people no longer defined by family relations and village hierarchies.

Rural youth recorded their experiences of this period of change in auto-biographies submitted to state-sponsored memoir competitions organized by the ZMW in conjunction with popular magazines.[6] Memoir competitions were not new in communist Poland. Left-wing intellectuals had started them before the war in an effort to seek out voices of the lower classes.[7] What was new after 1945, however, was the swelling volume and diversity of the participating rural actors who were able and willing to write, including increased numbers of women.[8] Females made up one-quarter to half of all the participants, and many belonged to the first generation of rural women who were able to read and write.[9]

The very act of writing testified to the new role of rural actors as both subjects and agents of modernity. This role included new conceptions of the self and the importance of personal voice. The desire to express themselves to a larger, nonvillage audience was visible in the materiality of the memoirs. Most of these authors wrote in schoolbooks, filling in almost every line with elaborate handwriting. Some sent in pictures and drawings. Villagers often spoke about what they considered their undeserved inferior position in Polish society. In this sense, the act of writing was the act of becoming visible to the larger world.

Picking up a pen was not always motivated by the eagerness to prove one-self in the eyes of the commission or to see one's story published in a mag-azine. Writing often served a deeply intimate and therapeutic purpose.[10] Some young women used the act of writing to lift the taboo of domestic vi-olence they experienced or witnessed. This was yet another way the chan-ging culture of the sixties and the stress on modernity enabled young women not only to relieve their emotional distress but also to expose the cruelty of gender norms within traditional rural milieux.

The Long Road to School

What had enabled so many to participate in these competitions and share their memoirs was a dramatic expansion in literacy in the postwar years. The socialist state rapidly brought elements of modernity to villages across Poland, insisting that peasants read, write, and develop a socialist

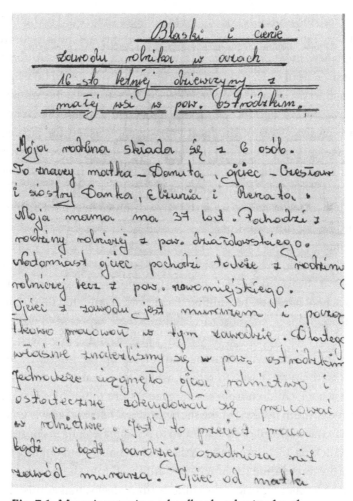

Fig. 7.1 Memoir entry in a schoolbook, submitted to the Memoirs of Rural Youth competition, 1972. Irena L., "The Ups and Downs of a Farmer's Occupation in the Eyes of a Sixteen-Year-Old Girl from a Small Village in the District of Ostróda." AAN, TPP, PMW, 5228, no. 88.

consciousness. By the early 1960s, as a result of mass schooling, illiteracy in rural areas dropped from 20 percent, where it had hovered in the late 1930s, to a mere 2.7 percent.[11] The literacy campaign brought discrete modernizing forces into the insular lives of villagers, forces often met with resistance. To accommodate the growing number of students, the state built numerous primary schools in rural areas. But even as new schools were constructed, they often serviced several villages that could be half a dozen miles apart. Take the village of Łukowo near the city of Chojnice in western Poland, where most children had to walk almost four miles to the closest elementary school in Czersk. During winter, the walk could take up to two hours each way. Going by bike reduced the time to forty-five minutes, but biking was not an option during the snowy winter months. When concerned representatives of the local Party chapter asked for farmers who would take children to school in a horse-driven wagon for a payment of 1,500 zloty per month, no volunteers came forward. Instead, the farmers told the Party officials "it is a waste to keep a horse in the cold like that" or that they themselves had to walk the same distance to school as their children and "everything was fine."[12]

The education drive was also hindered by widespread poverty and the nature of farm work. When a freshly minted female teacher moved to a village in 1965, she found that her students were poorly dressed and some even came to school barefoot. In addition, farm work dominated their daily lives. As the teacher observed, most rural children were expected to wake up at 6 AM. After they had breakfast, they let the chickens out, helped feed younger siblings, and assisted with cleaning and tidying up the house. By 9:30 AM, children were on their way to school, where they remained until 2:30 PM. While at school, children from several grades were sometimes crammed together in one room because of the shortage of teachers and space. Once their school day was over, children continued to participate in farm chores such as feeding chickens, picking eggs from the chicken house, and tending to cattle. They hardly found time for homework until well into the evening. By that time, as the teacher reported, the child "is tired, sleepy, makes mistakes, and hurries, or gives up on the homework and goes to sleep."[13]

Family life rarely provided a nurturing environment for village children. Many female authors of the memoirs recounted growing up with alcoholic and violent fathers. In describing instances of violence against themselves, their mothers, and their siblings, these women authors usually considered these experiences painful but nevertheless a "normal" part of rural life that they had no choice but to suffer and endure. One author, Weronika, tried to explain why she thought the violence she experienced was worth mentioning at all. "Maybe you think what I've written is unimportant," she wrote,

but I did not write this in hopes of winning the prize. I am only writing in order to express myself since you won't judge or laugh at me, because

I haven't even written the half of what I have experienced cause I would not even know how to describe it. There were fights, and I was maltreated not only with harsh words but also with beatings from my brothers, but I don't want to open old wounds. . . . Please, don't publish my letter in your magazine, unless you change something, because they would find out and I would be in trouble.[14]

Such statements confirm the widespread tolerance of domestic violence in postwar Polish society, despite condemnation from the state. It was common for rural communities, for example, to accept wife-beating if the wife was suspected of laziness or disobedience of her husband.[15] Rural wives and children who suffered domestic violence found fewer escape routes than those in the cities from harmful circumstances. The village cultural tradition and limited economic opportunities for women meant that children had to learn to adjust to the situation, at least until they moved out of the family household. In that context, mass schooling instituted by the state had a distinct emancipatory effect for rural youth. It helped equip village kids with writing skills and enabled them to pursue a pathway to further education. It instilled the desire and a way to leave the village.

But the road to further education after the compulsory seven years of primary school was not easy.[16] This endeavor required either relocation or a lengthy daily commute. No wonder rural youth were underrepresented in secondary and higher education. In 1968, as many as 44 percent of students in the college-preparatory high schools, the lycée, came from the urban intelligentsia, while 27 percent came from working-class households, and only 17.7 percent from villages.[17]

In many cases, rural parents simply could not afford to send their children off to school in the city. Coming from a farm family of eight kids, Zofia wrote in her memoirs that to attend a secondary school, "the eagerness . . . good academic standing . . . were not enough." She needed financial resources, and "in my parents' material situation this was extremely difficult."[18] Eventually, she became one of two from her village at the time to attend a secondary school in a nearby town. Another young woman, Józefa, from Silesia, was lucky to receive financial aid from the secondary school she attended and a room in a dormitory. She dreamt of studying Oriental philology at the prestigious Jagiellonian University in Kraków but instead settled for the Higher School of Education in the nearby city of Cieszyn, because the latter offered her financial support.[19]

It was not unusual for parents to undercut their children's intellectual aspirations. Rural parents tended to accept the need for vocational training, which usually required from one to three years beyond the primary school, but they had a harder time understanding the purpose of education at the secondary or university level. One young woman complained that she had not been able to "fulfill her dreams" of attending a secondary school, "only because my parents did not let me study . . . there weren't any hands to do the work on our property." Intervention from her teachers did not help. After completing elementary school, she remained in her parents' household "with bitterness in my heart and a hatred for the farm."[20] Yet the very fact that she had "dreams" suggested that education had brought new worldviews and a sense of possibility to young villagers.

Generational conflict, while not new to the village, came to be marked by the educational superiority of the youth to their elders. Many young people not only craved education but sought to implement what they had learned in school in their environment. A young woman tried to persuade her father to replace a horse with a tractor and to modernize the front yard, the kitchen, and the cowshed, all to no avail. Her father snapped at her: "you're just a brat and I am the boss here!"[21] A young man complained that he was treated by his parents "like a serf" as they gave him little money even though he worked hard on the farm. What was most upsetting to him, however, was that his input on farming was unwelcome. Instead, the father told him to wait until he inherited the farm. The young man was torn: "how do I change my fate?" he asked. "Shall I wait for my father to die or shall I run away from the village?"[22]

Such conflicts with parents prompted many young people to permanently leave their villages. But those who stayed still resisted the outdated rural hierarchies based on age, gender, and family relations. By the early 1960s, rural youth was in a full-fledged rebellion that embraced adopting new technologies, challenging traditional gender relations, and incorporating urban lifestyles.

Rural Rebels

Although it was the urban youth, mostly university students, who stood at the center of the March 1968 demonstrations, in a metaphorical sense the village also had its "generation of 1968," or rather, multiple rebellious generations who came of age during the long sixties. Their formative experiences were grounded in economic, cultural, and technological transformations that swept the Polish countryside at the time and often began in the schoolhouse.

The experience of one's youth was shaped differently in urban and rural areas. The students who protested in 1968 had mostly been born between 1944 and 1949. By that time, the same generational cohort in the country-side was already at a different stage in life, with many village women getting married and forming families at eighteen or nineteen. For young men, the completion of compulsory military service, usually at the age of twenty or twenty-one, marked the time when they looked for a wife. When they returned home from the army, they often married younger women.[23]

Władysław, from a village in the province of Opole, turned twenty-eight in 1968. Like many of his peers, he had a wife and child, and he was a little older than most of the protesting students. His memoir gives a sense of rural concerns at the time. When students demonstrated in Warsaw, he noted the building of a new road that connected his village to the nearby city. The opening of the road in May was attended by local officials: "there were speeches, flowers, ribbon cutting, a bottle of wine and dancing. . . . Everyone was so delighted that guests came all the way from Opole to our rundown little village of Osiek. "[24] For Władysław and many others, opportunities for mobility and connection to the urban world elevated individuals and communities.

In addition to new roads and transportation networks, popular culture helped rural people engage with the outside world. Urban-based youth magazines made their way to rural libraries alongside books, newspapers, and specialized farming publications.[25] In 1956, the ZMW launched the il-lustrated weekly *New Village* (Nowa Wieś), specifically intended for rural audiences. By 1967, it was publishing close to 300,000 copies.[26] Designed to bridge differences between rural and urban environments, *New Village* fea-tured some material from the West but tended to focus on domestic forms of popular culture. Its pages were filled with news and photographs of Polish big beat bands, domestic song festivals, and Polish film actors.[27] The maga-zine also facilitated an exchange of ideas and personal experiences among the readers by publishing their letters and encouraging discussion under the rubric "Give us your thoughts." The topics ranged from family problems and challenges faced by rural migrants in the city to sex education, fashion, rock music, and the hippies.[28]

Opportunities for personal mobility expanded for the village young. Organized vacations, youth camps, and visits to relatives in the city allowed many young people to temporarily experience urban ways of life. When high school students in a small town of Bielsk Podlaski in rural eastern Poland submitted essays about their summer vacations to a memoir competition in 1965, they often wrote about participating in traditional farm labor such as haymaking and harvest. At the same time, almost every student reported traveling to the nearby city of Białystok or to other parts of Poland, for example the Mazurian Lakes or the Baltic coast. Such ventures sometimes resulted in interaction not only with Poles from other parts of the country but also with foreigners. Zdzisława, for example, went to visit her uncle in the coastal city of Gdynia, where she saw the sea for the first time and seamen from Germany and America disembarking at the Gdynia port.[29] Her classmate, Anna, traveled by train to western Poland, where she met a high school student from East Germany, with whom she began exchanging letters.[30]

Not only trains and buses took young people away from the village but also a more individualized and exciting means of transportation: the motorcycle. By the early 1960s, the motorcycle had become an important element of youth culture and a powerful symbol of modern masculinity in the countryside. By 1964, 800,000 private owners of motorcycles could be found in rural areas, most of them young men.[31] The vehicle soon became a commodity imbued with mythical qualities, as it liberated young people from community supervision while offering new sensations of high-speed driving and mastery over technology.

The motorcycle helped construct Polish masculinity as embedded in global connections. Countless young men in Poland coveted Italian-made scooters such as Vespas or Lambrettas, images of which they saw in popular publications and film.[32] The Polish popular automotive magazine *Motor* often reinforced the global dimension of the motorcycle. In 1963, for example, *Motor* published an illustrated report by Franciszek Burdzy, who embarked on a solo adventure in Africa on the Polish-made WFM motorcycle, designed particularly for use in the countryside, "starting from Morocco and finishing in equatorial Cameroon."[33] He reported that the WFM "performed excellently" on the challenging African terrain but, above all, made a lasting impression on locals. "When I entered checkpoints, I expected to be asked to show my passport," Burdzy wrote. "None of the officials, however, were interested in my identification documents; rather, everyone surrounded me and looked over my Polish motorcycle. How efficient is it? How much does it cost? Can they buy it from me?"[34] The motorcycle, especially when inserted into the postcolonial world, helped define

Polish masculinity as distinctly mobile, modern, and superior to other, especially non-European, masculinities.

For young rural men, the motorcycle meant not only personal independence and imagined proximity to the world but also respectability in the local community. It was not uncommon for users and observers to refer to the motorcycle as the "iron steed" and to motorcyclists as "knights."[35] No one better expressed the mythical status of the motorcycle than Józef, a young man from a village in the province of Suwałki in northeastern Poland, who devoted no less than two pages of his memoir to his emotional bond with the Polish-produced Junak, which could be translated as "Daredevil." The name of the motorcycle projected a particular type of masculinity.

Like most young men in the countryside, Józef had craved this motorcycle for a long time before he was able to secure a loan of 5,500 zloty to pay for it in May 1962. The loan, combined with his savings and money he borrowed from his parents, finally allowed him to "become motorized." The new motorcycle excited him so much that he could not stop thinking of it day and night. "I would get up extra early in the morning," he confessed,

Fig. 7.2 "The Polish Motorcycle Republic." Illustration by Zdzisław Jankowski. *Polityka*, 21 July 1962. Warsaw University Library, Warsaw. Courtesy of *Polityka*.

"just to touch it, to hit the kickstarter, to hear the distinct rumble of the engine."[36]

From that time on, Józef commuted to his work at the local Communal National Council on the motorcycle. The distance was only two kilometers, but walking, as he explained, "went out of fashion." The motorcycle created a local sensation. "Everyone admired my motorcycle," he reported, "the head of the Council, the secretary, and the fellow employees. No one had a motorcycle like mine. Even the local girls started noticing me more." After work, he rode the motorcycle to a nearby lake, the city, the movie theater, and soccer matches.[37]

Notwithstanding the motorcycle's strong masculine associations, young women, too, rode it for a similar sensation of personal independence, high speed, and a connection to the outside world. Young female singer Karin Stanek best expressed young women's right to ride motorcycles when she sang a popular song, "Me and My Motorcycle." The lyrics were printed on the cover of *New Village* in October 1964:

> I don't want a Skoda or an Opel
> Ford? Fiat? For what?
> I just hop on my motorcycle!
> And I speed down the highway
> They won't catch me
> either in a Warszawa [a Polish-made car] or a Pobeda [a Soviet-made car]!
> . . .
> My motorcycle, my friend, what sweet music you play/
> We speed into the sunset, just he and I!
> . . .
> I go where I please
> I don't want a Cadillac
> I have my motorcycle[38]

While it is hard to tell how much influence the song "Me and My Motorcycle" had on young women's appropriation of motorcycle culture, numerous rural young women became adept at riding. Some of them "secretly" borrowed motorcycles from their brothers in an effort to escape the watchful eye of the village community. One eighteen-year old young woman from a village in eastern Poland sneaked out of her home in this way, together with her girl-friend, to attend a dance party in a neighboring village, something her family would not allow. Other young women rode motorcycles to isolated lakes or rivers, where they sunbathed and swam in scanty bathing suits, free from the disapproving eyes of village elders.[39]

Starting in 1963, *New Village* organized the national Golden Helmet Competition for male and female motorcyclists riding in pairs. The first such competition attracted 5,000 participants. A year later, the number grew to as many as 18,000. The competition involved riding a motorcycle for more than forty miles and then taking a series of tests, including one on mechanics, for which participants were required to replace a spark plug, start the engine, and perform regular maintenance.[40] *New Village* was unique in encouraging women to ride motorcycles. Other media tended to promote motorbikes, for example the Polish-produced OSA, as more appropriate vehicles for young women to own and utilize.[41]

Enthusiasm for the motorcycle was not equally shared by everyone. Some commentators worried that the passion for the motorcycle impeded other, perhaps more important, standards of modernity, such as hygiene. One female journalist sarcastically commented in 1968 that "the motorcycle had made a spectacular success in the village as opposed to soap."[42] The "spectacular success" of the motorcycle was of equal, if not greater, concern to those who saw themselves as moral guardians of the young. Some village priests vilified the motorcycle as dangerous to moral and religious values, as more and more young people skipped Sunday Mass in favor of riding their motorcycles. "In the old days," one priest remarked, "youth came to the church out of religiosity or a habit, or even as a way to socialize with others. Today, they hop on a motorcycle . . . and they disappear into the wide world."[43]

From the Church to the Club-Café

This priest was not alone in worrying about the potential of the motorcycle to draw young people away from the Church. Although religion continued to inform village culture, secular alternatives increasingly dominated young people's lives. Both could be combined in creative ways, however. Urban visitors often expressed astonishment and frustration at the seeming ease with which villagers reconciled the ostentatious devotion to Catholic rituals with relaxed morals in their private lives. Some believed that the nature of agricultural work made it particularly difficult for the rural population to separate themselves from religion. In 1959, a discussant at the meeting of the Party Press Bureau devoted to the secularization of culture argued that even if a farmer "had a degree in Art History and knew everything about . . . abstract art, and listened to Bartók . . . and had a car . . . that farmer would still be religious."[44] This was because his life depended on natural elements to a degree unimaginable to city dwellers. "Everyone, including you, comrades, gathered at this meeting," the speaker contended, "if you had a small farm . . . you would pray for there not to be any rain; you would pray for the lightening not to strike the hay bales, and for your cow not to get sick." For farmers, the speaker concluded, religion was "a sort of insurance policy."[45]

Religion not only undermined rational thinking, in the eyes of urban elites, but also signaled a dubious cultural taste prevalent in the countryside. To be sure, the communist state cultivated the original folk culture exemplified in regional costumes, crafts, songs, and dances but rejected what it saw as the antiintellectual folk Catholicism. Politicians and intellectuals alike condemned "the heinous display of plastic flowers, figurines of the Virgin Mary made out of papier-mâché . . . and the pseudo-intellectual gibberish of village sermons." Even more dangerous, as villagers migrated to cities, they brought with them "devotional artifacts" and "intellectual backwardness" that poisoned the cultural taste of urban "workers' and intelligentsia milieux."[46] Unrefined peasants seemed to pose no less a threat to the socialist project of "mass culture" than Western pulp.

Traditionally, the Catholic Church exerted tremendous influence on rural communities. Edward Ciupak, who conducted ethnographic research on rural parishes in the 1950s, characterized Roman Catholicism in Poland as more "peasant" than "Roman."[47] Polish Catholicism, according to Ciupak, was "more emotional and practical, and less philosophical and doctrinal."[48] Regular church attendance and religious events governed the social life of peasants. Baptisms, weddings, and funerals were "understood as family-social gatherings rather than liturgical rituals."[49] He noted a deep identification with one's own village, parish, and family, often stemming from strong feelings against the "other," not only city dwellers or people of different religions but even fellow Catholics in the neighboring village. Parishioners from one village looked down on Catholics in a neighboring village whose church had a different patron saint who was deemed "less generous" and "less protective" of his or her worshipers than theirs.[50]

Regardless of the strong feelings about their own exceptionalism, villagers wanted to know more about the world. Church-related social rituals included interactions over the exchange of global news. In one parish, as Ciupak noted, younger villagers, predominantly men, gathered at a cemetery before Sunday

Mass to discuss current events. At the center of these conversations were the village men known as "worldly," who attracted a particular interest because "of their contacts with other milieux." These were individuals who often traveled to the nearby town or city or had lived away from the village at some point in their lives. These men "remained outside the church during the Mass and would enter only for the Elevation, and then go back to the cemetery" to continue the conversation.[51]

This religion-centered village landscape was already changing with postwar migration and urbanization. Transportation networks and industrialization brought new factories and new people to the villages. New "outsiders," such as teachers, doctors, and Party activists, arrived. Newcomers often distinguished themselves by not attending church services and by exposing rural communities to alternative lifestyles and beliefs.

Secularization propelled by the communist state went hand in hand with modernizing efforts within the Church. The 1960s was a turbulent time for Catholics, as the Vatican II Council, held between 1962 and 1965, sought to change the way the Church related to the modern world. A total of sixty-one Polish bishops participated in the Council, including primate Stefan Wyszyński and Kraków bishop Karol Wojtyła, who would become Pope John Paul II in 1978.[52] Although village priests were obliged to read and explain Vatican II documents to the faithful, the Catholic "revolution" had a limited impact on the Polish countryside.

In the late 1960s, the liberal Catholic weekly, Tygodnik Powszechny, lamented the poor knowledge about Vatican II among villagers and widely circulated rumors about "revolutionary changes" within the Church, for example doing away with priests' celibacy. Villagers were also noted for criticizing the newly introduced shorter liturgy. As one farmer explained, he and his neighbors now missed the opportunity to spend more time in the church as a way to relax after a long week's hard work.[53] Some faithful parishioners actively resisted reforms. It was not unusual for groups of older women from rural parishes to travel around the country to check on priests to make sure they did not "modernize the liturgy too much" and that they adhered to "the cult of the Virgin Mary."[54]

Alongside Vatican II, the village was affected by the Church-led celebrations of "the Baptism of Poland" in 1966. According to historian Piotr Kosicki, it was the primate's prioritizing of the Millennium, which also entailed the struggle against communists "for the soul of the Polish nation," that affected the slow implementation of the Vatican II reforms. Not until

early 1968 was the first missal containing prayers and instructions for celebrating the Holy Mass that was not entirely in Latin printed in Poland.[55]
Rather, the Polish Church was busy launching massive religious celebrations
of the "Baptism of Poland" to counter the communist state's secular
celebrations of "One Thousand Years" of the Polish state. The Church's initiative had a strong folk Catholic component, as it included, for example,
a peregrination of the Virgin Mary of Częstochowa icon among different
parishes.[56] The icon began its travels in 1957, and villagers of all ages were
drawn to these celebrations.

Even as practicing Catholics, rural young people increasingly looked for
education, socialization, and leisure outside the religious space. In 1959,
the ZMW launched a national movement to create so-called club-cafés
(*klubokawiarnie*) in the countryside as new spaces to facilitate cosmopolitan urban culture and secular social interaction. Between 1962 and 1965, the
number of club-cafés skyrocketed from 700 to 6,755.[57] The village club-café
offered a variety of activities, from reading the press to pursuing amateur artistic activities. The club-café was typically equipped with a radio and television and featured a retail space where one could purchase snacks, office
supplies, and other consumer goods.[58]

The club-café disrupted rural ways of life by displacing the church and the
village inn from the center of peasant social life. To a large extent, this goal
was accomplished by promoting the urban culture of coffee drinking, thus
far little known to the villagers. Club-cafés popularized natural coffee as a
modern replacement for the hickory coffee traditionally consumed in rural
households. This exotic coffee was not only a drink and a ritual but a vehicle
for altering village culture. The club-cafés were alcohol-free spaces specifically intended to root out the perceived excessive consumption of vodka by
rural men.

The media lauded coffee drinking in the countryside as an unmistakable sign of cultural progress. Headlines such as "A Shot of Espresso Brings
the Village Forward" or "Coffee at a Village Club—The Village Saves Itself
from Cultural Backwardness" regularly appeared in the press. One youth activist from the Poznań area noted the globalizing effect of coffee drinking.
As a frequent traveler between the city and the village on organizational
assignments, he was glad to be able "to spend time feeling civilized in some
godforsaken village the same way one does in Warsaw." Some activists in the
ZMW worried about the "consumer" orientation of the club-cafés, but such
concerns were usually met with counterarguments from other members who

believed that products and services offered there contributed to "the awakening of the cultural and civilizational needs" of the villagers.[59]

With the acquisition of television sets, club-cafés often became a major gathering point for villagers of all ages.[60] Indeed, the village was introduced to the world primarily through television, in contrast to the cities, where other information outlets and forms of entertainment such as theater or concerts were more readily available. In remote areas, one sociologist claimed, television became "a certain kind of ritual, celebrated with great reverence. It not only signified a form of entertainment and relaxation but also satisfied the hunger for knowledge about what was happening outside the village, in the world at large."[61] While in urban areas the television was often perceived as a destructive force taking people away from "the radio, cinema, books, and lectures," in the countryside in the words of Stefan Żółkiewski, "the purpose of the television is different; it activates all the forms of civilized life, including amateur art. . . . It awakens the need for education and information [and] gets people excited about upcoming films they could watch in a traveling cinema."[62]

Watching television at a club-café became a new village ritual. It was customary to remain silent, and smoking was not permitted. Many dressed up for the occasion.[63] Some commentators compared this behavior to that of theater audiences.[64] Television transformed not only village social life but also work patterns. During harvest, farmers made sure to clear the fields at a certain hour so as to watch the evening feature film or episode of a favorite series.[65] Many people of all ages were willing to walk several miles to the nearest club-café to watch their favorite programming. For the most popular shows, such as the Polish mystery series *Kobra*, smaller clubs could not fit in everyone who showed up.[66]

Gendering Rural Modernity

While many rural women migrated to urban areas to take jobs in newly built factories during the Stalinist industrial drive in the early 1950s, women and girls who stayed in the village did not get to experience the economic and personal freedoms associated with the urban environment. Not until the Thaw in the late 1950s did young village women find opportunities to break free from the restrictive gender roles that defined agricultural communities. This was due, in part, to the restoration of the ZMW in 1956, which provided new ways to invigorate these young women's activism. By 1963, 300,000 young women belonged to the ZMW nationwide: 40 percent of the total membership.[67] This was at a time when the total number of rural women between the ages of fifteen and twenty-five was estimated at 1 million.[68] Girls' Councils (Rady Dziewcząt) within the organization provided a framework for empowering these young women. While there is no doubt that the Councils promoted the state agenda, their focus on education, leisure, and cultural uplift provided new tools for members and fellow travelers to use to redefine traditional gender norms in the village. Girls' Councils did not "organize" young women to serve the state. Rather, young rural women used the opportunities and authority of the organization to assert their subjectivity in new ways.

Strong links existed between the club-café and young women. No less than 90 percent of club workers and managers were female, and 54 percent of them were younger than twenty-six.[69] This overrepresentation was not a coincidence. Youth activists and villagers alike thought of women as more qualified than men to educate others on modern values and "civilized" manners. To this effect, young hostesses at the club-café were expected to maintain order and cleanliness, believed to induce the "cultured" behavior of customers. Club-cafés aimed, to a large degree, at uprooting specifically masculine vices such as excessive drinking, cursing, and rude behavior. In one club in the village of Stryszków, a "courageous" young female manager was praised for making "civilized behavior" her priority. As one youth activist reported, "when some guy would stumble in reeking of alcohol, she did not ask for help, but would take him by the collar and walk him out."[70]

The actions of the club hostess showed that young women themselves affirmed and practiced the gendered nature of the civilizing project. Referring to themselves as "the heart of the village," members of the Girls' Councils marked their presence in explicitly feminine ways, such as cultivating special breeds of flowers in their home gardens. This activity was intended not only to beautify the landscape but also to create recognizable symbols of rural young women committed to the civilizing mission in the village.[71]

In memoirs, female authors often referred to boys in their village as "peasants," juxtaposing them against their own presumed position as modern. The peasant, according to this designation, was someone who is "uncultured, primitive, and . . . does not see anything other than messing about in the dirt." Moreover, these "peasants" were not capable of "complex emotions," and needed to be educated in "manners and chivalry."[72] For many young women,

Fig. 7.3 A club-café at the People's House under the patronage of the Rural Youth Association, Kozłowa Góra, near Piekary Śląskie, 1960s. The sign on the wall reads: "Service provided by the ZMW brigades." Photo by Kazimierz Seko. Seko_170_12. Courtesy of KARTA Center Foundation.

the notion of civilization was embedded in specific emotional abilities that village boys lacked and needed to learn from their female counterparts.

In addition to promoting education in state-run agricultural schools and courses to gain "knowledge about the totality of agricultural economy," the modern rural young woman demanded improvements within the household and expanded access to leisure.[73] A delegate to the national congress of Girls' Councils insisted on the access to "modern technology" as an important part of "liberating the village woman" from "the bondage of traditional habits, backward views, and the yoke of hard labor." Technological innovation included not only the household equipment prevalent in urban areas, such as a washing machine, electric iron, and gas stovetop, but also "a tractor, radio, and television."[74] Young females demanded as much access to the mass media as to the mechanized farm and household equipment, all understood as critical to shaping modern lifestyles.

For many young women, modernity started at home. It included not only a fair division of work and access to modern consumerism but also moral and sexual autonomy. By the early 1960s, a quiet sexual revolution had descended on the Polish countryside in which rural young women took personal control over their own bodies away from the traditional village community. Traditionally, family and village communities regulated gender relations and sexual expression. Female premarital sex was accepted, but only according to prescribed norms and local customs. What rural parents feared was not so much their daughters' premarital sexual activity as new, more explicit expressions of sexuality associated with the urban lifestyle.

Fig. 7.4 The People's House under the patronage of the Rural Youth Association, Kozłowa Góra, near Piekary Śląskie, 1960s. A young woman is reading a popular magazine, sitting by a Polish-made radio of the model "Śląsk" (Silesia). Photo by Kazimierz Seko. Seko_170-56. Courtesy of KARTA Center Foundation.

Contemporary ethnographic research pointed to a variety of gender mixing in traditional rural communities. In the Podhale region in the Tatra Mountains, for example, official interactions between young women and men took place in communal farm work and when individual men visited a young woman's family house. But there were also unofficial contacts that sometimes involved sexual activity. If the boy came from a respectable family from the same or a neighboring village, such interaction was usually accepted. For example, in many households the oldest daughter customarily slept in a separate room so that she could receive unsupervised visits from her boyfriend. In traditional rural societies in other parts of Poland, too, mothers were known for instructing their daughters to "get to know the boy better" before entering marriage.[75] These practices were known to everyone in the village but were not acknowledged in public or private conversations.

Premarital pregnancy was not considered a scandal. As ethnographers have noted, getting pregnant "was perceived as a form of social faux pas" by the young woman's family, but usually she would be married off to the child's father or "to someone else, who consciously or unconsciously accepted the parental responsibility."[76] Sexually active young women were stigmatized only if they broke the rules, for example if they refused to marry. By the 1960s, these customs were increasingly being challenged by urban influences and rural young women's aspirations for personal autonomy.

Young women increasingly displayed their sexuality through urban fashion, which village communities rejected. When Józefa, a teenager, and her classmates put on miniskirts, the village older women condemned them for "transgression against tradition." She noted the double standard for city and village: "what is allowed for urban youth is not allowed for us, because our mothers and grandmothers are offended."[77] Another rural young woman, who signed her name as Lolobrygida after an Italian actress, described local outrage when a family's visiting relative from the nearby city of Lublin went outside "in a bikini to get a tan." Village people agreed that "this was a sin, a shame, and God's punishment." Lolobrygida expressed a different opinion: "what I would do to lay down in that same bikini and read a book!" She decided not to do so, however, because she feared the villagers "would poison my life, and this is too much of a price to pay for this one pleasure."[78]

Rules for female modesty were deeply ingrained in village communities and could bring shame and dishonor to a young woman's family. Sometimes parents threatened their daughters with physical punishment or even death if they dared to display their bodies in a nontraditional way. When, on another occasion, Lolobrygida finally decided to put on a swimsuit and "go to the field to weed out beets," her father stopped her. The father told her to "take that trash off" or otherwise he would "pour kerosene over my body and set me on fire."[79] Another village father got upset at his daughter, Marianna, when she refused to marry the man he chose for her. The father reportedly shouted: "you are not my daughter if you do not do as I say!"[80]

The fathers acted in accordance with village tradition that made offspring, regardless of age or sex, nearly completely dependent on parental will as a sign of "respect." But young women found it increasingly difficult to accept unquestionable parental control. Like Marianna, many young women rejected the traditional custom of matchmaking, where parents or other village elders found a suitable husband for them. Young women now considered matchmaking not only outdated but "offensive to the dignity of the human being." Some said that the custom was a kind of "selling . . . that was simply undignified for a modern person."[81]

The story of eighteen-year-old Leokadia illustrates the clash of rural tradition with young women's new understanding of love and marriage. A young man named Edward, who owned a sizeable farm, complete with 20,000 zloty in savings and a motorcycle, asked Leokadia's father for his daughter's hand. But the young woman hardly knew the suitor. When she went out with him to a restaurant in the nearby town of Pacanów, she found him boorish and too forthcoming. "He took a swig of vodka," she reported, "chased it with a pickle, and asked when the wedding was going to happen." She reacted with surprise and instead expressed her desire to continue her education. "How can I get married at the age of eighteen," she explained in her diary, "when I don't yet know anything . . . except only how to work on the farm and in the home, and when I have not yet been really kissed by anyone. And this vodka of his, and this behavior, after all I had only seen him once before." When her date tried to convince her that she "needed no school" and insisted that she drink the vodka with him, she got up and left the restaurant. To the surprise of her parents, she refused to marry Edward.[82]

While taking control over her destiny, the modern rural young woman also sought medical and scientific knowledge about her body. Girls' Councils organized health courses (*szkoły zdrowia*), which featured lectures by doctors and other medical professionals on female anatomy, hygiene, and reproductive health. The courses provided basic medical knowledge as well as more practical information on the specific locations of pharmacies and the help centers of the state-sponsored Society for Conscious Motherhood, where one could obtain contraceptives and advice on birth control and abortion. Female rural leaders believed that health courses were necessary to make young women "truly modern, on all accounts."[83] Such assistance was especially urgent given villagers' limited access to state medical insurance.[84]

At the same time, such science-based knowledge posed a direct threat to Catholic Church teachings and locally produced knowledge based on tradition and villagers' social experience. The very idea of discussing the female body in the form of a public lecture was already considered an attack on rural ways of life and an encouragement for young women to engage in sexual promiscuity. No wonder health courses were met with strong resistance, especially from rural mothers and local priests. In some villages, only boys were allowed to attend the lectures while mothers kept their daughters at home, claiming that they were "too young to be learning about conscious motherhood." In another village in the Olsztyn province, young women were allowed to attend the health courses, but the village priest ordered a compulsory "general confession" shortly after the instructions concluded. The female attendees felt humiliated and complained to the local chapter of the ZMW.[85]

Although village communities resisted sex education, the health courses expanded through the 1960s. By January 1960, Girls' Councils had helped set up 438 such courses in different parts of Poland, attended by 18,000 rural women. Four years later, the number of courses had increased to 778.[86] In this way, thousands of young rural women gained knowledge about their reproductive health and access to medical advice.

While modern ways of life penetrated the village, gender roles were slow to change. In the early 1970s, twenty-three-year-old Daniela reflected on the persistent inferior status of women in rural communities. She wrote in her memoir: "machines are replacing men in farm work, but domestic work for women has not changed. The woman has to feed the family and take care of the children; how difficult it is to do the laundry since not every household has a washing machine; how hard it is to milk the cows in unbearable heat; how heavy the baskets full of potatoes are that need to be steamed and then carried to the pigs. Even after all of this, I need to go out into the field with my father and brother to collect and plant the harvest of potatoes and wheat."[87] Alongside the drudgery of traditional rural women's work, by the early 1970s, the club-café had almost disappeared from the rural landscape. With the availability of private television sets, there was little need to frequent a club-café. As in the city, many villagers preferred to watch television at home.

More and more young women left their villages as the city offered a more certain path to personal independence and a different way of life. In 1967, Teresa, like so many other schoolgirls in her village, could not wait to graduate from elementary school and move to the city to attend a vocational school. Achieving economic independence was an important motivation, but she also admitted to feeling suffocated by the physical and mental constraints of her home village. "I was simply fed up with seeing the same faces again and again," she recalled in 2011. Rather, she wanted "to be in a place where there are new people, perhaps more interesting people."[88]

Between the Global and the National

A visitor in the mid-1960s who came to a Polish village on a Sunday would see a stark contrast between the older and younger generations. While older women wore traditional outfits, such as a head-kerchief and a simple skirt with an apron, their daughters would be attired in miniskirts and high heels, their hair combed back in the form of a rounded bouffant. While older men wore hats, vests, and galoshes, young men often dressed in casual pants, sweaters, and tennis shoes. Some grew longer hair and styled them in a "mop top" after the Beatles. In many front yards, sitting next to traditional farming equipment were colorful motorcycles of Polish makes such as the WFM or Junak. Wooden houses still dominated village architecture, especially in eastern and southern Poland, and long stretches of fields and forests would surround the settlement. But there were new buildings such as schools, small grocery stores, and club-cafés. Many villages would also have a paved road and a regular bus service to the nearby city. If one visited the local club-café, one was sure to find the latest issues of popular magazines, hear big beat songs on the radio, or get a glimpse of *Bonanza* on television. The smell of coffee would permeate the air, and a young hostess would take an order for an espresso and perhaps a biscuit to go with it.

While villages became more connected to urban culture, bringing modernity to the countryside did not always result in more open or cosmopolitan outlooks among those who lived there. Nor was cosmopolitanism the intention of youth organizations and cultural activists. Rather, the foremost

Fig. 7.5 "Youth of the Lubusz area," around the city of Lubusz
in western Poland, May 26, 1966. Judging from the style of dress
and of the musical instruments, the group are on their way to an
evening dance. Photo by Zbigniew Staszyszyn. Courtesy of Polish
Press Agency.

concern was to overcome the regionalism associated with cultural "backwardness" and to integrate villagers into the broader national culture.

As such the Polish village in the global sixties presents an intriguing case of
cultural globalization in the service of strengthening national identity. Youth
leaders expressed this view at a meeting in 1962 as they discussed the role of
radio and television in rural areas. The head of the Committee for Radio and
Television, Włodzimierz Sokorski, gave a speech at the meeting in which he
argued that exposing villagers to global cultural trends would not result in
"the cosmopolitan politicization of the national culture, the trend we observe
in various capitalist states." In the Polish village, by contrast, the media propelled "a different process" in which "a singular national culture" was being

formed "under our socialist conditions." This new national culture "absorbs all the traditions: folk, those of the forward-looking nobility, contemporary, and modern."[89] In other words, political leaders consciously used the exposure of people to the world through radio and television as a tool to foster a modern national identity.

Popular magazines, radio, and television gave the villagers exposure to global events. Television regularly showed Poles domestic and international news and Western popular programming. Because there were so few domestic or other Eastern European productions, Polish television relied on American and British shows such as *Bonanza, Dr. Kildare,* and *The Saint.*[90] Thanks to the television, world news became part of the emotional world of young villagers. Leokadia recorded in her diary on November 23, 1963: "I keep myself busy so as not to think. I was shocked by the news that . . . Kennedy was assassinated. The president [of the United States] is dead, and the assassins have not been caught. He was a great statesman, the protector of peace, (and of Blacks), and he was the most sympathetic of all political leaders. It is such a shame."[91]

Although the state censored and manipulated the news so as to paint a black-and-white picture of the Cold War, television had the capacity to bridge East-West divisions. Like the Kennedy assassination as Leokadia described it, the American landing on the moon in July 1969 made a powerful impact on many villagers. Poland was the only country in the Eastern bloc to provide a live broadcast of the Apollo 11 mission.[92] The landing on the moon, often watched in a communal setting of the club-café, left a lasting impression on rural individuals as they felt elevated by joining the global audience of this momentous event. One such individual was Władysław, who wrote in his memoir in 1972: "I remember when there was a live broadcast from the Silver Globe, and although this was a time of harvest and everyone was overworked, they still came to the village club before 3 AM to be actively present for this historical moment—the first steps on the moon being taken by a representative of the human race. And I don't know about anyone else, but I was very emotional, because a human stood on the moon and millions could see it on television—how marvelous is the human mind and the era in which we live."[93]

Many villagers imagined the future as a time of growing consumer opportunities and international connections. In 1970, when a journalist from *New Village* asked young people in the village of Łysa Góra in southern Poland to write about their visions of the year 2000, many hoped for the opening of a large department store in their village, so "no one would have to travel to Tarnów to buy a pair of shoes or a coat." Others wanted to open their village to international tourism, including constructing hotels, restaurants, and indoor swimming pools. They also hoped every home would be equipped with a color television projecting three-dimensional images. One young male respondent planned to become "a famous soccer player" and "to score goals [at a stadium] in Brazil, while my wife and children would watch me on television."[94]

While some young people became more aware of global connections, as is exemplified in their visions of the year 2000, for others, opening the village to the outside world first and foremost strengthened the rural bond with the nation. Sociologists soon found that rural readers devoured, alongside television programming and popular magazines such as *New Village*, nineteenth-century Polish novels by Henryk Sienkiewicz, Ignacy Kraszewski, Eliza Orzeszkowa, Maria Konopnicka, Bolesław Prus, and others.[95] Prominent sociologist Józef Chałasiński was not surprised by this development but rather pointed to a distinct way through which villagers finally became modern Poles. "The discovery of one's own nation," he wrote in 1968, "at the same time as obtaining freedom, is the history of our socialist revolution from the point of view of the people." It was only natural for rural youth "to want to catch up on national history." He continued: "a generation from the rural masses, no longer marginalized by their nation, not tempered by class warfare, reaches for books presenting them, suggestively in a literary style, with their birthright, the history of their fatherland."[96] What Chałasiński failed to note, however, was that "the history of their fatherland" through literature rarely included villagers, as most nineteenth-century Polish novels focus on the nobility and urban intelligentsia. The spreading of "national culture" through canonical Polish novels therefore tacitly encouraged rural communities to turn away from their own history as disempowerd peasants and serfs, and identify with traditional Polish elites.[97]

Mobility often meant the discovery of the Polish national culture embedded in the language and literature. Many of those who left the village came back not only with education and urban clothing styles but also with strong national attachments they wanted to transfer to the rest of the village. Such transfer often took place through the linguistic process. Zofia, who grew up speaking the mountain dialect of her village, worked hard at her secondary school in the city to learn Polish, which she described as "our true, correct speech style." She spoke Polish with her classmates in the city, but when she went back home for Sunday or vacation, she would revert to the village dialect. "I could not have done otherwise," Zofia explained, "because I was afraid to make a fool of myself, that I was pretending to be some village lady. But again, at the dormitory and the school I would speak in a correct way." She finally realized her "mistake" of not speaking Polish at home and decided to "contribute to the changing of speech style among my peers." Surprisingly, she learned, "no one laughed at me." On the contrary, she gained prestige among the young women in the village, who flocked to her home "to ask a lot about my school, and the city."[98] She felt elevated within her rural social circle because of her new-found education in the wider national culture. The exposure to school, "correct" speech, and urban ways of life set the young generation even more apart from their elders.

Zofia's testimony as a self-proclaimed bearer of national culture in her village is significant. Desires to participate in global culture, including access to consumerism and urban lifestyles, could be accompanied by an increasing identification with the modern nation. For rural women and men, globalizing the village often meant "entering" the world as modern Poles.

* * *

For Zofia and others, the emergent school system, television, the motorcycle, and the club-café shaped the ways rural young people embraced the global sixties. For many, exposure to the outside world brought a realization of personal autonomy and a sense that their own paths could diverge from those of their parents and past generations. For rural young women, these included not only choosing their education or work but also controlling their own bodies. Taking the health courses in which they learned about reproduction and birth control became a unique effort to assert their rights and desires for the future.

Yet embracing the modern world was more challenging in the village than in the city, as it required overcoming strong prejudices against urban culture and the control of the local community and the Church. Although many rural young women devoted themselves to "civilizing" the village, this project eventually fell short of their expectations. Many of the young women who enthusiastically managed club-cafés or set up sex education in rural areas eventually relocated to the city.

Opening the village to global influences produced ambivalent outcomes. Motorcycles, television, and club-cafés provided new ways for young people to liberate themselves from the restrictions of rural tradition and to think of themselves as part of the modern world rather than as part of a narrow family unit or a village. At the same time, through their interactions with the outside world, young villagers encountered not only youth magazines and international news but also the "nation," which spoke Polish and practiced urban ways of life. Ironically, the global sixties thus provided new opportunities for the state to nationalize rural actors. The state and youth organizations used modern forms of education, leisure, and the media to elevate rural young people to seeing themselves as Poles, no less deserving of all the benefits of modernity than other global citizens.

8

Domesticating the Sixties

Youth Culture, Globalization, and Consumer Socialism in the 1970s

In January 1970, the Polish weekly *Polityka* reflected on the closing 1960s as the years of "the progress frenzy." In four columns on just one page, author Jan Zakrzewski presented a dizzying list of events. He recorded the Cuban Missile Crisis, the wars in Algeria and Vietnam, the disarmament agreements between the Soviet Union and the United States, the U.S. civil rights movement, the first space exploration by Soviet cosmonaut Yuri Gagarin, and the American landing on the moon. There was also a place for "a record number" of train and plane crashes and the environmental devastation exemplified by the "300 million tons of toxic substances emitted by European factories, and 200 million tons of carbon dioxide produced by the continent's cars." Cultural changes occupied a prominent place in the account. Zakrzewski noted "changes in the thinking of individuals" and "the abandonment of old ways and traditions." In the sphere of sexual mores, "the sixties were the years of absolute 'freedom' and the rejection of all taboo." Miniskirts and "the obligatory sexual act" on the silver screen were among the examples. "In the West," he continued, "drug consumption increased tenfold, moral standards had collapsed . . . pornography had become a commodity for export." As if this was not enough, hippies could be found in every corner of the world ceasing "to turn heads," while the Beatles "were being knighted by the Queen."[1]

The vision of the progress frenzy was one in which political and cultural upheavals became normalized. But the article also presented two separate narratives of the sixties: one for the West and the Global South, the other for the socialist camp. In "socialist Europe," the sixties had ushered in an era of peace, material improvements, and increased cooperation among socialist states "as equals for the common good." Wars, military coups, and moral havoc had all happened outside the socialist camp.

A powerful narrative of harmonious socialist modernity would guide the politics of the new regime in Poland under Gierek, who came to power

Imagining the World from Behind the Iron Curtain. Malgorzata Fidelis, Oxford University Press. © Oxford University Press 2022. DOI: 10.1093/oso/9780197643402.003.0009

in December 1970. Soon afterward, Poles became beneficiaries of unprecedented consumer opportunities, economic growth, and a more extensive global opening. Scholars have traditionally viewed the "consumer socialism" that Poland and other countries in the Eastern bloc adopted as a strategy to legitimize the power of communist regimes. But the politics of the early 1970s were also intended to mitigate the cultural and political upheavals of the sixties. The new approach to socialism was prompted by broader challenges, not limited to the 1960s reform movements in the Eastern bloc such as Prague Spring.[2] In Poland, the 1970s—commonly associated with "liberalization"—were in fact full of anxieties about the effects of the global movements of the previous decade.

This chapter looks at the early 1970s as a distinct attempt to domesticate the developments of the global sixties in Poland, in line with the efforts at stabilizing society that were pursued by governments both East and West. Protest movements in the West often culminated in the 1970s with changes in legislation and expanded definitions of citizenship and human rights. Alongside these popular gains, however, the American and Western European ruling elites "repaired their own structures and re-asserted their hegemony."[3] Restructuring labor relations, by means of which European leaders of both social-democratic and communist parties kept workers' demands in check, in exchange for positions of power as trade union leaders, members of the Parliament, and government officials, was one example. The socialist camp also attempted to neutralize the liberationist impulses of the previous decade in a variety of ways.[4]

Alongside buying societal compliance with consumer goods and social benefits, the Polish ruling regime claimed to have fulfilled its distinct vision of modernity, which had been debated since the mid-1950s. A new national narrative reinterpreted the turbulent 1960s as standing in opposition to the "collapse of moral standards" that had plagued the West. Instead, the sixties became associated with a healthy cultural rebellion that, in Poland in contrast to the West, had resulted in more authentic human expression and an affirmation of the existing social and political model. In a way, the regime of the early Gierek era did not reject but assimilated the sixties upheavals by claiming that they had fulfilled many of these movements' aspirations, including the quest for authenticity and personal liberation. According to this new narrative, while the capitalist West seemed to be disintegrating due to political conflicts, environmental pollution, and deteriorating morality, "socialist Europe" had supposedly emerged from the sixties closer to the ideal of modernity than ever before.

A Generation in Revolt?

The need to stabilize society was once again reinforced in December 1970 when another revolt broke out in Poland, this time in the coastal cities of Gdańsk, Gdynia, Elbląg, Szczecin, and Słupsk, among others. As in 1968, the Gomułka regime resorted to force. This time, however, in addition to riot police and voluntary militia, the Polish military, including several tank divisions, were sent to deal with the unrest. In the end, an estimated forty-four people were killed and 1,164 were wounded, almost half of them militiamen and soldiers.[5] On December 20, after this military action against workers, Gomułka was forced to resign.

March 1968 and December 1970 are often seen as two distinct revolts: one was led by students and intellectuals, the other by workers. According to conventional interpretations, these protests exposed the disparity between the intelligentsia and the workers, who did not come together until 1980 to form the Solidarity movement. In 1968, workers supposedly not only did not join the students but were mobilized to beat them. In 1970, students supposedly stood aside. From the generational angle, however, the two revolts had much in common. Like the revolt in March 1968, the revolt in December 1970 was staged by the young.[6]

The Politburo decision to significantly raise the prices of basic foodstuffs, announced on December 12, 1970, prompted the protest. Polish workers were already facing a deteriorating economic situation. In the late 1960s, real wages had grown by a meager 1.5 percent per year, less than in other countries of the Eastern bloc.[7] When strikes and demonstrations erupted in shipyards and other workplaces on the Baltic coast, the riot police used clubs and tear gas against the demonstrators. On December 15, a crowd marched on the provincial Party committee building in Gdańsk and set it on fire. Demonstrations turned into street fights between the protestors and the riot police. On December 17, a day that came to be remembered as Black Thursday, the army fired on unarmed shipyard workers in Gdynia as they walked to their morning shift. Ten workers were killed. Street fights and demonstrations continued through December 22. The state dispatched more than 500 tanks, close to 100 military planes and helicopters, 5,000 militiamen, and 27,000 soldiers to quell the rebellion.[8] In addition to human casualties, nineteen public buildings were set on fire, and more than 100 civilian and military vehicles were destroyed.[9]

Young men dominated the riots. Some used violence and put themselves in danger. For example, they would drive an empty tram into a cordon of militiamen. Several young workers would stop a transport truck, throw out the drivers, drive the truck at full speed into a riot police cordon, and attempt to jump out of the driver's cabin at the last moment. At least one young man died jumping out of the cabin straight under the wheels of another truck.[10]

Nearly half of those arrested during and after the protests were men under the age of twenty, and two out of three protesters were under twenty-five.[11] In shipyards, young workers led the strikes, including Lech Wałęsa, aged twenty-seven. In the wake of these demonstrations, 700 young men in Gdańsk and Gdynia were forcibly conscripted into the army.[12]

In addition, a number of students from the Gdańsk Polytechnic, university, and medical school joined the protests.[13] According to personal testimonies, the memory of March 1968 sparked their decisions. Too young to have participated in the March rebellion, they adopted December 1970 as part of their "generational experience." One female student, who took part in the demonstrations in Gdańsk, explained her motivation in this way: "we were less cautious, because first, we did not have a personal experience of 'March'; and second, we wanted to show that we were no less brave than our older colleagues, who got beaten by the militia two years earlier." Even for those students who lived in other parts of Poland and learned about the demonstrations through the mass media, the revolt of December 1970 deepened their mental connection to March 1968, providing further proof that in 1968 the students had been right.[14]

The revolt of December 1970 gave some students new impetus to act. In Kraków, on the other side of the country, students took to the streets to express their solidarity with the protesting workers. The Kraków demonstrations were cut short by state authorities, who arrested student leaders and closed the Jagiellonian University for a holiday break a few days earlier than originally planned.[15] Echoes of the December revolt could still be heard in the summer of 1971, when a popular joke among students announced a fictional sightseeing tour to the Baltic coast organized by the ZMS. The tour's slogan promised to take students "along the trail of the burnt Party committee [buildings]."[16]

The Polish Road to Globalization

The use of force against workers was the final blow to Gomułka's regime, who resigned as the first secretary. The new leader, Edward Gierek, had already enjoyed a reputation as a relatively liberal and Western-oriented politician, having built his career in Upper Silesia, a major industrial area. An anonymous observer from the West who traveled to Poland in the summer of 1971 reported on the widespread popularity of the new first secretary among the Polish public, partly because of his perceived weak links to the Soviets and poor knowledge of the Russian language. According to the report, many Poles took pride in his "fluent French" and "rather Western demeanor."[17] Coming to power at a moment of national crisis, Gierek promised to build a "Second Poland" that would not only mitigate conflicts but also create a materially prosperous and globally prominent modern state. Young people would be the backbone of this project. Under his leadership, the communist regime itself underwent a generational change. Older communists with prewar or wartime roots passed away or retired. In 1971, out of nineteen members of the Central Committee of the Party, fifteen had been born after 1920.[18] Many of the new Party members came from rural backgrounds. Their advancement was a direct result of postwar communist policies aimed at elevating the lower classes.

While continuing to glorify Polish national traditions, Gierek's regime embraced global trends in a new way. They ostentatiously opened Poland to participating in global culture and the global economy as a "morally and politically unified nation."[19] While Gomulka had promoted the Polish Road to Socialism, Gierek championed the Polish Road to Globalization. Much of the economic and material progress was enabled by the regime's skillful maneuvering during the economic and financial turmoil that engulfed the capitalist world in the early 1970s. Amid the breakdown of the Bretton Woods economic system in 1971, Poland took advantage of Western bankers' search for investment opportunities in Eastern Europe, which brought the promise of high returns and thus enabled Polish leaders to obtain loans from Western banks at favorable rates. At the same time, Poland was shielded from the oil crisis of 1973 and the recession that followed because Poland imported its oil from the Soviet Union at a relatively low price.[20] Inserting itself into the global market, Poland finally had a chance to become a modern nation of prosperous people.

Some of the regime's most significant domestic legislation in its first years in power was aimed at pronatalism. Women who entered their childbearing years in the early 1970s could count on more maternity benefits than their mothers. In 1972, paid maternity leave was extended from twelve to sixteen weeks or up to twenty-eight weeks in the case of a multiple birth. The length of the maternity leave was made the same for blue- and white-collar female workers. All women were also entitled to an unpaid leave of up to three years to raise a child or children. In addition, the Polish state granted paid leaves for mothers to care for sick children under the age of fourteen. This legislation helped women combine their professional with their domestic roles, though it did not offer similar paternity benefits to men. For the Gierek regime, however, as for Christian Democrats in Western Europe in the 1950s, facilitating women's commitment to the household and family was an unmistakable sign of stability and prosperity. In 1970s Poland, unlike 1950s Western Europe, women remained active in the public sphere as workers and professionals under the official principle of equal rights.[21]

Elements of egalitarianism guided Polish prosperity. The Gierek regime raised wages for nearly everyone and ensured that there was no significant disparity between incomes. In the first half of the 1970s, individual wages grew by as much as 42 percent, while the cost of living only rose by 12 percent.[22] Farmers received special attention: Gierek ended compulsory deliveries of agricultural products and extended the state's healthcare and pension system to the rural population. His policies also stressed social equality within the younger generation. The university student population, for example, steadily grew, reaching slightly more than 300,000 by the end of the 1970s.[23] As a result of post-1968 policies, admissions programs privileged young people from peasant and working-class backgrounds to counterbalance the overrepresentation, in the state's view, of the intelligentsia. By 1972, the percentage of students from rural and working-class families reached 35 percent in the humanities and more than 50 percent in engineering.[24] In addition to these initiatives, Gierek took up building a modern infrastructure based on new technologies and mass investment. As a result, the gross national product rose on average by more than 5 percent per year between 1971 and 1975, while domestic production grew by 11 percent on average.[25] What Gierek proposed was a model of relative material comforts without the downsides of capitalism, for example unemployment and deep social stratification.

The most tangible changes were registered in the sphere of consumption and material standard. Consider the ownership of private cars. In 1971, the number of private cars in Poland stood at 556,000, and by the end of the decade it reached 2 million.[26] In June 1973, Poland started the production of the Fiat 126P, under Italian licensing, popularly known as the *maluch* (little one). It was designed as an affordable family car. Although buying the car from state-owned shops required prepayments and queueing, owning a "little one" became a realistic aspiration for many families.

Private cars not only equipped individuals and families with a means of transportation but also allowed them to emotionally connect to the modern world. The tiny *maluch*, with limited seating and storage space, was hardly functional as a family car. Yet it was advertised as a world-class product that placed Poles almost on par with Western elites. In March 1975, the *New Village* contended that Polish owners of a *maluch* should feel elevated since "Brigitte Bardot drives a car of the same caliber through the streets of Paris."[27]

More and more Western consumer products made their way to Poland. In 1972, Coca-Cola appeared in Polish stores, and Marlboro cigarettes arrived shortly afterward. The hard-currency store Pewex opened in 1972, selling Western food, clothes, cosmetics, electrotechnical equipment, and even Western-made cars. By 1975, the amount of Polish trade with the West surpassed trade with countries of the Eastern bloc, consisting of 55 percent of all of Poland's international trade.[28]

While Gierek's modernity expanded consumerism and social benefits, it also projected the image of Poland as a global success story affirmed by outsiders. Glorifying Polish international achievements had been a regular part of Polish media messaging but was taken to even higher levels. Reportedly, Poland's prosperity enjoyed unprecedented admiration from foreigners. A typical press commentary read: "since 1970, the recognition of Poland's economic and political successes has been on the rise.... The world mass media devote much attention to the People's Republic of Poland. And these are not reports on fleeting impressions, but extended studies on the development of specific branches of our industry or our development plans and cooperation with other countries.... Even the bourgeois press writes with respect about our leaders and the First Secretary Edward Gierek.... Poles are no longer depicted as 'romantic,' but as 'realist thinkers,' pragmatic and flexible in action."[29] The pages of newspapers and periodicals were populated with pictures of Polish leaders meeting their foreign counterparts and actors and singers attending international festivals or simply strolling through the streets of European cities. When Fidel Castro visited Poland for the first time in July 1972, the media disseminated images of him playing basketball with Polish players and parading around in traditional Upper Silesian miners' clothing.[30] Just five weeks earlier, Poland had hosted Richard Nixon, marking its first official U.S. presidential visit.[31] Poland seemed to be friends with everyone and a magnet for leaders from all geopolitical orientations.

Poland was bridging Cold War divisions and basking in the possibilities of détente. When the weekly *Perspectives* (Perspektywy), devoted to international politics, presented several pages of photographic panoramas of Polish international successes, it included pictures of leaders from all over the world paying respects to Poland. The panorama showed, for example, Willy Brandt bowing in front of the Polish flag during his visit to Warsaw in December 1970. The caption lauded the "normalization" of Polish–West German relations. Next to this photo was one of Richard Nixon being saluted by the Polish military in Warsaw. Nixon's visit, as the caption read, "was proof of Poland's position and authority in the world."[32] The panorama also included photos from the Conference on Security and Cooperation in Europe, the International Commission of Control and Supervision in Vietnam, and a gathering of socialist state leaders in Crimea, all events in which Poles participated. There was also coverage of Yugoslav leader Josip Bros Tito and Fidel Castro visiting Warsaw, and finally a photograph of a handshake between the Polish foreign minister, Stefan Olszowski, and the pope in the Vatican.[33]

Poles did not have to be content with only flipping through the pages of color magazines with international content but increasingly could interact directly with foreign cultures. Travel abroad had been on the rise through the 1960s. The number of travelers to socialist countries increased fivefold between 1960 and 1970, while the number of people going to the West more than doubled during the same time. Travel to socialist countries became less restricted as many countries within the bloc ceased to require passports from citizens of other socialist countries. Select Western European states also opened their doors to Polish tourists. Austria lifted its visa requirements in 1972 and Finland in 1974.[34] In 1980, the Polish state recorded 700,000 trips by Polish citizens to the West, six times as many as during the previous decade.[35] The most popular Western destinations were France, Great Britain, and West Germany.[36] But the United States also came within easier reach when LOT Polish airlines opened direct flights between Warsaw and New York in April 1973.[37]

In addition, opportunities to meet foreign tourists in Poland expanded. The number of foreign travelers to Poland had steadily increased from 78,200 in 1955 to nearly 2 million in 1969 and to as many as 8 million ten years later. This occurred in tandem with the expansion of the tourist industry in Western Europe.[38] The number of tourists who came from outside the Eastern bloc grew from 280,000 in 1969 to slightly over a million ten years

Fig. 8.1 Photographic panorama of Polish international achievements.
From top left: youth from the Polish diaspora meeting with two
Polish officials; a visit of the Czechoslovak delegation to Warsaw; the
Polish military saluting Josip Broz Tito at the Warsaw airport, 1972;
Fidel Castro in Nowa Huta, 1972; Polish delegates at the European
Conference on Security and Cooperation in Helsinki, July 1973; a
meeting between Stefan Olszowski and Pope Paul VI, November 1973;
a Polish officer socializing with his South Vietnamese counterparts
as part of the International Commission of Control and Supervision
formed in 1973; Polish soldiers in UN peacekeeping forces in the
Middle East, October 1973. *Perskpektywy*, 5 April 1974. National
Library, Warsaw.

later.[39] More personal interactions with foreigners, whether through travel or with visitors from abroad, formed another step in building a new relationship between the Gierek regime and the young generation.

As in the West, young people became a separate group of consumers with distinct desires and tastes. Discussions about the need for a domestic "youth market" appeared in *Around the World* in December 1968. Focusing on clothing and footwear, the discussants asserted the state's obligation to address the consumer needs of young people. A telling photograph depicted two young women trying on shoes at a small store. The caption read: "how much longer will girls have to buy fashionable shoes only in private stores?"[40] The illustration reinforced the point of the discussion: the Polish state would have to take responsibility for providing desired consumer products or else it would legitimize private entrepreneurs and the superiority of Western goods. That same year, a newly built retail store, Junior, opened in the center of Warsaw with the specific aim of selling youth clothes.[41]

The Gierek regime expanded youth production lines. By 1972, the Polish state enterprises, such as Odra in Szczecin and Sprawność in Kraków were producing blue jeans using a Polish-made fabric they called *texas*. Although the press admitted the quality did not match that of Levi's or Wrangler jeans, these Polish blue jeans were affordable, and their quality was steadily improving. Female fashion designers Barbara Hoff and Grażyna Hasse became especially well known for designing collections specifically for young people inspired by Western youth fashions.[42] They helped promote the hippie fashions that became popular among young men and women as part of *hipisowanie*.

The new generational cohort was defined as exceptional in a different sense from the cohort of the early 1960s. Not only their lack of wartime experiences made them distinct but also the fact that they were products of "extensive education by socialist institutions." *Around the World* argued that the meaning of the concept of "generation" had changed, as young people no longer experienced "upheavals and conflicts larger than their family, school, and local community." This generation, the magazine declared, was "a product of education" rather than of "their own struggles for survival."[43] The young people of the Gierek era could finally enjoy life to its fullest. Now there was no need for political upheaval, *Around the World* argued; instead there was the need to perfect personal goals: "a good and beautiful love, a well-functioning marriage—all that shapes the personal and everyday actions of young people."[44]

Ambiguous Counterculture

At the threshold of the 1970s, many students and members of the young intelligentsia described themselves as a new generation entering a new era. These
voices, of course, reflected the state's agenda to build the "Second Poland,"
but they also indicated a subjective empowerment that some young people
found in the expanding cultural opportunities, which often intersected with
the counterculture. In a sense, the early years of Gierek's rule resembled the
Thaw, as new outlets for youth self-expression became available, including a
revival of critical journalism. One outlet for the ambiguous counterculture
that operated on the edges of official culture was the Kraków-based monthly
Student.

Student had begun publishing in November 1967, under the patronage of
the ZSP, but acquired a new editorial leadership on the ascendance of the
Gierek regime and established a new reputation for voicing the interests and
concerns of the larger student community.[45] In addition to topics ranging
from students' everyday life to new directions in literature and art, *Student*
devoted extensive space to social and political issues in a global context.
One striking feature was the periodical's coverage of international student
movements, the New Left, and "the sexual revolution" in the West. Although
the articles often critiqued the New Left as misguided and infantile, they provided a plethora of information, stimulating commentary, and perspectives
from the Western press.[46]

Contributors to *Student* included a variety of young journalists, writers,
poets, and artists. Outside official channels, most of them identified with
the post-1968 search for new forms of protest, including politicized art and
literature. Many of them, such as poets Adam Zagajewski and Stanisław
Barańczak, later joined the organized political opposition. Almost all would
go on to become prominent writers and artists of the post-1989 era.[47] At least
two future controversial politicians published in *Student*: Leszek Balcerowicz
and Janusz Korwin-Mikke.[48]

Like the critical journalism of the Thaw, *Student* bridged genres and styles,
politics and culture, serious discussion and satirical drawings. Because of its
relatively small circulation, censors tended to be more lenient toward it. Each
issue was 10,000 copies, usually distributed only in large cities.[49] Editors and
contributors built on the Thaw tradition in addition to international countercultural inspirations. A series of articles in 1972 discussed the short-lived
student periodicals of the Thaw as an important generational experience and

a model of critical journalism that had helped young audiences make sense of the "post-October [1956] reality" as it was taking shape.[50] The evocation of the critical journalism of the mid-1950s attested to the persistent memory of the Thaw and its significance in laying the groundwork for young educated elites' modes of expression in the years to come.

Domesticating the Sexual Revolution

For *Student*, however, the counterculture was not just a subject of analysis but something its staff actively participated in. Editors and contributors often adopted hippie fashion, attended student clubs, and traveled to Wrocław for the international student theater festivals. They also made use of explicit sexuality, which, ironically, became a safe way to interrogate established social and political norms. By the early 1970s, *Student* regularly featured graphic sexual images and texts, some of them reprinted from the Western press.[51] This signaled a broader change in the public representation of sexuality under the Polish Road to Globalization.

The Polish press usually used the term "sexual revolution" to describe the increasing sexual permissiveness that was prevalent in the West and whose echoes were noticeable in the countries of the Eastern bloc. Polish commentators, however, believed that the desire to form families was inevitable for all young people. In 1971, medical doctor Mariusz Popielarski argued that even American hippies eventually looked for marital stability as soon as they approached their late twenties. At that time, he explained, "the unshaved, bearded and unkempt 'hippie,' who used to walk around barefoot—or sometimes as a way of protest—even completely naked, who practiced a messy sexual life and often used drugs, was able to change 'overnight.'" He was bound to transform into "a short-haired traditional white-shirt-wearing respectable young man" and "an exemplary father."[52]

Long-haired young Polish men populated youth and student magazines. In March 1974, to celebrate International Women's Day, *ITD* featured a young father on the cover who looked like a hippie. He was wearing a colorful shirt, had long hair and a beard, and was feeding a baby from a bottle. In the background, one could see a guitar lying on the couch as if he had just put it down to feed the baby.[53] Inside this issue of *ITD* were additional photographs of this man and his wife, both university students, taking care of their two small children.[54] Although the actual hippie groups were still a target of state repression, men and women who looked like hippies were accepted and even glamorized. As the photographs and the text in *ITD* indicated, the hippie style did not have to interfere with forming an exemplary loving family.

Elements of sexual freedom became part of a depoliticized personal lifestyle. The state condemned the commodification of sex under capitalism but accepted similar practices at home, for example the use of explicit sexual imagery in the popular press. Commentators agreed that modern people

Fig. 8.2 Cover of *ITD*, 10 March 1974. A modern father. Photo by Hanna Musiał (Anna Musiałówna). National Library, Warsaw. Courtesy of Hanna Musiał.

deserved fulfilling sexual lives. But as historian Katarína Lišková has argued for Czechoslovakia during the same time, "new accents on sex, complete with graphic description of sexual positions," did not necessarily signal progressive attitudes toward sex, as was the case in the West. The new openness about intimate life still reinforced gender hierarchy and the necessity of forming stable families.[55] A similar trend unfolded in Poland. The sexual revolution, in other words, was domesticated in a peculiar way to serve the goals of communist regimes seeking to "normalize" societies.

Student magazines were among the first in Poland to feature photos of topless and nude women on their pages. The trend took off in June 1969, when *Student*, for the first time in its short history, featured a photo of a topless woman on its back cover. *ITD* soon followed with similar erotic images. In the following years, graphic images of female nudes could be found on the back covers of nearly every issue of *Student*, *ITD*, and numerous other popular publications.

It may be tempting to see the turn toward graphic sexuality as a contemporary Western influence, but these popular magazines were walking a well-trodden path, from the time of the Thaw, of objectifying women and glamorizing their sexuality as explosive. In a way, the early 1970s revived that trend, reaffirmed by the sexual revolution in the West and the strong linkage of "healthy" sexuality with the modern lifestyle. Magazines such as *Student* and *ITD* helped normalize erotic imagery as part of appropriate leisure and entertainment.

In addition, sexual advice became an integral part of the student and youth press. Such advice no longer focused on moral guidelines and emotionality, as in *Radar* a few years earlier, but now on physiology and technique. Starting in 1967, *ITD* published a regular column that reaffirmed premarital sex in meaningful heterosexual relationships as positive and offered advice to couples on how to best shape their intimate lives so as to avoid future marital discord.

While earlier publications featured sexual advice from educators and writers, many of them female, now male sexologists and medical doctors dominated the field. The column in *ITD* was initially written by medical doctor Kazimierz Imieliński, who in 1963 became the first officially recognized sexologist in Poland. Two years later, sexologist Zbigniew Lew-Starowicz, who was close in age to his student readers, took over.[56] His column, "A Sexologist Responds" (Odpowiedzi seksuologa), appeared on the next-to-last page of every issue of *ITD*. Readers just flipped the back cover to see a salacious photograph of a nude female. It is hard to see this layout as accidental. Rather, this pairing reinforced the heterosexual masculine perspective on sexuality.

As in the early 1960s, narrow notions of sexual normativity continued to guide sexual advice. Masturbation, homosexuality, and generally anything that did not involve coitus were considered abnormal and detrimental to one's personal health and happiness. As Lew-Starowicz argued, the very purpose of sex was to assert and explore gender difference. "Sexual intercourse," he wrote, "releases a passion for the psychophysical distinction of the other person; it is the communication of masculinity and femininity in its fullest form."[57]

Although Lew-Starowicz asserted the right of women to sexual pleasure, his advice often replicated traditional assumptions about gender roles. Women were blamed for male sexual problems such as impotence.[58] Moreover, the sexual advice in *ITD* tended to undercut women's control over reproduction, a major departure from the advice of the early 1960s, when Irena Krzywicka and other female writers repeatedly articulated the central place of reproductive choice in healthy sex life. Lew-Starowicz accepted the use of contraception but only on a temporary basis, as a way to postpone pregnancy rather than avoid it. "Contraception cannot lead to the rejection of the value of motherhood," he wrote in April 1972. Those who consciously decide not to have children "derail the concept of love, marriage, and in the long run, work against themselves (one only needs to look at the divorce statistics)," he wrote. Even marriages with one child, he argued, "caused great harm" because they produced people whose "emotions and societal attitudes are often immature" and for whom "egoism and narcissism prevail."[59] Although sex was now firmly connected to pleasure and heterosexual love, ultimately it served a reproductive purpose. Women had the right to contraception and abortion, but this did not relieve them of the duty to become mothers. The shift in the focus of popular advice from female autonomy and reproductive rights to the language of motherhood as a duty is striking. It confirms the ways that expert discourse aided the state agenda in boosting birth rates, which had begun to drop in Poland in the late 1960s.

The idea of sexual liberation offered by the student periodicals asserted heterosexual male prowess. Analyzing the sexual "liberation" among New Left activists in West Germany, historian Dagmar Herzog has argued that "misogyny has been woven into the very fabric of sexual revolution."[60] In Poland, a similar pattern developed, albeit in a different way, as part of "official" culture. Depicting women as sexual objects while at the same time questioning their reproductive choice underscored the subjectivity of heterosexual men and their control over the female body.

Reorganizing Youth

Granting more personal autonomy and consumer choice to young people was only one side of the new approach to them in the early 1970s. The Gierek regime continued to suppress dissidents while also seeking to strengthen the state's control over the organized student and youth movement.

Although most of the Commandos and their allies left prison under the amnesty of August 1969, Gierek did not hesitate to crack down on youth dissent. In October 1971, several young activists of a small underground organization, Ruch (the Movement), were put on trial for attempting to destroy the monument of Lenin located in the mountain town of Poronin in southern Poland. The leaders, Andrzej Czuma and Stefan Niesiołowski, were sentenced to seven years in prison; their associates got three and a half to six.[61] The official youth movement also became a target of the Gierek regime as it aimed to reduce the autonomy of the youth organizations. In 1973, the ZSP was abolished and replaced with a new body under a different name: the Socialist Polish Student Association (Socjalistyczny Związek Studentów Polskich; SZSP). University chapters of the ZMS and the ZMW were incorporated into the new SZSP. According to historian Tom Junes, the act "marked the end of an era as organizational pluralism was terminated and for the first time in the history of the Communist regime in Poland there was to be only one, monopolistic student organization—the SZSP."[62] The process eventually culminated in the creation of the Association of Polish Socialist Youth (Socjalistyczny Związek Młodzieży Polskiej; ZSMP) in 1976.

The restructuring of the official youth organizations was, to a large extent, a response to the youth and student unrest of March 1968. The last national Congress of the old ZSP took place in March 1973, when the delegates voted to restructure and rename their organization. This was just a rubber stamp on the decision made at the Party headquarters. At the same time, the Party established a central body, the Federation of Socialist Polish Youth Associations (Federacja Socjalistycznych Związków Młodzieży Polskiej), ostensibly aimed at promoting closer cooperation within the youth movement.[63] In practice, this change meant centralization and control. The Congress was preceded by an extensive propaganda campaign in the press, in which activists and regular students expressed support for reorganizing the student movement. The decision was thus presented as an initiative from below.[64]

The press reports on the Congress appropriated the language of the international counterculture in an intriguing way: by frequently referring to the quest for "authenticity," which was supposedly being fulfilled within the renewed youth movement. The new student organization would promote "the climate of openness, authenticity and democracy"; the newly established Federation would reflect "the authentic communal activism of the entire young generation."[65] The cover of *ITD* was devoted to the Congress and featured a portrait of an attractive female blonde, Krystyna Świder, who was described as one of the top sociology students at Adam Mickiewicz University in Poznań and a member of the ZSP's executive committee. A small photo at the upper right corner of the cover showed Krystyna sitting behind a conference table, holding papers and engaging in a discussion with male activists.[66] Feminine beauty again helped to enhance the attractiveness of a political product.

* * *

Edward Gierek, the new leader coming to power after the bloody crushing of the workers' revolt on the Baltic coast, wasted no time in instituting policies that departed from the antisemitic campaigning, xenophobic nationalism, and state violence that had characterized the last years of his predecessor. Gierek was especially ready to enlist young people in the new project of renewing socialism through providing greater personal freedoms and more openness to the world. The new era was conceptualized in surprisingly global terms: as the fulfillment of sixties' visions and desires. Young people were encouraged to express their subjectivity without fear of the state's backlash. The press no longer denounced long-haired men as social deviants or enemies of socialism. Elements of critical journalism and the counterculture were also coopted as natural expressions of the young generation and, indeed, as a proof that state socialism provided outlets for such expression.

The liberalization of the cultural and personal spheres, however, went hand in hand with the strengthening of political control over any potential organized youth and student movement. The end of organization pluralism constituted the flip side of cultural liberalization. New structures of centralization and control were created to ensure that the idea of "freedom" did not cross to the political realm.

Three years after the "unification" of the official student movement in 1973, the Gierek regime shut down *Around the World*. Its last issue came out on April 25, 1976.[67] By that time it no longer commanded the popularity it had during the sixties as an exciting "window to the world." No recorded outcry from the readers and no street demonstrations—such as those when *Po prostu* ceased publication in November 1957—occurred. This was not surprising. By the early 1970s, countless other colorful magazines were featuring attractive international material, while personal travel to the West had become increasingly possible for many young people.

One of the most enduring outcomes of the state's domestication of the sixties movements was the depoliticization of transnational imagination. Official publications no longer vilified young "cosmopolitans" but accommodated them. For many young people in the early 1970s, the desirable global connections came to be strongly associated with consumer commodities, the pleasures of travel and leisure, and the global market, all of which seemed to make possible a fulfilling life and a harmonious society. The shuttering of *Around the World*, a quintessential element of the Polish sixties, only confirmed what had already happened a few years earlier. The era that had started during the Thaw—an era of novelty and of imagining liberation through a more interconnected world—had come to an end.

Conclusion

Imagining the World after the Sixties

In 1989, the world looked on at revolutions across the Eastern bloc with surprise. But when analyzed through the stories of those behind the Iron Curtain, the collapse of communism may be seen less as a breakthrough moment and more as a continuation, expansion, and modification of previous trends, from youth culture and consumer practices to modernity and globalization. 1989 did not happen in a vacuum: it was part of a longer process of imagining the world and its possibilities from the other side of the Iron Curtain. That process did not end when communism collapsed. Rather, the question of how to relate to the outside world has played a critical role in shaping and reshaping Polish democracy since the transition.

This book has shown that the story of the global sixties in Poland is, to a large extent, a story of young people's desires and struggles to be part of the world on their own terms. Across the globe, new generations grappled with similar issues, seeking what they saw as more humane political and ideological frameworks for their societies. In Poland, the Thaw of the mid-1950s was an important turning point. Disillusioned by Stalinism, many young people threw themselves into new kinds of activism on behalf of anti-Stalinist democratic socialism. Student clubs, avant-garde theater, jazz, and critical journalism all became part of the youth carnival that engulfed the country between 1954 and 1956. The unprecedented meeting of cultures at the World Youth and Student Festival that took place in Warsaw in the summer of 1955 generated demands for more meaningful participation in the global community of youth, including personal mobility across borders. Tragically, the enthusiasm for transnational engagements was curbed by the Soviet invasion of Hungary in November 1956. The crushing of the Hungarian Revolution delineated the limits of the youth "internationalism" that was allowed in post-Stalinist Eastern Europe afterward but failed to eliminate alternative ways of imagining the world.

Imagining the World from Behind the Iron Curtain. Malgorzata Fidelis, Oxford University Press. © Oxford University Press 2022. DOI: 10.1093/oso/9780197643402.003.0010

As Poland became more open to outside influences after 1956, the political elites adopted a new vision of modernity that allowed young people to participate in aspects of global youth culture, including new forms of sociability, fashion, music, and dance, while retaining state socialist political and economic structures. In the process, the state became complicit in facilitating new expressions of young selfhood. The quest for a noncapitalist modernity, however, included not only matters of consumption and leisure but also progressive attitudes toward female identity and the body. A new genre of youth magazines provided models for a modern socialist behavior and became an important source of transnational imagination. These magazines, although printed by state publishing houses, projected the West as the exciting "core" of youth culture while also featuring material from other socialist countries and the Global South. For many young readers, these magazines, alongside foreign radio stations and visual media, became windows into a world. They felt empowered by them.

The outside world was not accessible to every young person in Poland in the same way. The exposure differed from the city to the countryside, and from one social group to another. University students had more access to transnational cultures, in urban spaces where they could frequent student clubs and participate in the artistic initiatives of the official Student Culture. Some formed discussion circles that engaged issues of domestic and international politics. Student groups such as the Commandos brought perspectives from the Global East to international leftist conversations. As the student and youth protests of March 1968 demonstrated, these conversations exposed cracks and tensions among young leftists. In Poland, defining alternative visions of internationalism to the one promoted by the communist state proved especially challenging. The dissident ideas expressed in The Open Letter about the common goal of de-Stalinization and decolonization and of breaking free from superpower dominance were never developed either in words or deeds. The Global South remained an inspiration for some groups in the 1970s, including countercultural movements, but alternative internationalism remained an unfinished project. After 1968, the transnational imagination took a predominantly cultural turn and became most visible among hippies, who searched for "authenticity" outside the boundaries of the nation or the geopolitical Cold War order. Hippies made themselves visible on Polish streets with long hair, colorful dress, and communal gatherings. They professed pacifism and love. Harassed by the state and their fellow citizens, they took pride in their status as social outcasts. And their style proved attractive to other young people.

The search for a liberated young subjectivity exploded with no less force in the Polish countryside, albeit in different ways. More isolated from the larger society, young rural people adopted modernity as an all-encompassing search for self-expression that no longer bowed to the family, the village community, or the local priest. The world that came to the Polish village took many forms, from technological improvements and the motorcycle to changing notions of gender relations and the female body, as is evinced in rural residents' auto-biographies. It is worth noting that young villagers did not rebel against the political establishment, as did leftist students or urban countercultural fig-ures. Rather, they defied their immediate communities and rural traditions. Young women used state organizations such as the Girls' Councils to liberate themselves from constraints on their personal autonomy. In this sense, they claimed their subjectivity with the help of the state rather than in opposition to it. Perhaps it is no wonder that the world in the village often took a national form. The state—an important agent in rural youth liberation—encouraged young people to identify with the Polish nation as a way to connect to the outside world, in their case, the rest of Poland.

The Polish sixties culminated in two upheavals: the student and youth pro-test of March 1968 and the workers' uprising on the Baltic coast in December 1970. Both were staged by the young; both were met with state violence. By the early 1970s, the Polish regime recognized a need for a different strategy to deal with the younger generation. The new leader Edward Gierek, who came to power after the tragic events of December 1970, attempted to co-opt young people into the new project of building a "Second Poland." This in-cluded projecting another version of socialist modernity: the fulfillment of many of the desires and aspirations of the global sixties.

By the mid-1970s, the Gierek regime had domesticated some of the major cultural trends of the global sixties. Young people could express their per-sonal rebellions through extravagant fashion and greater personal freedoms. They felt connected to the world through consumer choice and increased engagements with the West, including personal travel. From the perspective of the ruling elites, there was no longer a reason to search for alternative forms of socialism. These elites had found the right balance. And indeed, Marxist "revisionists" were nowhere to be found. Karol Modzelewski expressed the thinking of many leftists at the time when he pointed to the Warsaw Pact invasion of Czechoslovakia in August 1968 as a final blow to global revolu-tionary ideas he had once put forward in the *Open Letter*. "After we joined the Soviet Army in the invasion of Czechoslovakia," he recalled in 2013, "I no longer believed that a revolutionary flame, anywhere it appeared, would easily engulf the whole empire and reach Moscow." What he found particularly disheartening was the Soviets' ability to mobilize "friendly regimes" against one another.[1] His assessment no doubt was influenced by what he had seen: many young people were content with the cultural and consumer connections to the world that the Gierek regime promoted.

The year 1974, the peak of Gierek's consumer socialism, was thus a year marked by many celebrations. Starting on July 22, 85,000 young people came to Warsaw from all over Poland to participate in public celebrations of the thirtieth "birthday" of the "People's Poland." Hailed as "the parade of youth," the participants marched through the streets, took part in sports competitions, put on theater performances, sang, danced, and played guitar. They pledged an oath to dedicate themselves to working for Poland and socialism.[2] According to youth magazines, there was no better time to be young and to live in "a country rich with natural resources, modern infrastructure, and the support and cooperation of the family of socialist nations." Poland was said to command "considerable authority in the world" and to possess, "above all, a talented society."[3] That summer, the Polish soccer team won a bronze medal at the FIFA championship in West Germany. This was an unprecedented success for Polish soccer and was celebrated nationally.[4]

But 1974 was also the last year of relative prosperity and political quiescence. The sixties were over, but the liberationist impulses returned in a new form as anticommunist opposition emerged. Beneath the country's peace and prosperity, the Polish version of consumer socialism was under strain. To keep prices low, Gierek kept borrowing from the West. Consequently, Polish debt grew from $8.4 billion in 1975 to nearly $15 billion in 1977 and close to $24 billion in 1979.[5] Meanwhile, Poland's exports failed to earn the expected amounts of hard currency necessary to service these loans. In response, in June 1976 the Gierek regime finally decided to raise the prices of basic foodstuffs—by as much as 70 percent. As in December 1970, the decision provoked a workers' revolt, this time in Radom, Ursus, and Płock in central Poland. The revolt prompted an immediate response from the intellectuals and professionals who formed the Workers' Defense Committee (Komitet Obrony Robotników; KOR), which was led by many veterans of 1968, including Jacek Kuroń and Adam Michnik.

The leaders of this new political opposition domesticated the sixties in their own way. In the increasingly interconnected world, dissidents learned to use international forces to propel what they saw as a specifically Polish cause. In a way, détente, initially championed by Gierek, soon became his downfall. In August 1975, European countries (with the exception of Albania and Andorra), the United States, and Canada signed the Helsinki Accords, a diplomatic document aimed at reducing Cold War tensions. The agreement included a declaration to respect "human rights and fundamental freedoms, including the freedom of thought, conscience, religion or belief, for all without distinction as to race, sex, language or religion."[6] Although the Polish dissidents at first viewed the Helsinki Accords with suspicion as a document that legitimized communist rule in Eastern Europe, they soon began invoking the agreement to call out their government for violations of human rights.

In December 1975, oppositional circles submitted a protest letter to the government in which they demanded freedom of thought, independent labor unions, and the elimination of censorship, in addition to other civic rights. The document, signed by fifty-nine intellectuals and professionals, included this statement: "the respect for these freedoms, confirmed by the Helsinki Accords, is of a considerable international significance, because where there is no freedom there is neither peace nor security."[7] The dissidents called out the elephant in the room: Poland's socialist modernity was not abiding by the core principles of equality and justice.

Members of KOR assisted workers who experienced repression after the June 1976 revolt with legal advice and material support. They openly argued for their right to do so under international agreements. In a way, this new organization built on the sixties ethos of inclusion and political empowerment from below. Echoes of the hippie counterculture could be found in the peaceful nature of the movement.[8]

The opposition groups of the 1970s, while appealing to international human rights, understood their goals primarily in domestic terms. The letter of December 1975, in addition to referencing the Helsinki Agreement, expressed the idea that protection of human rights had to be a condition of maintaining "the continuation of national tradition." Suppression of human rights, the letter contended, "threatened the existence of the nation."[9] This language was different from the language that was used to speak of the democratic values espoused during the 1968 student demonstrations and the language used to speak of economic oppression and workers' rights in the 1970 workers' revolt on the Baltic coast. Now, the rhetoric connected human rights to the nation, showing how dissident movements could use transnational agendas to enhance nationalist thinking at home. Such eclectic use of national and international rhetoric dominated the Solidarity movement, which emerged as a result of the massive workers' strikes of August 1980, and would have a profound effect on the character of the opposition movements that developed in the late 1980s.

The end of communism in Poland in 1989 opened new possibilities for building a better world, the one that young people had so intensely imagined and fought for in previous decades.

It was the Solidarity leaders, many of them former participants in the sixties youth culture, who gained a unique opportunity to implement the visions they had cultivated in their imagination. Unlike their counterparts in the First World, they did achieve a political revolution that so many had desired and fought for during the global sixties. They helped topple the establishment in their own country and across the Eastern bloc. Finally, they contributed to the downfall of one of the Cold War superpowers, the Soviet Union. After 1989, they assumed positions of authority, including the power to reshape Poland's relationship with the world.

By that time, though, these dissidents' transnational imagination had already changed. They had become not only more fixated on anticommunism and the nation but also increasingly attracted to what they saw as the successes of the global neoliberal market.[10] Under their leadership, Poland shed communist authoritarianism through a fast-paced privatization, market reforms, and consumerism rather than the sort of democratic socialism or antiimperialist transnational solidarities that had galvanized many of these same people two decades earlier. This was also because the world around them had changed. Global connections in the early 1990s were seen through the prism of a triumphant capitalism. It was widely believed that liberal democracy and the market had produced a global community of peace-oriented and democratic nations—indeed, a fulfillment of the sixties' dreams.[11]

While the devastating impact of "shock therapy" has been well documented in scholarship, critical journalism, and even personal memoirs of those involved in its implementation, the popular notion that Poland "returned" to Europe after 1989 has rarely been questioned.[12] Exploring the global sixties in Poland problematizes this claim. First, as I have shown in this book, Poland never left Europe. Young Poles found ways to actively participate in global youth culture long before the end of the Cold War, including through spaces and commodities provided by the very state that sought to control and limit outside influences. Second, post-1989 Poland, while embarking on liberal democracy and opening borders and information channels, simultaneously closed some windows to the world that had been open during the global sixties. In January 1993, the post-Solidarity government revoked the 1956 liberalization of the abortion law. By curtailing reproductive rights, the new Polish state not only defied the contemporary European liberal norm but also undermined a crucial element of the way young women in Poland understood themselves as modern. That same year, the Polish state concluded a Concordat with the Vatican, helping the Catholic Church to consolidate its political power and exert enormous influence on public life. The Church's aim ever since has been to fight liberal trends seen as "foreign" and promote an exclusionary national identity in which "Poles" are equated with conservative Catholics. Moreover, the Polish right has elevated racism and Islamophobia as part of its antirefugee and antiimmigrant politics since 2015. Indeed, the calls for isolation from the world coming from the top echelons of the Polish government are stronger and louder than they ever were during the Cold War.

It is true that young Poles no longer need to rely on their imagination for how they connect to the world. As part of the European Union, Polish citizens freely cross borders within Europe. The transnationalism of youth has been expanded and normalized by social media. Young Poles participate in global cultural and political movements as well as virtual and real spaces, from Twitch to climate strikes. Despite these developments, young people in Poland still need to position themselves vis-à-vis the church-state official culture that increasingly permeates public institutions, including schools. In that sense, the global sixties can provide inspiration for young people to reclaim their subjectivity as individuals and as a community.

There are signs that young people in Poland are already doing that. While they were largely disengaged from conventional politics during the first twenty-five years after the transition, in recent years they have been taking to the streets in increasing numbers to protest the breaking of democratic norms by the ruling right-wing populists.[13] The government's assault on women's reproductive rights and on the LGBT community draws especially large crowds of young protestors. This is similar to what we see among younger generations in Belarus, Russia, Iran, Hong Kong, the United States, and other places who are challenging authoritarian politics. The global sixties might be analyzed as a distinct era in twentieth-century history, but the youthful energy, creativity, and dreams that manifested during that era have survived and continue to shape societies. They often resurface in moments of global crisis when the future of young generations is at stake.

Abbreviations

AAN	Archiwum Akt Nowych, Archive of New Documents, Warsaw
AIPN	Archiwum Instytutu Pamięci Narodowej, Archive of the Institute of National Remembrance, Warsaw
APBi	Archiwum Państwowe, State Archive in Białystok
APKr	Archiwum Państwowe w Krakowie, State Archive in Kraków
APWr	Archiwum Państwowe we Wrocławiu, State Archive in Wrocław
BFiS PAN	Biblioteka Filozofii i Socjologii Polskiej Akademii Nauk, Library of Philosophy and Sociology of the Polish Academy of Sciences in Warsaw
BP	Biuro Prasy, Press Bureau
CKŻP	Centralny Komitet Żydów w Polsce, Central Committee of Jews in Poland
DS	Dwa Starty, Two Beginnings (Memoir Competition)
GM	Gabinet Ministra, Minister's Office
HU OSA	Blinken Open Society Archives in Budapest
KC	Komitet Centralny, Central Committee
KK	Komisja Kultury, Commission of Culture
KM	Komitet Miejski, City Committee
KSM	Komisja do Spraw Młodzieży, The Commission for the Matters of Youth
KU	Komitet Uczelniany, Higher School Committee
KW	Komitet Wojewódzki, Provincial Committee
MBP	Ministerstwo Bezpieczeństwa Publicznego, Ministry of Public Security
MKiS	Ministerstwo Kultury i Sztuki, Ministry of Culture and Art
OBOP	Ośrodek Badania Opinii Publicznej, Center for Research on Public Opinion
ORMO	Ochotnicza Rezerwa Milicji Obywatelskiej, Voluntary Reserve of the Citizens' Militia
PMW	Pamiętniki Młodzieży Wiejskiej, Memoirs of Rural Youth
PAP	Polska Agencja Prasowa, Polish Press Agency
PWRN	Prezydium Wojewódzkiej Rady Narodowej, Presidium of the Provincial National Council
PZPR	Polska Zjednoczona Partia Robotnicza, Polish United Workers' Party
RFE	Radio Free Europe
RL	Radio Liberty

RKiS	Rada Kultury i Sztuki, Council of Culture and Art
RN	Rada Naczelna, Main Council
STS	Studencki Teatr Satyryków, Student Theater of Satirists
SZSP	Socjalistyczny Związek Studentów Polskich, Socialist Polish Student Association
TPP	Towarzystwo Pamiętnikarstwa Polskiego, Friends of Memoir Society
TŚM	Towarzystwo Świadomego Macierzyństwa, Society for Conscious Motherhood
TSKŻ	Towarzystwo Społeczno-Kulturalne Żydów w Polsce, Socio-Cultural Association of Jews in Poland
WrOK	Wrocław Center of Culture
WP	Wydział Prezydialny, Presidium Division
ZG	Zarząd Główny, Main Directorate
ZHP	Związek Harcerstwa Polskiego, Polish Scouts Association
ZMP	Związek Młodzieży Polskiej, Polish Youth Association
ZMS	Związek Młodzieży Socjalistycznej, Socialist Youth Association
ZMW	Związek Młodzieży Wiejskiej, Rural Youth Association
ZSMP	Socjalistyczny Związek Młodzieży Polskiej, Association of Polish Socialist Youth
ZSP	Związek Studentów Polskich, Polish Student Association
ŻTK	Żydowskie Towarzystwo Kultury, Jewish Cultural Association
ZW	Zarząd Wojewódzki, Provincial Directorate

Notes

Introduction

1. Jerzy Illg, interview by author, digital recording, Kraków, 22 June 2011.
2. Scholars such as Richard Ivan Jobs and David M. Pomfret have argued for transnationality as a quintessential feature of youth in the modern era. Not only had young people "embodied and exploited the global shifts and flows that accompanied the acceleration of commercial and cultural exchange," as they argue, but the socio-logical concept of "youth" took shape in the very same contexts of "transfer and ex-change." Richard Ivan Jobs and David M. Pomfret, "The Transnationality of Youth," in *Transnational Histories of Youth in the Twentieth Century*, edited by Jobs and Pomfret (New York: Palgrave Macmillan, 2015), 1–19, 2. For a definition of the "long sixties" see Arthur Marwick, *The Sixties: Cultural Revolution in Britain, France, Italy, and the United States, c. 1958–1974* (Oxford: Oxford University Press, 1998).
3. Timothy Scott Brown, *West Germany and the Global Sixties: The Anti-authoritarian Revolt, 1962–1978* (New York: Cambridge University Press, 2013), 4. On the global sixties as an emerging analytical framework see Eric Zolov, "Introduction: Latin America in the Global Sixties," *Americas* 70, no. 3 (January 2014): 349–362. On geographic and context-specific definitions of the global sixties see Tamara Chaplin and Jadwiga E. Pieper Mooney, eds., *The Global 1960s: Convention, Contest, and Counterculture* (New York: Routledge, 2018). The framework of the global sixties revises the conventional Polish periodization of the sixties, which typically centers on the political leadership of Władysław Gomułka (1956–1970). The Gomułka era has been dubbed the time of "small stabilization" after the political and economic upheavals of Stalinism. The term "small stabilization" (*mała stabilizacja*) comes from a play by Tadeusz Różewicz, *Świadkowie, albo nasza mała stabilizacja* [Witnesses, or our small stabilization], published in 1962, and first performed as a stage production on Polish television in January 1963 Tadeusz Różewicz, "Świadkowie albo nasza mała stabilizacja," *Dialog* no. 5 (1962): 5-26.
4. Historian Jeremy Prestholdt has defined transnational imagination as "a mode that frames local circumstances within a global historical trajectory and shapes collective desires and actions as a result." Jeremy Prestholdt, "Resurrecting Che: Radicalism, the Transnational Imagination, and the Politics of Heroes," *Journal of Global Studies* 7, no. 3 (2012): 506–526, 509. For a broader discussion of "icons of dissent" and their role in reflecting "a desire to be part of a trans-local collective," see Jeremy Prestholdt, *Icons of Dissent: The Global Resonance of Che, Marley, Tupac, and Bin Laden* (Oxford: Oxford University Press, 2019), 12. For a discussion of miniskirts as a global symbol of modernity see Andrew Ivaska, *Cultured States: Youth, Gender, and*

Modern Style in 1960s Dar es Salaam (Durham, NC: Duke University Press, 2011), esp. 86–123.

5. I use the terms "communism" or "state socialism" interchangeably to denote the Marxist-Leninist version of socialism modeled on the Soviet Union. It is important to note, however, that after 1956, the term "socialism" (*socjalizm*) was the predominant one used in Poland.

6. For recent works on the Global South see, for example, Heather Marie Stur, *Saigon at War: South Vietnam and the Global Sixties* (New York: Cambridge University Press, 2021); and Eric Zolov, *The Last Good Neighbor: Mexico in the Global Sixties* (Durham, NC: Duke University Press, 2020). I use designations such as *Third World* (and accordingly *First World* and *Second World*) to reflect the contemporary conceptualization of geopolitical divisions. The more recent categories of the Global South and Global North tend to exclude the former Soviet-dominated world. As Martin Müller has argued, the attempt to overcome the Cold War hierarchy of the "Three Worlds" by turning to the concepts of the Global South and Global North have created "a black hole" into which all the societies that do not fit into the South-North binary disappear. Martin Müller, "In Search of the Global East: Thinking between North and South," *Geopolitics* 25, no. 3 (2020): 734–755, 734.

7. See, for example, Anne E. Gorsuch and Diane P. Koenker, eds., *The Socialist Sixties: Crossing Borders in the Second World* (Bloomington: Indiana University Press, 2013); Anne E. Gorsuch, "'Cuba, My Love!' The Romance of Revolutionary Cuba in the Soviet Sixties," *American Historical Review* 120, no. 2 (April 2015): 497–526; James Mark, Péter Apor, Radina Vučetić, and Piotr Osęka, "'We Are with You, Vietnam': Transnational Solidarities in Socialist Hungary, Poland, and Yugoslavia," *Journal of Contemporary History* 50, no. 3 (2015): 439–464; and James Mark and Péter Apor, "Socialism Goes Global: De-colonization and the Making of a New Culture of Internationalism in Socialist Hungary, 1956–1989," *Journal of Modern History* 87 (December 2015): 852–891.

8. See, for example, Julianne Fürst, "From the Maiak to the Psichodrom: How Sixties Counterculture Came to Moscow," in Chen Jian, Martin Klimke, Masha Kirasirova, Mary Nolan, Marilyn Young, and Joanna Waley-Cohen, eds., *The Routledge Handbook of the Global Sixties:Between Protest and Nation Building* (New York: Routledge, 2018), 180–192; and Madigan Fichter, "Yugoslav Protest: Student Rebellion in Zagreb, Belgrade, and Sarajevo in 1968," *Slavic Review* 75, no. 1 (Spring 2016): 99–121.

9. Ryszard Dyoniziak, ed., *Młodzież epoki przemian. Z badań polskich socjologów* (Warsaw: Nasza Księgarnia, 1965).

10. On youth in interwar Poland see, for example, Kamil Kijek, *Dzieci modernizmu: Świadomość, kultura i socjalizacja polityczna modzieży żydowskiej w II Rzeczypospolitej* (Wrocław: Wydawnictwo Uniwersytetu Wrocławskiego, 2017); Katarzyna Sierakowska, *Rodzice, dzieci, dziadkowie . . . Wielkomiejska rodzina inteligencka w Polsce 1918–1939* (Warsaw: Wydawnictwo "DiG," 2003); and Hanna Świda-Ziemba, *Urwany lot. Pokolenie inteligenckiej młodzieży powojennej w świetle listów i pamiętników z lat 1945–1948* (Kraków: Wydawnictwo Literackie, 2003). On the significance of intelligentsia in Polish society see Janusz Żarnowski, *Inteligencja polska*

jako elita kulturalna i społeczna w ostatnich stu latach (od 1918 r. do współczesności) (Warsaw: Instytut Historii PAN, 2019).

11. Both the Nazis and the Soviets engaged in a systematic extermination of Polish educated elites during World War II. For a historical overview of the intelligentsia in Poland see, for example, Aleksander Gella, "The Life and Death of the Old Polish Intelligentsia," *Slavic Review* 30, no. 1 (March 1971): 1–27. On the Warsaw Uprising see Norman Davies, *Rising '44: The Battle for Warsaw* (New York: Penguin Books, 2005).

12. See, for example, Richard Ivan Jobs, *Riding the New Wave: Youth and the Rejuvenation of France after the Second World War* (Stanford: Stanford University Press, 2007); Leerom Medovoi, *Rebels: Youth and the Cold War Origins of Identity* (Durham, NC: Duke University Press, 2005); and Ivaska, *Cultured States.*

13. Joanna Sadowska, *Sercem i myślą związani z partią. Związek Młodzieży Socjalistycznej (1957–1976). Polityczne aspekty działalności* (Warsaw: TRIO, 2009), 11–12.

14. See, for example, Agata Zysiak, Kamil Śmiechowski, Kamil Piskała, Wiktor Marzec, Kaja Kaźmierska, and Jacek Burski, *From Cotton and Smoke: Łódź—Industrial City and Discourses of Asynchronous Modernity, 1897–1994* (Łódź and Kraków: Łódź University Press and Jagiellonian University Press, 2018); and Jerzy Jedlicki, *A Suburb of Europe: Nineteenth-Century Polish Approaches to Western Civilization* (Budapest: Central European University Press, 1999).

15. See, for example, Jerzy Hryniewiecki, "Kształt przyszłości," *Projekt* 1 (1956): 5–9; and Michał Głowiński and Grzegorz Wołowiec, *Czas nieprzewidziany. Długa rozprawa bez pana, wójta i plebana* (Warsaw: Wielka Litera, 2018), 140.

16. On multiple concepts of modernity see, for example, "AHR Roundtable. Historians and the Question of 'Modernity.' Introduction," *American Historical Review* 116, no. 3 (2011): 631–637; and Katherine Pence and Paul Betts, eds., *Socialist Modern: East German Everyday Culture and Politics* (Ann Arbor: University of Michigan Press, 2008).

17. Józef Tejchma, interview by author, digital recording, Warsaw, 1 July 2011. Throughout this book, I refer to the ruling PZPR (Polska Zjednoczona Partia Robotnicza) as the Party. This agrees with contemporary Polish usage, in which the "Party" was spelled either with an upper- or lowercase letter. Nominally, the Party was communist, but the term "communist" did not appear in the official name. Tejchma was head of the Main Directorate of the Rural Youth Association (1957–1963); secretary of the Party Central Committee (1964–1972); member of the Politburo (1968–1980); and minister of culture (1974–1978). He has been best known for authorizing the production and distribution of Andrzej Wajda's film *Man of Marble* in 1976–1977, an act that cost Tejchma his ministerial post. Although Tejchma insisted on "culture in socialism," other intellectuals and political officials, for example Stefan Żółkiewski, used both the form "culture in socialism" (*kultura w socjalizmie* or *kultura socjalizmu*) and the form "socialist culture" (*kultura socjalistyczna*). See, for example, Stefan Żółkiewski, "Walka o styl kultury socjalistycznej," *Kultura i Społeczeństwo* 7, no. 2 (1964): 3–25.

18. See, for example, Donald R. Wright, *The World and a Very Small Place in Africa: A History of Globalization in Niumi, the Gambia,* 4th ed. (New York: Routledge, 2018);

Michael Kwass, *Contraband: Louis Mandarin and the Making of a Global Underground* (Cambridge, MA: Harvard University Press, 2014); and Jeremy Prestholdt, *Domesticating the World: African Consumerism and the Genealogies of Globalization* (Berkeley: University of California Press, 2008).

19. Marshall McLuhan, *Understanding Media: The Extensions of Man* (New York: McGraw-Hill, 1964).

20. For further discussion of contradictions in the communist project of internationalism see Rachel Applebaum, *Empire of Friends: Soviet Power and Socialist Internationalism in Cold War Czechoslovakia* (Ithaca, NY: Cornell University Press, 2019); and Eleonory Gilburd, *To See Paris and Die: The Soviet Lives of Western Culture* (Cambridge, MA: Harvard University Press, 2018).

21. The concept of the Third World, first used by French anthropologist and demographer Alfred Sauvy, in his essay "Three Worlds, One Planet!," in August 1952, was adopted in Poland in the mid-1950s. By the 1970s, the term "Third World" (Trzeci Świat) was increasingly being replaced with the phrase "developing nations" (*kraje rozwijające się*) as more adequately reflecting the primacy of socioeconomic conditions. See *Encyklopedia Powszechna PWN*, vol. 4, 3rd ed. (Warsaw: PWN, 1987), 544; and Marcin Wojciech Solarz, *Trzeci Świat. Zarys biografii pojęcia* (Warsaw: Wydawnictwo Uniwersytetu Warszawskiego, 2009). For the history of the concept of the Third World see Christoph Kalter, *The Discovery of the Third World: Decolonization and the Rise of the New Left in France, c. 1950–1976* (Cambridge: Cambridge University Press, 2016).

22. For further discussion see Odd Arne Westad, *The Global Cold War: Third World Interventions and the Making of Our Times* (New York: Cambridge University Press, 2005). For discussion of East-South relations see, for example, Theodora Dragostinova, *The Cold War from the Margins: A Small Socialist State on the Global Cultural Scene* (Ithaca, NY: Cornell University Press, 2021); James Mark, Artemy M. Kalinovsky, and Steffi Marung, eds., *Alternative Globalizations: Eastern Europe and the Postcolonial World* (Bloomington: Indiana University Press, 2020); Theodora Dragostinova and Malgorzata Fidelis, "Introduction: Beyond the Iron Curtain: Eastern Europe and the Global Cold War," *Slavic Review* 77, no. 2 (Fall 2018): 577–587; and David C. Engerman, "The Second World's Third World," *Kritika: Explorations in Russian and Eurasian History* 12, no. 1 (Winter 2011): 183–211.

23. Radio Free Europe (RFE), also called Radio Free Europe/Radio Liberty (RFE/RL), was established and funded by the U.S. government in 1949 with the purpose of countering Soviet influence. Radio Free Europe broadcast news and political commentary to Eastern European countries from its headquarters in Munich. The materials I worked with ranged from summaries of radio broadcasts and press articles published in Poland and other Eastern European countries to eyewitness testimonies from Western visitors.

24. Most of my interlocutors were educated elites, though some grew up in villages and working-class environments. Nearly all of them engaged in activities and groups characteristic of the Polish sixties, from the Student Theater and hippies to official youth organizations and the rebellion of 1968. Similarly, most of the published collections feature testimonies from artists, writers, hippies, and participants in 1968 student demonstrations.

25. For further discussion see Jennifer Jones Wallach, "Building a Bridge of Worlds: The Literary Autobiography as Historical Source Material," *Biography* 29, no. 3 (Summer 2006): 446–461, 450–451.

26. See Krzysztof Kosiński, *Oficjalne i prywatne życie młodzieży w czasach PRL* (Warsaw: Rosner & Wspólnicy, 2006), 81; and Zofia Skórzyńska, "Młodzież w świetle ankiety 'Mój światopogląd,'" *Więź* 7–8 (July-August 1960): 89–98, 96.

27. Alexei Yurchak, *Everything Was Forever, Until It Was No More: The Last Soviet Generation* (Princeton, NJ: Princeton University Press, 2006); and Paulina Bren, *The Greengrocer and His TV: The Culture of Communism after the 1968 Prague Spring* (Ithaca, NY: Cornell University Press, 2010).

28. Fehérváry writes: "to posit consumer goods as simply status symbols or the products of advertisers' manipulations is to dismiss the important ways in which such goods can ease or increase labor burdens, prolong the life of foods and people, transport people or maim them, provide people with pleasures or poison them." Krisztina Fehérváry, *Politics in Color and Concrete: Socialist Materiality and the Middle Class in Hungary* (Bloomington: Indiana University Press, 2013), 7. For similar works that challenge strictly "capitalist" explanations of the meaning of consumer cultures under state socialism see Venelin I. Ganev, "The Borsa: The Black Market for Rock Music in Late Socialist Bulgaria," *Slavic Review* 73, no. 3 (Winter 2014): 514–537; and Patrick Hyder Patterson, *Bought and Sold: Living and Losing the Good Life in Socialist Yugoslavia* (Ithaca, NY: Cornell University Press, 2011).

Chapter 1

1. Leopold Tyrmand, *Dziennik 1954. Wersja Oryginalna* (Warsaw: Prószyński i S-ka, 1999), 92. At the time, *Around the World* was published under the patronage of the official Stalinist Polish Youth Association (Związek Młodzieży Polskiej; ZMP). Unless otherwise noted, all translations from Polish to English are mine. For an English-language edition of Tyrmand's diary see Leopold Tyrmand, *Diary 1954*, translated by Anita Shelton and A. J. Wrobel (Evanston, IL: Northwestern University Press, 2014). The title of the magazine, *Around the World* (Dookoła Świata), was the same as that of the Russian geographic magazine *Vokrug sveta*, first published in St. Petersburg in 1861. It continued publishing in the Soviet Union under the patronage of the Komsomol (the All-Youth Communist League). I have found no evidence to suggest that Polish editors of *Around the World* were inspired by the Soviet publication, although they were probably familiar with it because of the broader public promotion of contemporary Soviet culture in Stalinist Poland. The two magazines, however, differed significantly in content and format. The Soviet magazine was primarily devoted to geography, geology, and science and has been commonly compared to the *National Geographic*. In contrast, the Polish *Around the World* was more akin to popular magazines oriented toward educational entertainment. It primarily featured articles about contemporary popular culture and social and cultural trends. While travel reportage appeared in nearly every issue, geography was not the main focus of the magazine.

2. On the Bikini Boys or Bikiniarze, see Katherine A. Lebow, *Unfinished Utopia: Nowa Huta, Stalinism, and Polish Society, 1949–1956* (Ithaca, NY: Cornell University Press, 2013), esp. chap. 5; and Maciej Chłopek, *Bikiniarze. Pierwsza polska subkultura* (Warsaw: Wydawnictwo Akademickie "Żak," 2005).

3. Tadeusz Mazowiecki and Zygmunt Skórzyński, "Historia nie tylko złudzeń: Październik 56," in *Październik 1956. Pierwszy wyłom w systemie. Bunt, młodość, rozsądek*, edited by Stefan Bratkowski (Warsaw: Prószyński i S-ka, 1996), 215–243, 218. For Polish translation of Ilya Ehrenburg novel see Ilja Erenburg, *Odwilż*, transl. Jan Brzechwa (Warsaw: PIW, 1955).

4. The name came from Grigori Malenkov, who became the head of the Soviet state in the wake of Stalin's death. For the first few months, he shared power with Nikita Khrushchev and Lavrentiy Beria. For further discussion of the New Course see Zbigniew Brzezinski, *The Soviet Bloc: Unity and Conflict* (Cambridge, MA: Harvard University Press, 1967), esp. 155–268; and Elena Zubkova, *Russia after the War: Hopes, Illusions, and Disappointments, 1945–1957*, translated and edited by Hugh Ragsdale (New York: Routledge, 2015), 151–163.

5. Zubkova, *Russia after the War*, esp. 191. For further discussion of Soviet de-Stalinization see, for example, Polly Jones, ed., *The Dilemmas of De-Stalinization: Negotiating Cultural and Social Change in the Khrushchev Era* (London: Routledge, 2006).

6. Jacek Fedorowicz, "Kultura młodych. Teatry studenckie w połowie lat pięćdziesiątych," in *"Jesteście naszą wielką szansą." Młodzież na rozstajach komunizmu 1944–1989*, edited by Paweł Ceranka and Sławomir Stępień (Warsaw: IPN, 2009), 358–363, 361.

7. Vladislav Zubok, *Zhivago's Children: The Last Russian Intelligentsia* (Cambridge, MA: Harvard University Press, 2011), 21. See also Denis Kozlov and Eleonory Gilburd, eds., *The Thaw: Soviet Society and Culture during the 1950s and 1960s* (Toronto: University of Toronto Press, 2013); and Steven Bitner, *The Many Lives of Khrushchev's Thaw: Experience and Memory in Moscow's Arbat* (Ithaca, NY: Cornell University Press, 2008). Other scholars contest the view that the Soviet Thaw impacted primarily intellectual circles. Robert Hornsby, for example, argues for a broader definition and more diverse protest movements, including workers' revolts, farmers' protests, and underground political groups, among others. See Robert Hornsby, *Protest, Reform and Repression in Khrushchev's Soviet Union* (Cambridge: Cambridge University Press, 2013).

8. For discussion of the Polish Thaw as a primarily national movement see Paweł Machcewicz, *Rebellious Satellite: 1956 in Poland* (Stanford: Stanford University Press, 2011).

9. Before Gomułka assumed power in October 1956, the Polish leadership was shaken by the death of Bolesław Bierut, the "little Stalin" of Poland, who died from a heart attack on March 12, 1956, after attending Khrushchev's "Secret Speech" at the Twentieth Congress of the Soviet Communist Party in Moscow. He was replaced by Edward Ochab. See Machcewicz, *Rebellious Satellite*, 48–58.

10. Tadeusz Kurek, "Mały apokryf czyli jak było naprawdę," *Dookoła Świata*, 6 January 1974, 4.

11. Kurek, "Mały apokryf," 4.

12. Cover of *Dookoła Świata*, 15 December 1953. The issue was announced as a "test issue," but the same image appeared on the cover of the first official publication of *Around the World* on January 3, 1954.

13. Kazimierz Koźniewski, "Między nami," *Dookoła Świata*, 3 January 1954, 2–3, 2.

14. Koźniewski, "Między nami," 3.

15. See, for example, a series of articles by Jerzy Ros, who joined the crew of the Polish ocean liner *Batory* on a trade journey to South Asia. Jerzy Ros, "Przez morza i dżungle," *Dookoła Świata*, 3 January 1954, 3. See also correspondence from Brazil and Vietnam: L. Gasparra, "Kraj bezlitosny. Korespondencja własna 'Dookoła Świata' z Brazylii," *Dookoła Świata*, 6 March 1955, 10–12; and Bernhard Seeger, "Mieszkańcy górzystej krainy. Korespondencja własna 'Dookoła Świata' z Wietnamu," *Dookoła Świata*, 22 May 1955, 4–5.

16. See, for example, "Pewnego dnia w sobotę . . . Podpatrzył K. Barcz," *Dookoła Świata*, 3 January 1954, 9; and Wojciech Giełżyński and Andrzej Wasilkowski, "Dookoła Plantów," *Dookoła Świata*, 17 October 1954, 2–3.

17. See, for example, the covers of *Around the World* of 8 June 1954, 21 August 1955, and 25 September 1955.

18. J.z., "W obiektywie 'dookoła świata,'" *Dookoła Świata*, 20 June 1954, 2. On the Mau-Mau rebellion, see also Andrzej Bieńkowski, "Polowania na ludzi," *Dookoła Świata*, 28 November 1954, 2–3, and 4.

19. Henryk Malecha, "Od tego się zaczęło. Tak powstał STS," in *Kultura studencka. Zjawisko, twórcy, instytucje*, edited by Edward Chudziński (Kraków: Fundacja STU, 2011), 159–163.

20. Edward Chudziński, "W stronę teatru otwartego," in Chudziński, *Kultura studencka*, 125–133, 125.

21. Halina Mikołajska, "Rehabilitacja metafory," *Po prostu*, 8 May 1956, 6.

22. Stanisław Jonas, "Teatr o własnym obliczu," *Nowy Medyk*, 1 May 1956, 4. Emphasis in the original. For other reports on Student Theater see Jarosław Abramow i Andrzej Jarecki, "Przedstawiamy STS," *Po prostu*, 1 April 1956, 8; and Wojciech Giełżyński and Waldemar Kiwilszo, "Alarm: Bim! Bom!," *Dookoła Świata*, 24 February 1957, 6–7.

23. *Ashes and Diamonds*, directed by Andrzej Wajda and released in 1958, is a hallmark of the Polish Film School. It focuses on a young man from the anticommunist underground who is ordered in the first days after the war to assassinate a local communist leader. For further discussion of Cybulski as a symbol of the era see Iwona Kurz, *Twarze w tłumie. Wizerunki bohaterów wyobraźni zbiorowej w kulturze polskiej lat 1955–1969* (Warsaw: Świat Literacki, 2006). On the figure of the young rebel in postwar American film see Leerom Medovoi, *Rebels: Youth and the Cold War Origins of Identity* (Durham, NC: Duke University Press, 2005).

24. Machcewicz, *Rebellious Satellite*, 61.

25. Bogusław Litwiniec, interview by author, digital recording, Wilcza, 15 July 2013.

26. Jerzy Tejchma, interview.

27. Ryszard Turski, "Skoro nas nie sadzają, idziemy naprzód," in Bratkowski, *Październik 1956*, 9–21, 19.

28. Eugeniusz Lasota, "Jak to się zaczęło?," in Bratkowski, *Październik 1956*, 46–56, 51.

29. "Do czytelników," *Pod Wiatr*, 1 December 1956, 1.
30. Quoted in Orzechowski, "Prasa studencka," in Chudziński, *Kultura Studencka*, 279.
31. "Co robić?," *Po prostu*, 8 June 1956, 1–2. The title harkened back to the Russian radical tradition. "What Is To Be Done? Burning Questions of Our Movement" was the title of Lenin's political manifesto published in 1902. Lenin took the title from the 1863 novel by Russian socialist philosopher Nikolay Chernishevsky (1828–1889), who inspired generations of Russian revolutionaries.
32. The clubs often started in private apartments, for example the Crooked Circle Club, located on Crooked Circle street next to the Old Town market in Warsaw. See Jerzy Mikke, "Niczego nie żałuję," in Bratkowski, *Październik 1956*, 57–62.
33. Skórzyński, "Historia nie tylko złudzeń," 232.
34. "Dom mody męskiej 'AS,'" *Zebra*, 2 April 1957, 15.
35. "Pamiętnik Funia," *Zebra*, 2 April 1957, 15.
36. See, for example, "Prezentujemy . . . Miss Wrocławia," *Poglądy*, 18 July 1957, 8; "Każda Miss'ka z bliska," *Poglądy*, 20 August 1957, 8; and "Odkrycie Miss," *Od Nowa*, 8 February 1958, 8.
37. "Historia aktu. Krótki kurs," *Poglądy*, 20 August 1957, 8. For similar visual compositions see "Uf! Jak gorąco czyli koty w kąpieli," *Zebra*, 15 July 1957, 13. In September 1957, the front cover of *Zebra* featured artistic female nudes—some of them dismembered—and the announcement of an article inside: "Woman and Love as Inspiration for Artists." See *Zebra*, 23 September 1957, front cover.
38. Ewa Toniak, "Wstęp," in *Jestem artystką we wszystkim co niepotrzebne. Kobiety i sztuka około 1960*, edited by Ewa Toniak (Warsaw: Neriton 2010), 9.
39. For discussion of bombshells in Western European film see, for example, Dagmar Herzog, *Sexuality in Europe: A Twentieth-Century History* (Cambridge: Cambridge University Press, 2011), 107–108; and Elaine Tyler May, *Homeward Bound: American Families in the Cold War Era*, 3rd ed. (New York: Basic Books, 2008), esp. 104–106.
40. Only one student magazine, *Rough Road Ahead*, based in Poznań, abstained from featuring images of nude women or reporting on beauty pageants. The magazine openly criticized such practices as denigrating of women. Its editors ridiculed a variety of motivations behind publishing such photos, including "solidarity with freethinking decisions of the Twentieth Party Congress [of the Soviet Communist Party]" and the desire "to transplant a refined culture of the West" to Poland. One author argued: "let them treat the human body with the respect it deserves; and not, as they often do . . . by inserting certain photos among a mixture of sensational news and gossip. In that context, the nude Anita Ekberg is an additional attraction, and a spicy one at that. As a matter of fact, we know what is at stake. Considering the rapid explosion of various magazines and the increased price of paper, the problem of attracting readers comes into focus. In this situation pornographic pictures kill two birds with one stone." Iksy, "Miss Europa z przodu i z tyłu," *Wyboje*, 28 February 1957, 8.
41. Jerzy Ambroziewicz, Walery Namiotkiewicz, and Jan Olszewski, "Na spotkanie ludziom z AK," *Po prostu*, 11 March 1956, 2 and 5, 5.
42. The term "Holocaust" was rarely used in Poland at the time and did not appear in *Po prostu*. The most common Polish term to refer to the Nazi extermination of the Jews was Zagłada, which could be translated as "total annihilation."

43. For further discussion of postwar Polish-Jewish relations see, for example, Joanna Tokarska-Bakir, *Pod klątwą. Społeczny portret pogromu kieleckiego* (Warsaw: Czarna Owca, 2018); Marcin Zaremba, *Wielka trwoga, 1944–1947. Ludowa reakcja na kryzys* (Kraków: Znak, 2012); and Jan Tomasz Gross, *Fear: Antisemitism in Poland after Auschwitz* (New York: Random House, 2007).

44. The history of Polish-Jewish relations is beyond the scope of this book. For recent works see, for example, Antony Polonsky, Hanna Węgrzynek, and Andrzej Żbikowski, eds., *New Directions in the History of the Jews in the Polish Lands* (Brookline, MA: Academic Studies Press, 2018); William Hagen, *Anti-Jewish Violence in Poland, 1914–1920* (New York: Cambridge University Press, 2018); and Joanna Beata Michlic, *Poland's Threatening Other: The Image of the Jew from 1880 to the Present* (Lincoln: University of Nebraska Press, 2006).

45. Anat Plocker, "'Zionists to Dayan': The Anti-Zionist Campaign in Poland, 1967–1968" (Ph.D. diss., Stanford University, 2011), 23.

46. Dariusz Stola, *Kraj bez wyjścia? Migrajce z Polski, 1949–1989* (Warsaw: Instytut Studiów Politycznych PAN, 2010), 51. Zionist parties in postwar Poland created a network called Bricha that helped Jews leave for Palestine. The emigration was technically illegal but tolerated by Polish authorities.

47. Hanka Szwarcman, "Kartki z pamiętnika," *Po prostu*, 20 May 1956, 3.

48. Szwarcman, "Kartki z pamiętnika," 3.

49. Szwarcman, "Kartki z pamiętnika," 3. The original Polish word "Beriowszczyzna" (from the Russian "Berievshchina") refers to Lavrentiy Beria (1899–1953), a close associate of Stalin who is believed to have been responsible for the antisemitic purges during late Stalinism. The English translation "Beriaism" comes from Konstany A. Jeleński, "From National Democrats to Stalinists," in *Against Anti-Semitism: An Anthology of Twentieth-Century Polish Writings*, edited by Adam Michnik and Agnieszka Marczyk (New York: Oxford University Press, 2018), 151–161, esp. 156. Beria served as the head of the NKVD (*Narodnyy komissariát vnutrennikh del* or the People's Commissariat for Internal Affairs) between 1938 and 1946 and continued to control the Soviet security apparatus as deputy prime minister and curator of the organs of state security afterward. "Beriaism" is a derogatory term and seems to have been used in Poland in 1956 more frequently than in the Soviet Union. Most likely, this was the result of Khrushchev's "Secret Speech," in which the new Soviet leader devoted much attention to Beria's detrimental influence on Stalin. The "Secret Speech" was widely distributed and read in Poland. See Machcewicz, *Rebellious Satellite*, 16–47. On the antisemitic dimension of Eastern European purges see Paul Hanebrink, *A Specter Hunting Europe: The Myth of Judeo-Bolshevism* (Cambridge, MA: Harvard University Press, 2018), 182–191.

50. Szwarcman, "Kartki z pamiętnika," 3.

51. Leszek Kołakowski, "Antysemici. Pięć tez nienowych i przestroga," *Po prostu*, 27 May 1956, 1 and 7, 1.

52. Brown, *West Germany and the Global Sixties*, 127.

53. Lisa Jakelski, *Making New Music in Cold War Poland: The Warsaw Autumn Festival, 1956–1968* (Berkeley: University of California Press, 2016), 7.

54. Andrzej Krzywicki, *Poststalinowski karnawał radości. V Światowy Festiwal Młodzieży i Studentów o Pokój i Przyjaźń, Warszawa 1955* (Warsaw: TRIO, 2009), 310 and 246.

55. Pia Koivunen, "The World Youth Festival as an Arena of the 'Cultural Olympics': Meanings of Competition in Soviet Culture in the 1940s and 1950s," in *Competition in Socialist Society*, edited by Katalin Miklóssy and Melanie Ilic (New York: Routledge, 2014), 125–141, 125.

56. Krzywicki, *Poststalinowski karnawał*, 48–51.

57. Caption on the cover, *Dookoła Świata*, 7 August 1955, 1.

58. Eleonory Gilburd, *To See Paris and Die: The Soviet Lives of Western Culture* (Cambridge, MA: Harvard University Press, 2018), 55.

59. Quoted in Marcin Meller, "Szlafroki na placu defilad," *Polityka*, 12 August 1995, 12.

60. "Warszawskie spotkania," http://www.youtube.com/watch?v=7eoNEmX6qWI.

61. Kristin Roth-Ey pointed to the similar celebration of international romance during the Moscow festival in 1957. Unlike in Moscow, however, no significant surveillance of the young people's sexual behavior took place in Warsaw. For discussion of Soviet policing of sexual transgression, especially by Russian young women, during the Moscow festival, see Kristin Roth-Ey, "'Loose Girls' on the Loose? Sex, Propaganda and the 1957 Youth Festival," in *Women in the Khrushchev Era*, edited by Melanie Ilič, Susan E. Reid, and Lynne Atwood (New York: Palgrave Macmillan, 2004), 75–95. Documents of the Polish security apparatus suggest that state authorities were primarily interested in uncovering potential "political conspiracies" at the festival and recruiting secret informants from abroad rather than detecting sexual transgressions. See, for example, AIPN, 1583/282, MBP, Departament III, V Światowy Festiwal Młodzieży i Studentów, 1955–1956, kk. 1–151.

62. Wojciech Giełżyński, "Róże i orchidee," *Dookoła Świata*, 15 August 1955, 4–5, 4.

63. Giełżyński, "Róże i orchidee," 4.

64. As Anne Gorsuch has noted in the Soviet case, gendered and racialized discourses found their way to public Soviet portrayals of the Cuban Revolution in the early 1960s. These images included "the virile Cuban man, the consumptive pleasures of sex associated with Cuban women and the impoverished black body believed to be in special need of Soviet assistance." See Gorsuch, "Cuba, My Love!," 497.

65. Andrzej Konopacki, "Okno na świat," *Kontrasty*, 25 December 1956, 2.

66. Zespół Redakcji, *Dookoła Świata*, "Obywatelu Ministrze Spraw Wewnętrznych," *Dookoła Świata*, 6 May 1956, 3. Emphasis in the original.

67. Zespół Redakcji, *Dookoła Świata*, "Obywatelu Ministrze," 3.

68. In June 1956, the Ministry of Internal Affairs simplified passport application procedures, allowing one to apply for a passport at a local Citizens' Militia headquarters rather than through the centralized Passport Bureau. Jerzy Kochanowski, *Rewolucja międzypaździernikowa* (Kraków: Znak, 2017), 219. Starting in 1956, the Polish state allowed individual and organized tourism to selected countries in the Eastern bloc and to Yugoslavia. Although Western travel remained more restricted, in 1957, a record number of 177,000 Polish citizens traveled to the West. This was a 500 percent increase from 1956. See Paweł Sowiński, *Wakacje w Polsce Ludowej. Polityka władz i ruch turystyczny (1945–1989)* (Warsaw: TRIO, 2005), 90 and 149.

69. Jan Rzechowski, "A Szabadsaghoz* ... (Wpomnienia naocznego świadka)," *Pod wiatr*, 1 December 1956, 3 and 6, 3. The Hungarian word in the title was translated by the author as the Polish *ku wolności* ("toward freedom").

70. Rzechowski, "A Szabadsaghoz," 3.

71. Andrzej Bieńkowski and Leszek Moczulski, "Kronika Budapesztu," *Dookoła Świata*, 2 December 1956, 2–3, 2. The report by Bieńkowski and Moczulski cited above titled "Kronika Budapesztu" or "The Budapest Chronicle" was based on interviews with three Polish journalists—Hanka Adamiecka, Marian Bielicki, and Zygmunt Rzeżuchowski—conducted on November 15 and 16, 1956, after they returned from Hungary.

72. Bieńkowski and Moczulski, "Kronika Budapesztu," 3.

73. Paul Landvai, *One Day That Shook the Communist World: The 1956 Hungarian Uprising and Its Legacy* (Princeton, NJ: Princeton University Press, 2008), 201.

74. Wiktor Woroszylski, "Dziennik Węgierski," *Aneks*, no.13–14 (1977), 185-242, 193. According to her contemporaries, Hanka Adamiecka was a true communist believer, despite the fact that both of her parents had perished at Soviet hands during World War II. Hanka's father was executed in the Katyń massacre of approximately 20,000 Polish military and reserve officers, conducted on Stalin's orders in April 1940. The following year, her mother, a teacher, was shot by the NKVD. After the war, Hanka became a dedicated communist activist and a journalist. After Khrushchev's "Secret Speech," she passionately supported the Polish Thaw. See Hanna Wieczorek, "Dolny Śląsk po wojnie. Nasze dekady: 1951–1956," *Gazeta Wrocławska*, 4 August 2009, https://gazetawroclawska.pl/dolny-slask-po-wojnie-nasze-dekady-19511960/ar/148607.

75. Bieńkowski and Moczulski, "Kronika Budapesztu," 2.

76. Quoted in Bieńkowski and Moczulski, "Kronika Budapesztu," 2. The Hungarian Revolution included groups with diverse political orientations. In Polish journalistic reports, however, the revolt was depicted overwhelmingly as leftist.

77. By the end of the fighting, approximately 2,500 Hungarians and 700 Soviet soldiers had been killed. In the months that followed, thousands of Hungarians were imprisoned or executed, and approximately 200,000 fled the country for Western Europe and the United States. Nagy was arrested, secretly tried, and found guilty of treason and an attempt to overthrow socialism in Hungary. He was executed in June 1958 and was not rehabilitated until 1989. For further discussion of the Hungarian Revolution see, for example, John P. C. Matthews, *Explosion: The Hungarian Revolution of 1956* (New York: Hippocrine Books, 2007); and Miklos Molnar, *Budapest 1956* (London: Allen and Unwin, 1971).

78. Bieńkowski and Moczulski, "Kronika Budapesztu," 3.

79. Wieczorek, "Dolny Śląsk po wojnie." See also Michał Głowiński and Grzegorz Wołowiec, *Czas nieprzewidziany. Długa rozprawa bez pana, wójta i plebana* (Warsaw: Wielka Litera, 2018) , 93.

80. Stefan Bratkowski, "Pod znakiem pomidora," in Bratkowski, *Październik 1956*, 68–83, 78.

81. Bratkowski, "Pod znakiem pomidora," 77. For similar testimonies see Antoni Zambrowski, "Młody komunista w poszukiwaniu swojej rewolucji," in Bratkowski, *Październik 1956*, 113–126, 124–125.

82. Andrzej Bratkowski, "W Budapeszcie," in Bratkowski, *Październik 1956*,188–189.

83. Bratkowski, "W Budapeszcie."

84. Bratkowski, "W Budapeszcie."

85. Bratkowski, "W Budapeszcie."
86. Ludmila Alexeyeva and Paul Goldberg, *The Thaw Generation: Coming of Age in the Post-Stalin Era* (Pittsburgh: University of Pittsburgh Press, 1993), 74.
87. Machcewicz, *Rebellious Satellite*, 233.
88. Wiesław Głowacki, "Ofiary stabilizacji?," *Po prostu*, 12 May 1957, 1–2, 1.
89. AAN, KC, PZPR, BP, 237/XIX-234, *Po prostu*, 1957–1958, "Uwagi dotyczące czasopisma 'Po prostu' za okres od 15. XII. 56 do 10. II. 57," kk. 1–8, 1.
90. Władysław Gomułka, *Przemówienia. Wrzesień 1957-Grudzień 1958* (Warsaw, 1959).
91. Bogusław Litwiniec, interview.
92. Kathleen E. Smith, *Moscow 1956: The Silenced Spring* (Cambridge, MA: Harvard University Press, 2017).

Chapter 2

1. Roman Waschko, "Big Beat w Polsce," *Radar. Młodzież Świata* 7 (1962): 16–17, 16.
2. During the Thaw, jazz bands occasionally played rock 'n' roll in local settings. See Anna Idzikowska-Czubaj, *Rock w Polsce. O paradoksach współistnienia* (Poznań: Wydawnictwo Poznańskie, 2011), 132–133.
3. Waschko, "Big Beat w Polsce," 16.
4. The ritual of singing "One Hundred Years" was often performed to honor Party officials during public celebrations. One of the most memorable occurrences of spontaneous singing of "One Hundred Years" took place on October 24, 1956, during the historic speech by Władysław Gomułka as the new first secretary at the Parade Square in Warsaw.
5. Waschko, "Big Beat w Polsce," 16.
6. Teresa Bochwic, "Moja odpowiedź," in *Krajobraz po szoku*, edited by Anna Mieszczanek (Warsaw: Przedświt, 1989), 72–87, 73.
7. Włodzimierz Sokorski, *Współczesność i młodzież* (Warsaw: Iskry, 1963), 183.
8. Sokorski, *Współczesność i młodzież*, 185.
9. "Co robić?," *Po prostu*, 8 June 1956, 1-2. On youth revolutionary committees in 1956 see Joanna Sadowska, *Sercem i myślą związani z Partią. Związek Młodzieży Socjalistycznej (1957-1976). Polityczne aspekty działalności* (Warsaw: TRIO, 2009), 58.
10. Both the ZMW and ZHP existed in the interwar period and shortly after the war. The ZSP was first created in 1950 but dealt only with narrow administrative matters concerning students, for example conditions in the dormitories and distribution of stipends. In 1958, Circles of Military Youth (Koła Młodzieży Wojskowej) were added to the list of official youth organizations. Sadowska, *Sercem i myślą związani z Partią*, 70.
11. Andrzej Gwóźdź, "Nowa Fala w Polsce albo wola (nowoczesnego) stylu w Polskim kinie," in *W poszukiwaniu Polskiej Nowej Fali*, edited by Andrzej Gwóźdź and Margarete Wach (Kraków: Universitas, 2017), 43–74, 52.

12. Exploring wartime experiences was an important theme of the Polish Film School, between 1954 and 1963, usually with a young male protagonist faced with difficult existential choices. The best known examples include Andrzej Wajda's *Kanał* ("Sewer"; 1957) and *Ashes and Diamonds* (1958). For more discussion of the European and Polish cinema at the time see Geoffrey Nowell-Smith, *Making Waves: New Cinemas of the 1960s* (New York: Bloomsbury, 2008).

13. Gwóźdź, "Nowa Fala," 52.

14. Elżbieta Ostrowska, "Transgresje i regresje. Dylematy męskości we wczesnych filmach Romana Polańskiego, Jerzego Skolimowskiego, Andrzeja Żuławskiego i Grzegorza Królikiewicza," in *W poszukiwaniu Polskiej Nowej Fali*, edited by Gwóźdź and Wach, 171–191, 175.

15. "Geografia myślenia," *Radar* 1 (1959): 19.

16. AAN, ZMS, 11/XI/17, KC, ZG, Narada aktywu w sprawie pracy ideowo-wychowawczej, "Stenogram z narady odbytej w Rozalinie przedstawicieli Komitetu Centralnego i aktywu terenowego Związku Młodzieży Socjalistycznej," 3–4 February 1961, kk. 1–250, 6. The quote comes from the speech by Stanisław Kociołek.

17. AAN, ZMS, KC, ZG, 11/XI/17, "Stenogram z narady," k. 124. Starting in 1956, the Polish state liberalized "informational policy" by ceasing to jam foreign radio stations, by importing Western films, and by inviting Western artists to Poland. See Dariusz Stola, *Kraj bez wyjścia? Migracje z Polski, 1949–1989* (Warsaw: Instytut Studiów Politycznych PAN, 2010), 85.

18. AAN, ZMS, KC, ZG, 11/X/19, Turystyka Zagraniczna ZMS, 1958–1961, "Komitet Wojewódzki ZMS," Warsaw, 24 October 1959, kk. 32–33. During the first two years of the Bureau's activity, young Poles went on sightseeing tours to the GDR, Hungary, Czechoslovakia, the USSR, Bulgaria, and Yugoslavia. See AAN, ZMS, KC, ZG, 11/X/19, Turystyka Zagraniczna ZMS, 1958–1961, "Sprawozdanie z działalności Biura Zagranicznego Turystyki Młodzieży za okres od 1 stycznia do 15 listopada 1958 r. i wnioski za rok 1959," kk. 6–22, 7.

19. APKr, KM, PZPR w Krakowie, 29/2149/24, Protokoły posiedzeń plenarnych KM PZPR wraz z załącznikami, 4 June and 29 October 1959, "Stenogram z Plenarnego posiedzenia Krakowskiego Komitetu Miejskiego Polskiej Zjednoczonej Partii Robotniczej, odbytego w dniu 4 czerwca 1959 w sali obrad KW PZPR w Krakowie," kk. 1–98, 43.

20. Sokorski, *Współczesność i młodzież*, 5. Sokorski's essays in the collection were first printed in popular periodicals, including *Radar* and *Przegląd Kulturalny* (The Cultural Review).

21. John Clarke, Stuart Hall, Tony Jefferson, and Brian Roberts, "Subcultures, Cultures and Class," in *Resistance through Rituals: Youth Subcultures in Post-war Britain*, edited by Stuart Hall and Tony Jefferson (London: Hutchinson, 1976), 9–74, 9.

22. Richard Ivan Jobs, *Riding the New Wave: Youth and the Rejuvenation of France after the Second World War* (Stanford: Stanford University Press, 2007), 2.

23. Józef Chałasiński, *Społeczeństwo i wychowanie* (Warsaw: PWN, 1948), 46.

24. Some Polish sociologists and other commentators warned against using the term "youth culture" (*kultura młodzieżowa*) because it "elevated youth to the status of an

almost distinct and independent social class." See Mikołaj Kozakiewicz, "Młodzież a współczesność," *Polityka*, 16 May 1964, 3. Instead, some preferred to speak of "youth subculture" (*podkultura młodzieżowa*) as an outgrowth of specific desires and needs of the young. See Ryszard Dyoniziak, *Młodzieżowa "podkultura." Studium socjologiczne* (Warsaw: Wiedza Powszechna, 1965). The Polish term *podkultura,* which suggested a smaller cultural unit, did not necessarily evoke negative connotations that were later associated with the term *subkultura* (subculture) adopted from English.

25. See, for example, Axel Schildt and Detlef Siegfried, "Introduction: Youth, Consumption, and Politics in the Age of Radical Change," in *Between Marx and Coca-Cola: Youth Cultures in Changing European Societies, 1960–1980,* edited by Schildt and Siegfried (New York: Berghahn Books, 2006), 1–35.

26. Julian Stawiński, "Co sądzisz o USA?," *Dookoła Świata,* 5 August 1956, 12–13, 12.

27. Aleksander Kamiński, "Kultura mas a wczasy," *Kultura i Społeczeństwo* 8, no. 3 (1964): 95–109, 97.

28. For comparative analysis of European regimes' responses to youth culture and politics see, for example, Kathrin Fahlenbrach, Martin Klimke, Joachim Scharloth, and Laura Wong, eds., *The Establishment Responds: Power, Politics, and Protest since 1945* (New York: Palgrave Macmillan, 2012); Timothy Scott Brown and Lorena Anton, eds., *Between the Avant-garde and the Everyday: Subversive Politics in Europe from 1957 to the Present* (New York: Berghahn Books, 2011). For an excellent comparative analysis of youth culture and reactions to it in West Germany and East Germany in the 1950s see Uta G. Poiger, *Jazz, Rock, and Rebels: Cold War Politics and American Culture in a Divided Germany* (Berkeley: University of California Press, 2000). For other European countries see, for example, Carol Holoha, *Reframing Irish Youth in the Sixties* (Liverpool: Liverpool University Press, 2018); and Kostis Kornetis, *Children of the Dictatorship: Student Resistance, Cultural Politics and the "Long 1960s" in Greece* (New York: Berghahn Books, 2013). For the Global South, see Andrew Ivaska, *Cultured States: Youth, Gender, and Modern Style in 1960s Dar es Salaam* (Durham, NC: Duke University Press, 2011); and Eric Zolov, *Refried Elvis: The Rise of the Mexican Counterculture* (Berkeley: University of California Press, 1999).

29. Stanisław Widerszpil, *Skład polskiej klasy robotniczej. Tendencje zmian w okresie industrializacji socjalistycznej* (Warsaw: PWN, 1965), 110.

30. Winderszpil, *Skład polskiej klasy robotniczej,* 111.

31. Winderszpil, *Skład polskiej klasy robotniczej,* 112.

32. BFiS PAN, III Ogólnopolski Zjazd Socjologiczny, Warsaw, 2–6 February 1965, Polskie Towarzystwo Socjologiczne, 20641 [1–6], Stefan Nowak, "Obiektywne i psychologiczne parametry przemian struktury społecznej," 1–8, 2.

33. BFiS PAN, III Ogólnopolski Zjazd Socjologiczny, Warsaw, 2–6 February 1965, Nowak, "Obiektywne i psychologiczne parametry," 7.

34. On shared values in postwar Europe, East and West, see Tony Judt, *Postwar: A History of Europe since 1945* (New York: Penguin Books, 2006).

35. Antoni Sułek, *Sondaż polski. Przygarść rozpraw o badaniach ankietowych* (Warsaw: Wydawnictwo IFiS PAN, 2001), 44.

36. Stefan Nowak, "Studenci Warszawy—Uwagi o problematyce i metodzie badań," in *Studenci Warszawy. Studium długofalowych przemian postaw i wartości,* edited by

Nowak (Warsaw: Wydawnictwo Uniwersytetu Warszawskiego, 1991), 15. Nowak and his team aimed at identifying trends through several different generations of students. The first part of the study took place in 1958 and 1961 and was followed by a series of studies in 1978, 1983, and 1988. The study was not published at the time. Attacked by the Politburo and some of Nowak's colleagues as a product of "revisionism" and "a non-Marxist methodology," *The Students of Warsaw* appeared in print in only forty-nine copies in 1965 as an internal publication of the Institute of Sociology at Warsaw University. The wider public had no access to the study until its publication in 1991, two years after the collapse of the communist regime. Partial findings of the study were published in the West. See Emilia Wilder, "Impact of Poland's Stabilization of Its Youth," *Public Opinion Quarterly* 28, no. 3 (Autumn 1964): 447–452.

37. See, for example, Irena Nowak, "Środowisko towarzyskie i postawy wobec przyjaźni wśród warszawskich studentów," in Nowak, *Studenci Warszawy*, 411–443.

38. Sułek, *Sondaż polski*, 55. The center was created by a group of intellectuals associated with the Crooked Circle Club, first as a small "editorial board" for Polish Radio, to aid the section for correspondence with listeners. By late 1958, the center had become an independent entity.

39. See Zofia Skórzyńska, "Młodzież w świetle ankiety 'Mój światopogląd,'" *Więź* 7-8 (July-August 1960), 89–98.

40. Skórzyńska, "Młodzież w świetle ankiety," 91.

41. BiFiS PAN, OBOP, folder 3, Maria Szaniawska (opr), na podstawie materiałów 1 elaboratu Zofii Skórzyńskiej, "Światopogląd Młodzieży," Ośrodek Badania Opinii Publicznej przy "Polskie Radio," unpublished manuscript, Warsaw, 1960, 11.

42. Skórzyńska, "Młodzież w świetle ankiety," 92.

43. Jobs, *Riding the New Wave*, 33. The study surveyed 8 million young people between the ages of eighteen and thirty from different social classes to investigate attitudes and worldviews of French youth.

44. František Povolný, "Studenti a polednový vývoj," *Nová mysl* 4 (1969), quoted in Vladimir Kusin, *The Intellectual Origins of the Prague Spring: The Development of Reformist Ideas in Czechoslovakia, 1956-1967* (Cambridge: Cambridge University Press, 2002), 139 (originally published 1971).

45. HU OSA 300-8-11, box 20, RFE/RL Research Institute, Publication Department, Daily Information Bulletin no. 2100, "Moscow's Youth Apathetic to Communist Ideology," 11 October 1965, n.p.; HU OSA 300-8-11, box 16, RFE/RL Research Institute, Publication Department, Daily Information Bulletin no. 1809, "The Conflict of Generations in Soviet Society," 26 August 1964, n.p.; HU OSA 300-8-11, box 17, RFE/RL Research Institute, Publication Department, "Daily Information Bulletin no. 1883, "Does Soviet Youth Require a New Moral Code?," 17 November 1964, n.p.

46. Quoted in Włodzimierz Kołodziejczyk, "'Świat kina a aspiracje życiowe wybranej kategorii dziewcząt," in *Młodzież epoki przemian. Z badań polskich socjologów*, edited by Ryszard Dyoniziak (Warsaw: Nasza Księgarnia, 1965), 421–450, 443.

47. Quoted in Kołodziejczyk, "'Świat kina,'" 438.

48. Quoted in Kołodziejczyk, "'Świat kina,'" 438. In some cases, contestants included letters from family members and friends testifying to their beauty and talent.

49. Kołodziejczyk, " 'Świat kina,' " 442.
50. The vast literature on the subject of objectification cannot be cited here. For some classical work see, for example, Rae Langton, *Sexual Solipsism: Philosophical Essays on Pornography and Objectification* (Oxford: Oxford University Press, 2009); and Martha Nussbaum, "Objectification," *Philosophy and Public Affairs* 24, no. 4 (1995): 249–291.
51. Leerom Medovoi, *Rebels: Youth and the Cold War Origins of Identity* (Durham, NC: Duke University Press, 2005), 267. See also Lois Banner, *Marilyn: The Passion and the Paradox* (New York: Bloomsbury, 2012); and Kathleen Rowe Karlyn, *The Unruly Woman: Gender and the Genres of Laughter* (Austin: University of Texas Press, 1995).
52. Jobs, *Riding the New Wave*, 203.
53. On public reactions to Brigitte Bardot in France see Jobs, *Riding the New Wave*, 185–231.
54. Mikołaj Kozakiewicz, "O czym marzą?," *Polityka*, 23 May 1964, 3.
55. Kozakiewicz, "O czym marzą?," 3.
56. Jerzy Feliksiak, *Głos w sprawach młodzieży* (Warsaw: Książka i Wiedza, 1966), 98.
57. On fears of Americanization in the West see, for example, Rob Kroes, "American Mass Culture and European Youth Culture," in Schildt and Siegfried, *Between Marx and Coca-Cola*, 82–105; and Poiger, *Jazz, Rock, and Rebels*.
58. Gordon Thompson, *Please Please Me: Sixties British Pop, Inside Out* (Oxford: Oxford University Press, 2008), 6.
59. Waschko, "Big Beat w Polsce," 16.
60. Stefan Bratkowski, "Przypadek 'Big Beat,'" *Radar. Młodzież Świata*, 19 August 1962, 4.
61. Waschko, "Big Beat w Polsce," 17.
62. Franciszek Walicki quoted in Roman Waschko, "Big Beat w Polsce," 16.
63. Sokorski, *Współczesność i młodzież*, 19.
64. Sokorski, *Współczesność i młodzież*, 140–141.
65. Sokorski, *Współczesność i młodzież*, 148.
66. Sokorski, *Współczesność i młodzież*, 24.
67. Sokorski, *Współczesność i młodzież*, 138. Sokorski's moralistic writings contrasted with his personal conduct and a public reputation for being a playboy, all of which testified to the power of patriarchy in Polish society. Sokorski was married four times to much younger partners and often boasted of his popularity among eighteen-year-old women. He was also known to engage in conduct toward his female employees that by today's standards would be identified as sexual harassment. See Włodzimierz Sokorski, *Notatki* (Warsaw: PIW, 1975); and Aleksandra Szarłat, *Prezenterki* (Warsaw: Świat Książki, 2012).
68. See, for example, Anne Gorsuch, "The Dance Class or the Working Class: The Soviet Modern Girl," in *The Modern Girl Around the World: Consumption, Modernity, and Globalization*, edited by Alyse Eve Weinbaum, Lynn M. Thomas, Priti Ramamurphy, Uta G. Poiger, Madeleine Yue Dong, and Tani E. Barlow (Durham, NC: Duke University Press, 2008), 174–193.
69. Sokorski, *Współczesność i młodzież*, 27.
70. Irena Krzywicka, *Miłość . . . małżeństwo . . . dzieci . . .* (Warsaw: Iskry, 1962), 15.
71. Krzywicka, *Miłość*, 177.

72. Josie McLellan, *Love in the Time of Communism: Intimacy and Sexuality in the GDR* (Cambridge: Cambridge University Press, 2011), 11.

73. Hanna Malewska, *Kulturowe i psychospołeczne determinanty życia seksualnego* (Warsaw: PIW, 1969), 5–6.

74. Malewska, *Kulturowe i psychospołeczne determinanty*, 71.

75. Henry P. David and Robert McIntyre, *Reproductive Behavior: Central and Eastern European Experiences* (New York: Springer, 1981), 130. In addition, minors below age fifteen also had the right to abortion under the 1932 law.

76. For further discussion see Malgorzata Fidelis, *Women, Communism, and Industrialization in Postwar Poland* (New York: Cambridge University Press, 2010), chap. 5.

77. Barbara Klich-Kluczewska and Piotr Perkowski, "Obiekty biopolityki? Zdrowie, reprodukcja i przemoc," in Katarzyna Stańczak-Wiślicz, Piotr Perkowski, Malgorzata Fidelis, and Barbara Klich-Kluczewska, *Kobiety w Polsce, 1945–1989. Nowoczesność, równouprawnienie, komunizm*, (Kraków: Universitas, 2020), 337–405, 361.

78. On the history of the TŚM see Agnieszka Kościańska, *Gender, Pleasure, and Violence: The Construction of Expert Knowledge of Sexuality in Poland* (Bloomington: Indiana University Press, 2021).

79. Prof. dr med. Marcin Kacprzak, "To dopiero 10 lat!," in *Towarzystwo Świadomego Macierzyństwa, 1957–1967* (Warsaw: Państwowy Zakład Wydawnictw Lekarskich, 1967), 3–14, 3.

80. Malewska, *Kulturowe i psychospołeczne determinanty*, 98.

81. Marek Koreywo, "Pigułki," *Nowa Wieś*, 7 January 1968, 12–13, 13.

82. Wanda Jakubowska, "Działalność Towarzystwa Świadomego Macierzyństwa w okresie 1957–1967," in *Towarzystwo Świadomego Macierzyństwa*, 15–28, 21. According to a survey conducted in 1972, 57 percent of married women in Poland used some form of birth control. Withdrawal, which stood at 21 percent, was the most common method, followed by 19 percent, who used the rhythm method, and 11 percent, who preferred the condom. Fewer than 2 percent used the pill. See D. Peter Mazur, "Contraception and Abortion in Poland," *Family Planning Perspectives* 13, no. 4 (July-August 1981): 195–198, 195.

83. "List do Rad Zakładowych, June 1960," in *Towarzystwo Świadomego Macierzyństwa*, 63–65, 63.

84. See, for example, Wojciech Giełżyński, "Podnoszę szlabany," *Dookoła Świata*, 2 September 1958, 10–11.

85. Krzywicka, *Miłość*, 53.

86. Krzywicka, *Miłość*, 55.

87. Anna Lanota, *Słowo do rodziców o wychowaniu seksualnym* (Warsaw: Towarzystwo Świadomego Macierzyństwa, 1960), 8.

88. Elżbieta Jackiewiczowa, *O czym chcą wiedzieć dziewczęta*, 4th ed. (Warsaw: Państwowy Zakład Wydawnictw Lekarskich, 1961), 14.

89. Andrzej Dołęgowski, "Szkoła miłości," *Radar* 7 (1957), 18–19, 19. The choice of an interwar German text as a guide for Polish youth in socialist Poland seems puzzling. It may have reflected, however, the traditional popularity of German sexological writings in interwar Poland. For further discussion on German sexology in Poland see Kościańska, *Gender, Pleasure, and Violence*, 22.

90. A.D., "Diotima mówi o miłości," *Radar* 8 (1958): 29–30, 30.

91. D.M., "Lekarz ma głos," *Radar* 10 (1958), 31. Depathologizing of homosexuality did not take place in Poland until the mid-1980s. See Agnieszka Kościańska, *Zobaczyć łosia. Historia polskiej edukacji seksualnej od pierwszej lekcji do internetu* (Wołowiec: Wydawnictwo Czarne, 2017), esp. 237–239.

92. See, for example, Dr. Janusz Łopuski, *Co chce wiedzieć każdy chłopiec*, 4th ed. (Warsaw: Państwowy Zakład Wydawnictw Lekarskich, 1961); and Jackiewiczowa, *O czym chcą wiedzieć dziewczęta*.

93. A.D., "Diotima mówi o miłości," 29.

94. Krzywicka, *Miłość*, 17.

95. Krzywicka, *Miłość*, 18–19.

96. Łopuski, *Co chce wiedzieć każdy chłopiec*, 41.

97. Łopuski, *Co chce wiedzieć każdy chłopiec*, 48–49.

98. Jackiewiczowa, *O czym chcą wiedzieć dziewczęta*, 47.

99. Jackiewiczowa, *O czym chcą wiedzieć dziewczęta*, 41.

100. Katarína Lišková, *Sexual Liberation, Socialist Style: Communist Czechoslovakia and the Science of Desire, 1945–1989* (Cambridge: Cambridge University Press, 2018), 105.

101. AAN, KC, PZPR, BP, 237/XIX-223, Młodzież Świata, 1959, 1960, Janusz Kolczyński, "Młodzież Świata," Warsaw, 17 June 1959, kk. 1–16, 8.

102. Mikołaj Kozakiewicz, "Miłość i moda," *Radar* 7 (July 1960): 19–21.

103. See, for example, Hanna Świda-Ziemba, *Młodzież PRL. Portrety pokoleń w kontekście historii* (Kraków: Wydawnictwo Literackie, 2011).

104. For further discussion of the concept of "small stabilization" see Marcin Zaremba, "Społeczeństwo polskie lat sześćdziesiątych—między 'mała stabilizacją' a 'małą destabilizacją,'" in *Oblicza Marca 1968*, edited by Konrad Rokicki and Sławomir Stępień (Warsaw: IPN, 2004), 24–51, 25.

Chapter 3

1. Eleonory Gilburd, "The Revival of Soviet Internationalism in the Mid to Late 1950s," in *The Thaw: Soviet Society and Culture during the 1950s and 1960s*, edited by Denis Kozlov and Eleonory Gilburd (Toronto: University of Toronto Press, 2013), 362–401, 364.

2. Gerd-Rainer Horn, *The Spirit of '68: Rebellion in Western Europe and North America, 1956–1976* (Oxford: Oxford University Press, 2007), 36.

3. Antonina Kłoskowska, *Kultura masowa. Krytyka i obrona* (Warsaw: PWN, 2006). The original edition was published in 1963. For contemporary responses to Kłoskowska's book see "Antonina Kłoskowska. *Kultura masowa. Krytyka i obrona*," *Studia Socjologiczne* 4, no. 1 (1964): 249–262. On the expansion of mass culture in the post-1945 era see Michael Denning, *Culture in the Age of Three Worlds* (New York: Verso, 2004).

4. AAN, KC, PZPR, BP, 237/XIX-284, "Stenogram narady na temat laicyzacji kultury odbytej w SDP w dniu 25 czerwca 1959," kk. 1–68, 3. Stefan Żółkiewski (1911–1991) was a literary scholar; editor-in-chief of the periodicals *Kuźnica* (1945–1948), *Polityka* (1957–1958), *Nowa Kultura* (1958–1962), and *Kultura i Społeczeństwo* (1960–1968); minister of higher education (1956–59); and member of the Central Committee of the Polish United Workers' Party (1954–1968). See "Stefan Żółkiewski," in *Encyklopedia Powszechna*, 3rd ed., vol. 4 (Warsaw: Państwowe Wydawnictwo Naukowe, 1987), 916; and Andrzej Mencwel, *Przedwiośnie czy Potop. Studium postaw polskich w XX wieku* (Warsaw: Czytelnik, 1997), 484–495.

5. AAN, MKiS, GM, WP, RKiS, 49, "Stenogram plenarny z posiedzenia w dn. 18 maja 1964," 49, kk. 1–125.

6. AAN, MKiS, GM, WP, RKiS, 49, "Stenogram plenarny." See also AAN, MKiS, GM, WP, RKiS, 49, "Lista obecności na posiedzeniu plenarnym Rady Kultury i Sztuki dnia 18 maja 1964," kk. 126–129.

7. Tadeusz Mazowiecki, "Personalizm i skutery," *Więź* 7–8 (July-August 1960): 7–13, 7. Mazowiecki's essay opened the thematic issue "Contemporary Art and Mass Culture" in *Bond*. Other contributors included writers and journalists such as Jerzy Zawieyski, Leszek Prorok, Ryszard Matuszewski, Jan Józef Lipski, and Leopold Tyrmand.

8. Stefan Wilkanowicz, "Personalizm Mounicrowski wobec kultury masowcj," *Więź* 10 (October 1963): 3–15, 10.

9. Stefan Żółkiewski, "Walka o styl kultury socjalistycznej," *Kultura i Społeczeństwo* 7, no. 2 (1964): 3-25, 17.

10. AAN, MKiS, GB, WP, RKS, "Stenogram plenarnego posiedzenia w dniu 18 maja 1964," 49, k. 3.

11. The quote comes from Witold Figlewski, head of the Center for Film Leasing (part of the Center for Film Distribution). See "Kapitanowie kultury masowej w Polsce odpowiadają," *Więź* 2 (February 1964), 3–38, 7. Emphasis in the original.

12. Jerzy Adamski, "Refleksje o przesłankach polityki kulturalnej," *Nowe Drogi* 4 (April 1965): 186–192, 191–192.

13. For discussion of the gap between Party instructions and cultural practice see, for example, Andrzej Friszke, "Kultura czy ideologia? Polityka kulturalna kierownictwa PZPR w latach 1957–1963," in *Władza a społeczeństwo w PRL. Studia historyczne*, edited by Andrzej Friszke (Warsaw: Instytut Studiów Politycznych PAN, 2003), 115–145, 143.

14. See, for example, Urszula Jakubowska, ed., *Czasopisma społeczno-kulturalne w okresie PRL* (Warsaw: Instytut Badań Literackich, 2011).

15. Illustrated youth magazines existed side by side with dailies and weeklies designed primarily for youth activists, such as the *Banner of Youth* (Sztandar Młodych) or the *Struggle of Youth* (Walka Młodych), both run by the ZMS. All of them covered elements of international youth culture, but their primary focus was on political activism and organizational life. Other youth publications were designed for a middle-school-age audience. They included *Cross-country* (Na przełaj), which started publishing in 1957 under the patronage of the scout organization; *The World of the Young* (Świat

młodych), established in 1949; and *Sparkle* (Płomyk), published by the Teachers Association. In addition, a number of illustrated magazines addressed to the general public were widely read by young people. These included *Ty i Ja* (You and I) and *Przekrój* (Cross-section). The former, in particular, was a unique lifestyle magazine that emerged in 1960 and featured a substantial amount of material on Western cultural trends. Polish artists were responsible for the graphic design of the magazine's covers. One of them was prominent poster designer Roman Cieślewicz, who emigrated to France in 1963 and became a cofounder of Opus International, a New Left artistic group. For more information on *Ty i Ja* from the point of view of its editors see, for example, AAN, KC, PZPR, BP, "Ty i Ja," 237/XIX/250, Maria Borowska to Secretary, KC, PZPR, Jerzy Łukaszewicz, 28 December 1971, kk. 3–5, 3. On *Przekrój* see Justyna Jaworska, *Cywilizacja "Przekroju." Misja obyczajowa w magazynie ilustrowanym* (Warsaw: Wydawnictwo Uniwersytetu Warszawskiego, 2008).

16. AAN, KC, PZPR, BP, 237/XIX-165, Oceny i kierunki rozwoju prasy młodzieżowej, "Uwagi o prasie młodzieżowej," 9 October 1959, kk. 18–33, k. 31.

17. AAN, KC, PZPR, BP, 237/XIX-165, "Uwagi o prasie młodzieżowej," k. 32.

18. In addition to teenage girls, *Filipinka* was widely read by young female workers and university students. Zofia Sokół, *Prasa kobieca w Polsce w latach 1945–1995* (Rzeszów: Wydawnictwo Wyższej Szkoły Pedagogicznej, 1998), 125. See also AAN, KC, PZPR, BP, 237/XIX/212, Filipinka, Anna Pawłowska, "Dwutygodnik 'Filipinka,'" 17 November 1964, kk. 1–18.

19. See Malgorzata Fidelis, "Are You a Modern Girl? Consumer Culture and Young Women in 1960s Poland," in *Gender Politics and Everyday Life in State Socialist Eastern and Central Europe*, edited by Shana Penn and Jill Massino (New York: Palgrave, 2009), 171–184.

20. The new magazine replaced *Fresh Start*, one of the student periodicals of the Thaw era. See AAN, KC, PZPR, BP, 237/XIX-165, "Uwagi o prasie młodzieżowej," k. 31. See also AAN, KC, PZPR, BP, I.T.D., 1966, 1967, 237/XIX-216, Bohdan Roliński, "Uwagi o 'ITD,'" kk. 16–20, 16.

21. See, for example, Marek Konopka, "Rock around the Clock," *Dookoła Świata*, 9 August 1956, 6–7; Wojciech Giełżyński, "C'est Paris," *Dookoła Świata*, 31 March 1957, 16–17, and 20; Marek Konopka, "Pokolenie rytmu," *Dookoła Świata*, 13 July 1958, 16–17; Jerzy Sieniawski, "Pół nocy z Satchmo," *Dookoła Świata*, 5 July 1959, 3–4; Jerzy Segel, "Inwazja rytmu," *Dookoła Świata*, 11 October 1959, 5, and 14–15. In addition, Western film stars were sometimes featured on the cover, for example Marilyn Monroe on September 6, 1959.

22. AAN, KC, PZPR, BP, 237/XIX-223, Młodzież Świata, 1959, 1960, Janusz Kolczyński, "Młodzież Świata," Warsaw, 17 June 1959, kk. 1–16, 7.

23. "Dorośli nas peszą," *Filipinka*, 24 June 1962, 5.

24. Stefan Bratkowski and Wojciech Giełżyński, "Mocne uderzenie," *Dookoła Świata*, 3 January 1960, 2–3.

25. Axel Schildt and Detlef Siegfried, "Introduction: Youth, Consumption, and Politics in the Age of Radical Change," in *Between Marx and Coca-Cola: Youth Cultures in Changing European Societies, 1960–1980*, edited by Schildt and Siegfried (New York: Berghahn Books, 2006), 25.

26. Jonathyne Briggs, *Sounds French: Globalization, Cultural Communities and Pop Music*, 1958–1980 (Oxford: Oxford University Press, 2015), 29.

27. Horn, *The Spirit of '68*, 36. For further discussion of the youth underground press in Western Europe and the United States see Timothy Scott Brown, *West Germany and the Global Sixties: The Anti-Authoritarian Revolt, 1962-1978* (New York: Cambridge University Press, 2013); and John McMillian, *Smoking Typewriters: The Sixties Underground Press and the Rise of Alternative Media in America* (New York: Oxford University Press, 2011).

28. On moral censorship interventions in youth publications in France see Richard Ivan Jobs, *Riding the New Wave: Youth and the Rejuvenation of France after the Second World War* (Stanford: Stanford University Press, 2007), esp. 261–268.

29. AAN, KC, PZPR, BP, 237/XIX-165, "Uwagi o prasie młodzieżowej," k. 19.

30. AAN, KC, PZPR, BP, 237/XIX-165, "Uwagi o prasie młodzieżowej," k. 22.

31. AAN, PZPR, KC, BP, 237/XIX/-218, Kraj Rad, 1957, 1958, "Ocena pierwszego numeru czasopisma 'Kraj Rad,'" 17 December 1957, kk. 1–4, 1. In 1959, *Kraj Rad* published 60,000 copies. See also AAN, PZPR, KC, BP, 237/XIX-218, Kraj Rad, 1957, 1958, "Notatka w sprawie przejścia czasopisma 'Kraj Rad' na tygodnik i przesunięcia innych czasopism wykonywanych na Okopowej do zakładów poza RSW 'Prasa,'" 4 December 1958, k. 17.

32. AAN, PZPR, KC, BP, 237/XIX/-218, Kraj Rad, 1957, 1958, "Ocena pierwszego numeru," kk. 2–3.

33. AAN, KC, PZPR, BP, 237/XIX-223, Kolczyński, "Młodzież Świata," k. 7. See also, APKr, KW, PZPR, 1370, Wydział Kultury Nauki i Oświaty, "Praca kulturalno-oświatowa a potrzeby społeczne," kk. 37–55.

34. For example, in 1962, *Around the World* published a series of articles on cities titled "Color Cities." The series featured, among others, Peking, Skopje, San Francisco, Singapore, Vienna, Berlin, Marseille, Bucharest, and Warsaw. See, for example, Janusz Mazur, "San Francisco. Daleko od Nowego Jorku," *Dookoła Świata*, 3 June 1962, 11; and Zygmunt Broniarek, "Kolorowa wystawa. Seattle," *Dookoła Świata*, 8 July 1962, 11. For other reports on foreign culture see, for example, Zygmunt Szymański, "Louvre," *Dookoła Świata*, 8 July 1956, 10–11; Janusz Mazur, Leszek Moczulski, "Ludzie, samochody, mitologia," *Dookoła Świata*, 4 November 1956, 10–11; Olgierd Budrewicz, "Moj prywatny 'Digest.' Korespondencja własna 'DŚ'z USA," *Dookoła Świata*, 18–25 December 1960, 22–23, and 26; Włodzimierz Sokorski, "Spotkania z młodzieżą USA," *Radar. Młodzież Świata* 7 (1961): 13–14; and "Las Vegas. Bajkowe miasto," *Radar. Młodzież Świata* 9 (1962): 17–18.

35. See, for example, "Afryka 1957," *Dookoła Świata*, 4 August 1957, 8; Bogdan Szczygieł, "Metryka z Dogondoutchi. Korespondencja własna z Nigru," *Dookoła Świata*, 15 January 1967, 4–5. In addition to youth magazines, books and reportage on Third World countries by Polish foreign correspondent Ryszard Kapuściński enjoyed popularity. Kapuściński's reports from Africa during decolonization were published in *Polityka* and the internal newsletter of the Polish Press Agency (Biuletyn Specjalny; PAP) in 1962–66. His first books on his experiences in Africa were *The Black Stars* (Czarne gwiazdy) and *If the Entire Africa* (Gdyby cała Afryka), published in 1963 and 1969, respectively. His most famous books, such as *Chrystus z karabinem na*

ramieniu (The Christ who carried a rifle) and *Wojna futbolowa* (The soccer war), were published in 1975 and 1978, respectively. For discussion of Kapuściński's life and writings see Artur Domosławski, *Kapuściński Non-fiction* (Warsaw: Świat Książki, 2010). For further discussion of public representations of the Global South in post-1945 Poland, especially in literature, art, and the social sciences, see Adam F. Kola, *Socjalistyczny postkolonializm. Rekonsolidacja pamięci* (Toruń: Wydawnictwo Uniwersytetu Mikołaja Kopernika, 2018).

36. "35 dni w Azji. Fotoreportaż własny 'Dookoła Świata' z Birmy, Kambodży i Indii," *Dookoła Świata*, 28 April 1957, 4–5. The visit also included China, Vietnam, and Korea.

37. Quoted in "35 dni w Azji," 4.

38. See, for example, Szczygieł, "Metryka z Dogondoutchi," 4; and Jerzy Solecki, "Egipt na 1/50 sekundy," *Dookoła Świata*, 30 January 1966, 8–9, 8. On Polish economic experts' engagement in India see Małgorzata Mazurek, "Polish Economists in Nehru's India: Making Science for the Third World in an Era of De-Stalinization and Decolonization," *Slavic Review* 77, no. 3 (Fall 2018): 588–610.

39. *ITD*, 9 December 1962, 1. Brigadas Conrado Benitez were named after Conrado Benitez, a teacher who had been murdered by counterrevolutionaries. More than 100,000 young volunteers from urban areas, most of them women, joined the Brigadistas. They lived and worked in the countryside building schools, teaching villagers how to read and write, and training new teachers. For further discussion see Rebecca Herman, "An Army of Educators: Gender, Revolution and the Cuban Literacy Campaign of 1961," *Gender and History* 24, no. 1 (April 2012): 93–111.

40. Beata Tyszkiewicz, "Hawana jaką widziałam," *Dookoła Świata*, 24 February 1963, 19.

41. *ITD*, 23 September 1962, 2–3.

42. Elaine Tyler May, *Homeward Bound: American Families in the Cold War Era*, 3rd ed. (New York: Basic Books, 2008), 104.

43. Tyler May, *Homeward Bound*, 105.

44. Kristin Roth-Ey, *Moscow Primetime: How the Soviet Union Built a Media Empire That Lost the Cultural Cold War* (Ithaca, NY: Cornell University Press, 2011), 115.

45. AAN, KC, PZPR, BP, 237/XIX-216, Roliński, „Uwagi o 'ITD,'" kk. 17–18.

46. AAN, PZPR, KC, BP, 237/XIX-165, "Uwagi o prasie młodzieżowej," k. 27.

47. AAN, KC, PZPR, BP, 237/XIX/210, Dookoła Świata, "Notatka informacyjna ze spotkania z kierownictwem 'Dookoła świata' poświęconemu ocenie pisma," January 1959, kk. 1–4, 2.

48. AAN, PZPR, KC, BP, 237/XIX/120, Dookoła Świata, "Uwagi o 12-tu numerach 'Dookoła Świata,'" kk. 5–10, 8.

49. AAN, KC, PZPR, BP, 237/XIX-165, "Uwagi o prasie młodzieżowej," k. 28.

50. AAN, PZPR, KC BP, 237/XIX/210, Dookoła Świata, "Notatka informacyjna ze spotkania," k. 3.

51. Jane Leftwich Curry points to the remarkable pluralism of the Polish media after 1956 and Polish journalists' surprisingly significant influence on policy decisions. As she explains, this was due, in part, to political instability and frequent changes of leadership, which allowed journalists to be allied with different factions within the Party and to contribute to a "quasi-pluralistic authoritarian" state. Jane Leftwich Curry,

Poland's Journalists: Professionalism and Politics (New York: Cambridge University Press, 1990), esp. 32–33. For further discussion of the hierarchy of censorship see Jan Tomkowski, "Lata 1961–70," in Jakubowska, *Czasopisma społeczno-kulturalne*, 169–234, esp. 183.

52. Sławomir Tabkowski, interview by author, digital recording, Kraków, 26 June 2012.
53. Wojciech Mann, *Rock-Mann. Czyli jak nie zostałem saksofonistą* (Kraków: Znak, 2010), 34.
54. Mann, *Rock-Mann*, 60. For similar personal memories of the Rolling Stones' concert in Warsaw in April 1967 see Marcin Sitko, *The Rolling Stones za żelazną kurtyną. Warszawa 1967* (Warsaw: Wydawnictwo c2, 2012).
55. For comparison, the most widely read periodical, *Girlfriend* (Przyjaciółka), reached a circulation of about 2 million at the time. The main Party daily, *Trybuna Ludu*, was publishing 1.5 million copies by the first half of the 1970s. See Sokół, *Prasa kobieca*, 403; and "Trybuna Ludu," in Encyklopedia interia, https://encyklopedia.interia.pl/dzienniki-czasopisma/news-trybuna-ludu,nId,1998729.
56. Irena Nowakowa, "Przemiany społeczno-kulturalne w miastach województwa warszawskiego," *Kultura i Społeczeństwo* 1 (1966): 163–178, 172.
57. Sławomir Tabkowski, interview.
58. Tomasz Tłuczkiewicz, interview by author, digital recording, Warsaw, 12 February 2013.
59. Sokół, *Prasa kobieca w Polsce*, 127.
60. "Przebój," *Radar. Młodzież Świata* 2 (1962): 16–17, 16.
61. Sławomir Tabkowski, interview.
62. Andrzej Sadowski, interview by author, digital recording, Białystok, 11 February 2013.
63. Alicja Imlay, interview by author, digital recording, Szalejów Górny, 13 July 2013.
64. As Krisztina Fehérváry has noted for postcommunist Hungary, "In constructing certain material worlds and consumer practices as 'normal,' [Hungarians] disassociated themselves from stigmatized material culture of the 'not normal' state socialist modernity." Krisztina Fehérváry, *Politics in Color and Concrete: Socialist Materiality and the Middle Class in Hunagry* (Bloomington: Indiana University Press, 2013), 41.
65. The self-description "the merriest barrack" was also used by Hungarians to describe the Kádár era after 1968.
66. On the consuming of Polish reading material by Soviet citizens, including the magazine *Jazz*, see Gleb Tsipursky, *Socialist Fun: Youth, Consumption, and State Sponsored Popular Culture in the Cold War Soviet Union, 1945–1970* (Pittsburgh: University of Pittsburgh Press, 2016), esp. 191. For similar examples of Soviet citizens reading the Polish press, see William J. Risch, *The Ukrainian West: Culture and the Fate of Empire in Soviet Lviv* (Cambridge, MA: Harvard University Press, 2011); Sergei I. Zhuk, *Rock and Roll in the Rocket City: The West, Identity, and Ideology in Soviet Dnepropetrovsk, 1960–1985* (Baltimore: Johns Hopkins University Press, 2010), esp. 1–3; and Vladislav Zubok, *Zhivago's Children: The Last Russian Intelligentsia* (Cambridge, MA: Harvard University Press, 2011), esp. 90.
67. HU OSA, 300-8-47, box 28, RFL/RL Research Institute, Publications Department, "Polish Situation Report," 7 June 1962, n.p. The Fair presented 2,000 publishing houses from twenty countries, the UN, and UNESCO.

68. HU OSA, 300-8-47, box 28, RFE/RL Research Institute, Publications Department, "Polish Situation Report," 7 June 1962.

69. HU OSA, 300-8-47, box 28, RFE/RL Research Institute, Publications Department, "Polish Situation Report," 7 June 1962.

70. HU OSA, 300-8-47, box 30, RFE/RL Research Institute, Publications Department, "Polish Situation Report," 5 August 1965, n.p.

71. HU OSA, 300-8-47, box 30, RFE/RL Research Institute, Publications Department, "Polish Situation Report," 5 August 1965.

72. HU OSA, 300-8-47, box 30, RFE/RL Research Institute, Publications Department, "Polish Situation Report," 5 August 1965.

73. AAN, KC, PZPR, BP, 237/XIX-223, Młodzież Świata, 1959, 1960, "Notatka w sprawie angielskiego wydania 'Młodzieży Świata,'" n.d., kk. 17–18, 17.

74. The Polish government seems to have built on a relatively strong presence of Poles in Indonesia under the Dutch in the interwar period, where Polish geologist Józef Zwierzycki contributed to the discovery of repositories of oil, solder, gold, and silver. In 1955, Poland initiated diplomatic relations with Indonesia, and in 1959, the first president of independent Indonesia, Sukarno (born Koesno Sosrodihardjo) visited Poland. For more information see "Indonezja," Serwis Rzeczypospolitej Polskiej, https://www.gov.pl/web/indonezja/relacje-dwustronne.

75. AAN, KC, PZPR, BP, 237/XIX-223, Młodzież Świata, 1959, 1960, Zarząd Główny RSW Prasa, Prezes, to Tow. Artur Starewicz, Kierownik Biura Prasy, KC, PZPR, Warsaw, 13 July 1960, k. 25.

76. HU OSA, 300-8-47, box 28, RFE/RL Research Institute, Publications Department, "Polish Situation Report," 28 May 1962, n.p. For further discussion of the monthly *Poland* see Marta Przybyło, "Oddziaływanie przez fotografię. Miesięcznik 'Polska' w latach 1954–1968," in *Początek przyszłości. Fotografia w miesięczniku "Polska" w latach 1954–1968*, edited by Marta Przybyło and Karolina Puchała-Rojek (Warsaw: Zachęta – Narodowa Galeria Sztuki, 2019), 23–31.

77. Anna Idzikowska-Czubaj, *Rock w Polsce. O paradoksach współistnienia* (Poznań: Wydawnictwo Poznańskie, 2011), 137.

78. Friszke, "Kultura czy ideologia," 115-145.

Chapter 4

1. See, for example, Tom Junes, *Student Politics in Communist Poland: Generations of Consent and Dissent* (London: Lexington Books, 2015); Hanna Świda-Ziemba, *Młodzież PRL. Portrety pokoleń w kontekście historii* (Kraków: Wydawnictwo Literackie, 2011); and Piotr Osęka, *My, ludzie z Marca. Autoportret pokolenia '68* (Wołowiec: Wydawnictwo Czarne, 2015).

2. This chapter builds on the critique of the concept of the intelligentsia as a unique intellectual community in the Soviet Union and Eastern Europe. As historian Benjamin Tromly has suggested, rather than approaching the intelligentsia through the prism of the group's own myth-making about themselves, scholars need to examine the

intelligentsia as "an historically constructed set of identifications and ideas." Benjamin Tromly, *Making the Soviet Intelligentsia: Universities and Intellectual Life under Stalin and Khrushchev* (New York: Cambridge University Press, 2014), 12.

3. Timothy Scott Brown and Lorena Anton, introduction to *Between the Avant-garde and the Everyday: Subversive Politics in Europe from 1957 to the Present,* edited by Brown and Anton (New York: Berghahn Books, 2011), 1–8, 5.

4. See, for example, Chelsea Szendi Schieder, "Left Out: Writing Women Back into Japan's 1968," in *The Global 1960s: Convention, Contest, and Counterculture,* edited by Tamara Chaplin and Jadwiga Pieper Mooney (New York: Routledge, 2018), 176–195; Mary Kay Vaughan, "Mexico 1968: Events, Assessments, and Antecedents," in *The Routledge Handbook of the Global Sixties: Between Protest and Nation Building,* edited by Chen Jian, Martin Klimke, Masha Kirasirova, Mary Nolan, Marilyn Young, and Joanna Waley-Cohen (New York: Routledge, 2018), 146–148; Colin Barker, "Some Reflections on Student Movements of the 1960s and Early 1970s," *Revista Crítica de Ciências* 81 (2008): 1–35, 6–7; Axel Schildt and Detlef Siegfried, "Introduction: Youth, Consumption, and Politics in the Age of Radical Change," in *Between Marx and Coca-Cola: Youth Cultures in Changing European Societies, 1960–1980,* edited by Schildt and Siegfried (New York: Berghahn Books, 2006), 19; Kostis Kornetis, *Children of the Dictatorship: Student Resistance, Cultural Politics and the "Long 1960s" in Greece* (New York: Berghahn Books, 2013), 14; and Howard Brick, *The Age of Contradictions: American Thought and Culture in the 1960s* (Ithaca, NY: Cornell University Press, 1998), esp. 23–43.

5. Adam and Zofia Mazurek, interview by the author, Warsaw, 16 June 2011. The Party School was funded by Marxist intellectual Adam Schaff and offered a two-year postgraduate program to train the Party cadres. The School was closed in September 1968.

6. AAN, RN, ZSP, KW, 1/15, Posiedzenia KW, materiały na posiedzenie KW dotyczące prasy studenckiej, 1969, "Studenci studiów dziennych wg. typów uczelni i ośrodków. Stan w dn. 31.12.1966 r.," k. 14. This number amounted to approximately 3 percent of young people between the ages of fifteen and twenty-nine. AAN, KC, PZPR, XIB/57 [Kancelaria Sekretarza KC i Członków Biura Politycznego, 1945–1981, 1988], Ruch młodzieżowy, notatki, analizy, 1967, „Propozycje Zarządów Głównych ZMS i ZMW w sprawie prasy młodzieżowej w związku z przewidywaną reorganizacją w dziedzinie wydawnictw," Warsaw, 30 October 1967, kk. 10–13, 10.

7. AAN, RN, ZSP, KW, 1/15, "Studenci studiów dziennych.," k. 14.

8. Jan Poprawa, "Na studenckiej stradzie (jazz-piosenka-kabaret)," in *Kultura studencka. Zjawisko, twórcy, instytucje,* edited by Edward Chudziński (Kraków: Fundacja STU, 2011), 201–233, 202.

9. APKr, KM, PZPR, Kraków, 29/2149/60, Protokoły posiedzeń egzekutywy KM wraz z załącznikami, 14 August–18 December 1959, "Praca ideologiczna w uczelnianych organizacjach partyjnych," n.d., kk. 317–325, 317.

10. For discussion of continuities between the interwar and postwar Polish university culture see John Connelly, *Captive University: The Sovietization of Czech, East German, and Polish Higher Education, 1945–1956* (Chapel Hill: University of North Carolina Press, 2000).

11. The interwar professoriate remained prominent at traditional universities such as Warsaw University and the Jagiellonian University in Kraków. New academic centers, however, such as Łódź, which acquired its first university in 1945, became "a magnet for interwar leftist intellectuals." See Agata Zysiak, *Punkty za pochodzenie. Powojenna modernizacja i uniwersytet w robotniczym mieście* (Kraków: Znak, 2016), esp. 50.

12. Reintroducing Marxism into university curricula after 1956 was a gradual process and differed from one school to another. For example, in 1958 in Kraków, not all higher education institutions, including the Academy of Fine Arts and the State Higher School of Theater, offered them. See APKr, KM, PZPR, Kraków, 29/2149/60, "Praca ideologiczna," k. 321.

13. On interwar antisemitic policies in Polish higher education, for example "ghetto benches" and "numerus clausus," see Szymon Rudnicki, "Anti-Jewish Legislation in Interwar Poland," in *Antisemitism and Its Opponents in Modern Poland*, edited by Robert Blobaum (Ithaca, NY: Cornell University Press, 2005), 148–170.

14. The TSKŻ was formed in 1950 as a result of the unification of the Central Committee of Jews in Poland (Centralny Komitet Żydów w Polsce, CKŻP), a political organization representing Jews in postwar Poland, and the culturally oriented Jewish Cultural Association (Żydowskie Towarzystwo Kulturalne, ŻTK). In 1953, the Socio-Cultural Association of Jews in Poland had thirty-three regional branches and more than 11,000 members. Piotr Pęziński, *Na rozdrożu. Młodzież żydowska w PRL, 1956–1968* (Warsaw: Żydowski Instytut Wydawniczy, 2014), 24.

15. Interview with Ewa, pt. 1, in Joanna Wiszniewicz, *Życie przecięte. Opowieści pokolenia Marca* (Wołowiec: Wydawnictwo Czarne, 2008), 53–64, 58.

16. The most significant increase in the number of students from working-class and peasant backgrounds was registered during the Stalinist era, 1948–1953, when the proportion of such students reached 59 percent of a total student body. This number, however, dropped to 51 percent between 1954 and 1957. APKr, KU, PZPR, Akademia Ekonomiczna w Krakowie, 29/2432/42, Korespondencja przychodząca, 1949–1953, 1958, "Struktura społeczna studentów w szkołach wyższych podległych M. Sz. W. w latach 1953–1957," March 1958, n.p.

17. Kazimierz Z. Sowa, "Dom studencki jako środowisko społeczne," in *Z badań nad środowiskiem domu studenckiego. Raporty z badań*, edited by Irena Kurzela, Aleksander Kamiński, and Sowa (Warsaw: Państwowe Wydawnictwo Naukowe, 1967), 45–105, esp. 85.

18. "Mezalians," in *Awans pokolenia. Młode pokolenie wsi polskiej*, edited by Józef Chałasiński (Warsaw: Ludowa Spółdzielnia Wydawnicza, 1964), 609–652, 648.

19. AAN, TPP, PMW, 1972, 5239, no. 129, n.p.

20. Andrzej Sadowski, interview by author, digital recording, Białystok, 11 February 2013.

21. HU OSA, 300-8-47, box 30, RFE/RL Research Institute, Publications Department, Situation Report, Poland, 4 November 1966, n.p.

22. David C. Engerman, "The Second World's Third World," *Kritika: Explorations in Russian and Eurasian History* 12, no. 1 (Winter 2011), 206.

23. Quoted in Mieczysław Andrzej Węgrzynowski, "Obyczajowość młodzieży studenckiej. Zwyczaj chodzenia," in *Młodzież epoki przemian. Z badań polskich*

socjologów, edited by Ryszard Dyoniziak (Warsaw: Nasza Księgarnia, 1965), 451–477, 461.

24. Andrzej Baranowski, "Pałacykiada," *Pałacyk. Konfrontacje*, Wrocław, 11 May 2002, 3. The original Polish word, *dzicz*, used in this personal recollection could refer to both a savage place and a savage people.

25. Katarzyna Stańczak-Wiślicz, " 'Być dziewczyną.' Wychowanie, dorastanie i edukacja dziewcząt," in Katarzyna Stańczak-Wiślicz, Piotr Perkowski, Malgorzata Fidelis, and Barbara Klich-Kluczewska, *Kobiety w Polsce, 1945–1989. Nowoczesność, równouprawnienie, komunizm* (Kraków: Universitas, 2020), 217–279.

26. *ITD*, 12 January 1964, 1.

27. *ITD*, 7 June 1964, 1.

28. "Stały kącik. Moja dziewczyna," *ITD*, 25 February 1962, 14.

29. Examples of the headlines in Kraków newspapers include: "She Gave Herself Away for Go Go Boots [Oddała się za kozaki]"; "A Super-comfortable Place for Trysts [Superkomfortowy dom schadzek]"; and "Free Love or Student Self-Rule [Wolna miłość czy samorządność studencka]." Quoted in Maciej Szumowski, "Ciotka w mini czy działacz w spódnicy," *Student* 1 (January 1968): 8–9, 9.

30. Węgrzynowski, "Obyczajowość młodzieży studenckiej," 467. The dormitory, consisting of five apartment buildings, housed as many as 3,000 students attending Łódź University, the Polytechnic, and the Medical Academy.

31. Quoted in Węgrzynowski, "Obyczajowość młodzieży studenckiej," 455.

32. Węgrzynowski, "Obyczajowość młodzieży studenckiej," 459.

33. Węgrzynowski, "Obyczajowość młodzieży studenckiej," 460.

34. Węgrzynowski, "Obyczajowość młodzieży studenckiej," 461.

35. Konrad Rokicki, *Kluby studenckie w Warszawie, 1956–1980* (Warsaw: IPN, 2018), 22.

36. Leopold René Nowak, "Szwedzkie kłopoty z nastolatkami," *Przekrój*, 5 September 1965, 11.

37. For further discussion of Hybrydy as a unique bohemian place in communist Poland see, for example, Tomasz Dominik and Marek Karewicz, *Złota młodzież, niebieskie ptaki. Warszawka lat 60* (Warsaw: Twój Styl, 2003); and Cezary Pasek, *Złota młodzież w PRL-u i jej obraz w literaturze i filmie* (Warsaw: Bellona, 2010). For discussion of the political dimension of student clubs in Poland and Czechoslovakia in the 1960s, see Zdeněk Nebřenský, *Marx, Engels, Beatles. Myšlenkový svět polských a československých vysokoškoláků, 1956–1968* (Prague: Akademie Masarykův ústav AV ČR, 2017).

38. Eugeniusz Mielcarek, "Dwudziestolecie kultury studenckiej (1956–1976). Romans z mecenasem," in Chudziński, *Kultura Studencka*, 329–345, 340.

39. AAN, RN, ZSP, Wydział Organizacyjny, 2/4, III Krajowy Zjazd ZSP, "Stenogram z posiedzenia Komisji Kulturalno-Oświatowej," 1957, kk. 1–53, 13.

40. Andrzej Ostoja-Sojecki, "Miejsce magiczne," *Pałacyk. Konfrontacje*, 11 May 2002, 2.

41. Krzysztof Miklaszewski, "Kwestia rodowodu," in Chudziński, *Kultura studencka*, 61–73, 64–65. For a detailed report on the activity of a total of twenty-two student clubs located in Wrocław in 1969 see APWr, Wrocławiu WrOK, 15, "Ogólna analiza stanu działalności studenckich klubów w m. Wrocławiu," Wrocław, 10 December 1969, kk. 1–15.

42. Piotr Wierzbicki, "Dyskusja o klubach. W obronie elitarności," *ITD*, 15 October 1967, 6–7.

43. Baranowski, "Pałacykiada," 3.

44. Wiesław Misiek, "16 moich miesięcy," *Pałacyk. Konfrontacje*, 11 May 2002, 13.

45. Jan Miodek, "Przyjaźń przetrwała," *Pałacyk. Konfrontacje*, 31 May 2003, 18.

46. Quoted in Magdalena Grzebałkowska, *Komeda. Osobiste życie jazzu* (Kraków: Znak, 2018), 248.

47. Jurek Lukierski, "Pałacyk jest jeszcze w Sewilli," *Pałacyk. Konfrontacje*, 31 May 2003, 7.

48. Marek Demiański, "Richard P. Feynman—urwisowaty geniusz," in Richard Feynman, *Pan raczy żartować, panie Feynman!* transl. Tomasz Bieroń (Kraków: Znak, 2018), 3–9, esp. 5–6..

49. Jolanta Wachowicz-Makowska, *Panienka w PRL-u* (Warsaw: Czytelnik, 2007), 147. Former male students often recall excessive drinking and partying as a way of resisting the stern reality of communism. See, for example, Dominik and Karewicz, *Złota młodzież*.

50. Quoted in Dominik and Karewicz, *Złota młodzież*, 71.

51. Krzysztof Piasecki, "Kocham Cię, Marian!," *Pałacyk. Konfrontacje*, 11 May 2002, 11.

52. Starting in 1956, Poland became an important site for international jazz events such as the All-Polish Jazz Festival in Sopot, first held in August 1956, and the annual Jazz on the Odra in Wrocław, initiated in 1964. On the history of jazz in Poland see Igor Pietraszewski, *Jazz w Polsce. Wolność improwizowana* (Warsaw: Nomos, 2012).

53. "Jazz to nie moda lecz epoka w muzyce," *Jazz*, February 1956, 4.

54. Jerzy Rudke and Franciszek Lipowicz, "Jazz-kluby—organizacje nie masowe," *Jazz*, January 1959, 2.

55. Tomasz Tłuczkiewicz, interview by author, digital recording, Warsaw, 12 February 2013.

56. Roman Waschko, "Jazz Fan," *Radar* 1 (January 1961), 16–17, 17.

57. Roman Waschko, "Jazzowe dziewczęta. Płeć silniejsza," *Radar* 7 (July 1961), 15.

58. Urszula Dudziak, *Wyśpiewam Wam wszystko* (Warsaw: Kayax, 2011), 200.

59. Dudziak, *Wyśpiewam Wam wszystko*, 200.

60. Andrzej Friszke, *Anatomia buntu. Kuroń, Modzelewski i komandosi* (Kraków: Znak, 2010), 167. Readers did not necessarily adopt a particular ideological program promoted by those authors. For example, only a handful of students were interested in Maoism, while a more significant Maoist fraction developed within the Polish ruling party under the leadership of Kazimierz Mijal, who founded an illegal Communist Party of Poland (Komunistyczna Partia Polski) in 1965. Mijal left Poland for Albania in 1966, but his associates in Poland continued to distribute anti-Soviet and pro-Chinese leaflets until 1969, when they were arrested and sentenced to several years in prison. See Przemysław Gasztold, "Maoizm nad Wisłą? Działalność Komunistycznej Partii Polski Kazimierza Mijala," *Pamięć i sprawiedliwość* 2, no. 32 (2018): 290–318. For official images of Maoism in Poland see David Tompkins, "The East Is Red? Images of China in East Germany and Poland through the Sino-Soviet Split," *Zeitschrift für Ostmitteleuropa-Forschung* 62, no. 3 (2013): 393–424.

61. Stefan Nowak, "Treść i struktura wewnętrzna postaw społecznych," in *Studenci Warszawy. Studium długofalowych przemian postaw i wartości*, edited by Nowak (Warsaw: Wydawnictwo Uniwersytetu Warszawskiego, 1991), 93–186, 98.

62. Nowak, "Treść i struktura," 99.

63. Quoted in Zofia Józefowicz, "Aneks 1. Wybrane sylwetki studentów Warszawy 1958 w wywiadach otwartych," in Nowak, *Studenci Warszawy*, 537–637, 548–49.

64. Quoted in Józefowicz, "Aneks 1," 547.

65. In November 1956, the Gomułka regime concluded an agreement with the Church under the leadership of Primate Stefan Wyszyński. This included lifting state interference in Church appointments below the rank of bishop, reestablishing the Joint Commission between the Episcopate and the state, and granting autonomy to the Catholic press. For more discussion, see, for example, A. Kemp-Welch, *Poland under Communism: A Cold War History* (New York: Cambridge University Press, 2008), 118.

66. APKr, KM, PZPR, Kraków, 29/2149/59, Protokoły posiedzeń egzekutywy KM wraz z załącznikami, 3 January–29 July 1959, "Informacja dot. działalności kleru na terenie m. Krakowa," n.d., kk. 280–287, 285.

67. Anna Pawełczyńska, "Treść, dynamika i funkcja postaw wobec religii," in Nowak, *Studenci Warszawy*, 315–350, esp. 316–317.

68. APKr, KM, PZPR w Krakowie, 29/2149/24, Protokoły posiedzeń plenarnych KM PZPR wraz z załącznikami, 4 June and 29 October 1959, "Stenogram z Plenarnego posiedzenia Krakowskiego Komitetu Miejskiego Polskiej Zjednoczonej Partii Robotniczej, odbytego w dniu 4 czerwca 1959 w sali obrad KW PZPR w Krakowie," kk. 1–98, 79. On the interaction between Catholic and leftist intelligentsia clubs see, for example, Friszke, *Anatomia buntu*.

69. The Oaza movement was officially established in 1976. In addition to elementary and secondary school students, it extended its activity to university students, young professionals, and later families. See Krzysztof Kosiński, *Oficjalne i prywatne życie młodzieży w czasach PRL* (Warsaw: Rosner & Wspólnicy, 2006), 82–83.

70. Karol Modzelewski, *Zajeździmy kobyłę historii. Wyznania poobijanego jeźdźca* (Warsaw: Iskry, 2013), 98–99.

71. Junes, *Student Politics in Communist Poland*, 75.

72. Irena Grudzińska Gross, interview by author, Boston, 23 November 2013.

73. The attack on Modzelewski and Michnik came from Gomułka himself in a speech at the plenary meeting of the Party Central Committee in July 1963.

74. The Commandos were one of several informal (and often overlapping) leftist groups active at Warsaw University at the time. Historian Andrzej Friszke estimates the number of students involved in such groups at approximately 100. Friszke, *Anatomia buntu*, 499.

75. Paula Sawicka quoted in Osęka, *My, Ludzie z Marca*, 134.

76. Barbara Toruńczyk, "Opowieść o pokoleniu marca. Przesłanie dla nowej lewicy," pt. 1, *Krytyka Polityczna* 15 (2008): 208–230, 211.

77. Jan Lityński quoted in Rokicki, *Kluby studenckie*, 46.

78. For recent works on the sexual revolution in the West see, for example, Rebecca Clifford, Robert Gildea, and Anette Warring, "Gender and Sexuality," in *Europe's*

1968: Voices of Revolt, edited by Robert Gildea, James Mark, and Anette Warring (Oxford: Oxford University Press, 2013), 239–257; and Dagmar Herzog, *Sex after Fascism: Memory and Morality in Twentieth-Century Germany* (Princeton, NJ: Princeton University Press, 2007).

79. Quoted in Osęka, *My, Ludzie z Marca,* 301.

80. Herzog, *Sex after Fascism,* 231.

81. Adam Michnik, "Anti-authoritarian Revolt: A Conversation with Daniel Cohn-Bendit," in Adam Michnik, *Letters from Freedom: Post–Cold War Realities and Perspectives,* edited by Irena Grudzińska Gross, with a foreword by Ken Jowitt (Berkeley: University of California Press, 1998), 29–67, 34.

82. Interview with Małgosia Tal, pt. 1, in Wiszniewicz, *Życie Przecięte,* 95–133, 107.

83. Interview with Małgosia Tal, in Wiszniewicz, *Życie Przecięte,* 132.

84. See, for example, Hanna Samson, "Subiektywny alfabet (ducha) lat siedemdziesiątych," in *Buntownicy. Polskie lata 70. i 80,* edited by Anna Grupińska and Joanna Wawrzyniak (Warsaw: Świat Książki, 2011), 454–460, 456.

Chapter 5

1. The most intense wave of nationwide demonstrations took place from March 9 to March 20, 1968, but other forms of protest, such as leaflet distribution, persisted until early May. For a chronology of events, see, for example, Jerzy Eisler, *Polski Rok 1968* (Warsaw: IPN, 2006); Piotr Osęka, *Marzec '68* (Kraków: Znak, 2008); and Tom Junes, *Student Politics in Communist Poland: Generations of Consent and Dissent* (London: Lexington Books, 2015), 103–122.

2. The antisemitic campaign (also known as the anti-Zionist campaign) in 1967–1968 terminated the Jewish community in Poland. For further discussion see, for example, Dariusz Stola, "Fighting against the Shadows: The Anti-Zionist Campaign of 1968," in *Anti-Semitism and Its Opponents in Modern Poland,* edited by Robert Blobaum (Ithaca, NY: Cornell University Press, 2005), 284–300; Dariusz Stola, *Kampania antysyjonistyczna w Polsce, 1967–1968* (Warsaw: Instytut Studiów Politycznych PAN, 2000); and Hans Christian Dahlmann, *Antisemitismus in Polen 1968. Interaktionen zwischen Partei und Gesellschaft* (Osnabrück: Fibre, 2013).

3. Adam Michnik, "Anti-authoritarian Revolt: A Conversation with Daniel Cohn-Bendit," in Adam Michnik, *Letters from Freedom: Post–Cold War Realities and Perspectives,* edited by Irena Grudzińska Gross, with a foreword by Ken Jowitt (Berkeley: University of California Press, 1998), 50. The conversation between Adam Michnik and Daniel Cohn-Bendit took place in May 1987 and first appeared in Daniel Cohn-Bendit, *Nous l'avons tant aimée, la révolution* (Paris, 1987). Like Michnik, former students began publishing their personal accounts of 1968 in the late 1970s and 1980s. By that time, many of the testimonies were influenced by the authors' experiences in their anticommunist opposition activities of the 1970s and 1980s. See, for example, Jakub Karpiński, *Krótkie spięcie (Marzec 1968)* (Paris: Polski

Instytut Literacki, 1977); *Marzec 1968. Relacje. Procesy* (Warsaw: NZS PW, 1981); and Anna Mieszczanek, ed., *Krajobraz po szoku* (Warsaw: Przedświt, 1989).

4. See, for example, Eisler, *Polski Rok 1968*, 15; and Andrzej Friszke, "Miejsce Marca 1968 wśród innych 'polskich miesięcy,'" in *Oblicza Marca 1968*, edited by Konrad Rokicki and Sławomir Stępień (Warsaw: IPN, 2004), 15–23.

5. See, for example, Robert Gildea, James Mark, and Anette Warring, eds., *Europe's 1968: Voices of Revolt* (Oxford: Oxford University Press, 2013); Kostis Kornetis, *Children of the Dictatorship: Student Resistance, Cultural Politics and the "Long 1960s" in Greece* (New York: Berghahn Books, 2013); and Gerd-Rainer Horn, *The Spirit of '68: Rebellion in Western Europe and North America, 1956–1976* (Oxford: Oxford University Press, 2007). An important strand of transnational scholarship has traced networks of activists and ideas between specific countries within and beyond Europe. See, for example, Martin Klimke, *The Other Alliance: Student Protest in West Germany and the United States in the Global Sixties* (Princeton, NJ: Princeton University Press, 2010).

6. For nation-specific cases see, for example, Martin Klimke and Joachim Scharloth, eds., *1968 in Europe: A History of Protest and Activism, 1956–1977* (New York: Palgrave Macmillan, 2008). For comparative approaches within Eastern Europe and between East and West see, for example, Aleksandra Konarzewska, Anna Nakai, and Michał Przeperski, eds., *Unsettled 1968 in the Troubled Present: Revisiting 50 Years of Discussions from East and Central Europe* (New York: Routledge, 2020); and Vladimir Tismaneanu, ed., *Promises of 1968: Crisis, Illusion, Utopia* (Budapest: Central European University Press, 2011). For an analysis of personal testimonies and the extent to which Polish students identified with their Western counterparts, see Osęka, Piotr Osęka, *My, ludzie z Marca. Autoportret pokolenia '68* (Wołowiec: Wydawnictwo Czarne, 2015), esp. 296–316. For a new integrative interpretation of sixties movements in Western, Eastern, and southern Europe see Timothy Scott Brown, *Sixties Europe* (Cambridge: Cambridge University Press, 2020). According to Brown, "what 1968 in East and West had in common was not just a set of globalizing commitments but a set of revolutionary problems that had yet to be resolved in either location." Brown, *Sixties Europe*, 26.

7. In the most notable case of the period, Czechoslovak students accused student leader Rudi Dutschke from West Germany, on his visit to Prague in April 1968, of "radical" and "utopian" ideas that reminded them of Stalinism in their own country rather than pointing the way toward genuine freedom and democracy. See Paulina Bren, "1968 East and West: Visions of Political Change and Student Protest from across the Iron Curtain," in *Transnational Moments of Change: Europe 1945, 1968, 1989*, edited by Gerd Rainer-Horn and Padraic Kenney (New York: Rowman and Littlefield, 2004), 119–135.

8. Expanding on Victoria Langland's study of the Brazilian student movement, I explore "how contemporaneous beliefs, fears, and suspicions about such [transnational] connections affected the course of local events." Victoria Langland, *Speaking of Flowers: Student Movements and the Making and Remembering of 1968 in Military Brazil* (Durham, NC: Duke University Press, 2013), 9. See also Victoria Langland,

"Transnational Connections of the Global Sixties as Seen by a Historian of Brazil," in *The Routledge Handbook of the Global Sixties: Between Protest and Nation Building*, edited by Chen Jian, Martin Klimke, Masha Kirasirova, Mary Nolan, Marilyn Young, and Joanna Waley-Cohen (New York: Routledge, 2018), 15–26.

9. On Third Worldism in Europe and the United States, see, for example, Quinn Slobodian, *Foreign Front: Third World Politics in Sixties West Germany* (Durham, NC: Duke University Press, 2012); Nico Slate, ed., *Black Power beyond Borders: The Global Dimensions of the Black Power Movement* (New York: Palgrave Macmillan, 2012); and Cynthia Young, *Soul Power: Culture, Radicalism, and the Making of a U.S. Third World Left* (Durham, NC: Duke University Press, 2006).

10. The term "global consciousness" comes from Scott Rutherford, Sean Mills, Susan Lord, Catherine Krull, and Karen Dubinsky, "Introduction: The Global Sixties," in *New World Coming: The Sixties and the Shaping of Global Consciousness*, edited by Karen Dubinsky, Catherine Krull, Susan Lord, Sean Mills, and Scott Rutherford (Toronto: Between the Lines, 2009), 1–6, 3.

11. Burleigh Hendrickson, "The Politics of Colonial History: Bourguiba, Senghor, and the Student Movements of the Global 1960s," in *The Global 1960s: Convention, Contest, and Counterculture*, edited by Tamara Chaplin and Jadwiga Pieper Mooney (New York: Routledge, 2018), 13–32, 28.

12. Until 1990, the Soviet government did not officially acknowledge the Katyń massacre, maintaining that it was the work of the Nazis. This was also the official line of the communist regime in Poland. For further discussion, see Wojciech Materski, Anna Cienciała, and Natalia S. Lebedeva, eds., *Katyń: A Crime without Punishment* (New Haven, CT: Yale University Press, 2008).

13. The Polish word *pokój* used in this phrase phonetically doubles as both "peace" and "room." Hence the jocular effect produced by the word play. The phrase "room with a kitchen" also alludes to the endemic shortage of housing in communist Poland, and the high demand for living spaces with individual rather than communal kitchens. For further discussion of living space in Eastern Europe and the Soviet Union see, for example, David Crowley and Susan E. Reid, eds., *Socialist Spaces: Sites of Everyday Life in the Eastern Bloc* (New York: Berg, 2002); and Steven Harris, *Communism on Tomorrow Street: Mass Housing and Everyday Life after Stalin* (Baltimore: Johns Hopkins University Press, 2013).

14. Michnik, "Anti-authoritarian Revolt," 36–37.

15. Irena Grudzińska Gross, interview by author, Boston, 23 November 2013..

16. Michnik, "Anti-authoritarian Revolt," 34.

17. Between 1952 and 1976, the legendary Polish émigré and World War II veteran Jan Nowak Jeziorański headed RFE's Polish section, which functioned as an important center for Polish émigré politics. In 1965, an estimated one-third of the Polish population regularly tuned in to RFE broadcasts. Andrzej Friszke, *Anatomia buntu. Kuroń, Modzelewski i komandosi* (Kraków: Znak, 2010), 68.

18. Barbara Toruńczyk, "Opowieść o pokoleniu marca. Przesłanie dla nowej lewicy," pt. 1, *Krytyka Polityczna* 15 (2008): 208–230; and Friszke, *Anatomia buntu*, 463.

19. See Jacek Kuroń and Karol Modzelewski, *Open Letter to the Party: Revolutionary Marxist Students in Poland Speak Out (1964–1968)*, trans. Gerard Paul (New York: Merit,

1968). The *Open Letter* was the collective work of many people, most of whom were involved in the Thaw movement, including Grażyna Kuroń (Jacek Kuroń's wife), Stanisław Gómułka, Joanna Majerczyk-Gómułkowa, Lechosław Goździk, and others. See Bartłomiej Starnawski, "Reformacja popaździernikowa. O strukturze argumentacji manifestu lewicowej opozycji politycznej w *Liście otwartym do Partii* Jacka Kuronia i Karola Modzelewskiego," in *Rok 1966. PRL na zakręcie. Idee-Dyskursy-Praktyki*, edited by Katarzyna Chmielewska, Grzegorz Wołowiec, and Tomasz Żukowski (Warsaw: Instytut Badań Literackich PAN, 2014), 169–190.

20. Kuroń and Modzelewski, *Open Letter to the Party*, 74.

21. See, for example, Bartłomiej Starnawski, "'Tu stoję, inaczej nie mogę ... ' Wokół *Listu Otwartego do Partii* oraz pojęcia 'rewizjonizmu' w perspektywie analizy retorycznej dyskursu o opozycji politycznej lat 60. w Polsce," in *Komunizm. Idee i praktyki w Polsce 1944–1989*, edited by Katarzyna Chmielewska, Agnieszka Mrozik, and Grzegorz Wołowiec (Warsaw: Instytut Badań Literackich PAN, 2018), 377–433.

22. Kuroń and Modzelewski were released in 1967 but then were imprisoned again for their involvement in March 1968.

23. Friszke, *Anatomia buntu*, 222.

24. Andrzej Paczkowski, interview by author, digital recording, Warsaw, 22 June 2012.

25. James Mark, Péter Apor, Radina Vučetić, and Piotr Osęka, "'We Are with You, Vietnam': Transnational Solidarities in Socialist Hungary, Poland, and Yugoslavia," *Journal of Contemporary History* 50, no. 3 (2015), 444.

26. Quoted in Junes, *Student Politics in Communist Poland*, 94.

27. Currently Szlajfer denies that he wanted to go to Cuba in 1967. He claims that he only called the Cuban embassy to ask for assistance in organizing a meeting at the student dormitory to discuss Cuban-Soviet relations after the death of Che Guevara in October 1967. Documents of the security apparatus, however, confirm Szlajfer's meeting with a security officer and his sending a letter to the Ministry of Internal Affairs in 1965. Friszke, *Anatomia buntu*, 492.

28. International Workers' Day on May 1 was a public holiday in state socialist countries. The celebrations included street marches of workers and students. The main parade typically took place in the capital city with the participation of Party-state leaders.

29. Friszke, *Anatomia buntu*, 418–419.

30. Quoted in Friszke, *Anatomia buntu*, 420.

31. "Dokument nr. 235," in *Marzec 1968 w dokumentach MSW*, edited by Franciszek Dąbrowski, Piotr Gontarczyk, and Paweł Tomasik (Warsaw: IPN, 2008), 822.

32. Osęka, *Marzec '68*, 169.

33. Barbara Dąbrowska (Anna Dodziuk), "Musiałam to wybrać," in Mieszczanek, *Krajobraz po szoku*, 88–98, 90.

34. Article 71 of the Constitution of the People's Republic of Poland, adopted in 1952, stated: "the People's Republic of Poland guarantees its citizens the right to freedom of speech, print, assembly and rallies, marches and manifestations," http://prawo.sejm. gov.pl/isap.nsf/download.xsp/WDU19520330232/O/D19520232.pdf.

35. "Wiec w obronie swobód demokratycznych. Piątek godz 12-ta. Dziedziniec UW. Precz z represjami. Autonomia uniwersytetu zagrożona!" in *Marzec 1968. Dokumenty. Odezwy i ulotki* (Warsaw: NZS PW, 1981), 7–8.

36. Quoted in Osęka, *Marzec '68*, 173.
37. Scholars have debated the identities of the attackers. Most likely, many of these workers belonged to the Party or to the Voluntary Reserve of the Citizens' Militia (Ochotnicza Rezerwa Milicja Obywatelskiej; ORMO), a paramilitary organization established in 1946 to assist the national police. In addition, the group probably included functionaries of the political education section of the Polish army dressed as civilians. See Osęka, *Marzec '68*, 174.
38. Teresa Bochwic, "Moja odpowiedź," in Mieszczanek, *Krajobraz po szoku*, 72–87, here 76.
39. The Polish word "Żydówa" is a derogatory term for a Jewish woman. Krystyna Starczewska, "'W jakimś sensie byłam pierwszą ofiarą tej napaści.' Krystyna Starczewska o tym jak rozpoczął się Marzec 1968," 6 March 2018 http://wyborcza.pl/10,82983,23151201,w-jakims-sensie-bylam-pierwsza-ofiara-tej-napasci-krystyna.html.
40. For a transnational perspective on gender in 1968, see Sara M. Evans, "Sons, Daughters, and Patriarchy: Gender and the 1968 Generation," *American Historical Review* 114, no. 2 (2009): 331–347. On antifeminist reactions to 1968, see, for example, Mary Kay Vaughan, "Mexico 1968: Events, Assessments, and Antecedents," in Jian et al., *The Routledge Handbook of the Global Sixties*, 146–148; and Langland, *Speaking of Flowers*.
41. Quoted in "Wypisy," in Mieszczanek, *Krajobraz po szoku*, 34–60, here 34. The male name "Dżery" is used here as a Polish phonetic spelling of "Jerry," which had strong American connotations.
42. Jacek Kuroń, *Wiara i wina. Do i od komunizmu* (Wrocław: Wydawnictwo Dolnośląskie, 1995), 294.
43. AAN, KC, PPZPR, KSM, 237/XXXV-24, "Informacja o wydarzeniach na Wyższych Uczelniach w marcu 1968 r.," kk. 18–49, esp. 32. Students from Warsaw Polytechnic included the following point in their resolution in support of university students: "we protest against the use of violence and beatings of women." See "Rezolucja studentów zgromadzonych w auli Politechniki Warszawskiej w dn. 9 marca 1968 r.," in *Marzec 1968. Dokumenty*, 11–13, 11.
44. Osęka, *Marzec '68*, 184.
45. Julian Kwiek, *Marzec 1968 w Krakowie* (Kraków: Księgarnia Akademicka, 2008), 52.
46. Włodzimierz Suleja, "Wrocław," in Rokicki and Stępień, *Oblicza marca 1968*, 199–223, esp. 199–202.
47. Text by Natan Tenenbaum reprinted in Grażyna Jaworska and Henryk Głowacki, *Folklor marcowy. Marzec 1968* (Warsaw: NZS PW, 1981), 10. Cardinal Stefan Wyszyński was the head of the Catholic Church in Poland from 1948 to 1981. The original text read: "Sławne to były dzieła, sławne były czasy / A jak było—opowiem—bo wszystko znam z prasy. / Więc Wyszyński z Kuroniem za pieniądze Mao / Chcieli Żydom zaprzedać naszą Polskę całą." I thank Jan Fidelis for translating the poem.
48. Interview with Lena, pt. 2, in Joanna Wiszniewicz, *Życie Przecięte. Opowieści Pokolenia Marca* (Wołowiec: Wydawnictwo Czarne, 2008), 403–408, 405.
49. Tomasz Tłuczkiewicz, interview by author, digital recording, Warsaw, 12 February 2013.
50. Suleja, "Wrocław," 223.

51. Ryszard Terlecki, "Kraków," in Rokicki and Stępień, *Oblicza Marca 1968*, 131–140, esp. 139–140.

52. Edyta Wróbel, "Kielecczyzna," in Rokicki and Stępień, *Oblicza marca 1968*, 115-130, 120–122.

53. Wróbel, "Kielecczyzna," 120–121.

54. "Szyfrogram nr. 158, 9 April 1968," in *Marzec '68 w Białymstoku. Wybór źródeł*, edited by Urszula Gierasimiuk (Białystok: IPN, 2008), 209. On the popular reception of the antisemitic campaign, see, for example, Marcin Zaremba, "Biedni Polacy 1968. Społeczeństwo polskie wobec wydarzeń marcowych w świetle raportów KW i MSW dla kierownictwa PZPR," *Więź* 3 (1998): 161–172; and Osęka, *Marzec '68*, 207–266.

55. HU OSA, 300-8-47, box 30, RFE/RL Research Institute, Publications Department, "Polish Situation Report," March 14, 1968, n.p. The Polish Military Mission in Germany was formed in 1945 as part of the Allied Control Council for Germany. The Mission then served as a Polish diplomatic post in West Germany until the establishment of the Polish Embasssy in the Federal Republic of Germany in 1974.

56. Factional struggles were the modus operandi of communist parties in Eastern Europe, and the only way to gain power or advance in the Party structures was to discredit (or physically purge, as under Stalinism) the opposing group. Under Stalinism, the main dividing line ran between the Muscovites (those who had spent the war years in the Soviet Union) and the home communists (those who had remained in their own countries). During de-Stalinization in Poland in the mid-1950s, the two dominant factions were the "liberal" Puławianie, who supported reforms, and the "hardline" Natolińczycy, who opposed them. Although Gomułka came to power in 1956 as a reformer, he eventually allied himself with the hardliners. For further discussion of internal struggles within communist parties in Eastern Europe see, for example, Zbigniew Brzeziński, *The Soviet Bloc: Unity and Conflict*, rev. ed. (Cambridge, MA: Harvard University Press, 1967). Moczar's faction was new in the early 1960s, and it consisted mainly of World War II veterans from both the communist and noncommunist anti-Nazi resistance (the People's Army and the Home Army, respectively). They bonded over their wartime experiences and apotheosized soldiering. Historians have often described the Partisans as antiintelligentsia, promilitary, and seeking to combine extreme nationalism with communist doctrine. For key political figures behind the antisemitic campaign, see Mikołaj Kunicki, *Between the Brown and the Red: Nationalism, Catholicism, and Communism in Twentieth-Century Poland; The Politics of Bolesław Piasecki* (Athens: University of Ohio Press, 2012).

57. See Tomasz Żukowski, "Ustanowienie nacjonalistycznego pola dyskursu społecznego. Między partią a Kościołem w roku 1966," in Chmielewska, Wołowiec, and Żukowski, *Rok 1966*, 11–38; and Zbigniew Marcin Kowalewski, "Posłowie. Polska między rewolucjami a czystkami etnicznymi," in Michał Siermiński, *Dekada przełomu. Polska lewica opozycyjna, 1968–1980*, (Warsaw: Książka i Prasa, 2016), 303–352, esp. 348.

58. Żukowski, "Ustanowienie nacjonalistycznego pola dyskursu społecznego," 17.

59. The National Democratic Party, or Endecja, was established in 1893 by Roman Dmowski, who condemned military uprisings staged by Polish elites against the Russian empire in the nineteenth century as self-destructive and turned instead to integral nationalism as the most effective way to strengthen the nation. Endecja

leaders were known for inciting popular hatred against minorities—especially Jews, blaming them for undermining the Polish nation from within. For further discussion, see Brian Porter, *When Nationalism Began to Hate: Imagining Modern Politics in Nineteenth-Century Poland* (New York: Oxford University Press, 2002).

60. Maria Janion, "Wprowadzenie. Trudna klasa w ciężkiej szkole," in *Rzeczy mgliste. Eseje i studia,* edited by Joanna Tokarska-Bakir (Sejny: Fundacja Pogranicze, 2004), 5–10, 7.

61. Marek Nowakowski, *Syjoniści do Syjamu. Zapiski z lat 1967–1968* (Warsaw: Świat Książki, 2009), 6.

62. Jérôme Bourdon has argued that the state of Israel was distinctively alluring to the global mass media in the 1960s, including sexualized female soldiers and the idealized community of the kibbutz. The Six-Day War and the subsequent occupation of the West Bank was a turning point in "shifting sympathies" from Israel to the Palestinians, especially in Western Europe. Jérôme Bourdon, "The Export of Zionism? Global Images of Israel in the 1960s," in Chaplin and Mooney, *The Global 1960s,* 236–254.

63. Mieczysław Rakowski, *Dzienniki polityczne 1967–1968* (Warsaw: Iskry, 1999), 63.

64. Nowakowski, *Syjoniści do Syjamu,* 6.

65. Daniel Blatman, "Polish Jewry, the Six-Day War, and the Crisis of 1968," in *The Six-Day War and World Jewry,* edited by Eli Lederhendler (College Park: University Press of Maryland, 2000), 291–310. Romania was the only socialist country that did not break diplomatic relations with Israel.

66. Historians consider Gomułka's speech at the Congress of the Trade Unions on June 19, 1967, to be the beginning of the antisemitic campaign. The speech included the following: "we cannot ignore the people who, when facing a threat to world peace and Poland's security and peaceful existence, take the side of the aggressors, the havoc-wreakers and the imperialists. We do not want to have a fifth column in our country. I urge those who feel that these words are directed at them—regardless of their nationality—to draw appropriate conclusions." See Stola, *Kampania antysyjonistyczna w Polsce,* 39. The translated quote comes from Martyna Rusiniak-Karwat, "Fifth Column," Museum of History of Polish Jews Polin, Vitual Shtetl, Estranged: March '68 and Its Aftermath https://marzec68.sztetl.org.pl/en/slowo/piata-kolumna/.

67. AAN, KC, PZPR, KSM, 237/XXXV-24, untitled document, kk. 1–9, k. 3.

68. In this case, the name Radio Free Europe, commonly referred to in Poland, including by the official media, as Radio Wolna Europa, was deliberately written in German.

69. "Ulotki ORMO. Kogo popieracie?," in *Marzec 1968. Dokumenty,* 59–60. Many of the Commandos were raised in a cosmopolitan Polish-Jewish intelligentsia environment. On the family backgrounds of the Commandos, see, for example, Piotr Osęka, Polymeris Voglis, and Anna von der Goltz, "Families," in Gildea, Mark, and Warring, *Europe's 1968,* 46–71; and Agnes Arndt, *Rote Bürger: Eine Milieu- Und Beziehungsgeschichte Linker Dissidenz in Polen (1956–1976)* (Göttingen: Vandenhoeck & Ruprecht, 2013). The derogatory term "banana youth" (*bananowa młodzież*) was commonly used with regard to urban elite youth, who supposedly practiced luxurious lifestyles symbolized by the eating of bananas, a fruit that was rarely accessible in Polish stores at the time.

70. "List Beaty Dąbrowskiej do I sekretarza KC PZPR, Władysława Gomułki," in *Marzec '68. Między tragedią a podłością*, edited by Grzegorz Sołtysiak and Józef Stępień (Warsaw: PROFI, 1998), 360–363. Dąbrowska also complained of physical abuse while under arrest, including beatings in the face and forced starvation.

71. The topic of sexual violence—actual or implied—in the state's treatment of female students in 1968 has not been explored. Available sources say little about sexual assault, as this is still a taboo topic in Poland. Some women, however, have recently come forward with their stories, which hint at verbal threats of sexual violence. Krystyna Starczewska, for example, has recounted an incident from March 1968, when a group of men approached her near her apartment building. They started shoving her around and threatened to do "something to me," all in the presence of passive onlookers. Krystyna Starczewska, " 'W jakimś sensie byłam pierwszą ofiarą tej napaści,' " 6 March 2018 http://wyborcza.pl/10,82983,23151201,w-jakims-sensie-bylam-pierwsza-ofiara-tej-napasci-krystyna.html.

72. Jan Guranowski, "Pod sztandarem Marksa przeciw Marksowi," *Trybuna Ludu*, June 2, 1968, 5.

73. For further discussion, see Jerzy Jedlicki, *A Suburb of Europe: Nineteenth-Century Polish Approaches to Western Civilization* (Budapest: Central European University Press, 1999).

74. Włodzimierz Sokorski, "Integracja narodowa," *Radar*, no. 7 (July 1968): 6–7, 6.

75. Marian Jakubowski, "O precyzyjne rozumienie pojęć: patriotyzm, internacjonalizm, kosmopolityzm, nacjonalizm," in *Patriotyzm, ideologia, wychowanie. Dyskusja na temat patriotycznego i internacjonalistycznego wychowania*, edited by Wojciech Pomykało (Warsaw: Ministerstwo Obrony Narodowej, 1968), 70–81, 76.

76. See, for example, Wojciech Pomykało, "Jaką mamy młodzież," *Wychowanie*, 16–31 August 1968, 4–12.

77. Krzysztof M. Gawlikowski, "Bitwa naszego pokolenia," *ITD*, 7 July 1968, 4–5, 4.

78. Between March 8 and April 6, the security forces apprehended a total of 2,725 people nationwide, including 641 university students, 487 secondary school students, 272 white-collar workers, 937 blue-collar workers, and 215 unemployed persons. Out of this number, 319 people were placed under arrest, including 82 university students; 1,224 people were subject to further investigation, including 280 university students. By the end of October 1968, seventy-eight university students had been put on trial, and sixty-three of them had received prison sentences (of 6–18 months) in conjunction with financial penalties. The political trials of leading Commandos, including Adam Michnik, Irena Grudzińska, and Barbara Toruńczyk, took place in late 1968 and early 1969. For further discussion see Andrzej Friszke, "Rok 1968—koniec i początek," *Zeszyty Literackie* 142, no. 2 (2018): 76–96, esp. 83–84.

79. Eisler, *Polski Rok 1968*, 320; and "Dyskusja," in *Oblicza marca 1968*, 230–243, 236.

80. Osęka, *Marzec '68*, 285–306.

81. Dariusz Stola, *Emigracja pomarcowa* (Warsaw: Instytut Studiów Społecznych UW, 2000), 9.

82. Friszke, "Rok 1968—koniec i początek," 89.

83. Stola, *Emigracja pomarcowa*, 14–17.

84. The travel documents stated that the owner "did not possess citizenship of the People's Republic of Poland." Stola, *Emigracja pomarcowa*, 7–8.

85. Michnik, "Anti-authoritarian Revolt," 45.

86. Michnik, "Anti-authoritarian Revolt," 48. In the eyes of communist states, assigning an intellectual to manual labor, as happened to many dissidents in Eastern Europe, was a form of punishment.

87. On Polish Marxist intellectual traditions see, for example, Eric Blanc, "Anti-imperial Marxism: Borderland Socialists and the Evolution of Bolshevism on National Liberation," *International Socialist Review*, no. 100 (2016), https://isreview.org/issue/100/anti-imperial-marxism; Piotr Laskowski, *Szkice z dziejów anarchizmu* (Warsaw: Muza, 2006); Timothy Snyder, *Nationalism, Marxism, and Modern Central Europe: A Biography of Kazimierz Kelles-Krauz* (Oxford: Oxford University Press, 1997); and Andrzej Walicki, *Stanisław Brzozowski and the Polish Beginning of "Western Marxism"* (New York: Clarendon Press, 1989). For a discussion of 1968 as the demise of the Polish oppositional Left, see Katarzyna Chmielewska and Tomasz Żukowski, "Trauma marca," in Chmielewska, Wołowiec, and Żukowski, *Rok 1966*, 380–395.

88. HU OSA, 300-50-13, box 1, RFE Confidential Reports on Poland, 1971–1972, "Wrażenia z Polski," September 29, 1971, n.p.

89. Kacper Szulecki, "'Freedom and Peace Are Indivisible': On the Czechoslovak and Polish Dissident Input to the European Peace Movement, 1985–1989," in *Entangled Protest: Transnational Approaches to the History of Dissent in Eastern Europe and the Soviet Union*, edited by Robert Brier (Osnabrück: Fibre, 2013), 199–228, esp. 207.

90. See, for example, Aldona Jawłowska and Zofia Dworakowska, eds., *Wolność w systemie zniewolenia. Rozmowy o polskiej kontrkulturze* (Warsaw: Wydawnictwo Uniwersytetu Warszawskiego, 2008).

91. Michnik, "Anti-authoritarian Revolt," 39.

92. Michnik, "Anti-authoritarian Revolt," 41–42.

Chapter 6

1. Bogusław Tracz, *Hippiesi, kudłacze, chwasty. Hipisi w Polsce w latach 1967–1975* (Katowice-Kraków: IPN, 2014), 150–151.

2. Theodore Roszak, *The Making of a Counter Culture: Reflections on the Technocratic Society and Its Youthful Opposition* (New York: Anchor Books, 1969). On more recent definitions of "counterculture" see, for example, Jeremi Suri, "The Rise and Fall of the International Counterculture," *American Historical Review* 114, no. 1 (February 2009): 45–68. The Polish term *kontrkultura* emerged in the early 1970s, but it tended to be exclusively applied to the West, at least in official discourses and scholarly publications. For a pioneering Polish-language study of countercultural movements in the West see Aldona Jawłowska, *Drogi kontrkultury* (Warsaw: PIW, 1975).

3. Juliane Fürst, "Love, Peace and Rock 'n Roll on Gorky Street: The 'Emotional Style' of the Soviet Hippie Community," *Contemporary European History* 23 (November 2014): 565–587, 584. See also Fürst, *Flowers through Concrete: Exploration in Soviet Hippieland* (Oxford: Oxford University Press, 2021).

4. Joachim C. Häberlen, "Dropping Out of Socialism? A Western Perspective," in *Dropping out of Socialism: The Creation of Alternative Spheres in the Soviet Bloc*, edited by Juliane Fürst and Josie McLellan (Lanham, MD: Lexington Books, 2017), 303–318, 315.

5. Joachim C. Häberlen and Mark Keck-Szajbel, introduction to *The Politics of Authenticity: Countercultures and Radical Movements across the Iron Curtain, 1968–1989*, edited by Häberlen and Keck-Szajbel (New York: Berghahn Books, 2019), 1–23, 9.

6. The pioneering Polish-language monograph on the hippie movement by Bogusław Tracz has provided invaluable insights on the hippie community but has relied heavily on the reports produced by the security apparatus. The book often replicates the language found in institutional documents. See Tracz, *Hippiesi, kudłacze, chwasty.* For an interesting comparative analysis of hippie communities in Poland and Ukraine, see William Jay Risch, "Only Rock 'n' Roll? Rock Music, Hippies, and Urban Identities in Lviv and Wrocław, 1965–1980," in *Youth and Rock in the Soviet Bloc: Youth Cultures, Music, and the State in Russia and Eastern Europe*, edited by William Jay Risch (Lanham, MD: Lexington Books, 2015), 81–99.

7. I was inspired by American historian David Farber, who has urged scholars to "move past the label [of counterculture] and instead historicize the countercultural project." This involves "tracing what was laid out in real time in words and deeds by many in the sixties era as they struggled to find spaces in which they might feel less complicit in practices and beliefs they saw as destructive of their own freedom and that of others in American society." David Farber, "Building the Counterculture, Creating Right Livelihoods: The Counterculture at Work," *The Sixties: A Journal of History, Politics and Culture* 6, no. 1 (2013): 1–24, 2–3.

8. In 1973, the Wrocław festival was renamed the International Festival of Open Theater.

9. The name Empik came from the abbreviation for the Klub Międzynarodowej Prasy i Książki (Club of International Press and Book) established in 1948. The Empiks could be found in all large cities in Poland, and they usually featured a bookstore, a reading room for domestic and international press, and a café. These clubs also served as centers for cultural events such as art exhibitions or meetings with renowned writers and artists. In addition, some Empiks offered foreign language courses. In personal interviews, Empiks have prominently figured as places where people acquired foreign reading material, fashion journals, or vinyl records. See, for example, Mieczysław Janowski, interview by the author, Wrocław, 17 July 2013; and Adam and Zofia Mazurek, interview.

10. Fanfan was a protagonist in the 1952 French period comedy *Fanfan la Tulipe*. Gérard Philipe played Fanfan.

11. The name *bitnicy* was probably adopted from the contemporary Polish popular press, which featured articles about American beatniks. The beatniks were usually depicted as anti-capitalist, but also decadent and misguided. The term "beatnik" was used in other European countries such as France to denote "a hippie, drifter, or young itinerant." Richard Ivan Jobs, *Backpack Ambassadors: How Youth Travel Integrated Europe* (Chicago: University of Chicago Press, 2017), 148.

12. Wasz Andrzej, "Długowłosi," *Nowa Wieś*, 25 September 1966, 15. The Polish word *obojniak* (plural *obojniacy*) is a derogatory term for someone whose gender is unrecognizable, possessing both female and male attributes.

13. "O hippies źle i lepiej," *Forum*, 24–31 December 1967, 28–29.

14. "Prorok," in *Hipisi w PRL-u,* edited by Kamil Sipowicz (Warsaw: Baobab, 2008), 161–169, 165. Prorok (Prophet) is a pseudonym of Józef Pyrz (1946-2016) considered to be a founder of the hippie movement in Poland.

15. After 1945, religion lessons were taught at Polish schools in agreement with the Polish interwar constitution of March 1921. They were not obligatory, however. The Polish communist government began gradually withdrawing religion from schools in the late 1940s, but the process was not complete until 1961. Religious instruction returned to Polish schools in 1990. See "Ustawa z dnia 15 lipca 1961 r. o rozwoju system oświaty i wychowania," http://prawo.sejm.gov.pl/isap.nsf/DocDetails.xsp?id= WDU19610320160.

16. Milo Kurtis, interview by author, digital recording, Warsaw, 15 February 2013.

17. Milo Kurtis, interview.

18. Jerzy Illg, interview by author, digital recording, Kraków, 22 June 2011.

19. Olga Jackowska and Kamil Sipowicz, *Kora, Kora. A planety szaleją* (Warsaw: Agora, 2011), 47.

20. Most of the Polish citizens of Ukrainian ethnicity found themselves in the Western Territories as a result of the so-called Operation Vistula, conducted by the Polish military in 1947. An estimated 140,000 Ukrainians and other Ruthenian regional groups were deported and scattered throughout western Poland. For more discussion see Timothy Snyder, "'To Resolve the Ukrainian Question Once and for All': The Ethnic Cleansing of Ukrainians in Poland, 1943-1947," *Journal of Cold War Studies* 1, no. 2 (Spring 1999): 86–120.

21. Padraic Kenney, *Rebuilding Poland: Workers and Communists, 1945–1950* (Ithaca, NY: Cornell University Press, 1997), 156. In 1947, an estimated 47,000 Jews lived in Lower Silesia, including 20,000 in Wrocław. This was 40–50 percent of all the Polish Jews who survived the Holocaust. By the late 1940s, the majority of Polish Jews had emigrated. For further discussion see Marek Ordyłowski, *Życie codzienne we Wrocławiu 1945–1948* (Wrocław: Zakład im. Ossolińskich, 1991), esp. 46; and Bożena Szaynok, *Ludność Żydowska na Dolnym Śląsku, 1945–1950* (Wrocław: Uniwersytet Wrocławski, 2000), esp. 27. For a general discussion of postwar Wrocław see Gregor Thum, *Uprooted: How Breslau Became Wrocław during the Century of Expulsions* (Princeton, NJ: Princeton University Press, 2011).

22. Alicja Imlay, interview by the author, digital recording, Szalejów Górny, 13 July 2013.

23. Natalia LL, interview by Tomasz Raczek, Szczerotok, Radio TOK FM, 29 April 2015. The avant-garde artist and photographer Natalia LL studied at the Academy of Fine Arts in Wrocław in the late 1950s and early 1960s. In the interview, she spoke, in particular, about artistic experimentation and exhibitions of Consumer Art with limited access to the public taking place in Wrocław at the time. Similar views were expressed by the musician, composer, and journalist Bogusław Klimsa. Bogusław Klimsa, interview by author, digital recording, Wrocław, 12 May 2016.

24. Alicja Imlay, interview.

25. Artur Trapszyc, *Lokalny pejzaż kontrkultury. Peace, Love i PRL (komentarz do wystawy)* (Toruń: Muzeum Etnograficzne, 2013), 40.

26. AIPN, 0224/656/4, "Informacja. Dotyczy: negatywnych zjawisk wystepujących wśród młodzieży szkolnej na tle narkomanii i tzw. ruchu 'hippies,'" Warsaw, 20 October 1971, kk. 93–100, 96.

27. Irena Groblewska, interview by author, digital recording, Emilianówka, 27 July 2013.

28. According to Eric Zolov, in the aftermath of the student massacre in Mexico City in June 1968, the young Mexicans' turn to the counterculture "offered the possibility for continued protest, only now by repudiating rather than engaging society as a strategy for change." Eric Zolov, *Refried Elvis: The Rise of the Mexican Counterculture* (Berkeley: University of California Press, 1999), 132.

29. Jan Poprawa, interview by author, digital recording, Kraków, 28 June 2012.

30. Jerzy Illg, "Polskie lato miłości," heh.pl forum, 8 October 2008 http://f.heh.pl/ftopic7 031.html.

31. Interview with Tomasz Rodowicz by Zofia Dworakowska in Aldona Jawłowska and Zofia Dworakowska, eds., *Wolność w systemie zniewolenia. Rozmowy o polskiej kontrkulturze* (Warsaw: Wydawnictwo Uniwersytetu Warszawskiego, 2008), 220–238, 222.

32. Arthur Marwick, *The Sixties: Cultural Transformation in Britain, France, Italy and the United States, c. 1958–c. 1974* (Oxford: Oxford University Press, 2000), 480–481.

33. AIPN, 0224/656/4, "Informacja. Dotyczy: negatywnych zjawisk występujących wśród mlodzieży," k. 94.

34. Trapszyc, *Lokalny pejzaż kontrkultury*, 21.

35. AIPN, 0224/656/3, "Zestawienie zdjęć fotograficznych wykonanych w dniu 1. IV. 1971 r., na miejscu ujawnienia rysunków i napisów," kk. 138–139.

36. Irena Groblewska, interview.

37. Krzysztof Jerzy Baranowski, „Powiedziałem, że w Peerelu to ja do wojska nie pójdę," in *Buntownicy. Polskie lata 70 i 80*, edtied by Anna Grupińska and Joanna Wawrzyniak (Warsaw: Świat Książki, 2011), 168–175, 170.

38. See, for example, "Prezes," in Sipowicz, *Hipisi w PRL-u*, 311–316, 315; and AIPN, 0224/656/3, "Informacja o społecznych nieprzystosowaniach i przestępczości młodzieży," 31 December 1971, kk. 150–166, 161.

39. The security apparatus recorded a case in which Polish hippies engaged in global politics in a more explicit way, but this was a rare instance. In September 1969, a group of more than fifty hippies staged a demonstration against the Vietnam War at the American embassy in Warsaw. They carried banners with the following signs: "The world has cast us aside, because we speak the truth," "Stop War in Vietnam," and "Everyone wants to live, end all war." See AIPN, 0224/656/1, Komendant stołeczny MO w Warszawie, "Meldunek specjalny dot. Wydarzeń szczególnego znaczenia zaistniałych w m.st. Warszawie w dniu 14.IX.1969 r.," Warsaw, 14 September 1969, kk. 89–90, 89.

40. Aldona Jawłowska, "Kontrkultura w poszukiwaniu nowych koncepcji człowieka i ludzkiego świata," in Jawłowska and Dworakowska, *Wolność w systemie zniewolenia,*

15–47. For example, Jerzy Grotowski (1933–1999), the legendary director of the experimental theater in Wrocław Teatr Laboratorium, traveled to India in the early 1970s, where he became immersed in Hindu philosophy and culture. See Zbigniew Osiński, *Grotowski's Journeys to the East* (New York: Routledge, 2014).

41. Jawłowska, "Kontrkultura w poszukiwaniu nowych koncepcji," 36–37.

42. Interview with Jacek Ostaszewski by Adam Rubczak in Jawłowska and Dworakowska, *Wolność w systemie zniewolenia*, 289–302, 293.

43. On cross-border international hippie travel see, for example, Jobs, *Backpack Ambassadors*, 136–193; and Mark Liechty, *Far Out: Counterculture Seekers and the Tourist Encounter in Nepal* (Chicago: University of Chicago Press, 2017).

44. AIPN, 0224/656/2, "Wykaz osób należacych do ruchu hippies z terenu kraju i z zagranicy, utrzymujących kontakty z hippiesami krakowskimi," n.d., kk. 19–22, 22.

45. AIPN, 0224/656/1, "Informacja dot. grupy młodzieżowej 'hippies,'" Warsaw, 23 September 1969, kk. 72–81, 76.

46. Tracz, *Hippiesi, kudłacze, chwasty*, 243.

47. In May 1965, Ginsberg was crowned the King of May by students in Prague at the annual May celebrations. The incident provoked a strong reaction from the Czechoslovak government. Ginsberg was beaten by the secret police and expelled from the country on the basis of "moral as well as political danger" to the young generation. For further discussion see Petr Kopecký, "Czeching the Beat, Beating the Czech: Ginsberg and Ferlinghetti in Czechia," *The Sixties: A Journal of History, Politics, and Culture* 3, no. 1 (June 2010): 97–103. See also Allen Ginsberg, *Iron Curtain Journals, January–May 1965*, edited by Michael Schumacher (Minneapolis: University of Minnesota Press, 2018). The Polish security apparatus recorded no inappropriate behavior from Ginsberg during his stay in April 1965. After the Czechoslovak incident, however, the Polish authorities placed him on the list of people "undesirable in the People's Republic of Poland." See Andrzej Pietrasz, *Allen Ginsberg w Polsce* (Warsaw: Semper, 2014), 186–192.

48. Pietrasz, *Allen Ginsberg w Polsce*, 153–157.

49. While in Warsaw, the Polish Ministry of Culture and Art accorded Ginsberg an official status of "Guest of the Ministry of Culture," which gave him free hotel and per diem funds. Ginsberg, *Iron Curtain Journals*, 260.

50. Ginsberg, *Iron Curtain Journals*, 271.

51. Quoted in Pietrasz, *Allen Ginsberg w Polsce*, 80. According to another account, by artist and hippie Jacek Gulla, Niemczyk indeed hosted Ginsberg, but the American poet left no trace of his visit in the apartment. Rather, after a few years, Niemczyk himself painted the autograph on the wall of his kitchen. For further discussion, see Pietrasz, *Allen Ginsberg w Polsce*, 81.

52. Illg, "Polskie lato miłości," heh.pl forum, 8 October 2008 http://f.heh.pl/ftopic7 031.html.

53. See Ks. Bolesław Saduś, "Big-beat w katedrze?," and Father Tomasz Pawłowski and Adam Macedoński, "Msza beatowa w Krakowie," *Tygodnik Powszechny*, 19 January 1969, 6.

54. HU OSA, 300-50-13, box 1, RFE Confidential Reports on Poland, 1971–1972, "Attitudes of Polish Young Intelligentsia," 20 August 1971, n.p.

55. See, for example, Ks. Adam, "Rozmowy niedokończone," *Tygodnik Powszechny*, 25 May 1969, 4.

56. AIPN, 0224/656/3, Komenda Milicji Obywatelskiej, woj. Poznańskie to Dyrektor Biura Śledczego Ministerstwa Spraw Wewnętrznych w Warszawie, Poznań, 18 June 1970, kk. 107–112.

57. AIPN, 0224/656/4, Komenda Stołeczna Milicji Obywatelskiej. Służba Bezpieczeństwa, "Informacja. Dotyczy: przeprowadzonej w dniu 4 i 5 X 1971 operacji przeciwko 'hippiesom.'" Warsaw, 7 October 1971, kk. 29–31, k. 29. Capital letters in the original.

58. AIPN, 0224/656/1, "Informacja," 23 September 1969, kk. 72–81, 76.

59. "Prorok," in Sipowicz, *Hipisi w PRL-u*, 162.

60. "Kasiarz," in Sipowicz, *Hipisi w PRL-u*, 239–242, 240.

61. "Belfegor," in Sipowicz, *Hipisi w PRL-u*, 397–404, 398.

62. "Psycholog," in Sipowicz, *Hipisi w PRL-u*, 253–268, 266.

63. Alicja Imlay, interview.

64. AIPN, 01299/882, "Notatka dotyczy: grup młodzieżowych tzw. hippies," Warsaw, 23 April 1969, in *"Jesteście naszą wielką szansą." Młodzież na rozstajach komunizmu 1944–1989*, edited by Paweł Ceranka and Sławomir Stępień (Warsaw: IPN, 2009), 369.

65. AIPN, 0224/656/2, "Wyciąg z doniesienia 'Michał' z dnia 19. VI. 1970 r.," k. 115. The name Allen Ginsberg is misspelled in the document.

66. AIPN, 0224/656/2, Stanisława Zakrzewska, "Tragiczne kwiaty," kk. 129–132, 129.

67. AIPN, 0224/656/2, "Notatka służbowa," Warsaw, 15 June 1970, k. 128

68. "Zappa," in Sipowicz, *Hipisi w PRL-u*, 405–412, 409.

69. "Zappa," in Sipowicz, *Hipisi w PRL-u*, 409.

70. Trapszyc, *Lokalny pejzaż kontrkultury*, 23.

71. For personal testimonies of Polish hitchhikers see *Autostop polski. PRL i współczesność*, edited by Jakub Czupryński (Kraków: Halart, 2005).

72. Trapszyc, *Lokalny pejzaż kontrkultury*, 20–21.

73. Tracz, *Hipiesi, Kudłacze, chwasty*, 151.

74. The story of Polish female hippies is yet to be written. In my research, I encountered similar issues of a lesser visibility of female hippies to the ones described by Juliane Fürst in the Soviet context. See Fürst, *Flowers Through Concrete*, chap. 9.

75. Kamil Sipowicz, interview by author, digital recording, Warsaw, 26 June 2013.

76. Milo Kurtis, interview.

77. See, for example, Andrzej Łarski, "Mit 'hippies,'" *ITD*, 16 April 1969.

78. Jackowska and Sipowicz, *Kora, Kora*, 49.

79. Magdalena, interview by author, Warsaw, 18 February 2013. Magdalena is a fictitious name, as the interviewee asked for anonymity.

80. Wojciech "Tarzan" Michalewski, *Mistycy i narkomani* (Warsaw: ETHOS, 1992), 24.

81. Michalewski, *Mistycy i narkomani*, 67.

82. "Piotr Dmyszewicz," in Sipowicz, *Hipisi w PRL-u*, 349–359, 355.

83. Michalewski, *Mistycy i narkomani*, 62.

84. Michalewski, *Mistycy i narkomani*, 34.

85. Alice Echols, *Scars of Sweet Paradise: The Life and Times of Janis Joplin* (New York: Holt, 2000), ix.

86. Kamil Sipowicz, interview.

87. AIPN, 0224/656/3, Informacja. Dotyczy: ruchu tzw. "hippies" oraz narkomanii wśród młodzieży," Warsaw, 26 June 1971, kk. 95–105.
88. Magdalena, interview; and Jackowska and Sipowicz, *Kora, Kora*, 57.
89. Sipowicz, *Hipisi w PRL-u*, 155.
90. See *Stowarzyszenie Monar. O nas*, achttp://www.monar.org/o-nas/historia/.
91. AIPN, 0224/656/1, "Informacja," 23 September 1969, kk. 72–81, 72. The statement has "nihilism" added by hand and misspelled in Polish as "nichilizm."
92. AIPN, 0224/656/1, "Informacja," 23 September 1969, k.73.
93. Sipowicz, *Hipisi w PRL-u*, 396. The gauntlet was also used against political dissidents in the second half of the 1970s. See Jan Skórzyński, *Siła bezsilnych. Historia Komitetu Obrony Robotników* (Warsaw: Świat Książki, 2012), 89.
94. "Zappa," in Sipowicz, *Hipisi w PRL-u*, 399.
95. Sipowicz, *Hipisi w PRL-u*, 156–158.
96. AIPN, 0224/656/1, "Informacja," 23 September 1969, k. 78.
97. The collection of the security apparatus documents used in this study comes from the first surveillance action under the name "Kudłacze," conducted in 1968–1971.
98. AIPN, 0224/656/1, "Oświadczenie," kk. 65–66, 66.
99. AIPN, 0224/656/1, anonymous statement, no title, n.d., kk. 123–127, esp. 126.
100. Jerzy Lovell, *Jak żyć? Zbiór reportarzy* (Warsaw: Iskry, 1972), 110.
101. Irena Groblewska, interview.
102. Baranowski, „Powiedziałem, że w Peerelu," in Grupińska and Wawrzyniak, *Buntownicy*, 170.
103. Interview with Tomasz Rodowicz, in Jawłowska and Dworakowska, *Wolność w systemie zniewolenia*, 221.
104. Bolesław Kuźniak, "Mieszkaliśmy w muzyce i to był nasz świat – taka enklawa zamknięta," in Grupińska and Wawrzyniak, *Buntownicy*, 117–124, 118.
105. Interview with Tomasz Rodowicz, in Jawłowska and Dworakowska, *Wolność w systemie zniewolenia*, 222.
106. Kuźniak, "Mieszkaliśmy w muzyce," in Grupińska and Wawrzyniak, *Buntownicy*, 117–124, 118.
107. In the words of Jan Poprawa, radicalized student artists after 1968 "found the need to start speaking their mind." Jan Poprawa, *Fama—1966-1977. Historia imprezy* (Warsaw, Kraków, Świnoujście: Zarząd Główny SZSP, 1983), 9.
108. Elżbieta Matynia, *Performative Democracy* (New York: Paradigm, 2009), 5.
109. Matynia, *Performative Democracy*, 21.
110. Bogusław Litwiniec, interview by author, digital recording, Wilcza, 15 July 2013..
111. David Looseley, "The World Theatre Festival, Nancy, 1963–1988: A Critique and a Retrospective," *New Theatre Quarterly* 6, no. 22 (May 1990): 141–153.
112. Bogusław Litwiniec, interview.
113. APWr, Komitet Wojewódzki PZPR (KW PZPR) 979, Wydział Propagandy, Oświaty i Kultury, "Założenia programowo-ideowe III Międzynarodowego Festiwalu Festiwali Teatrów Studenckich we Wrocławiu," 17 October 1970, kk. 143–147, 146.
114. AAN, RN, ZSP, Komisja Kultury KK, 6/18, II Międzynarodowy Festiwal Festiwali Teatrów Studenckich, "Program ramowy II Międzynarodowego Festiwalu Festiwali Teatrów Studenckich," Wrocław, 18–26 października 1969 r., kk. 25–30, 25.

115. AAN, RN, ZSP, KK, 6/18, Kurier. Biuletyn Prasowy nr. 1, 18–26 October 1969, kk. 72–81, 73. AAN, RN, ZSP, KK, 6/18, "Program ramowy," k. 28.

116. APWr, KW, PZPR 979, Wydział Propagandy, Oświaty i Kultury, Współpraca z Wydziałem Kultury PWRN w zakresie działalności kulturalnej insytucji artystycznych, 1970, "Założenia programowo-ideowe," k. 145.

117. AAN, RN, ZSP, KK, 6/18, II Międzynarodowy Festiwal Festiwali Teatrów Studenckich, Wrocław, 18–26 October 1969, Lista gości honorowych festiwalu, k. 10.

118. APWr, KW, PZPR 979, Wydział Propagandy, Oświaty i Kultury, "Założenia programowo-ideowe," k. 147.

119. AAN, RN, ZSP, KK, 6/18, Kurier. Biuletyn Prasowy nr. 1, kk. 72–81, 81. The Bread and Puppet Theater moved from New York to Vermont in 1970.

120. APWr, KW, PZPR, 982, Wydział Propagandy, Oświaty i Kultury, Korespondencja i informacje dot. działalności instytucji artystycznych, 1971, "III Międzynarodowy Festiwal Festiwali Teatrów Studenckich—Wrocław, 17.X–24.X. 1971 r.—analiza i wnioski," kk. 95–100, 95.

121. AAN, RN, ZSP, KK, 6/18, Kurier. Biuletyn Prasowy nr. 7, 18–26 October 1969, kk. 56–65, 57.

122. AAN, RN, ZSP, KK, 6/18, Kurier. Biuletyn Prasowy nr. 7, k. 65.

123. APWr, KW, PZPR 979, Wydział Propagandy, Oświaty i Kultury, "Założenia programowo-ideowe," k. 143.

124. AAN, RN, ZSP. KK, 6/18, "Program ramowy," k. 27.

125. Leszek Budrewicz, interview by author, digital recording, Wrocław, 12 May 2016.

126. Edward Chudziński, interview by author, digital recording, Kraków, 27 June 2012.

127. Interview with Lech Raczak by Zofia Dworakowska, in Jawłowska and Dworakowska, *Wolność w systemie zniewolenia*, 169–186, 172–173. Raczak and his experimental theater group, the Eighth Day Theater, did not participate in the festival in 1969. The group traveled to Wrocław on their own to watch the performances.

128. Farber, "Building the Counterculture," 3.

Chapter 7

1. Andrzej Sadowski, interview by author, digital recording, Białystok, 11 February 2013.

2. Hanna Jaworowska, "Wsie jak miasta," *Nowa Wieś*, 2 October 1969, 2–3, 2.

3. Kamila Chylińska, "Kiedy mydło zrobi na wsi karierę?," *Zwierciadło*, 31 March 1968, 3.

4. Arthur Marwick, *The Sixties: Cultural Transformation in Britain, France, Italy and the United States, c. 1958–c. 1974* (Oxford: Oxford University Press, 2000), 360–365.

5. APWr, KW, PZPR, 989, Wydział Propagandy, Oświaty i Kultury KW PZPR, Praca kulturalno-oświatowa w miejscu zamieszkania. Wytyczne KW oraz onformacje z powiatów na ten temat, 1965, "Referat," kk. 21–27, 21.

6. I use original submissions to two rural memoir competitions: Dwa Starty (Two Beginnings) conducted in 1969, and Pamiętniki Młodzieży Wiejskiej. Perspektywy

młodego pokolenia wsi (Memoirs of Rural Youth: Perspectives of the Young Rural Generation), held in 1972. The first competition asked young rural people to compare their experiences with those of their parents. The second asked young people to reflect on their experiences and beliefs as members of a young generation in the rural "People's Poland." The collections are housed at the Archive of New Documents in Warsaw. For further discussion of the archival collection of the Friends of Memoir Society, see Dariusz Wierzchoś, "Zwyczajne życie zwykłych ludzi. Losy Archiwum Towarzystwa Przyjaciół Pamiętnikarstwa," Histmag.org, 10 April 2008, https://hist mag.org/Zwyczajne-zycie-zwyklych-ludzi.-Losy-archiwum-Towarzystwa-Przyjac iol-Pamietnikarstwa-1750.

7. On interwar Polish memoirs see Katherine Lebow, "The Conscious of the Skin: Interwar Polish Autobiography and Social Rights," *Humanity: An International of Human Rights, Humanitarianism, and Development* 3, no. 3 (Winter 2012): 297–319.

8. When Polish sociologists organized the first memoirs competition specifically aimed at the rural population in the early 1930s, men accounted for 97 percent of all the authors; only 7 submissions out of a total of 488 came from women. Ludwik Krzywicki, "Nieco o pamiętnikach i pamiętnikarzach," in *Pamiętniki chłopów*, edited by Krzywicki(Warsaw: Instytut Gospodarstwa Społecznego, 1935), XIX–XLII, XXXVII. Subsequent rural memoir competitions in the 1930s registered a growing number of submissions from women, reaching 30 percent in memoir contests addressed to young people. Anna Dzierzgowska, "Pamiętniki kobiet w pamiętnikach chłopów," paper presented at the Gender History Seminar (over Zoom), Warsaw University, 12 April 2021.

9. The number of female authors differed from one rural memoir competition to another. In Two Beginnings, women were 26 percent of the 510 authors. See Mieczysław Pisarek, "Wstęp," in *Dwa starty. Wypowiedzi nadesłane na konkurs ogłoszony przez ZG ZMW i redakcję "Zarzewie,"* edited by Henryk Maziejuk, Mieczyslaw Pisarek, and Stanisław Wiechno (Warsaw: Książka i Wiedza, 1970), 5–17, 9. Other competitions generated more entries from women. For example, A Month of my Life (*Miesiąc mojego życia*), a competition aimed at rural inhabitants of the Western Territories, launched in 1962, resulted in close to 2000 submissions, half of which came from women. See Józef Chałasiński, "Społeczno-kulturalny awans prowincji w świetle konkursu 'Jeden miesiąc mojego życia,'" in *Miesiąc mojego życia. Wybór pamiętników,* edited by Chałasiński (Warsaw: Ludowa Spółdzielnia Wydawnicza, 1964), 5–44, 7. In my rough estimate from reading the surviving memoirs of the 1972 competition Memoirs of Rural Youth, approximately 55 percent of the submissions came from women.

10. A young woman from a village in southeastern Poland articulated this motivation in the closing paragraph of her autobiography: "I wrote down my recollections somewhat in a stream of consciousness. Until that point in time I had never written to a magazine, and I decided to summarize my life [by] pouring it out onto the page. Sometimes one gets a sense of relief letting go of the weight of years gone by. Please, keep my name and address confidential." AAN, TPP, PMW, 1972, 5272, no. 498, n.p.

11. Mirosław Sanigórski, "Polna droga do indeksu," *Kulisy*, 2 June 1968, 1 and 3, 1.
12. Hanna Jaworowska, "Polną drogą do szkoły," *Nowa Wieś*, 2 February 1969, 2–3, 2.
13. "Losy dziecka. Dlaczego 'trudne'?," *Nowa Wieś*, 26 September 1965, 2.
14. AAN, TPP, DS, 2751, no. 97, 1 February 1969, n.p.
15. Barbara Klich-Kluczewska, *Rodzina, tabu i komunizm w Polsce*, 1956-1989 (Kraków: Libron, 2015), 220.
16. The seven-grade primary school was established in 1948. Between 1962 and 1971, compulsory primary education was gradually extended to eight grades. See "Polska. Oświata. Polska Rzeczpospolita Ludowa," in *Encyklopedia PWN*, https://encyklope dia.pwn.pl/haslo/Polska-Oswiata-Polska-Rzeczpospolita-Ludowa;4575102.html.
17. Sanigórski, "Polna droga do indeksu," 1 and 3.
18. AAN, TPP, PMW, 5239, no. 129, n.p.
19. AAN, TPP, PMW, 5248, no. 226, 25 May 1972, n.p.
20. Quoted in Eugenia Jagiełło-Łysiowa, "Od chłopa do rolnika (Niektóre problemy młodzieży rolniczej w świetle materiałów konkursu na pamiętnik młodego pokolenia wsi)," *Wieś Współczesna* 6 (June 1963): 36–50, 40.
21. Quoted in Mirosław Sanigórski, "Milion do wzięcia," *Kulisy. Express Wieczorny*, 5 January 1964, 1 and 3, 3.
22. Stanisław Zagórski, "W stronę wyzwolonego uczucia," *Nowa Wieś*, 29 March 1970, 13.
23. On marriage patterns in postwar Poland see Barbara Klich-Kluczewska, "Kobieta wobec rodziny," in Katarzyna Stańczak-Wiślicz, Piotr Perkowski, Małgorzata Fidelis, and Barbara Klich-Kluczewska, *Kobiety w Polsce, 1945-1989. Nowoczesność, równouprawnienie, komunizm* (Kraków: Universitas, 2020), 255–293.
24. AAN, TPP, PMW, 5261 no. 371, n.p.
25. For lists of popular periodicals and other publications available in rural libraries see, for example, APKr, PWRN, Kr KI 817, 1962-1964, Prezydium Wojewódzkiej Rady Narodowej w Krakowie Wydział Rolnictwa i Leśnictwa, Oddział Oświaty Rolniczej to Prezydium Wojew. Rady Norodowej, Wydział Kultury, Kraków, 4 July 1963, k. 93; and APBi, ZW, ZMS, 329, Związek Młodzieży Socjalistycznej, KW to Komitet Powiatowy ZMS, Białystok, 15 January 1964, k. 52.
26. AAN, KC, PZPR, XIB/57, [Kancelaria Sekretarza KC i Członków Biura Politycznego, 1945-1981, 1988], Ruch młodzieżowy, notatki, analizy, 1967, "Propozycje Zarządów Głównych ZMS i ZMW," kk. 10-13, 11; and APKr, PWRN Kr KI 817, "Spis czasopism zalecanych do prenumeraty na rok 1964," kk. 109 -113. The title *New Village* published between 1948 and 1956 under the patronage of ZMP, but its formula was significantly different, oriented toward political propaganda and the collectivization of agriculture.
27. For articles on Western Europe and the United States see, for example, L.M., "W cieniu drapaczy chmur," *Nowa Wieś*, 8 April 1962, 14–15; Eugeniusz Buczek, "Ptaki. Niesamowita wojna ludzi z ptakami," *Nowa Wieś*, 23 May 1965, 4; and Franciszek Nietz, "Gniewna Ameryka," *Nowa Wieś*, 23 August 1970, 12–13. On Polish popular culture see, for example, Eugeniusz Buczek, "Jazz klub 'Zarzewie,'" *Nowa Wieś*, 28 January 1962, 18–19; "Co sądzisz o telewizji?," *Nowa Wieś*, 2 January 1966; and "Opolskie impresje," *Nowa Wieś*, 23 July 1967, 4–5.

258 NOTES

28. See, for example, "Kto jest nowoczesny?," *Nowa Wieś*, 6 December 1964, 15; "Tradycja i nowoczesność," *Nowa Wieś*, 20–27 December 1964, 51–52; and "Obyczaje w klubie," *Nowa Wieś*, 21 April 1968, 15.

29. APBi, ZW, ZMS, 309, Zdzisława T. "Wspomnienia z wakacji," kk. 76–88, 78.

30. APBi, ZW, ZMS, 309, Anna D., "Moje wakacje," kk. 37–42. On meeting a young woman from France see APBi, ZW, ZMS, 309, Krystyna K. "Moje wakacje," kk. 67–70.

31. L. Manicki "Kaski złote, srebrne, brązowe," *Nowa Wieś*, 4 October 1964, 4–5.

32. For example, the Lambretta was featured in the Polish film *Innocent Sorcerers,* as was described in chapter 2 as an element of masculine rebellion. The Italian scooter was a status symbol among young urban professionals. One of the best known Polish owners of a Lambretta was jazz musician and composer Krzysztof Komeda. See Magdalena Grzebałkowska, *Komeda. Osobiste życie jazzu* (Kraków: Znak, 2018), 294–296.

33. Franciszek Burdzy, "WFM-ką do równika," *Motor*, 22 September 1963, 6. The name WFM stands for the Warsaw Factory of Motorcycles (Warszawska Fabryka Motocykli). The global dimension of the motorcycle was also reinforced by Che Guevara's memoir *Motorcycle Diaries*, parts of which appeared in a Polish translation in 1969. See Che Guevara, *Dziennik z Boliwii*, translated by Ryszard Kapuściński (Warsaw: Książka i Wiedza, 1969).

34. Burdzy, "WFM-ką do równika," 6.

35. Krzysztof Kąkolewski "Polska Rzeczpospolita motocyklowa," *Polityka*, 21 July 1962, 3.

36. AAN, TPP, PMW, 5280, no. 555, n.p.

37. AAN, TPP, PMW, 5280, no. 555.

38. Lyrics by Włodzimierz Patuszyński, music by Mateusz Święcicki, "Motor i ja," *Nowa Wieś*, 4 October 1964, 1.

39. Eugenia Jagiełło-Łysiowa, "W pogoni za nowym 'stylem życia' (Z materiałów konkursu na pamiętniki młodzieży wiejskiej)," *Wieś Współczesna* 5 (May 1965): 80–93, 89.

40. Manicki, "Kaski złote, srebrne, brązowe," 4–5.

41. See, for example, Emilia Krzyżanowska, "Prowadziłam Osę nad Adriatyk," *Motor*, 18 October 1964, 7.

42. Chylińska, "Kiedy mydło zrobi na wsi karierę?," 3.

43. HU OSA, 300-50-13, box 1, RFE Confidential Reports on Poland, 1971–1972. "Prymas a duchowieństwo," 30 December 1971, n.p.

44. AAN, KC, PZPR, BP, 237/XIX-284, "Stenogram narady na temat laicyzacji kultury odbytej w SDP w dniu 25 czerwca 1959," kk. 1-68, 26.

45. AAN, KC, PZPR, BP, 237/XIX-284, "Stenogram narady na temat laicyzacji kultury," k. 27.

46. AAN, KC, PZPR, BP, 237/XIX-284, "Stenogram narady na temat laicyzacji kultury," k. 8.

47. Edward Ciupak, *Kultura religijna wsi. Szkice socjologiczne* (Warsaw: Iskry, 1961), 6.

48. Ciupak, *Kultura religijna wsi*, 87.

49. Ciupak, *Kultura religijna wsi*, 103.

50. Ciupak, *Kultura religijna wsi*, 104–105.

51. Ciupak, *Kultura religijna wsi*, 96–97.

52. For further discussion of Vatican II in Poland see Piotr H. Kosicki, "Vatican II and Poland," in *Vatican II behind the Iron Curtain*, edited by Piotr H. Kosicki (Washington, DC: Catholic University of America Press, 2016), 127–198.

53. Ks. Zdzisław Lewandowski, "Sobór w wiejskiej parafii," *Tygodnik Powszechny*, 5 May 1968, 4.

54. HU OSA, 300-50-13, box 1, RFE Confidential Reports on Poland, "Prymas a duchowieństwo."

55. Kosicki, "Vatican II in Poland," 192–193.

56. The Virgin Mary icon of Częstochowa was named Queen of Poland in 1656 by Polish king Jan Kazimierz.

57. Waldemar Winkiel, "Kluby i działalność kulturalna na wsi," *Wieś Współczesna* 6 (June 1965), 107–114, 109.

58. AAN, TPP, 126, Materiały dotyczące klubów na wsi, n.p.

59. AAN, ZG, ZMW, 12/X/7, "Stenogram z Krajowej Narady Działaczy Klubów Kultury na wsi w dniu 10 stycznia 1965," 10 January 1965, n.p.

60. In 1966, 2.3 million television sets were registered in Poland, reaching an estimated 10 million viewers, or one-third of the population. Leszek Goliński, "Telewizja—partner pierwszej rangi," *Kultura i Społeczeństwo* 4 (October–December 1966): 161–170, 161. On the history of Polish television in the 1960s, see Patryk Pleskot, *Wielki mały ekran. Telewizja a codzienność Polaków lat sześćdziesiątych* (Warsaw: TRIO, 2007).

61. Jerzy Rudzki, "Telewizja wśród młodzieży wiejskiej," *Wieś Współczesna* 5 (May 1964): 57–71, 59.

62. AAN, MKiS, GM, WP, RKiS, 49, "Stenogram plenarny," k. 16.

63. Rudzki, "Telewizja wśród młodzieży wiejskiej," 68.

64. AAN, ZG, ZMW, 12/X/4, "Wpływ radia i telewizji na przemiany w środowisku wiejskim. Stenogram z drugiego wieczoru dysusyjnego Klubu ZG ZMW i red. Zarzewia," 16 November 1962, kk. 1–55, 29.

65. Bolesław Gołębiowski, *Kultura i życie społeczne wsi* (Warsaw: Iskry, 1964), 44.

66. AAN, ZG, ZMW, 12/X/4, "Wpływ radia i telewizji," k. 35.

67. AAN, ZG, ZMW, 12/IV/117d, III Narada Krajowa Dziewcząt ZMW, Stenogram, 16-17 November 1963, "Referat Kol. Haliny Krzywdzianki na III Krajową Naradę Dziewcząt ZMW," Warsaw, 16–17 November 1963, n.p.

68. Sanigórski, "Milion do wzięcia," 1.

69. AAN, ZG, ZMW, 12/X/7, "Stenogram z Krajowej Narady Działaczy Klubów Kultury," n.p.

70. AAN, ZG, ZMW, 12/X/7, "Stenogram z Krajowej Narady Działaczy Klubów Kultury," n.p.

71. APBi, ZW, ZMW w Białymstoku, 1957–1976, 40, "Jesteśmy sercem wsi," n.d., kk. 121–122, 121. See also AAN, ZG, ZMW, 12/VI/117b, II Krajowa Narada Dziewcząt-Członkiń ZMW, Stenogram, 25 February 1961, "Stenogram II Krajowego Zjazdu Dziewczat—Członkiń Związku Młodzieży Wiejskiej odbytego w dniu 25 lutego 1961

r.," kk. 1–100, 37. For further discussion on cultivating flower gardens as a distinct sign of young women's activism in the village see APBi, ZW, ZMW, 95, "Protokół z wojwódzkiej narady dziewcząt odbytej w Białymstoku w dniach 5–6 marca 1970," kk. 84–93, 86; and Kozicki, "Zbuntowane dziewczęta," 4.

72. Quoted in Eugenia Jagiełło-Łysiowa, "Dziewczęta wiejskie a małżeństwo," *Wieś Współczesna* 6 (June 1965): 75–88, 80.

73. AAN, ZMW, ZG, 12/IV/117d, "III Narada Krajowa Dziewcząt ZMW," 16–17 November 1963 r., n.p.

74. AAN, ZG, ZMW, 12/IV/116, Krajowa Narada Dziewcząt ZMW. Materiały informacyjne, 1958–1968, "Do wszystkich dziewcząt polskiej wsi," n.p. On the role of technology, consumption, and fashion in Polish rural women's concept of modernity see also Maria Bartnik, "Ku nowoczesności," *Nowa Wieś*, 9 March 1969, 4.

75. Anna Kowalska-Lewicka, "Tradycyjne normy obyczajowe w kontaktach młodzieży na Podhalu," *Problemy Rodziny*, September-October 1971, 16–22, 22.

76. Kowalska-Lewicka, "Tradycyjne normy obyczajowe," 21.

77. AAN, TPP, PMW, 5248, no. 226.

78. Lolobrygida, "Pamiętnik dziewczyny z lubelskiego," *Nowa Wieś*, 13 May 1962, 11.

79. Lolobrygida, "Pamiętnik dziewczyny z lubelskiego," 11.

80. AAN, TPP, PMW, 5266, no. 455, n.p.

81. Quoted in Jagiełło-Łysiowa, "Dziewczęta wiejskie a małżeństwo," 82.

82. AAN, TPP, PMW, 5234, no. 107, 1 November 1962, n.p.

83. AAN, ZG, ZMW, 12/VI/117b, II Krajowa Narada Dziewcząt-Członkiń ZMW, "Stenogram II Krajowego Zjazdu," k. 5.

84. For further discussion of healthcare in rural areas see Ewelina Szpak, *"Chory człowiek jest wtedy jak coś go boli." Społeczno-kulturowa historia zdrowia i choroby na wsi polskiej po 1945r.* (Warsaw: Instytut Historii PAN, 2016). Although villagers were not eligible for state medical insurance, prenatal care and childbirth were free of charge.

85. AAN, ZG, ZMW, 12/VI/117b, II Krajowa Narada Dziewcząt-Członkiń ZMW, "Stenogram II Krajowego Zjazdu Dziewczat—Członkiń Związku Młodzieży Wiejskiej odbytego w dniu 25 lutego 1961, drugi dzień obrad," n.p.

86. AAN, ZG, ZMW, 12/VI/116, Krajowa Narada Dziewcząt ZMW. Materiały informacyjne, 1958–1968, "Informacje na Sekretariat ZG ZMW z działalności szkół zdrowia," n.p.

87. AAN, TPP, 5248, PMW, no. 219, n.p.

88. Teresa, interview by author, digital recording, Białystok, 16 July 2011. Teresa is a fictitious name, as the interviewee asked for anonymity.

89. AAN, ZG, ZMW, 12/X/4, "Wpływ radia i telewizji na przemiany w środowisku wiejskim," k. 25.

90. Goliński, "Telewizja," 166.

91. AAN, TPP, PMW, 5234, no. 107, 23 November 1963, n.p.

92. See Paweł Wroński, "Gdyby nie wyścig Ameryki z ZSRR, może człowiek w ogóle nie stanąłby na Księżycu," *Wyborcza.pl*, 19 July 2019, https://wyborcza.pl/7,90535,25003 078,zimna-wojna-i-ladowanie-na-ksiezycu-w-polskiej-tv-decyzje.html.

93. AAN, TPP, PMW, 5261, no. 371.

94. Quoted in R.Ł. "Za 30 lat," *Nowa Wieś*, 29 November 1970, 5.

95. Zdzisław Grzelak, "Młodzież a kultura (próba podsumowania badań)," *Kultura i Społeczeństwo*, April-June 1969, 213–224, esp. 216–221.

96. Józef Chałasiński, *Kultura i naród* (Warsaw: Książka i Wiedza, 1968), 11.

97. For further discussion of disseminating the Polish elite history and culture as part of popular culture in postwar Poland, see Aleksandra Sekuła, "Chłop Kmicicem. Zmiana wyobrażeń tożsamościowych (1960–1999 i dalej)," in *Rok 1966. PRL na zakręcie. Idee-Dyskursy-Praktyki*, edited by Katarzyna Chmielewska, Grzegorz Wołowiec, and Tomasz Żukowski (Warsaw: Instytut Badań Literackich PAN, 2014), 299–312.

98. AAN, TPP, PMW, 5239, no. 129.

Chapter 8

1. Jan Zakrzewski, "Sześćdziesiąte lata szaleństwa postępu," *Polityka*, 17 January 1970, 10. In 1965, the Beatles were appointed Members of the Order of the British Empire.

2. For discussion of the Czechoslovak regime's attempt to depoliticize society through consumerism and television shows as an antidote to Prague Spring, see Paulina Bren, *The Greengrocer and His TV: The Culture of Communism after the 1968 Prague Spring* (Ithaca, NY: Cornell University Press, 2010).

3. Colin Barker, "Some Reflections on Student Movements of the 1960s and Early 1970s," *Revista Crítica de Ciências* 81 (2008), 24.

4. On the commonality of responses to upheavals from below by political elites East and West see Jeremy Suri, *Power and Protest: Global Revolution and the Rise of Détente* (Cambridge, MA: Harvard University Press, 2005). On interpretations of the 1970s as an era of contradictions see, for example, Duco Hellema, *The Global 1970s: Radicalism, Reform, and Crisis* (New York: Routledge, 2019); and Thomas Borstelmann, *The 1970s: A New Global History from Civil Rights to Economic Inequality* (Princeton, NJ: Princeton University Press, 2012).

5. Antoni Dudek and Tomasz Marszałkowski, *Walki uliczne w PRL* (Kraków: Geo, 1999), 219.

6. Piotr Perkowski, *Gdańsk. Miasto od nowa* (Gdańsk: Terytoria, 2013), 193.

7. For example, in Czechoslovakia, real wages rose by 3.5 percent during the same time and in Bulgaria by 4.1 percent. Dudek and Marszałkowski, *Walki uliczne*, 168.

8. Andrzej Paczkowski, *Pół wieku dziejów Polski, 1939–1989* (Warsaw: PWN, 1995), 390.

9. Dudek and Marszałkowski, *Walki uliczne*, 219.

10. Dudek and Marszałkowski, *Walki uliczne*, 177.

11. Perkowski, *Gdańsk*, 193.

12. Perkowski, *Gdańsk*, 195.

13. An estimated 100 students from Gdańsk Polytechnic were apprehended during the protests, and 80 were expelled. HU OSA, 300-50-13, box 3, RFE Confidential Reports on Poland, 1972, "University Students' Attitudes," Munich, 29 August 1972, n.p.

14. HU OSA, 300-50-13, box 3, RFE Confidential Reports on Poland, "University Students' Attitudes."

15. Tom Junes, *Student Politics in Communist Poland: Generations of Consent and Dissent* (Lanham, MD: Lexington Books, 2015), 130–131.

16. HU OSA, 300-50-13, box 1, RFE Confidential Reports on Poland, "Attitudes of Polish Young Intelligentsia," Munich, 20 August 1971, n.p.

17. HU OSA, 300-50-13, box 1, RFE Confidential Reports on Poland, "Wrażenia z podróży do Polski," 9 September 1971, n.p.

18. Jerzy Eisler, *Grudzień 1970. Geneza, przebiegi konsekwencje* (Warsaw: IPN, 2012), 476.

19. Quoted in Marcin Zaremba, "'Bigosowy socjalizm.' Dekada Gierka," in *Polacy wobec PRL. Strategie przystosowawcze*, edited by Grzegorz Miernik (Kielce: Akademia Świętokrzyska, 2003), 184–200, 192.

20. Lukas Dovern, "Investing in Socialist Poland: A Transnational History of Finance in the Cold War, 1944–1991," (Ph.D. diss., Stanford University, 2019), chap. 6.

21. For more discussion of pronatalist policies in Poland see Piotr Perkowski, "Wedded to Welfare? Working Mothers and the Welfare State in Communist Poland," *Slavic Review* 76, no. 2 (2017): 455–480.

22. Paweł Sasanka, *Czerwiec 1976. Geneza-przebieg-konsekwencje* (Warsaw: IPN, 2006), 56.

23. Junes, *Student Politics in Communist Poland*, 144.

24. HU OSA, 300-50-13, box 3, RFE Confidential Reports on Poland, "Students' and Workers' Moods," Munich, 22 August 1972, n.p. The increase, however, was predominantly in the numbers of working-class youth. The percentage of young people from rural areas within the student population grew only slightly from 10 percent in 1971 to 12.4 percent two years later. This prompted the ZMW to establish university preparatory courses in some villages. See Jan Andrykiewicz, *Związek Młodzieży Wiejskiej w latach 1957–1976* (Warsaw: Muzeum Historii Polskiego Ruchu Ludowego, 2002), 93.

25. Andrzej Friszke, *Polska Gierka* (Warsaw: Wydawnictwo Szkolne i Pedagogiczne, 1995), 33.

26. Zaremba, "Bigosowy socjalizm," 199.

27. R.Z., "Mały Fiat," *Nowa Wieś*, 16 March 1975, 4–5, 4.

28. Janusz Rolicki, *Przerwana Dekada. Wywiad rzeka* (Warsaw: Wydawnictwo FAKT, 1990), 84.

29. Ewa Boniecka, "Pożegnania z mitami," *Perspektywy*, 2 August 1973, 19–23, 22.

30. Ewa Boniecka, "Światy różne, ale bliskie," *Perspektywy*, 16 June 1972, 4–5.

31. Eventually, all three American presidents of the 1970s decade visited Poland, including Gerald Ford in 1975 and Jimmy Carter in 1977. Paczkowski, *The Spring Will Be Ours: Poland and the Poles from Occupation to Freedom*, translated by Jane Cave (University Park PA: Pennsylvania State University Press, 2003), 362.

32. "Polska polityka zagraniczna," *Perspektywy*, 5 April 1974, 9–15, 11.

33. "Polska polityka zagraniczna," 13.

34. Dariusz Stola, *Kraj bez wyjścia? Migrajce z Polski, 1949–1989* (Warsaw: Instytut Studiów Politycznych PAN, 2010), 167. On trasnational mobility in the Eastern bloc in the 1970s see, for example, Mark Keck-Szajbel, "A Cultural Shift in the 1970s: 'Texas' Jeans, Taboos, and Transnational Tourism," *East European Politics and Society and Cultures* 29, no. 1 (2015): 212–225.

35. Stola, *Kraj bez wyjścia?*, 260.
36. Stola, *Kraj bez wyjścia?*, 263.
37. Stola, *Kraj bez wyjścia?*, 167.
38. Between the late 1960s and the late 1970s, the number of West Germans who spent their vacations abroad rose from 35 to 60 percent. See Hellema, *The Global 1970s*, 15.
39. Paweł Sowiński, *Wakacje w Polsce Ludowej. Polityka władz i ruch turystyczny (1945–1989)*. (Warsaw: TRIO, 2005), 285–286.
40. "Młodzieżowy klient wart uwagi," *Dookoła Świata*, 22–29 December 1968, 3, and 12–13, 13.
41. Anna Pelka, *Texas-land. Moda młodzieżowa w PRL* (Warsaw: TRIO, 2007), 59.
42. Danuta Wilhelmi, "Kariera dżinsów," *Perspektywy*, 11 July 1972, 35.
43. Zbigniew Jurkiewicz, "Refleksje nad życiorysem pokolenia," *Dookoła Świata*, 13 June 1971, 5–6, 5.
44. "Bilans roku 1971," *Dookoła Świata*, 5 December 1971, 6–7, 7.
45. Edward Chudziński, interview by author, digital recording, Kraków, 27 June 2012. In 1971, *Student* became a biweekly.
46. See, for example, Marianna Bocian, "Bunt francuskich studentów," *Student*, January-February 1971, 4; Kazimierz Rydzewski, "Siła i słabość kontestacji," *Student*, 22 March–4 April 1973, 4; Sławomir Magala, "Norman Mailer," *Student*, 13–21 December 1973, 5; Wit Jaworski, "Nowa Lewica i inni," *Student*, 26 June 1974, 3–4; and Magala, "Muzeum Kontestacji. Wyznania kustosza," *Student*, 15 August–4 September 1974, 4–5.
47. Examples include illustrator Andrzej Mleczko, who has been best known for his satirical drawings; poster artist Jan Sawka; actor, director, and satirist Krzysztof Materna; and journalist and satirist Michał Ogórek.
48. Leszek Balcerowicz became minister of finance under the first Solidarity government in Poland in 1989, responsible for the radical transition to a neoliberal market economy, known as "shock therapy." Janusz Korwin-Mikke formed several political parties after 1989, all with a similar platform of extreme nationalism and support for an unbridled free market. He served as an MP in the European Parliament in 2014–2018.
49. AAN, RN, ZSP, Komitet Wykonawczy, 1/15, Posiedzenia KW. Materiały na posiedzenie KW dotyczące prasy studenckiej, 1969, "Ocena aktualnej sytuacji oraz założenia rozwojowe prasy studenckiej," Warsaw, 10 June 1969, kk. 2–24, 4.
50. Emil Orzechowski, "Czarno na białym czyli Zebra," *Student*, 15 January–14 February 1972, 19. See also Lothar Herbst, "'Poglądy,'" *Student*, 17 July–13 August 1972, 17.
51. For example, *Student* featured parts of a book about a hippie commune in Munich originally published in German: Wolf Mein and Lisa Wegen, *Die Pop-Kommune: Dokumentation über Theorie u. Praxis e. neuen Form d. Zusammenlebens* (Munich: Heyne, 1971). See J.Z., "Raport z życia komuny (II). Portrety uczestników," *Student*, 15 August–4 September 1974, 4; and J.Z. (opr), "Public relations z wilekim biustem. Raport z życia Komuny—2," *Student*, 5–18 September 1974, 1, 4–5.
52. Lek. Med. Mariusz Popielarski, "Niektóre zagadnienia współczesnej seksuologii," *Problemy Rodziny* (November-December 1971): 30–36, 33. For further analysis of public discussions of the sexual revolution in Poland see Paweł Rams, "Bitwa o

młodych. Dyskursy władzy wobec przemian życia młodzieży w Polsce w latach 70," *Teksty Drugie* 1 (2020): 320–336.

53. Cover of *ITD*, 10 March 1974.

54. Barbara Olak, "Studia we dwoje . . . A dzieci u babci?," *ITD*, 10 March 1974, 5–6.

55. Katarína Lišková, *Sexual Liberation, Socialist Style: Communist Czechoslovakia and the Science of Desire, 1945–1989* (Cambridge: Cambridge University Press, 2018), 180.

56. Kazimierz Imieliński (1929–2010) received his degree in medicine in 1954. In 1965, he published a pioneering book on sexology titled *Życie seksualne. Psychohigiena* [Sexual life: psycho-hygiene]. He became a frequent interviewee and author of articles in the popular press. In 1973, he helped open the Sexology Department at the Medical Academy in Kraków, which trained the subsequent generations of Polish sexologists, including Lew-Starowicz. For more discussion on Imieliński, Lew-Starowicz, and the Polish School of Sexology see Agnieszka Kościańska, *Gender, Pleasure, and Violence: The Construction of Expert Knowledge of Sexuality in Poland* (Bloomington: Indiana University Press, 2021), esp. 41–55.

57. Dr. Zbigniew L. Starowicz, "Cel i sens współżycia," *ITD*, 2 April 1972, 14. In a similar way, Kazimierz Imieliński stressed gender difference as essential to healthy sex. See "Z Psychohigieny życia seksualnego," *Magazyn Studencki*, March 1974, 3.

58. Zbigniew L. Starowicz, "Matriarchat?," *ITD*, 30 April 1972, 14.

59. Dr. Zbigniew L. Starowicz, "Antykoncepcja," *ITD*, 31 October 1971, 14.

60. Dagmar Herzog, *Sex after Fascism: Memory and Morality in Twentieth-Century Germany* (Princeton, NJ: Princeton University Press, 2007), 231.

61. Jan Skórzyński, *Siła bezsilnych. Historia Komitetu Obrony Robotników.* (Warsaw: Świat Książki, 2012), 25. Gierek released the activists of the Movement in September 1974 shortly before his official visit to the United States.

62. Junes, *Student Politics in Communist Poland*, 136.

63. JW, "Przed zjednoczeniem," *ITD*, 18 February 1973, 3.

64. See, for example, "Jakiej chcemy organizacji," *ITD*, 21 January 1973, 5; and "Jakiej chcemy organizacji," *ITD*, 1 April 1973, 3 and 8–9.

65. Józef Grabowicz, "Jednością silni," *Nowa Wieś*, 15 April 1973, 2.

66. Cover, *ITD*, 22 April 1973.

67. Zbigniew Jurkiewicz, "Od Redakcji," *Dookoła Świata*, 25 April 1976, 2.

Conclusion

1. Karol Modzelewski, "Socjalizm z twarzą Gierka," in *Dekada Gierka. Blaski i cienie*, edited by Paweł Bożyk (Warsaw: Wydawnictwo "Kto jest kim," 2013), 47–76, 58.

2. Ewa Kacprzycka and Elżbieta Mardosiewicz, "Idzie młodość," *ITD*, 28 July 1974, 10–11, 10.

3. Redakcja *ITD*, "Ojczyzna to wielki zbiorowy obowiązek," *ITD*, 21 July 1974, 3.

4. See, for example, Zdzisław Pietrasik, "Przyżyjmy to jeszcze raz," *ITD*, 26 July 1974, 15.

5. Andrzej Paczkowski, *Pół wieku dziejów Polski, 1939–1989* (Warsaw: PWN, 1995), 404.

6. "The Final Act of the Conference on Security and Cooperation in Europe," 1 August 1975, 14 I.L.M. 1292, Helsinki Declaration, University of Minnesota Human Rights Library, http://hrlibrary.umn.edu/osce/basics/finact75.htm.

7. The letter was prompted, in part, by Gierek's announcement of planned amendments to the Polish constitution. The government intended to add a declaration of "permanent alliance" with the Soviet Union and specified that the condition for respecting civic rights in Poland would depend on the citizens' fulfillment of "duties toward the state." "List 'pięćdziesięciu dziewięciu' wysłany 5 grudnia 1975 przez prof. E. Lipińskiego do Marszałka Sejmu PRL," *Aneks*, no.11 (1976):11-14.

8. A number of former hippies participated in KOR activities, especially in underground publishing. Mirosław Chojecki and Magdalena Bocheńska-Chojecka, interview by author, digital recording, Konstancin-Jeziorna, 30 July 2013. Some former hippies claim that they influenced KOR by providing models of acting outside the state structures. These included underground publishing and communal meetings in private spaces. See, for example, "Prorok," in Sipowicz, *Hipisi w PRL-u*, 163.

9. "List 'pięćdziesięciu dziewięciu,'" 13.

10. Interestingly, many Eastern European economists, including Leszek Balcerowicz, the architect of the Polish "shock therapy," took their economic models from contemporary Latin America, especially Pinochet's Chile, rather than Western Europe. James Mark, Bogdan C. Iacob, Tobias Rupprecht, and Ljubica Spaskovska, *1989: A Global History of Eastern Europe* (Cambridge: Cambridge University Press, 2019), esp. 58–59.

11. These ideas were powerfully expressed in Francis Fukuyama, "The End of History," *National Interest*, no. 16 (Summer 1989), 3–18, 3.

12. In Poland, the best known memoir critical of the economic policies during the transition is the one by Marcin Król, who participated in the 1968 student rebellion and later in the Solidarity movement and Round Table negotiations of 1989. The title of the book translates as "We were stupid." See Marcin Król, *Byliśmy głupi* (Warsaw: Wydawnictwo Czerwone i Czarne, 2015).

13. On young people's distance from politics after the postcommunist transition see Jakub Sawulski, *Pokolenie '89. Młodzi o polskiej transformacji* (Warsaw: Wydawnictwo Krytyki Politycznej, 2019).

Bibliography

Personal Interviews

Leszek Budrewicz, Wrocław, 12 May 2016

Mirosław Chojecki and Magdalena Bocheńska-Chojecka, Konstancin-Jeziorna, 30 July 2013

Edward Chudziński, Kraków, 27 June 2012

Irena Groblewska, Emilianówka, 27 July 2013

Irena Grudzińska Gross, Boston, 23 November 2013

Jan Güntner, Kraków, 26 June 2012

Jerzy Illg, Kraków, 22 June 2011

Alicja Imlay, Szelejów Górny, 13 July 2013

Mieczysław Janowski, Wrocław, 17 July 2013

Bogusław Klimsa, Wrocław, 12 May 2016

Milo Kurtis, Warsaw, 15 February 2013

Bogusław Litwiniec, Wilcza, 15–16 July 2013

Magdalena, Warsaw, 18 February 2013

Adam and Zofia Mazurek, Warsaw, 16 June 2011

Hanna Musiał (Anna Musiałówna), Warsaw, 26 June 2013

Andrzej Paczkowski, Warsaw, 22 June 2012

Jan Poprawa, Kraków, 28 June 2012

Andrzej Sadowski, Białystok, 11 February 2013

Kamil Sipowicz, Warsaw, 26 June 2013

Sławomir Tabkowski, Kraków, 26 June 2012

Józef Tejchma, Warsaw, 1 July 2011

Teresa, Białystok, 16 July 2011

Tomasz Tłuczkiewicz, Warsaw, 12 February 2013

Archives and Libraries

Archiwum Akt Nowych, Warsaw

Archiwum Instytutu Pamięci Narodowej, Warsaw

Archiwum Państwowe w Białymstoku

Archiwum Państwowe w Krakowie

Archiwum Państwowe we Wrocławiu

Biblioteka Filozofii i Socjologii Polskiej Akademii Nauk, Warsaw

Biblioteka Narodowa, Warsaw

Biblioteka Uniwersytetu Warszawskiego, Warsaw

Vera and Donald Blinken Open Society Archive, Budapest

Periodicals and Newspapers

Dookoła Świata
Express Wieczorny
Filipinka
Forum
Gazeta Wrocławska
ITD
Jazz
Kontrasty
Kulisy
Kultura i Społeczeństwo
Motor
Nowa Wieś
Nowe Drogi
Nowy Medyk
Pałacyk. Konfrontacje
Perspektywy
Pod Wiatr
Poglądy
Polityka
Po prostu
Problemy Rodziny
Projekt
Przekrój
Radar
Student
Studia Socjologiczne
Sztandar Młodych
Trybuna Ludu
Tygodnik Powszechny
Ty i Ja
Wieś Współczesna
Więź
Wyboje
Wychowanie
Zebra
Zwieciadło

Published Primary Sources

"Antonina Kłoskowska. *Kultura masowa. Krytyka i obrona.*" *Studia Socjologiczne* 4, no. 1 (1964): 249–262.

Chałasiński, Józef. *Kultura i naród*. Warsaw: Książka i Wiedza, 1968.

Chałasiński, Józef. _____. *Społeczeństwo i wychowanie*. Warsaw: PWN, 1948.

Ciupak, Edward. *Kultura religijna wsi. Szkice socjologiczne*. Warsaw: Iskry, 1961.

Dąbrowski, Franciszek, Piotr Gontarczyk, and Paweł Tomasik, eds. *Marzec 1968 w dokumentach MSW*. Warsaw: IPN, 2008.

Dyoniziak, Ryszard, ed. *Młodzież epoki przemian. Z badań polskich socjologów.* Warsaw: Nasza Księgarnia, 1965.

Dyoniziak, Ryszard. *Młodzieżowa "podkultura." Studium socjologiczne.* Warsaw: Wiedza Powszechna, 1965.

Erenburg, Ilja. *Odwilż.* Translated by Jan Brzechwa. Warsaw: PIW, 1955.

Encyklopedia Powszechna PWN, vol. 4. 3rd edition. Warsaw: PWN, 1987.

Feliksiak, Jerzy. *Głos w sprawach młodzieży.* Warsaw: Książka i Wiedza, 1966.

"Fifth Column." https://marzec68.sztetl.org.pl/en/slowo/piata-kolumna/.

"The Final Act of the Conference on Security and Cooperation in Europe." 1 August 1, 1975. 14 I.L.M. 1292. Helsinki Declaration. University of Minnesota Human Rights Library. http://hrlibrary.umn.edu/osce/basics/finact75.htm.

Gierasimiuk, Urszula, ed. *Marzec '68 w Białymstoku. Wybór źródeł.* Białystok: IPN, 2008.

Gomułka, Władysław. *Przemówienia. Wrzesień 1957–Grudzień 1958.* Warsaw, 1959.

Hall, Stuart, and Tony Jefferson, eds. *Resistance through Rituals: Youth Subcultures in Postwar Britain.* London: Hutchinson, 1976.

Jackiewiczowa, Elżbieta. *O czym chcą wiedzieć dziewczęta.* 4th ed. Warsaw: Państwowy Zakład Wydawnictw Lekarskich, 1961.

Jawłowska, Aldona. *Drogi kontrkultury.* Warsaw: PIW, 1975.

Jaworska, Grażyna, and Henryk Głowacki. *Folklor marcowy. Marzec 1968.* Warsaw: Studencka Oficyna Wydawnicza, 1981.

Kłoskowska, Antonina. *Kultura masowa. Krytyka i obrona.* Warsaw: PWN, 2006.

Krzywicka, Irena. *Miłość... małżeństwo... dzieci...* Warsaw: Iskry, 1962.

Kuroń, Jacek, and Karol Modzelewski. *Open Letter to the Party. Revolutionary Marxist Students in Poland Speak Out (1964–1968).* Translated by Gerard Paul. New York: Merit, 1968.

Kurzela, Irena, Aleksander Kamiński, and Kazimierz Z. Sowa, eds. *Z badań nad środowiskiem domu studenckiego. Raporty z badań.* Warsaw: PWN, 1967.

Kusin, Vladimir. *The Intellectual Origins of the Prague Spring: The Development of Reformist Ideas in Czechoslovakia, 1956–1967.* Cambridge: Cambridge University Press, 2002.

Lanota, Anna. *Słowo do rodziców o wychowaniu seksualnym.* Warsaw: Towarzystwo Świadomego Macierzyństwa, 1960.

"List 'pięćdziesięciu dziewięciu' wysłany 5 grudnia 1975 przez prof. E. Lipińskiego do Marszałka Sejmu PRL." *Aneks,* no.11 (1976):11–14.

Lovell, Jerzy. *Jak żyć? Zbiór reportarzy.* Warsaw: Iskry, 1972.

Łopuski, Janusz. *Co chce wiedzieć każdy chłopiec.* 4th ed. Warsaw: Państwowy Zakład Wydawnictw Lekarskich, 1961.

Malewska, Hanna. *Kulturowe i psychospołeczne determinanty życia seksualnego.* Warsaw: PIW, 1969.

Marzec 1968. Dokumenty. Odezwy i ulotki (Warsaw, NZS PW, 1981).

Marzec 1968. Relacje. Procesy. Warsaw: NZS PW, 1981.

McLuhan, Marshall. *Understanding Media: The Extensions of Man.* New York: McGraw-Hill, 1964.

Mein, Wolf and Lisa Wegen, *Die Pop-Kommune: Dokumentation über Theorie u. Praxis e. neuen Form d. Zusammenlebens.* Munich: Heyne, 1971.

Nowak, Stefan, ed. *Studenci Warszawy. Studium długofalowych przemian postaw i wartości.* Warsaw: Wydawnictwo Uniwersytetu Warszawskiego, 1991.

Pomykało, Wojciech, ed. *Patriotyzm, ideologia, wychowanie. Dyskusja na temat patriotycznego i internacjonalistycznego wychowania.* Warsaw: Ministerstwo Obrony Narodowej, 1968.

Poprawa, Jan. *Fama—1966–1977. Historia imprezy.* Warsaw: Zarząd Główny SZSP, 1983.

Roszak, Theodore. *The Making of a Counter Culture: Reflections on the Technocratic Society and Its Youthful Opposition.* New York: Anchor Books, 1969.

Różewicz, Tadeusz. „Świadkowie, albo nasza mała stabilizacja." *Dialog* no. 5 (1962): 5-26.

Sokorski, Włodzimierz. *Współczesność i młodzież.* Warsaw: Iskry, 1963.

Towarzystwo Świadomego Macierzyństwa, 1957–1967. Warsaw: Państwowy Zakład Wydawnictw Lekarskich, 1967.

Widerszpil, Stanisław. *Skład polskiej klasy robotniczej. Tendencje zmian w okresie industrializacji socjalistycznej.* Warsaw: PWN, 1965.

Wilder, Emilia. "Impact of Poland's Stabilization of Its Youth," *Public Opinion Quarterly* 28, no. 3 (Autumn 1964): 447–452.

Wydarzenia marcowe 1968. Z przedmową Prof. Zygmunta Baumana. Paris: Instytut Literacki, 1969.

Published Memoirs and Interviews

Alexeyeva, Ludmila, and Paul Goldberg. *The Thaw Generation: Coming of Age in the Post-Stalin Era.* Pittsburgh: Pittsburgh University Press, 1993.

Bratkowski, Stefan, ed. *Październik 1956. Pierwszy wyłom w systemie. Bunt, młodość, rozsądek.* Warsaw: Prószyński i S-ka, 1996.

Chałasiński, Józef, ed. *Awans pokolenia. Młode pokolenie wsi polskiej.* Warsaw: Ludowa Spółdzielnia Wydawnicza, 1964.

Chałasiński, Józef, ed. *Miesiąc mojego życia. Wybór pamiętników.* Warsaw: Ludowa Spółdzielnia Wydawnicza, 1964.

Czupryński, Jakub, ed. *Autostop polski. PRL i współczesność.* Kraków: Ha!art, 2005.

Dasko, Henryk. *Dworzec Gdański. Historia niedokończona.* Kraków: Wydawnictwo Literackie, 2008.

Demiański, Marek. „Richard P. Feynman – urwisowaty geniusz." In Richard Feynman, *Pan raczy żartować, panie Feynman!* Translated by Tomasz Bieroń. Kraków: Znak, 2018, 3-9.

Dominik, Tomasz, and Marek Karewicz. *Złota młodzież, niebieskie ptaki. Warszawka lat 60.* Warsaw: Twój Styl, 2003.

Dudziak, Urszula. *Wyśpiewam Wam wszystko.* Warsaw: Kayax, 2011.

Fedorowicz, Jacek. *Ja jako wykopalisko.* Warsaw: Świat Książki, 2011.

Ginsberg, Allen. *Iron Curtain Journals, January–May 1965.* Edited by Michael Schumacher. Minneapolis: University of Minnesota Press, 2018.

Głowiński, Michał, and Grzegorz Wołowiec. *Czas nieprzewidziany. Długa rozprawa bez pana, wójta i plebana.* Warsaw: Wielka Litera, 2018.

Grupińska, Anna, and Joanna Wawrzyniak, eds. *Buntownicy. Polskie lata 70. i 80.* Warsaw: Świat Książki, 2011.

Guevara, Ernesto Che. *Dziennik z Boliwii.* Translated by Ryszard Kapuściński. Warsaw: Książka i Wiedza, 1969.

Illg, Jerzy. "Polskie lato miłości." Heh.pl forum, 8 October 2008 http://f.heh.pl/ftopic7031.html.

Jackowska, Olga, and Kamil Sipowicz. *Kora, Kora. A planety szaleją.* Warsaw: Agora, 2011.

Jawłowska, Aldona and Zofia Dworakowska, eds. *Wolność w systemie zniewolenia. Rozmowy o polskiej kontrkulturze.* Warsaw: Wydawnictwo Uniwersytetu Warszawskiego, 2008.

Karpiński, Jakub. *Krótkie spięcie (Marzec 1968).* Paris: Instytut Literacki, 1977.

Król, Marcin. *Byliśmy głupi.* Warsaw: Wydawnictwo Czerwone i Czarne, 2015.

Krzywicki, Ludwik. Pamiętniki chłopów. Warsaw: Instytut Gospodarstwa Społecznego, 1935.

Kuroń, Jacek. *Wiara i wina. Do i od komunizmu.* Wrocław: Wydawnictwo Dolnośląskie, 1995.

Landvai, Paul. *One Day That Shook the Communist World: The 1956 Hungarian Uprising and Its Legacy.* Princeton, NJ: Princeton University Press, 2008.

LL, Natalia. Interview by Tomasz Raczek, Szczerotok, Warsaw, Radio TOK FM, 29 April 2015.

Mann, Wojciech. *Rock-Mann. Czyli jak nie zostałem saksofonistą.* Kraków: Znak, 2010.

Michalewski, Wojciech. "Tarzan." *Mistycy i narkomani.* Warsaw: ETHOS, 1992.

Michnik, Adam. "Anti-authoritarian Revolt: A Conversation with Daniel Cohn-Bendit." In Adam Michnik, *Letters from Freedom: Post–Cold War Realities and Perspectives*, edited by Irena Grudzińska Gross with a foreword by Ken Jowitt. Berkeley: University of California Press, 1998, 29–67.

Michnik, Adam, and Agnieszka Marczyk, eds. *Against Anti-Semitism: An Anthology of Twentieth-Century Polish Writings.* New York: Oxford University Press, 2018.

Mieszczanek, Anna, ed. *Krajobraz po szoku.* Warsaw: Przedświt, 1989.

Modzelewski, Karol. "Socjalizm z twarzą Gierka." In *Dekada Gierka. Blaski i cienie.* edited by Paweł Bożyk. Warsaw: Wydawnictwo "Kto jest kim." 2013, 47–76.

Modzelewski, Karol. *Zajeździmy kobyłę historii. Wyznania poobijanego jeźdźca.* Warsaw: Iskry, 2013.

Nowakowski, Marek. *Syjoniści do Syjamu. Zapiski z lat 1967–1968.* Warsaw: Świat Książki, 2009.

Rakowski, Mieczysław. *Dzienniki polityczne 1967–1968.* Warsaw: Iskry, 2002.

Rolicki, Janusz. *Przerwana Dekada. Wywiad rzeka.* Warsaw: Wydawnictwo FAKT, 1990.

Sipowicz, Kamil. *Hipisi w PRL-u.* Warsaw: Baobab, 2008.

Sokorski, Włodzimierz. *Notatki.* Warsaw: PIW, 1975.

Sołtysiak, Grzegorz, and Józef Stępień, eds. *Marzec '68. Między tragedią a podłością.* Warsaw: PROFI, 1998.

Starczewska, Krystyna. "'W jakimś sensie byłam pierwszą ofiarą tej napaści' Krystyna Starczewska o tym jak rozpoczął się Marzec 1968." wyborcza.pl, 6 March 2018. http:// wyborcza.pl/10,82983,23151201,w-jakims-sensie-bylam-pierwsza-ofiara-tej-napasci-krystyna.html.

Szarłat, Aleksandra. *Prezenterki.* Warsaw: Świat Książki, 2012.

Toruńczyk, Barbara. "Opowieść o pokoleniu marca. Przesłanie dla nowej lewicy." Pt. 1. *Krytyka Polityczna* no. 15 (2008): 208–230.

Tyrmand, Leopold. *Dziennik 1954. Wersja Oryginalna.* Warsaw: Prószyński i S-ka, 1999.

Tyrmand, Leopold. *Diary 1954.* Translated by Anita Shelton and A. J. Wrobel. Evanston, IL: Northwestern University Press, 2014.

Wachowicz-Makowska, Jolanta. *Panienka w PRL-u.* Warsaw: Czytelnik, 2007.

Wiszniewicz, Joanna. *Życie przecięte. Opowieści pokolenia Marca.* Wołowiec: Wydawnictwo Czarne, 2008.

Woroszylski, Wiktor. "Dziennik Węgierski." *Aneks*, no.13–14 (1977), 185–242.

Secondary Sources

"AHR Reflections: 1968." *American Historical Review* 123, no. 3 (June 2018): 706–778.

Andrykiewicz, Jan. *Związek Młodzieży Wiejskiej w latach 1957–1976*. Warsaw: Muzeum Historii Polskiego Ruchu Ludowego, 2002.

Applebaum, Rachel. *Empire of Friends: Soviet Power and Socialist Internationalism in Cold War Czechoslovakia*. Ithaca, NY: Cornell University Press, 2019.

Arndt, Agnes. *Rote Bürger: Eine Milieu- Und Beziehungsgeschichte Linker Dissidenz in Polen (1956–1976)*. Göttingen: Vandenhoeck & Ruprecht, 2013.

Barker, Colin. "Some Reflections on Student Movements of the 1960s and Early 1970s." *Revista Crítica de Ciências* 81 (2008): 1–35.

Bitner, Steven. *The Many Lives of Khrushchev's Thaw: Experience and Memory in Moscow's Arbat*. Ithaca, NY: Cornell University Press, 2008.

Blobaum, Robert, ed. *Antisemitism and Its Opponents in Modern Poland*. Ithaca, NY: Cornell University Press, 2005.

Bodnár, Judith. "Making a Long Story Longer: Eastern Europe and 1968 as a Global Moment, Fifty Years Later." *Slavic Review* 77, no. 4 (Winter 2018): 873–880.

Borstelmann, Thomas. *The 1970s: A New Global History from Civil Rights to Economic Inequality*. Princeton, NJ: Princeton University Press, 2012.

Bren, Paulina. *The Greengrocer and His TV: The Culture of Communism after the 1968 Prague Spring*. Ithaca, NY: Cornell University Press, 2010.

Brick, Howard. *The Age of Contradictions: American Thought and Culture in the 1960s*. Ithaca, NY: Cornell University Press, 1998.

Brier, Robert, ed. *Entangled Protest: Transnational Approaches to the History of Dissent in Eastern Europe and the Soviet Union*. Osnabrück: Fibre, 2013.

Briggs, Jonathyne. *Sounds French: Globalization, Cultural Communities and Pop Music, 1958–1980*. Oxford: Oxford University Press, 2015.

Brown, Timothy Scott. *Sixties Europe*. Cambridge: Cambridge University Press, 2020.

Brown, Timothy Scott. *West Germany and the Global Sixties: The Anti-authoritarian Revolt, 1962–1978*. New York: Cambridge University Press, 2013.

Brown, Timothy Scott, and Lorena Anton, eds. *Between the Avant-Garde and the Everyday: Subversive Politics in Europe from 1957 to the Present*. New York: Berghahn Books, 2011.

Brzezinski, Zbigniew. *The Soviet Bloc: Unity and Conflict*. Cambridge, MA: Harvard University Press, 1967.

Ceranka, Paweł, and Sławomir Stępień, eds. *"Jesteście naszą wielką szansą." Młodzież na rozstajach komunizmu 1944–1989*. Warsaw: IPN, 2009.

Chaplin, Tamara, and Jadwiga Pieper Mooney, eds. *The Global 1960s: Convention, Contest, and Counterculture*. New York: Routledge, 2018.

Chłopek, Maciej. *Bikiniarze. Pierwsza polska subkultura*. Warsaw: Wydawnictwo Akademickie "Żak," 2005.

Chmielewska, Katarzyna, Agnieszka Mrozik, and Grzegorz Wołowiec, eds. *Komunizm. Idee i praktyki w Polsce, 1944–1989*. Warsaw: Instytut Badań Literackich PAN, 2018.

Chmielewska, Katarzyna, Grzegorz Wołowiec, and Tomasz Żukowski, eds. *Rok 1966. PRL na zakręcie. Idee-Dyskursy-Praktyki*. Warsaw: Instytut Badań Literackich PAN, 2014.

Chudziński, Edward, ed. *Kultura studencka. Zjawisko, twórcy, instytucje*. Kraków: Fundacja STU, 2011.

Connelly, John. *Captive University: The Sovietization of Czech, East German, and Polish Higher Education, 1945–1956.* Chapel Hill: University of North Carolina Press, 2000.

Crowley, David, and Susan E. Reid, eds. *Socialist Spaces: Sites of Everyday Life in the Eastern Bloc.* New York: Berg, 2002.

Curry, Jane Leftwich. *Poland's Journalists: Professionalism and Politics.* New York: Cambridge University Press, 1990.

Dahlmann, Hans Christian. *Antisemitismus in Polen 1968. Interaktionen zwischen Partei und Gesellschaft.* Osnabrück: Fibre, 2013.

David, Henry P., and Robert McIntyre. *Reproductive Behavior: Central and Eastern European Experiences.* New York: Springer, 1981.

Davies, Norman. *Rising '44: The Battle for Warsaw.* New York: Penguin Books, 2005.

Denning, Michael. *Culture in the Age of Three Worlds.* New York: Verso, 2004.

Domosławski, Artur. *Kapuściński Non-fiction.* Warsaw: Świat Książki, 2010.

Dovern, Lukas. "Investing in Socialist Poland: A Transnational History of Finance in the Cold War, 1944–1991." Ph.D. diss., Stanford University, 2019.

Dragostinova, Theodora. *The Cold War from the Margins: A Small Socialist State on the Global Cultural Scene.* Ithaca, NY: Cornell University Press, 2021.

Dragostinova, Theodora, and Malgorzata Fidelis. "Introduction: Beyond the Iron Curtain: Eastern Europe and the Global Cold War." *Slavic Review* 77, no. 2 (Fall 2018): 577–587.

Dubinsky, Karen, Catherine Krull, Susan Lord, Sean Mills, and Scott Rutherford, eds. *New World Coming: The Sixties and the Shaping of Global Consciousness.* Toronto: Between the Lines, 2009.

Dudek, Antoni, and Tomasz Marszałkowski. *Walki uliczne w PRL.* Kraków: Geo, 1999.

Echols, Alice. *Scars of Sweet Paradise: The Life and Times of Janis Joplin.* New York: Holt, 2000.

Eisler, Jerzy. *Grudzień 1970. Geneza, przebiegi konsekwencje.* Warsaw: IPN, 2012.

Eisler, Jerzy. *Polski Rok 1968.* Warsaw: IPN, 2006.

Engerman, David C. "The Second World's Third World." *Kritika: Explorations in Russian and Eurasian History* 12, no. 1 (Winter 2011): 183–211.

Evans, Sara M. "Sons, Daughters, and Patriarchy: Gender and the 1968 Generation." *American Historical Review* 114, no. 2 (2009):331–347.

Fahlenbrach, Kathrin, Martin Klimke, Joachim Scharloth, and Laura Wong, eds. *The Establishment Responds: Power, Politics, and Protest since 1945.* New York: Palgrave Macmillan, 2012.

Farber, David. "Building the Counterculture, Creating Right Livelihoods: The Counterculture at Work." *The Sixties: A Journal of History, Politics and Culture* 6, no. 1 (2013): 1–24.

Fehérváry, Krisztina. *Politics in Color and Concrete: Socialist Materiality and the Middle Class in Hungary.* Bloomington: Indiana University Press, 2013.

Fichter, Madigan. "Yugoslav Protest: Student Rebellion in Zagreb, Belgrade, and Sarajevo in 1968." *Slavic Review* 75, no 1 (Spring 2016): 99–121.

Fidelis, Małgorzata. "Are You a Modern Girl? Consumer Culture and Young Women in 1960s Poland." In *Gender Politics and Everyday Life in State Socialist Eastern and Central Europe,* edited by Shana Penn and Jill Massino. New York: Palgrave, 2009.

Fidelis, Małgorzata. "The Other Marxists: Making Sense of International Student Revolts in Poland in the Global Sixties." *Zeitschrift für Ostmitteleuropa-Forschung* 62 (2013): 425–449.

Fidelis, Małgorzata. *Women, Communism, and Industrialization in Postwar Poland.* New York: Cambridge University Press, 2010.

Friszke, Andrzej. *Anatomia buntu. Kuroń, Modzelewski i komandosi.* Kraków: Znak, 2010.

Friszke, Andrzej. *Polska Gierka.* Warsaw: Wyadwnictwo Szkolne i Pedagogiczne, 1995.

Friszke, Andrzej. "Rok 1968—koniec i początek." *Zeszyty Literackie* 142, no. 2 (Summer 2018): 76–96.

Friszke, Andrzej, ed. *Władza a społeczeństwo w PRL. Studia historyczne.* Warsaw: Instytut Studiów Politycznych PAN, 2003.

Fürst, Juliane. *Flowers through Concrete: Exploration in Soviet Hippieland.* Oxford: Oxford University Press, 2021.

Fürst, Juliane. "Love, Peace and Rock'n Roll on Gorky Street: The 'Emotional Style' of the Soviet Hippie Community." *Contemporary European History* 23 (November 2014): 565–587.

Fürst, Juliane, and Josie McLellan, eds. *Dropping out of Socialism: The Creation of Alternative Spheres in the Soviet Bloc.* Lanham, MD: Lexington Books, 2017.

Ganev, Venelin I. "The Borsa: The Black Market for Rock Music in Late Socialist Bulgaria." *Slavic Review* 73, no. 3 (Winter 2014): 514–537.

Gasztold, Przemysław. "Maoizm nad Wisła? Działalność Komunistycznej Partii Polski Kazimierza Mijala." *Pamięć i sprawiedliwość* 2, no. 32 (2018): 290–318.

Gella, Aleksander. "The Life and Death of the Old Polish Intelligentsia," *Slavic Review* 30, no. 1 (March 1971): 1–27.

Gilburd, Eleonory. *To See Paris and Die: The Soviet Lives of Western Culture.* Cambridge, MA: Harvard University Press, 2018.

Gildea, Robert, James Mark, and Anette Warring, eds. *Europe's 1968: Voices of Revolt.* Oxford: Oxford University Press, 2013.

Gorsuch, Anne E. "'Cuba, My Love!' The Romance of Revolutionary Cuba in the Soviet Sixties." *American Historical Review* 120, no. 2 (April 2015): 497–526.

Gorsuch, Anne E. "The Dance Class or the Working Class: The Soviet Modern Girl." In *The Modern Girl around the World: Consumption, Modernity, and Globalization,* edited by Alyse Eve Weinbaum, Lynn M. Thomas, Priti Ramamurphy, Uta G. Poiger, Madeleine Yue Dong, and Tani E. Barlow. Durham, NC: Duke University Press, 2008, 174–193.

Gorsuch, Anne E., and Diane P. Koenker, eds. *The Socialist Sixties: Crossing Borders in the Second World.* Bloomington: Indiana University Press, 2013.

Grazia, Victoria de. *Irresistible Empire: America's Advance through Twentieth-Century Europe.* Cambridge, MA: Harvard University Press, 2005.

Gross, Jan Tomasz. *Fear: Antisemitism in Poland after Auschwitz.* New York: Random House, 2007.

Grzebałkowska, Magdalena. *Komeda, Osobiste życie jazzu.* Kraków: Znak, 2018.

Gwóźdź, Andrzej, and Margarete Wach, eds. *W poszukiwaniu Polskiej Nowej Fali.* Kraków: Universitas, 2017.

Häberlen, Joachim, and Mark Keck-Szajbel, eds. *The Politics of Authenticity: Countercultures and Radical Movements across the Iron Curtain, 1968–1989.* New York: Berghahn Books, 2019.

Hanebrink, Paul. *A Specter Hunting Europe: The Myth of Judeo-Bolshevism.* Cambridge, MA: Harvard University Press, 2018.

Hellema, Duco. *The Global 1970s: Radicalism, Reform, and Crisis.* New York: Routledge, 2019.

Herman, Rebecca. "An Army of Educators: Gender, Revolution and the Cuban Literacy Campaign of 1961." *Gender and History* 24, no. 1 (April 2012): 93–111.

Herzog, Dagmar. *Sex after Fascism: Memory and Morality in Twentieth-Century Germany.* Princeton, NJ: Princeton University Press, 2007.

Herzog, Dagmar. *Sexuality in Europe: A Twentieth-Century History.* Cambridge: Cambridge University Press, 2011.

Holoha, Carol. *Reframing Irish Youth in the Sixties.* Liverpool: Liverpool University Press, 2018.

Hornsby, Robert. *Protest, Reform and Repression in Khrushchev's Soviet Union.* Cambridge: Cambridge University Press, 2013.

Idzikowska-Czubaj, Anna. *Rock w Polsce. O paradoksach współistnienia.* Poznań: Wydawnictwo Poznańskie, 2011.

Ilič, Melanie, Susan E. Reid, and Lynne Atwood, eds. *Women in the Khrushchev Era.* New York: Palgrave Macmillan, 2004.

Ivaska, Andrew. *Cultured States: Youth, Gender, and Modern Style in 1960s Dar es Salaam.* Durham, NC: Duke University Press, 2011.

Jakelski, Lisa. *Making New Music in Cold War Poland.* Berkeley: University of California Press, 2016.

Jakubowska, Urszula, ed. *Czasopisma społeczno-kulturalne w okresie PRL.* Warsaw: Instytut Badań Literackich PAN, 2011.

Janion, Maria. "Wprowadzenie. Trudna klasa w ciężkiej szkole." In Joanna Tokarska-Bakir, *Rzeczy mgliste. Eseje i studia.* Sejny: Pogranicze, 2004.

Jaworska, Justyna. *Cywilizacja "Przekroju." Misja obyczajowa w magazynie ilustrowanym.* Warsaw: Wydawnictwo Uniwersytetu Warszawskiego, 2008.

Jedlicki, Jerzy. *A Suburb of Europe: Nineteenth-Century Polish Approaches to Western Civilization.* Budapest: Central European University Press, 1999.

Jian, Chen, Martin Klimke, Masha Kirasirova, Mary Nolan, Marilyn Young, and Joanna Waley-Cohen, eds. *The Routledge Handbook of the Global Sixties: Between Protest and Nation Building.* New York: Routledge, 2018.

Jobs, Richard Ivan. *Backpack Ambassadors: How Youth Travel Integrated Europe.* Chicago: University of Chicago Press, 2017.

Jobs, Richard Ivan. *Riding the New Wave: Youth and the Rejuvenation of France after the Second World War.* Stanford: Stanford University Press, 2007.

Jobs, Richard Ivan, and David M. Pomfret, eds. *Transnational Histories of Youth in the Twentieth Century.* New York: Palgrave Macmillan, 2015.

Jones, Polly, ed. *The Dilemmas of De-Stalinization: Negotiating Cultural and Social Change in the Khrushchev Era.* New York: Routledge, 2006.

Judt, Tony. *Postwar: A History of Europe since 1945.* New York: Penguin Books, 2006.

Junes, Tom. *Student Politics in Communist Poland: Generations of Consent and Dissent.* Lanham, MD: Lexington Books, 2015.

Kalter, Christoph. *The Discovery of the Third World: Decolonization and the Rise of the New Left in France, c. 1950–1976.* Cambridge: Cambridge University Press, 2016.

Kemp-Welch, A. *Poland under Communism: A Cold War History.* New York: Cambridge University Press, 2008.

Kenney, Padraic. *Rebuilding Poland: Workers and Communists, 1945–1950.* Ithaca, NY: Cornell University Press, 1997.

Kijek, Kamil. *Dzieci modernizmu: Świadomość, kultura i socjalizacja polityczna modzieży żydowskiej w II Rzeczypospolitej.* Wrocław: Wydawnictwo Uniwersytetu Wrocławskiego, 2017.

Klich-Kluczewska, Barbara. *Rodzina, tabu i komunizm w Polsce, 1956–1989*. Kraków: Libron, 2015.

Klimke, Martin. *The Other Alliance: Student Protest in West Germany and the United States in the Global Sixties*. Princeton, NJ: Princeton University Press, 2010.

Klimke, Martin, and Joachim Scharloth, eds. *1968 in Europe: A History of Protest and Activism, 1956–1977*. New York: Palgrave Macmillan, 2008.

Kochanowski, Jerzy. *Rewolucja międzypaździernikowa*. Kraków: Znak, 2017.

Kola, Adam F. *Socjalistyczny postkolonializm. Rekonsolidacja pamięci*. Toruń: Wydawnictwo Uniwersytetu Mikołaja Kopernika, 2018.

Konarzewska, Aleksandra, Anna Nakai, and Michał Przeperski, eds. *Unsettled 1968 in the Troubled Present: Revisiting 50 Years of Discussions from East and Central Europe*. New York: Routledge, 2020.

Kopecký, Petr. "Czeching the Beat, Beating the Czech: Ginsberg and Ferlinghetti in Czechia." *The Sixties: A Journal of History, Politics, and Culture* 3, no. 1 (June 2010): 97–103.

Kornetis, Kostis. *Children of the Dictatorship: Student Resistance, Cultural Politics and the "Long 1960s" in Greece*. New York: Berghahn Books, 2013.

Kościańska, Agnieszka. *Gender, Pleasure, and Violence: The Construction of Expert Knowledge of Sexuality in Poland*. Bloomington: Indiana University Press, 2021.

Kościańska, Agnieszka. *Zobaczyć łosia. Historia polskiej edukacji seksualnej od pierwszej lekcji do internetu*. Wołowiec: Wydawnictwo Czarne, 2017.

Kosicki, Piotr H., ed. *Vatican II behind the Iron Curtain*. Washington, DC: The Catholic University of America Press, 2016.

Kosiński, Krzysztof. *Oficjalne i prywatne życie młodzieży w czasach PRL*. Warsaw: Rosner & Wspólnicy, 2006.

Kozlov, Denis, and Eleonory Gilburd, eds. *The Thaw: Soviet Society and Culture during the 1950s and 1960s*. Toronto: University of Toronto Press, 2013.

Krzywicki, Andrzej. *Poststalinowski karnawał radości. V Światowy Festiwal Młodzieży i Studentów o Pokój i Przyjaźń, Warszawa 1955*. Warsaw: TRIO, 2009.

Kunicki, Mikołaj. *Between the Brown and the Red: Nationalism, Catholicism, and Communism in Twentieth-Century Poland. The Politics of Bolesław Piasecki*. Athens: University of Ohio Press, 2012.

Kurz, Iwona. *Twarze w tłumie. Wizerunki bohaterów wyobraźni zbiorowej w kulturze polskiej lat 1955–1969*. Warsaw: Świat Literacki, 2006.

Kwiek, Julian. *Marzec 1968 w Krakowie*. Kraków: Księgarnia Akademicka, 2008.

Langland, Victoria. *Speaking of Flowers: Student Movements and the Making and Remembering of 1968 in Military Brazil*. Durham, NC: Duke University Press, 2013.

Langton, Rae. *Sexual Solipsism: Philosophical Essays on Pornography and Objectification*. Oxford: Oxford University Press, 2009.

Laskowski, Piotr. *Szkice z dziejów anarchizmu*. Warsaw: Muza, 2006.

Lebow, Katherine A. "The Conscious of the Skin: Interwar Polish Autobiography and Social Rights." *Humanity: An International of Human Rights, Humanitarianism, and Development* 3, no. 3 (Winter 2012): 297–319.

Lebow, Katherine A. *Unfinished Utopia: Nowa Huta, Stalinism, and Polish Society, 1949–1956*. Ithaca, NY: Cornell University Press, 2013.

Lederhendler, Eli, ed. *The Six-Day War and World Jewry*. College Park, MD: University Press of Maryland, 2000.

Liechty, Mark. *Far Out: Counterculture Seekers and the Tourist Encounter in Nepal*. Chicago: University of Chicago Press, 2017.

Lišková, Katarína. *Sexual Liberation, Socialist Style: Communist Czechoslovakia and the Science of Desire, 1945-1989*. Cambridge: Cambridge University Press, 2018.

Looseley, David. "The World Theatre Festival, Nancy, 1963-1988: A Critique and a Retrospective." *New Theatre Quarterly* 6, no. 22 (May 1990): 141-153.

Machcewicz, Paweł. *Rebellious Satellite: 1956 in Poland*. Stanford: Stanford University Press, 2011.

Mark, James, and Péter Apor. "Socialism Goes Global: De-colonization and the Making of a New Culture of Internationalism in Socialist Hungary, 1956-1989." *Journal of Modern History* 87 (December 2015): 852-891.

Mark, James, Péter Apor, Radina Vučetić, and Piotr Osęka. "'We Are with You, Vietnam': Transnational Solidarities in Socialist Hungary, Poland, and Yugoslavia." *Journal of Contemporary History* 50, no. 3 (2015): 439-464.

Mark, James, Bogdan C. Iacob, Tobias Rupprecht, and Ljubica Spaskovska. *1989: A Global History of Eastern Europe*. Cambridge: Cambridge University Press, 2019.

Mark, James, Artemy M. Kalinovsky, and Steffi Marung, eds. *Alternative Globalizations: Eastern Europe and the Postcolonial World*. Bloomington: Indiana University Press, 2020.

Marwick, Arthur. *The Sixties: Cultural Transformation in Britain, France, Italy and the United States, c. 1958-c. 1974*. Oxford: Oxford University Press, 2000.

Materski, Wojciech, and Anna Cienciala, eds. *Katyń: A Crime without Punishment*. New Haven, CT: Yale University Press, 2008.

Matthews, John P. C. *Explosion: The Hungarian Revolution of 1956*. New York: Hippocrine Books, 2007.

Matynia, Elżbieta. *Performative Democracy*. New York: Paradigm, 2009.

May, Elaine Tyler. *Homeward Bound: American Families in the Cold War Era*. 3rd ed. New York: Basic Books, 2008.

Maziejuk, Henryk, Mieczyslaw Pisarek, and Stanisław Wiechno, eds. *Dwa starty. Wypowiedzi nadesłane na konkurs ogłoszony przez ZG ZMW i redakcję "Zarzewie."* Warsaw: Książka i Wiedza, 1970.

Mazuer, Peter D. "Contraception and Abortion in Poland," *Family Planning Perspectives* 13, no. 4 (July-August 1981): 195-8.

Mazurek, Małgorzata. "Polish Economists in Nehru's India: Making Science for the Third World in an Era of De-Stalinization and Decolonization." *Slavic Review* 77, no. 3 (Fall 2018): 588-610.

McLellan, Josie. *Love in the Time of Communism: Intimacy and Sexuality in the GDR*. Cambridge: Cambridge University Press, 2011.

McMillian, John. *Smoking Typewriters: The Sixties Underground Press and the Rise of Alternative Media in America*. Oxford: Oxford University Press, 2011.

Medovoi, Leerom. *Rebels: Youth and the Cold War Origins of Identity*. Durham, NC: Duke University Press, 2005.

Mencwel, Andrzej. *Przedwiośnie czy Potop. Studium postaw polskich w XX wieku*. Warsaw: Czytelnik, 1997.

Michlic, Joanna Beata. *Poland's Threatening Other: The Image of the Jew from 1880 to the Present*. Lincoln: University of Nebraska Press, 2006.

Miklóssy, Katalin, and Melanie Ilic, eds. *Competition in Socialist Society*. New York: Routledge, 2014.

Molnar, Miklos. *Budapest 1956*. London: Allen and Unwin, 1971.

Müller, Martin. "In Search of the Global East: Thinking between North and South." *Geopolitics* 25, no. 3 (2020): 734-755.

Nebřenský, Zdeněk. *Marx, Engels, Beatles. Myšlenkovy svět polskych a československych vysokoškoláků, 1956–1968*. Prague: Akademie Masarykův ústav AV ČR, 2017.

Nowell-Smith, Geoffrey. *Making Waves: New Cinemas of the 1960s*. New York: Bloomsbury, 2008.

Nussbaum, Martha. "Objectification," *Philosophy and Public Affairs* 24, no. 4 (1995): 249–291.

Osęka, Piotr. *Marzec '68*. Kraków: Znak, 2008.

Osęka, Piotr. *My, ludzie z Marca. Autoportret pokolenia '68*. Wołowiec: Wydawnictwo Czarne, 2015.

Osiński, Zbigniew. *Grotowski's Journeys to the East*. New York: Routledge, 2014.

Paczkowski, Andrzej. *Pół wieku dziejów Polski, 1939–1989*. Warsaw: PWN, 1995.

Paczkowski, Andrzej. *The Spring Will Be Ours: Poland and the Poles from Occupation to Freedom*. Translated by Jane Cave. University Park, PA: Pennsylvania State University Press, 2003).

Pasek, Cezary. *Złota młodzież w PRL-u i jej obraz w literaturze i filmie*. Warsaw: Bellona, 2010.

Patterson, Patrick Hyder. *Bought and Sold: Living and Losing the Good Life in Socialist Yugoslavia*. Ithaca, NY: Cornell University Press, 2011.

Pelka, Anna. *Texas-land. Moda młodzieżowa w PRL*. Warsaw: TRIO, 2007.

Pence, Katherine, and Paul Betts, eds. *Socialist Modern: East German Everyday Culture and Politics*. Ann Arbor: University of Michigan Press, 2008.

Perkowski, Piotr. *Gdańsk. Miasto od nowa*. Gdańsk: Terytoria, 2013.

Perkowski, Piotr. "Wedded to Welfare? Working Mothers and the Welfare State in Communist Poland." *Slavic Review* 76, no. 2 (2017): 455–480.

Pęziński, Piotr. *Na rozdrożu. Młodzież żydowska w PRL, 1956–1968*. Warsaw: Żydowski Instytut Wydawniczy, 2014.

Pietrasz, Andrzej. *Allen Ginsberg w Polsce*. Warsaw: Semper, 2014.

Pietraszewski, Igor. *Jazz w Polsce. Wolność improwizowana*. Warsaw: Nomos, 2012.

Pleskot, Patryk. *Wielki mały ekran. Telewizja a codzienność Polaków lat sześćdziesiątych*. Warsaw: TRIO, 2007.

Plocker, Anat. "'Zionists to Dayan': The Anti-Zionist Campaign in Poland, 1967–1968." Ph.D. diss., Stanford University, 2011.

Poiger, Uta G. *Jazz, Rock, and Rebels: Cold War Politics and American Culture in a Divided Germany*. Berkeley: University of California Press, 2000.

Polonsky, Antony, Hanna Węgrzynek, and Andrzej Żbikowski, eds. *New Directions in the History of the Jews in the Polish Lands*. Brookline, MA: Academic Studies Press, 2018.

"Polska. Oświata. Polska Rzeczpospolita Ludowa." In *Encyklopedia PWN*. https://encyklopedia.pwn.pl/haslo/Polska-Oswiata-Polska-Rzeczpospolita-Ludowa;4575102.html.

Porter, Brian. *When Nationalism Began to Hate: Imagining Modern Politics in Nineteenth-Century Poland*. Oxford: Oxford University Press, 2002.

Prestholdt, Jeremy. *Domesticating the World: African Consumerism and the Genealogies of Globalization*. Berkeley: University of California Press, 2008

Prestholdt, Jeremy. *Icons of Dissent: The Global Resonance of Che, Marley, Tupac, and Bin Laden*. Oxford: Oxford University Press, 2019.

Presholdt, Jeremy. "Resurrecting Che: Radicalism, the Transnational Imagination, and the Politics of Heroes." *Journal of Global Studies* 7, no. 3 (2012): 506–526.

Przybyło Marta, and Karolina Puchała-Rojek, eds. *Początek przyszłości. Fotografia w miesięczniku "Polska" w latach 1954–1968*. Warsaw: Zachęta—Narodowa Galeria Sztuki, 2019.

Rainer-Horn, Gerd. *The Spirit of '68: Rebellion in Western Europe and North America, 1956–1976*. Oxford: Oxford University Press, 2007.

Rainer-Horn, Gerd, and Padraic Kenney, eds. *Transnational Moments of Change: Europe 1945, 1968, 1989*. New York: Rowman and Littlefield, 2004.

Rams, Paweł. "Bitwa o młodych. Dyskursy władzy wobec przemian życia młodzieży w Polsce w latach 70." *Teksty Drugie* 1 (2020): 320–336.

Risch, William J. *The Ukrainian West: Culture and the Fate of Empire in Soviet Lviv*. Cambridge, MA: Harvard University Press, 2011.

Risch, William J., ed. *Youth and Rock in the Soviet Bloc: Youth Cultures, Music, and the State in Russia and Eastern Europe*. Lanham, MD: Lexington Books, 2015.

Rokicki, Konrad. *Kluby studenckie w Warszawie, 1956–1980*. Warsaw: IPN, 2018.

Rokicki, Konrad, and Sławomir Stępień, eds. *Oblicza Marca 1968*. Warsaw: IPN, 2004.

Roth-Ey, Kristin. *Moscow Primetime: How the Soviet Union Built a Media Empire That Lost the Cultural Cold War*. Ithaca, NY: Cornell University Press, 2011.

Sadowska, Joanna. *Sercem i myślą związani z partią. Związek Młodzieży Socjalistycznej (1957–1976). Polityczne aspekty działalności*. Warsaw: TRIO, 2009.

Sasanka, Paweł. *Czerwiec 1976. Geneza-przebieg-konsekwencje*. Warsaw: IPN, 2006.

Sawulski, Jakub. *Pokolenie '89. Młodzi o polskiej transformacji*. Warsaw: Wydawnictwo Krytyki Politycznej, 2019.

Schieldt, Axel, and Detel Siegfried, eds. *Between Marx and Coca-Cola: Youth Cultures in Changing European Societies, 1960–1980*. New York: Berghahn Books, 2006.

Sierakowska, Katarzyna. *Rodzice, dzieci, dziadkowie . . . Wielkomiejska rodzina inteligencka w Polsce 1918–1939*. Warsaw: Wydawnictwo "DiG." 2003.

Siermiński, Michał. *Dekada przełomu. Polska lewica opozycyjna, 1968–1980*. Warsaw: Książka i Prasa, 2016.

Sitko, Marcin. *The Rolling Stones za żelazną kurtyną. Warszawa 1967*. Warsaw: Wydawnictwo c2, 2012.

Skórzyński, Jan. *Siła bezsilnych. Historia Komitetu Obrony Robotników*. Warsaw: Świat Książki, 2012.

Slobodian, Quinn. *Foreign Front: Third World Politics in Sixties West Germany*. Durham, NC: Duke University Press, 2012.

Smith, Kathleen E. *Moscow 1956: The Silenced Spring*. Cambridge, MA: Harvard University Press, 2017.

Snyder, Timothy. *Nationalism, Marxism, and Modern Central Europe: A Biography of Kazimierz Kelles-Krauz*. Oxford: Oxford University Press, 1997.

Sokół, Zofia. *Prasa kobieca w Polsce w latach 1945–1995*. Rzeszów: Wydawnictwo Wyższej Szkoły Pedagogicznej, 1998.

Solarz, Marcin Wojciech. *Trzeci Świat. Zarys biografii pojęcia*. Warsaw: Wydawnictwo Uniwersytetu Warszawskiego, 2009.

Sowiński, Paweł. *Wakacje w Polsce Ludowej. Polityka władz i ruch turystyczny (1945–1989)*. Warsaw: TRIO, 2005.

Stańczak-Wiślicz, Katarzyna, Piotr Perkowski, Małgorzata Fidelis, and Barbara Klich-Kluczewska. *Kobiety w Polsce, 1945-1989. Nowoczesność, równouprawnienie, komunizm*. Kraków: Universitas, 2020.

Stola, Dariusz. *Emigracja pomarcowa.* Warsaw: Instytut Studiów Społecznych UW, 2000.

Stola, Dariusz. *Kampania antysyjonistyczna w Polsce, 1967–1968.* Warsaw: Insytut Studiów Politycznych PAN, 2000.

Stola, Dariusz. *Kraj bez wyjścia? Migrajce z Polski, 1949–1989.* Warsaw: Instytut Studiów Politycznych PAN, 2010.

Stur, Heather Marie. *Saigon at War: South Vietnam and the Global Sixties.* New York: Cambridge University Press, 2021.

Sułek, Antoni. *Sondaż polski. Przygarść rozpraw o badaniach ankietowych.* Warsaw: Wydawnictwo IFiS PAN, 2001.

Suri, Jeremi. *Power and Protest: Global Revolution and the Rise of Détente.* Cambridge, MA: Harvard University Press, 2005.

Suri, Jeremi. "The Rise and Fall of the International Counterculture." *American Historical Review* 114, no. 1 (February 2009): 45–68.

Szaynok, Bożena. *Ludność Żydowska na Dolnym Śląsku, 1945–1950.* Wrocław: Uniwersytet Wrocławski, 2000.

Szpak, Ewelina. *"Chory człowiek jest wtedy jak coś go boli." Społeczno-kulturowa historia zdrowia i choroby na wsi polskiej po 1945r.* Warsaw: Instytut Historii PAN, 2016.

Świda-Ziemba, Hanna. *Młodzież PRL. Portrety pokoleń w kontekście historii.* Kraków: Wydawnictwo Literackie, 2011.

Świda-Ziemba, Hanna. *Urwany lot. Pokolenie inteligenckiej młodzieży powojennej w świetle listów i pamiętników z lat 1945–1948.* Kraków: Wydawnictwo Literackie, 2003.

Thompson, Gordon. *Please Please Me: Sixties British Pop, Inside Out.* Oxford: Oxford University Press, 2008.

Tismaneanu, Vladimir, ed. *Promises of 1968: Crisis, Illusion, Utopia.* Budapest: Central European University Press, 2010.

Thum, Gregor. *Uprooted: How Breslau Became Wrocław during the Century of Expulsions.* Princeton, NJ: Princeton University Press, 2011.

Tokarska-Bakir, Joanna. *Pod klątwą. Społeczny portret pogromu kieleckiego.* Warsaw: Czarna Owca, 2018.

Tompkins, David G. "The East Is Red? Images of China in East Germany and Poland through the Sino-Soviet Split." *Zeitschrift für Ostmitteleuropa-Forschung* 62, no. 3 (2013): 393–424.

Toniak, Ewa, ed. *Jestem artystką we wszystkim co niepotrzebne. Kobiety i sztuka około 1960.* Warsaw: Neriton, 2010.

Tracz, Bogusław. *Hippiesi, kudłacze, chwasty. Hipisi w Polsce w latach 1967–1975.* Katowice-Kraków: IPN, 2014.

Trapszyc, Artur. *Lokalny pejzaż kontrkultury. Peace, Love i PRL (komentarz do wystawy).* Toruń: Muzeum Etnograficzne, 2013.

Tromly, Benjamin. *Making the Soviet Intelligentsia: Universities and Intellectual Life under Stalin and Khrushchev.* New York: Cambridge University Press, 2014.

"Trybuna Ludu." Encyklopedia interia. https://encyklopedia.interia.pl/dzienniki-czasopisma/news-trybuna-ludu,nId,1998729

Tsipursky, Gleb. *Socialist Fun: Youth, Consumption, and State Sponsored Popular Culture in the Cold War Soviet Union, 1945–1970.* Pittsburgh: University of Pittsburgh Press, 2016.

Walicki, Andrzej. *Stanisław Brzozowski and the Polish Beginning of "Western Marxism."* New York: Clarendon Press, 1989.

Wallach, Jennifer Jones. "Building a Bridge of Worlds: The Literary Autobiography as Historical Source Material." *Biography* 29, no. 3 (Summer 2006): 446–461.

Westad, Odd Arne. *The Global Cold War: Third World Interventions and the Making of Our Times*. New York: Cambridge University Press, 2005.

Wierzchoś, Dariusz. "Zwyczajne życie zwykłych ludzi. Losy Archiwum Towarzystwa Przyjaciół Pamiętnikarstwa." Histmag.org, 10 April 2008, https://histmag.org/Zwycza jne-zycie-zwyklych-ludzi.-Losy-archiwum-Towarzystwa-Przyjaciol-Pamietnikars twa-1750..

Wolin, Richard. *The Wind from the East: French Intellectuals, the Cultural Revolution, and the Legacy of the 1960s*. 2nd ed. Princeton, NJ: Princeton University Press, 2017.

Wright, Donald R. *The World and a Very Small Place in Africa: A History of Globalization in Niumi, the Gambia*, 4th ed. New York: Routledge, 2018.

Wroński, Paweł. "Gdyby nie wyścig Ameryki z ZSRR, może człowiek w ogóle nie stanąłby na Księżycu." *Wyborcza.pl*. 19 July 2019. https://wyborcza.pl/7,90535,25003078,zimna-wojna-i-ladowanie-na-ksiezycu-w-polskiej-tv-decyzje.html.

Young, Cynthia. *Soul Power: Culture, Radicalism, and the Making of a U.S. Third World Left*. Durham, NC: Duke University Press, 2006.

Yurchak, Alexei. *Everything Was Forever, until It Was No More: The Last Soviet Generation*. Princeton, NJ: Princeton University Press, 2006.

Zaremba, Marcin. " 'Bigosowy socjalizm.' Dekada Gierka." In *Polacy wobec PRL. Strategie przystosowawcze*, edited by Grzegorz Miernik. Kielce: Akademia Świętokrzyska, 2003, 184–200.

Zaremba, Marcin. *Komunizm, Legitymizacja, Nacjonalizm*. Warsaw: TRIO, 2005.

Zaremba, Marcin. *Wielka trwoga, 1944–1947. Ludowa reakcja na kryzys*. Kraków: Znak, 2012.

Zhuk, Sergei I. *Rock and Roll in the Rocket City: The West, Identity, and Ideology in Soviet Dnepropetrovsk, 1960–1985*. Baltimore: Johns Hopkins University Press, 2010.

Zolov, Eric. "Introduction: Latin America in the Global Sixties." *Americas* 70, no. 3 (January 2014): 349–362.

Zolov, Eric. *The Last Good Neighbor: Mexico in the Global Sixties*. Durham, NC: Duke University Press, 2020.

Zolov, Eric. *Refried Elvis: The Rise of the Mexican Counterculture*. Berkeley: University of California Press, 1999.

Zubkova, Elena. *Russia after the War: Hopes, Illusions, and Disappointments, 1945–1957*. Translated and edited by Hugh Ragsdale. New York: Routledge, 2015.

Zubok, Vladislav. *Zhivago's Children: The Last Russian Intelligentsia*. Cambridge, MA: Harvard University Press, 2011.

Zysiak, Agata. *Punkty za pochodzenie. Powojenna modernizacja i uniwersytet w robotniczym mieście*. Kraków: Znak, 2016.

Zysiak, Agata, Kamil Śmiechowski, Kamil Piskała, Wiktor Marzec, Kaja Kaźmierska, and Jacek Burski. *From Cotton and Smoke. Łódź—Industrial City and Discourses of Asynchronous Modernity, 1897–1994*. Łódź and Kraków: Łódź University Press and Jagiellonian University Press, 2018.

Żarnowski, Janusz. *Inteligencja polska jako elita kulturalna i społeczna w ostatnich stu latach (od 1918 r. do współczesności)*. Warsaw: Instytut Historii PAN, 2019.

Index

For the benefit of digital users, indexed terms that span two pages (e.g., 52–53) may, on occasion, appear on only one of those pages.

Tables, figures, and boxes are indicated by *t*, *f*, and *b* following the page number.

1968, 111–18
  and antisemitism, 102, 118–26
  in Europe, 103–4, 124–25
  and gender, 114, 121–22
  as a global phenomenon, 103–5, 124–26, 203
  and memory, 124–26, 187
  in Polish historiography, 103, 186
  in rural communities, 117–18, 162–63
  and student protests, 5–6, 8, 12, 102, 104–5, 112–17, 123, 199–200

abortion, 10, 54–56, 176–77, 198, 207–8
abortion law, 54–55, 207–8
Adamiecka, Hanka, 32–34
Adamski, Jerzy, 64
Africa, 7–8, 17, 29, 44, 52–53, 69, 71–72, 73–74, 75, 86, 105, 154, 164–65
Against the Wind (Pod Wiatr, periodical), 19, 20, 31–32
Albania, 117, 205–6
Alexeyeva, Ludmila, 35–36
Algeria, 71–72, 108, 184
Almatur (student tourist bureau), 82, 152–53
"Americanization," 50–51
Amnesty International, 107
Andrycz, Nina, 69–70
anti-Colonialism
  in public culture, 69–72
  in state policy, 7–8
  in student protest, 104–5, 106, 107–11, 124
anti-imperialism
  in public culture, 29, 38
  in state policy, 104–5
  in student protest, 104, 105–11, 124–25

antisemitism, 119–20, 236n.13
  and antisemitic campaign of 1967–1968, 118–26
  and cosmopolitanism, 122
  in the Party, 37, 118–26, 219n.49
  and the Thaw, 23–25, 38
"apolitics"
  in sociological research, 47, 75
  and youth magazines, 61, 62, 64–74
Armstrong, Louis, 93
Around the World (Dookoła Świata, periodical), 11–12, 14, 15–17, 27–31, 28*f*, 30*f*, 33, 37, 44, 61, 65–67, 69–74, 75–76, 140–41, 193, 201
Austria, 107, 191
"authenticity"
  in countercultural movements, 127, 130–32, 203
  in public culture, 185
  in student culture, 98–99, 104, 200

Balcerowicz, Leszek, 194, 263n.48, 265n.10
Baltic Coast, 19, 137–38, 149, 163–64, 186–87
  and workers' protests of 1970, 149, 186–87, 200, 204, 206–7
Baranowski, Krzysztof Jerzy, 149
Barańczak, Stanisław, 150, 194
Banner of Youth (Sztandar Młodych, newspaper), 32, 33–34, 39, 49–50
"Baptism of Poland" *see* Millennium (1966)
Bardot, Brigitte, 22, 48–49, 66*f*, 71–72, 72*f*, 190
Beatles, The, 50, 128–29, 133, 149–50, 178, 184

beatniks (*bitnicy*), 49, 128–29
beat poets, 2–3, 136
"Beautiful Girls to the Screen" (contest, 1957), 48
beauty culture
    during the Thaw, 21–22, 29
    in youth magazines, 21–22, 29, 87–89, 89*f*, 200
Belarus, 77, 132, 208
Bem, Józef, 31–32
Beria, Lavrentiy, 24, 219n.49
Białystok, 82–83, 163–64
Bielsk Podlaski, 163–64
Bierut, Bolesław, 212n.9
Bieszczady Mountains, 141–42, 144
big beat (Polish rock 'n' roll), 50–51, 66–67, 94, 163, 178. *See also* rock 'n' roll
Bikini Boys (*Bikiniarze*), 14, 128–29
birth control, 53–60, 144, 176–77, 198
"Black Thursday," 186
Blue and Blacks (Niebiesko–Czarni, band), 50, 51*f*, 52*f*, 79
blue jeans, 2, 3, 42, 75, 85, 90, 107, 193. *See also* fashion
Blumsztajn, Seweryn, 134
Bochwic, Teresa, 40, 114
Bogucka, Teresa, 110
"bombshells," 22
Bonanza (American miniseries), 178, 180
Bond (Więź, periodical), 63
Boniecki, Adam, 137
bossa nova (dance), 93
Brandt, Willy, 191
Bratkowski, Andrzej, 34–35
Bratkowski, Stefan, 34, 66–67
Bravo (West German periodical), 67–68
Brazil, 26–27, 152–53, 180–81
Bread and Puppet Theater, 152–54
Bren, Paulina, 10–11, 241n.7, 261n.2
Brown, Timothy Scott, 2, 231n.27
Brus, Włodzimierz, 97–98
Budapest, 25, 31–35, 38, 152–53
Buddhism, 135. *See also* countercultural movements
Bureau of Foreign Tourism for Youth, 43
Burma, 69–70
Bydgoszcz, 133

Cambodia, 69–70
Canada, 135, 205–6
Candide (French magazine), 129
Castro, Fidel, 70, 106, 190, 191, 192*f*
Catholic Church. *See* Catholicism
Catholicism
    and countercultural movements, 130, 136–37, 144
    and mass culture, 63
    and nationalism, 118–20, 124–25
    in postcommunist Poland, 10, 207–8
    practice among youth, 10, 96, 130, 170
    in rural communities, 167–71
    and sexuality, 54, 56–57, 177
    and student groups, 21, 96–97, 136–37
    and the Thaw, 36, 96–97
censorship, 10, 19–20, 74, 115, 206
Center for Research on Public Opinion (OBOP), 46
Chałasiński, Józef, 44, 181
Chęciny, 141–42
Chudziński, Edward, 154
Cieślewicz, Roman, 229–30n.15
China, 26–27, 78–79, 95–96, 117, 238n.60
cinema, 2–3, 18, 22, 41–43, 48–49, 61, 70–73, 82, 153, 171
    Ashes and Diamonds, 18, 217n.23
    Film magazine, 48
    Innocent Sorcerers, 41–42
    Knife in the Water, 41–42
    and masculinity, 42, 164–66
    and the Polish Film School, 41–42
Circles of Military Youth (Koła Młodzieży Wojskowej), 222n.10
Citizens Militia, 121, 244n.37
Ciupak, Edward, 168–69
class divisions, 63–64, 99–100, 154, 158
    and countercultural movements, 127, 133, 154
    among students, 81–83, 85, 99–100, 161, 189
Club of Seekers of Contradictions (Klub Poszukiwaczy Sprzeczności), 97–98. *See also* student clubs
Clubs of Catholic Intelligentsia, 21, 96–97
Clubs of Young Intelligentsia, 21
club-Cafés (*klubokawiarnie*)

and rural communities, 170–71, 172–73, 173f, 178
and young women, 172, 182–83
Coca-Cola, 50, 100, 107, 114, 190
coffee, 12–13, 15–16, 40, 170–71, 178
Cohn-Bendit, Daniel, 106, 125–26
Collectivization of agriculture, 15, 45, 157
Cold War
    and cultural diplomacy, 25, 29–30, 152–53, 191–93
    debates over, 107–9, 124, 214n.22
    and the global sixties, 40–41, 72–73, 104–5
colonialism. See also anti-Colonialism
    at the 1955 World Youth and Student Festival, 26–30
    and 1968, 117, 120, 124–26
    and media, 17, 42–43, 69–70, 86, 164–65
    and protests, 104–5, 109, 111
Commandos (Komandosi), 98–101, 105–14, 125–26, 134, 138–39, 199, 203
Commission for Radio and Television, 40–41, 43
Commission of Culture, 63
Communist Party. See Polish United Workers' Party
communist system
    collapse of, 207–8
    definitions of, 7, 20–21, 97–98, 107–8, 212n.5
    in Poland, 36, 46–47, 119, 123, 124, 187–88
consumption, 10–11, 45, 151, 156–57, 203, 207
    anxieties about, 49–50, 88–89, 98, 121, 175
    in socialist societies, 7, 15, 47
    under Gierek, 3–4, 184–85, 189–90, 193, 201, 204–5
    and foreign goods, 42–43, 50, 85, 107, 114, 180, 189–90, 193
    and youth culture, 5, 41–43, 47, 60, 75–76, 81, 87–88, 91, 93–90, 100–1, 193
contraception see birth control
Contrasts (Kontrasty, periodical), 19, 29–30

cosmopolitanism, 37–38, 170, 178–80
    and 1968, 121–23
Council of Culture and Art, 63–64
countercultural movements. See also hippies
    and Catholicism, 130, 136–37, 144
    and drugs, 128, 136, 144–48
    and eastern religions, 135
    and gender and sexuality, 142–45
    and hippies, 1, 3–4, 8, 12–13, 116, 125, 127–28, 138–45
    and identity, 128–33, 134–35
    and student theater, 151, 154
Cross-Section (Przekrój, periodical), 229–30n.15
Cuba, 2, 7–8, 70–71, 71f, 104–6, 108, 109–11, 136, 184, 190–91
    and the Cuban Missile Crisis, 70–71, 184
    and "literacy brigades," 70
cultural liberalization
    during the Thaw, 15–19
    under Gierek, 149, 187–93
cultural policy, 63–64, 79. See also mass culture
Cybulski, Zbyszek, 18
Cyrankiewicz, Józef, 69–70, 118
Czechoslovakia, 10–11, 47, 122, 135–36
    Prague Spring, 1, 79–80, 102–3, 133–34, 141–42, 204–5
    relations with Poland, 34–35
    sexual attitudes in, 59, 196–97
Częstochowa, 36, 141–42, 146–47
    and icon of Virgin Mary, 169–70
Czuma, Andrzej, 199

Davis, Angela, 1, 135
Dąbrowska, Beata, 121–22
de-Colonization, 7–8, 52–53, 61, 71–72, 107–9, 203, 231–32n.35
Demiański, Marek, 93
democratic socialism, 33, 36, 38, 95–96, 202, 207, see also socialism
Denmark, 135, 152–53
de-Stalinization, 45, 203. See also Thaw
détente, 7–8, 191, 205–6
dissidents, 35–36, 102–11, 199, 205–7
Djilas, Milovan, 97–98

Dmowski, Roman, 119–20
Dołęgowski, Andrzej, 57
Dodziuk, Anna, 112
domestic violence, 148, 158, 160–61
drugs, 128, 136, 144–48, 184
Dudas, Jozsef, 33
Dudziak, Urszula, 95
Duszniki, 141–42, 142f
Dyoniziak, Ryszard, 4, 223–24n.24
Dziady (The Forefathers' Eve), 111–12
Dzierżyński, Feliks, 134–35

East Germany, 78, 110–11, 163–64
Eastern bloc, 34–35, 43, 77, 83–84, 97–98,
    104–5, 180, 184–85, 186, 190, 191–
    93, 195, 202, 207
economics
    and postwar growth, 44–45
    and price increases, 186, 205
    and postcommunism, 207–8, 263n.48,
        265n.10
    and Western bank loans, 188, 205
education
    higher education, 81–85
    and literacy, 158–60
    in rural communities, 158–62, 173–74,
        178, 181–82
Ehrenburg, Ilya, 14
Eichelberger, Wojciech, 138–39
Elbląg, 186
Empik (Klub Międzynarodowej Prasy i
    Książki), 128–29, 249n.9
Endecja (National Democratic Party),
    119–20, 124–25, 245–46n.59
"Eurocentrism," 95–96, 124, 125–26, 135
"Extra-Parliamentary Opposition," 118

Fashion. See also blue jeans; miniskirt
    and countercultural movements, 1, 127,
        128–29, 131–33, 149, 151–52
    and magazines, 21, 71–72, 193, 195
    in rural communities, 175–76, 181–82
    and youth and students, 40, 42, 49, 83,
        94–95, 121, 193
Feliksiak, Jerzy, 49–50
Federation of Socialist Polish Youth
    Associations (Federacja
    Socjalistycznych Związków
    Mlodziezy Polskiej), 199–200

Fehérváry, Krisztina, 10–11, 233n.64
feminism, 48–49, 53–60, 87–90, 99–100,
    124–25, 155, 171–78, 197–99
festivals, 2, 11–13, 25–31, 38, 70–71, 78,
    83, 98, 128, 132, 141–42, 150–55,
    202, 238n.52
Feynman, Richard, 93
Fiat 126P (maluch), 189–90
Filipinka (periodical), 65–66, 67f, 75–76
Finland, 105–6, 191
First World, 3, 103–5, 207
Forum (weekly), 129
France, 24, 78, 97–98, 156–57
    travel to, 107, 152, 191
    and youth, 14, 47, 135, 249n.11
French May, 106, 109
Fresh Start (Od nowa, periodical), 19,
    230n.20
Friszke, Andrzej, 95–96, 239n.74

Gartner, Katarzyna, 136–37
Gawlikowski, Krzysztof, 122–23
Gdańsk, 39, 50–51
    and the Bim-Bom Theater, 17–
        19, 26–27
    and students, 17, 82–83, 91, 115
    and workers' protests of December
        1970, 137–38, 186–87
Gdynia, 163–64, 186–87
gender roles, 27–29, 44, 53, 57–58, 59–60,
    94–95, 198–99
    and 1968, 114
    and countercultural movements, 142–
        45, 148
    and higher education, 86, 87–90
    and masculinity, 21–22, 42, 58, 93–94,
        99, 121–22, 147–48, 164–66
    and rural communities, 171–78, 196–97
Generation (Pokolenie, periodical), 15–16
generational conflict, 35–37, 52–53, 60,
    103, 107–8, 119, 124, 128–29, 161–
        67, 178, 181–82, 187–88, 191–93
Gerő, Ernő, 31–32
Gest (pantomime theater), 154
Giedroyc, Jerzy, 107
Giełżyński, Wojciech, 29, 66–67
Gierek, Edward, 3–4, 12–13
    and consumer socialism, 184–85, 189–
        90, 193, 205

and globalization, 187–93
and rise to power, 149, 157, 184–85
Girls' Councils (Rady Dziewcząt), 171–74,
    176–77, 204
Ginsberg, Allen, 1, 2, 136, 140, 252n.47
"global consciousness," 104, 121
globalization, 187–93, 202
    cultural dimensions, 179–80
    definitions of, 7, 40–41
    under Gierek, 187–93
Global East, 203, 212n.6. *See also*
    Second World
Global North, 212n.6, *See also* First World
Global South, 3, 7–8, 17, 61, 69–70, 104,
    105, 106–7, 108, 126, 156–57, 184,
    203, 212n.6. *See also* Third World
Goldberg, Paul, 35–36
Gomułka, Władysław
    and 1968, 117, 118–19, 120–21
    and 1970 workers' protests, 149, 186
    rise to power, 3–4, 15, 35–37, 151–52, 157
Górecki, Wiktor, 110
Grotowski, Jerzy, 251–52n.40
Grudzińska, Irena (Irena Grudzińska
    Gross), 107, 121
Groblewska, Irena, 133, 135, 149
Guevara, Che, 2, 110–11, 243n.27

Hasse, Grażyna, 193
Health Courses (*szkoły zdrowia*), 176–
    77, 182
Hejmo, Konrad, 137
Helsinki Accords, 59, 206–7
Hendrix, Jimi, 1, 135, 137, 149–50
Herzog, Dagmar, 99, 198–99
Hippies. *See also* countercultural
    movements
    and communes, 138–45
    and drugs, 144–48
    and gender, 142–45
    and identity, 1, 116, 128–33
    in the press, 128–29
    and sexuality, 143–45
    and surveillance, 128, 134–35, 140, 146–48
    in the Soviet Union, 127
    in the United States, 129, 135–36,
        145, 155
hipisowanie (hippiness), 128, 149–50,
    195–96, 196f

Hiroshima, 137–38
hitchhiking. *See* travel
Ho Chi Minh, 135
Hoff, Barbara, 193
Holocaust
    and Auschwitz (Oświęcim), 137–38
    and memory, 23, 37, 38
    survivors in Poland, 23–24, 132
    and the Warsaw Ghetto Uprising, 24
Home Army (Armia Krajowa), 23, 24–25
human rights, 54, 59, 125, 185, 205–7
Hungary, 10–12
    1956 Revolution, 31–35, 105–6, 108,
        110–11, 125–26, 202
    and Polish reporting, 32–34
    relations with Poland, 34–35
Hybrydy (Hybrids), 90–91, 93–94, 98, 100.
    See also student clubs

Illg, Jerzy, 1, 131–32, 136
Imlay, Alicja, 76, 132
Imieliński, Kazimierz, 197–98, 264n.56
India, 16, 29, 69–70, 127
Indonesia, 78–79
internationalism, 7, 8–9, 27–31, 34–35,
    61–62, 67–68, 69–73, 118, 122–23,
    134–35, 202–3
International Book Fair (1962), 78
International Festival of Student Theater
    Festivals in Wrocław, 141–42, 151–
    54, 153f
International Union of Students (IUS), 25
International Women's Day (March 8),
    102, 112, 114, 195–96
Israel, 26–27
    diplomatic relations with, 23, 120–21
    and the Six-Day War, 104–5, 120–21, 123
Italy, 67–68, 78, 107, 135, 156–57
ITD (student periodical), 11–12, 65–66,
    70–73, 72f, 75, 87–88, 89f, 122–23,
    195–98, 196f

Jackiewiczowa, Elżbieta, 56, 58
Jagiellonian University, 85, 115, 161, 187
Janion, Maria, 119–20
jazz, 50–51, 63–64, 65, 131f
    and festivals, 78, 82, 83, 132
    and student clubs, 2–3, 90–95
    during the Thaw, 15–16, 21, 39

Jazz (monthly), 76, 233n.66
Jews *see* Polish Jews
Jonas, Stanisław, 18
Joplin, Janis, 137
journalists, 15–16, 19–25, 32–35, 56–60,
    61–62, 194–95
  relations with the state, 19–20, 35–
    37, 73–74
"Junak," 165, 178. *See also* motorcycles

Kamiński, Aleksander, 44
Katowice, 82–83, 115, 131–32
Katyń massacre, 105–6, 117
Kazimierz (town), 141–42
Kennedy, John Fitzgerald, 131*f*, 180
Kenya, 17
Kerouac, Jack, 136, 140–41
Kielce, 117, 143–44
Khrushchev, Nikita, 43
  and the "Secret Speech" (1956), 15,
    23, 216n.9
Kłodzko, 1
Kłoskowska, Antonina, 62, 63
"Kobra" (Polish mystery television
    series), 171
Kołakowski, Leszek, 24–25
Kolczyński, Janusz, 59
komis stores, 94, 121
Konopacki, Andrzej, 29–30
Kopaniec, 140, 141*f*
Kora (Olga Jackowska), 131–32, 142–43
Korwin-Mikke, Janusz, 194, 263n.48
Kozakiewicz, Mikołaj, 49, 59–60
Kołodziejczyk, Ryszard, 48
Kozłowski, Maciej, 98–99
Kozłowa Góra, 77*f*, 173*f*, 174*f*
Koźniewski, Kazimierz, 16
Kraj Rad (The Country of Councils,
    periodical), 68–69
Kraków, 34, 75, 133, 135–37, 143, 149,
    154, 193. *See also* Jagiellonian
    University
  and 1968, 115
  and students, 17, 19, 20, 76, 78, 82–83,
    85, 91, 96–97, 161, 187, 194
Krzywicka, Irena, 54, 56–60, 198
Kultura (émigré periodical), 107, 109
Kuroń, Jacek, 107–9, 115, 123, 134, 205

Kurtis, Milo, 130, 142–43
Kuźniak, Bolesław, 149–50

Lambretta, 258n.32
Lanota, Anna, 56
Lasota, Irena, 112
Latin America, 17, 44, 73–74, 86
Lew-Starowicz, Zbigniew, 198
Lišková, Katarína, 59, 196–97
Lithuania, 77, 132
Litwiniec, Bogusław, 19, 151–52
Lollobrigida, Gina, 48, 175
LSD, 145. *See also* drugs
Lublin, 19, 20, 31–32, 82–83, 132–33
Lubusz, 179*f*
Lukács, György, 33
Lukierski, Jerzy, 93
Lovell, Jerzy, 149
Łopuski, Janusz, 58
Łódź, 82–83, 85, 90, 92*f*, 115
Łysa Góra, 180–81

magazines, 64–74. *See also* press
  circulation of, 19, 194–95
  controversies over, 35–38, 59, 73–74
Malenkov's New Course, 15.
    See also Thaw
Malewska, Hanna, 54, 55–56
Mann, Wojciech, 75
Mao Tse Tung, 1, 115, 135
Margueritte, Bernard, 112
marijuana, 145–46. *See also* drugs
Marxism
  and 1968, 103, 117, 118, 124–25
  and dissidents, 97–98, 100–1, 103, 107,
    118, 125–26
  reform of, 83–84, 124–25
  and students, 43, 83–84
  during the Thaw, 19, 20–21
"Marxist revisionism," 64, 102, 204–5,
    224–25n.36
Marwick, Arthur, 134, 211n.2
mass culture, 5, 7–8, 10–11, 21–22, 25, 41–
    43, 60, 62–64, 75–80, 81, 91, 168
  definition of, 62
  debates over, 62, 63–64, 73–74
Matynia, Elżbieta, 150–51
Mau Mau Uprising, 17

May Day (International Labor Day), 110, 116

Mazowiecki, Tadeusz, 14, 21, 63

Mazurian Lakes, 141–42, 163–64

memoirs, 9, 86, 158, 160–61, 163–64, 165, 172–73, 177–78, 180

Mexico, 26–27, 81–82, 135

Mexico City, 133–34, 251n.28

migration
    after 1968, 123–24
    internal, 45, 132, 169

Michnik, Adam, 97–98, 99, 103, 105–6, 107, 112–13, 115, 121, 124, 125–26, 205

Michaluk, Eugeniusz, 151–52

Mickiewicz, Adam, 111–12

Mielno, 141–42

Mikołajska, Halina, 17, 18

Millennium (1966), 119, 169–70

Mingus, Charlie, 93

miniskirt, 2, 3, 10, 83, 175, 178, 184. See also fashion

Miodek, Jan, 91–92

Misiek, Wiesław, 91–92

Ministry of Culture and Art, 63, 136, 152

Ministry of Internal Affairs, 109–10

Moczar, Mieczysław, 119–20

modernity, 3–4, 44–50, 203
    debates over, 49–50, 51–53, 205–3
    and gender roles, 6, 48–49, 53–60, 171–78
    under Gierek, 184–85, 189–93
    in rural communities, 85–86, 157–58, 167, 171–78, 204
    and socialism, 6–9

Modzelewski, Karol, 97–98, 99, 107, 108–9, 123, 204–5

Mondo Beat (Italian periodical), 67–68

morality
    in sex education, 53–60
    and socialism, 49–53, 98–99, 185

motorcycles
    and Golden Helmet Competition, 167
    and masculinity, 164–66
    in rural communities, 165–67, 176, 178, 182, 204
    and young women, 166–67

Moscow, 15, 19–20, 27–29, 99–100, 106, 124, 204–5

Motyka, Julian, 152

Mounier, Emmanuel, 21

Nagy, Imre, 31, 32, 33–34, 221n.77

Namiotkiewicz, Walery, 105–6

nationalism
    and 1968, 102–3, 118–26
    and anticommunist opposition, 102–3, 124
    and postcommunism, 126, 207–8
    and rural communities, 117–18, 178–83

Nauman-Hoffer, Gilbert Otto (Diotima), 56–60

Nehru, Jawaharlal, 69–70

Nepal, 135

New Left, 8, 99, 105–11, 122

New York, 61, 93, 132, 152–53, 191

New Wave, 44

New Village (Nowa Wieś, periodical), 128–29, 163, 166, 167, 180–81, 190

Niemczyk, Krzysztof, 136

Niesiołowski, Stefan, 199

Nixon, Richard, 190–91

North Vietnam, 109–10

Nowak, Stefan, 46, 96

Nowe Drogi (New Paths, monthly), 64

Oasis (The Light and Life Movement), 97. See also Catholicism

OBOP. See Center for Research on Public Opinion

Olszowski, Stefan, 191, 192f

"Open Letter to the Party," 107–9, 203, 204–5

Opole, 82–83, 115, 163
    Polish song festival, 141–42, 257n.27

ORMO. See Voluntary Reserve of the Citizens' Militia

Ostaszewski, Jacek, 135

Ostróda, 141–42, 159f

Ożarów, 139, 139f

pacifism, 8, 127, 134–35, 137–38, 146, 203

Pałacyk (Little Palace), 91–92, 94, 95, 98, 132. See also student clubs

"Partisans" (Party faction), 118–20, 245n.56

Passport Bureau, 30–31, 220n.68

Paszkiewicz, Bogumił, 92
Pawełczyńska, Anna, 96–97
"Peaceful Coexistence," 7–8, 43, 105–6
People's Tribune (Trybuna Ludu, newspaper), 32, 233n.55
Perspectives (Perspektywy, weekly), 191
Petőfi, Sándor, 31–32
Pewex (hard currency store), 190
Piasecki, Romuald, 116
Podkowa Leśna, 136–37
Poland (periodical), 79
Po prostu (Straight talk, periodical), 17, 19–25
Polish Jews
    and 1968, 102–5, 118–26
    and identity, 84–85
"Polish Road to Socialism," 3–4, 15, 37, 188
Polish Scouts Association (Związek Harcerstwa Polskiego, ZHP), 41, 79, 107
Polish Socialist Party (Polska Partia Socjalistyczna, PPS), 107
Polish Student Association (Zrzeszenie Studentów Polskich, ZSP), 2–3, 18–19, 41, 84, 91, 108–9, 152
    and cultural patronage, 65
    and the "unification" congress of 1973, 200
Polish United Workers' Party (Polska Zjednoczona Partia Robotnicza, PZPR), 6–7, 15, 19–20, 35–36, 37, 45, 59, 62–63, 64, 68, 74, 79, 82, 118–26, 151, 154, 157–60, 187–88
Polish Youth Association (Związek Młodzieży Polskiej, ZMP), 20–21, 41, 97–98
Political Discussion Club, 97–98. *See also* student clubs
Polityka (periodical), 49, 165f, 184
popular culture. *See* mass culture
Popielarski, Mariusz, 195
postcommunism, 126, 207–8
Poznań, 48, 137, 149, 170–71
    and 1956 workers' uprising, 15, 103, 146–47
    and 1968, 115
    and students, 17, 19, 82–83, 150, 200
Prague, 25, 103

Prague Spring. *See* Czechoslovakia
press. *See also* student press
    crackdowns on, 37, 73–74
    during the Thaw, 19–25
    and photojournalism, 15–17, 21–22, 29, 48, 61, 69–73, 76, 87–88, 163, 191–93, 192f, 195–96, 197, 200
    and sex education columns, 56–60, 197–99
    and travelogues, 15–17, 73–74, 93
Press Bureau, 35–37, 59, 62, 64, 68–69, 73–74, 76, 78–79, 167–68
Pronatalism, 188–89, 198
Prophet (Józef Pyrz), 129, 134, 137–38

race
    at the 1955 World Youth and Student Festival, 27–29
    and 1968, 118–26
    and international students, 86
    and sexuality, 27–29, 86
Raczak, Lech, 154
Radar (periodical), 11–12, 42–43, 56–57, 59–60, 64–67, 66f, 69, 75–76, 78–79, 197
Radio Free Europe, 107, 214n.23
Radio Luxembourg, 2–3, 75, 76, 79
Radom, 116–17, 205
Rákosi, Matyas, 31
Réalité (French magazine), 129
Red and Blacks (Czerwono–Czarni, band), 50, 136–37
Red Guitars (Czerwone Gitary, band), 50
regionalism, 8–9, 178–80
reproductive rights, 53–60, 176–77, 198–99, 207–8. *See also* abortion
Riot police (ZOMO), 113–14, 115, 116–17, 186–87
Rough Road Ahead (Wyboje, periodical), 19, 218n.40
rock 'n' roll. *See also* big beat
    concerts, 39, 50–51, 51f, 52f, 66–67, 75, 116
    "polonization" of, 50–51
    reactions to, 39, 75, 149–50
    in youth magazines, 66–68, 76, 94–95
Rolling Stones concert in Warsaw (1967), 75

Roszak, Theodore, 127
Różewicz, Tadeusz, 211n.3
Ruch (The Movement), 199
Ruciane Nida, 141–42
Runowicz, Roman, 116
Rural Youth Association (Związek
    Młodzieży Wiejskiej, ZMW), 5, 41,
    77f, 158, 163, 170–72, 173f, 174f,
    177, 199
rural communities
    and Catholicism, 167–71
    and childhood, 158–62
    and gender roles, 171–78
    and memoir competitions, 158
    and modernization, 85–86, 157–58,
      167, 171–78, 189, 204
    and national identity, 178–83, 204
Russia, 111–12, 117, 208
Rodowicz, Tomasz, 134, 149–50

Sadowski, Andrzej, 76, 85–86, 156
Sagan, Francoise, 78
Sandomierz, 116–17
Sartre, Jean Paul, 39–40
Sawicka, Paula, 98
Salut les Copains (French
    magazine), 67–68
secularization, 6, 10, 54, 56–57, 167–71
"Second Poland," 5, 187–88, 194, 204
Second World, 3–4
security apparatus, 154, 220n.61,
    252n.47
    and countercultural movements, 128,
      134–35, 140, 146–48
    and treatment of women, 114, 121–
      22, 147–48
sex education
    in print, 56–60, 197–99
    and reproductive rights, 55–59, 176–77
sexology, 59–60, 264n.56
sexual revolution, 54, 195–99
    and hippies, 144–45
    in rural communities, 174–77
    and students, 98–99
"shock therapy," 207–8, 263n.48, 265n.10
Sipowicz, Kamil, 131f, 142–43
Six-Day War (1967), 104–5, 120–21,
    246n.62

sixties, 124, 134
    interpretations of, 1–2, 103–4, 184
    and socialism, 5–6, 124–25
"small stabilization" (mała stabilizacja),
    60, 211n.3
Socialism. See also Marxism
    attitudes among youth, 8–9, 46–47,
      96, 124–26
    consumer, 184–85, 189–90, 193, 205
    and students, 97–101, 105–11, 199–201
Socialist Youth Association (Związek
    Młodzieży Socjalistycznej, ZMS),
    5, 41, 42–43, 65
Socialist Polish Student Association
    (Socjalistyczny Związek Studentów
    Polskich, SZSP), 199
Society for Conscious Motherhood
    (Towarzystwo Świadomego
    Macierzyństwa, TŚM), 55, 176–77
sociology
    as an academic discipline, 45–46
    studies of youth and students, 46–48,
      51–53, 86
Socio-Cultural Association of Jews in
    Poland (Towarzystwo Społeczno-
    Kulturalne Żydów w Polsce,
    TSKŻ), 84, 236n.14
Sokorski, Włodzimierz, 40–41, 43, 51–53,
    54, 179–80
Solidarity (Solidarność), 103, 125, 206–8
Sopot, 39, 238n.52
Soviet Union, 3, 7–8, 10–11, 96, 184, 204–5
    and imperialism, 34, 104, 105–6, 107–8,
      110–11, 117–18, 120
    invasion of Hungary, 31–35, 38, 125–
      26, 202
    relations with Poland, 15, 19–20, 26–27,
      32, 34, 68–69, 77, 79, 117–18,
      120, 188
Soviet Screen (periodical), 73
Spain, 110, 156–57
Spanish Civil War, 107
Stalin, Iosif, 2, 14, 15, 21, 32, 34–35
Stalinism, 3–4, 5–6, 14, 15–16, 20–21, 22–
    24, 31, 34, 37–38, 41–42, 44, 45–46,
    48, 54–55, 60, 103, 107–8, 122, 157,
    171–72, 202
Stanek, Karin, 166

Starczewska, Krystyna, 114, 247n.71
state violence, 146–48, 186, 204, 206
  and 1968, 113–15, 121–22, 123–24
Student (periodical), 154, 194–95, 197
student clubs
  and gender roles, 90, 93–95
  and memory, 91–92
  and student culture, 41–42, 81, 83,
    84, 90–95
  and the Thaw, 15–16, 17–19, 26–27,
    36, 202
student press. *See also* ITD
  and critical journalism, 19–25, 36–37,
    151–52, 194–95, 200, 202
  crackdowns on, 35–37
  during the Thaw, 19–25
  under Gierek, 195, 197–99
student protests. *See* 1968
students
  demographic profile, 81–83, 85,
    87, 96–97
  and dormitories, 81, 83, 86
  female, 87–90
  international, 86
  and organizations, 41–42, 81, 83, 84,
    90–95, 97–101, 105–14, 125–26,
    134, 138–39, 199, 203
  from rural backgrounds, 85–86,
    156, 189
Student Theater, 17–19, 26–27, 78, 83, 93–
    94, 128, 141–42, 150–55
  Bim-Bom Theater, 17, 18, 26–27, 151
  Eighth Day Theater, 150–51, 255n.127
  Kalambur, 91, 151–52
  Student Theater of Satirists (Studencki
    Teatr Satyryków, STS), 17, 26–
    27, 151
Sudety Mountains, 140
Sweden, 96, 135
Switzerland, 96
Szabad Nep (Hungarian newspaper), 33
Szczecin, 65–66, 76, 131*f*, 186, 193
Szczecinek, 133
Szlajfer, Henryk, 109–10
Szumowska, Dorota, 139
Szwarcman, Hanka, 24–25, 33
Świętokrzyskie Mountains, 141–
    42, 146–47

Święty Krzyż, 141–42
Świnoujście, 141–42

Tabkowski, Sławomir, 74, 76
Tal, Malgosia, 99–100
Tarnów, 116–17, 180–81
"Tarzan" (Michalewski), 143–45, 146
Tatra Mountains, 78, 175
technology
  in the household, 12–13, 156, 171, 173–
    74, 180
  and youth culture, 49, 54, 69, 164–
    67, 189–90
Thaw, 3–4, 14–19, 31–38, 194–95,
    197, 201
  effects on the press, 19–25
  and gender and sexuality, 21–22
  in the Soviet Union, 15, 35–38
Third World, 3, 7–9, 27–29, 65–66, 69,
    73–74, 104, 106, 107–11, 124,
    135, 191
television, 51–53, 77
  and the Apollo 11 mission, 180
  and international programming, 2–3,
    77, 178, 180
  in rural communities, 170, 171, 173–
    74, 177–78, 179–81, 182–83,
    259n.60
Tejchma, Józef, 6–7, 152
Tenenbaum, Natan, 115
Tito, Josip Bros, 191, 192*f*
Tłuczkiewicz, Tomasz, 76, 94, 116, 127
tourism, 3, 180–81. *See also* travel
  expansion under Gierek, 191–93
  organized for youth, 43, 82
"transnational imagination," 2, 8–9, 104–5,
    124, 201, 207
travel. *See also* tourism
  domestic, 51–52, 54, 56, 85, 154, 163–
    64, 168–69, 170–71
  and hitchhiking, 39–40, 98, 140–41
  international, 30–31, 34–35, 99–100,
    107, 121, 135, 201
  loosening of restrictions, 2, 3, 30–31, 43,
    77, 191–93
  Polish delegations abroad, 34, 69–70
  in press, 15–17, 69, 73–74, 93, 164–65
Toruń, 133

Toruńczyk, Barbara, 98, 107
Trotskyism, 95–96, 107, 109
Troubadours (Trubadurzy, band), 50
twist (dance), 2–3, 10, 39–40, 67f, 93
Tygodnik Powszechny (periodical), 169
Tyrmand, Leopold, 14, 229n.7
Tyszkiewicz, Beata, 70–71

Ukraine, 77, 132
United Nations, 25
United States, 27, 54, 71–72, 78, 81–82,
    96, 105, 117, 122, 180, 184, 191,
    205–6, 208
  cultural influence of, 14, 50–52, 67–68,
    69, 72–73, 145, 151
  protests against, 104, 109–11
  and the Six-Day War, 104–5
  and youth, 26–27, 44, 50–52, 82, 129, 195

Vatican, 191, 192f, 207–8
Vatican II Council, 97, 169–70
"Vietnamese" (Wietnamczycy), 109–11
Vietnam leaflet, 110–11, 125–26
Vietnam War, 7–8, 104–5, 106, 109–11,
    117, 121, 125–26, 154, 184
Views (Poglądy, periodical), 19, 21, 22f, 37,
    151–52, 263n.50
Voluntary Reserve of the Citizens' Militia
    (Ochotnicza Rezerwa Milicji
    Obywatelskiej, ORMO), 121,
    244n.37

Wachowicz-Makowska, Jolanta, 93
Wajda, Andrzej, 41–42, 70–71, 213n.17
Walicki, Franciszek, 50–51
Wałęsa, Lech, 187
Warsaw, 14, 19, 24, 37, 45, 51f, 52f, 63–64,
    66–67, 75, 78, 82–83, 84–85, 90–
    91, 96–97, 130–31, 130f, 133, 134–
    37, 138–39, 140, 148, 149, 170–71,
    191, 192f, 193, 205
  and the 1944 Uprising, 4–5
  and the 1955 World Youth and Student
    Festival, 2, 25–31, 38, 202
  and 1968, 81, 102, 111–18, 119–20, 121,
    124, 137–38, 163
Warsaw Pact, 1, 33–35, 102–3, 133–34,
    141–42, 204–5

Warsaw University, 17, 46–47, 76, 82, 85–
    86, 87–88, 87f, 97–100, 102, 105–6,
    108–11, 119–20, 121, 130, 156
Waschko, Roman, 39, 50–51, 94–95
welfare state, 157, 188–89
West Germany, 25, 67–68, 78, 118, 191,
    198–99, 205
WFM (motorcycle brand), 164–65, 178
workers' protests
  and 1968, 116–17
  on the Baltic Coast (1970), 137–
    38, 186–87
  in Poznań (1956), 15, 103
Workers' Defense Committee (Komitet
    Obrony Robotników, KOR),
    205, 206
World Federation of Democratic Youth
    (WFDY), 25, 65
World War II, 10, 44
  memory of, 4–5, 17, 23, 117, 120
World Youth and Student Festival
  in Moscow (1957), 27–29
  in Warsaw (1955), 2, 25–31, 38, 202
Woroszylski, Wiktor, 32
Wrocław, 19, 76, 82–83, 86, 91–92,
    93, 94, 132–33, 139, 140, 151–
    52, 157–58
  and 1968, 115–16, 127
  and the International Festival of Student
    Theater Festivals, 141–42, 151–
    54, 153f
  territorial changes and
    demographics, 132
Włocławek, 133
Wojtyła, Karol (Pope John Paul II), 169
Wyszyński, Stefan, 115, 169, 239n.65

Yugoslavia, 33–34, 96, 106, 223n.18
Yurchak, Alexei, 10–11
You and I (Ty i Ja, periodical),
    229–30n.15
youth culture, 2, 44–50
  debates over, 41
  emergence of, 4–5, 40–41, 44
  and politics, 5–6, 8, 12, 102, 104–5, 112–
    18, 123, 199–200
  in rural communities, 77f, 157–58, 162–
    67, 179–82

294   INDEX

  and the Thaw, 17–19, 41
  restructuring under Gierek,
    199–201

Zagajewski, Adam, 194
Zakopane, 78

Zakrzewska, Stanisława, 140, 148
Zakrzewski, Jan, 184
Zebra (periodical), 19, 20, 37
Zionism, 12, 26–27, 102, 115, 117–26.
    See also antisemitism
Żółkiewski, Stefan, 62, 63–64, 171,
    213n.17